Music Therapy Groupwork
with Special Needs Children

MUSIC THERAPY GROUPWORK WITH SPECIAL NEEDS CHILDREN

The Evolving Process

By

KAREN D. GOODMAN, M.S., R.M.T., L.C.A.T.

Associate Professor of Music Therapy
Montclair State University

CHARLES C THOMAS • PUBLISHER, LTD.
Springfield • Illinois • U.S.A.

Published and Distributed Throughout the World by

CHARLES C THOMAS • PUBLISHER, LTD.
2600 South First Street
Springfield, Illinois 62794-9265

© 2007 by CHARLES C THOMAS • PUBLISHER, LTD.

ISBN 978-0-398-07739-6   (hard)
ISBN 978-0-398-07740-2   (paper)

Library of Congress Catalog Card Number: 2007002914

With THOMAS BOOKS *careful attention is given to all details of manufacturing
and design. It is the Publisher's desire to present books that are satisfactory as to their
physical qualities and artistic possibilities and appropriate for their particular use.*
THOMAS BOOKS *will be true to those laws of quality that assure a good name
and good will.*

Printed in the United States of America
MM-R-3

Library of Congress Cataloging in Publication Data

Goodman, Karen D.
    Music therapy groupwork with special needs children : The evolving
process / by Karen D. Goodman.
        p. cm.
    Includes bibliographical references and index.
    ISBN 978-0-398-07739-6 (hard cover) – ISBN 978-0-398-07740-2 (pbk.)
    1. Child mental health services. 2. Music therapy for children. 3.
Children with disabilities–Rehabilitation. I. Title.
    [DNLM: 1. Music Therapy–methods. 2. Child. 3. Disabled Persons. 4.
Psychotherapy, Group–methods. WM 450.5.M8 G653m 2007]

RJ499.G663 2007
618.92'891654--dc22   2007002914

This book is written in honor of my parents,
Ruth and Daniel Goodman,
who continue to teach me love, optimism, and industry.

Preface

I write the preface to *Music Therapy Groupwork with Special Needs Children* after having written the book. Writing the book has crystallized my ideas after so many years of groupwork and yet raised more thoughts and even controversy. This is gratifying for it demonstrates that the material remains stimulating to me, even after so many years of practice.

I continue to be inspired by the moments of sheer joy while making music, my original impetus to enter the field of music therapy, and trust that you can provide some of these moments for your clients. I continue to be impressed with the value of the music itself in reaching children, and helping to mobilize a group

The field of music therapy continues to grow and, along with that growth, birth new applications of music therapy in groupwork. Whereas many therapists in the field began working with children of special needs, previously referred to as "handicapped," we also work with children in medical settings, in hospice, in dysfunctional families and in community crisis. Further, the move toward inclusion places many higher-functioning special needs children in the music room of the music educator where the music therapist frequently consults. These additional clinical settings are a statement about our added perspective in helping children as well as changes in society over the past decades. In writing the book, I found it difficult to delimit the focus. Nevertheless, I did. Therefore, please be certain that while the focus of the book is with children in self-contained educational settings and child psychiatric settings, this is a beginning, not an end. I chose to focus on these latter areas because, frankly, they are the areas of practice I spent so many years practicing.

In working effectively and thoughtfully with the children, I developed many concepts over the years and share these with you in the book. Since most of the book is not written in the first person, please understand that any idea that is not referenced in the book is an original idea on my part.

Above all, I hope to develop the therapist's sensibility *to work effectively toward the formation of a cohesive group with children who have different functioning levels, different temperaments and different musical preferences.* In order to achieve this end, *the therapist must employ different developmental expectations (goals and objectives) for each child, adaptation in the presentation of the music and varying methods while simultaneously encouraging the sense of group.* These concepts stand in contrast to an approach where the clinician establishes the same generic goals for group members and presents material, without adaptation, on a uniform level with the hope that the group will become cohesive as time passes.

I have also made a concerted effort in the book to convey my integration of multiple approaches in music therapy. Music therapy, particularly in the group, can feel like a balancing act. The art and science of music therapy encourages the therapist to find a relationship-based approach with the children through making music, much of which is a creative spontaneous process. At the same time, we are called upon to structure and document changing behaviors, which allow the children to find increasing independence as they make their ways in the world. This balancing act, between structure and freedom, can call upon different approaches, approaches gleaned from the worlds of cognitive-behavioral, humanism, psychodynamic theory and group theory.

Throughout the eight chapters, I provide multiple clinical vignettes from my clinical work, which will serve to demonstrate my theoretical perspectives. Certainly the review of many years of my case notes has given me an additional opportunity to reflect on, and be thankful for my work.

The first chapter, "The Story of a Group," presents my thinking process as I proceed with a seemingly disparate group of children. This thought process brings the reader through the various stages of working with a group: assessment of individual children within the prospective group, considering the children as a potential group, organization of long-term goals, formulation of music therapy objectives, methods and materials for beginning sessions, considerations regarding how to evaluate the music therapy sessions and problem solving as sessions proceed over the following year. The first chapter, in effect, is the groundwork for all subsequent chapters.

The second chapter, on assessment, provides a healthy review of the literature. The area of assessment is one that has actually received a great deal of attention in the last two decades, more so than evaluation. Assessment works most effectively when the tool used is specific to the developmental level of the child and theoretical purpose of the music therapy work itself. Using published or previously published assessment tools, including an assessment I authored for disturbed children in 1989, casework is presented to demonstrate some of the very real questions about the efficacy of various assessment tools. The task of music therapy assessment for provision of services on the Individual Education Plan (IEP), a consulting role I am frequently asked to provide, is also discussed.

The third chapter, the writing that actually started the entire book, reflects on the clinician's choices in providing individual or group therapy. It explains the structure of the group in the special education and the child psychiatric settings, presents ideas regarding developmental prerequisites for groupwork and helps the clinician consider what I term "core considerations in forming a group," including developmental appropriateness, sensory appropriateness, musical appropriateness, and last but not least, the practical realities of the facility.

The fourth and fifth chapters bring the reader through the process of long-term goal planning and short-term music therapy objective planning, a necessary process for many school systems and hospitals that hold the therapist accountable for progress. While these chapters may try the patience of the reader and seem contrary to an artistic process, they are necessary details toward the documentation of progress. They also demonstrate the variability of how goals were presented in the Individual Education Plan in the past versus the federal mandate for their presentation in the present. Although many therapists practice groupwork with generic types of goals for the children, the option to clearly conform to following the IEP goals, although problematic, is presented along with practical suggestions to simplify the process (i.e., Chapter 4 presents my suggestions for organizing the IEP goals and prioritizing them for use as group music therapy goals). Most importantly, music therapists, from the unique perspective of music therapy, have a role in changing or adding goals to the individual education plan; a seasoned clinician will exercise this prerogative.

The sixth chapter, "Materials," begins to introduce the reader to the myriad of possibilities for interventions through music, the primary tool of the music therapist or "musical therapist" as some innocently refer to us. The considerations in selecting and creating vocal, instrumental, movement and listening materials are presented to the therapist as part of an overall effort in the book to emphasize the thoughtful use of the music as a selective tool. As a practical measure, I include a listing of materials I used over a five-year period with multiply handicapped children. While it was not possible to detail all the ways in which I adapted almost all of the materials to suit the spontaneous reactions of the children in the group, I hope that the reader will, through a series of case examples in this chapter (see my "General and Specific Continuum of Music Response"), begin to understand the necessity for simultaneously using music with different expectations from members of the group, a necessity that requires musical reactivity and improvisation on the part of the therapist.

Chapter 7, "Methods," dense as it is, draws on possibilities which all involve basic principles of music therapy. In this chapter I identify and discuss all the variables that have to be considered as the therapist devises music therapy methods: 1) the space being used for music therapy; 2) the physical arrangement of the group; 3) activity levels consistent with developmental functioning; 4) diagnosis of the child; 5) goals and objectives for all group members; 6) how to incorporate other professionals into the music therapy session; 7) strategies promoting group process, 8) suggested session format;

9) adaptive nature of methodology; and 10) consideration of the therapist's knowledge base and philosophy of helping. Methods are as variable as the plethora of clinical situations we find ourselves in. Suggestions for the beginning therapist to detail method in a session plan are included in this chapter. This chapter will stimulate the clinician to think in terms of many kinds of challenging conditions requiring different emphases in methodology. The concept of working with the group as a group of children with individual needs is vital to understanding the juggling act of using different methods with different children in the group even while the children work together to become a group.

Finally, the eighth chapter reflects on evaluation, the objective and subjective pieces of this process, and the issues regarding documentation in a creative arts process. Evaluation is multifaceted and serves not only to keep track of how the children are doing in the session week-to-week but also to educate the clinician in a continuing effort for self-growth. The celebration of subjective evaluation in this chapter recognizes that part of evaluation that helps the therapist in terms of self-growth and examining the process of music therapy.

Music Therapy Groupwork with Special Needs Children, The Evolving Process, is broad in scope. Not only do the children in the group change as a result of the music therapy process but so does the therapist in understanding and adapting to the needs of the group. The book presents a combination of beginning, intermediate and advanced level concepts. Feel free to focus on the chapters that appeal to your level of training. It is an ideal resource for the student entering the field of music therapy (who will profit from the study guide questions at the end of each chapter), the beginning therapist beginning to cope with the demands of group practice, the seasoned clinician reconsidering long-standing ways of conducting the group and the allied professional working with the music therapist.

Writing this book has provided an opportunity to share, beyond my immediate classroom at Montclair State University, all the ideas I have formulated over the many years working with groups of children. I sincerely hope that the reader finds value in the ideas I present and uses these ideas to further the profession of music therapy.

KAREN D. GOODMAN
October 18, 2006

Acknowledgments

Writing this book has been a true learning experience with many stops and starts. I acknowledge the support of many individuals along the way. Without their help, this book might not have come to fruition.

- To my husband and children, Jonathan, Sara, and Adam Lautman for their love and encouragement.
- To dear academic colleagues and friends: Donna Chadwick, Maureen Carr, and Donald Mintz for enriching my personal and professional life, encouraging me to write this book, and listening to me.
- To invaluable professionals who impacted my clinical work: Elaine Barden, SLP, Linda Gottlieb, SLP, Maureen Hunt, O.T., Stanley Greenspan, M.D., Daniel Stern, M.D., Cynthia Pfeffer, M.D.
- To dearly missed colleagues and friends who played a vital role in my professional development: Jack Sacher, Lucille Weistuch, Lucy Greene, Vera Moretti, Florence Tyson, Judith Kestenberg, M.D., and Silvano Arieti, M.D.
- To Clive Robbins, Kenneth Bruscia, Cynthia Briggs, Stanley Greenspan, M.D., Donald Michel, and Michael Rohrbacher for generously providing permissions to reprint previously published work.
- To Barbara Wheeler in appreciation for the music therapy programs we built together over a 22-year period at Montclair State University and for the initial encouragement to write this book while recognizing the value of my clinical work.
- To Montclair State University for providing the necessary release time to write this book.
- To Michael Thomas, Charles C Thomas, Publisher for his efforts in publishing this book.
- To Claire Slagle, Charles C Thomas, Publisher for her patience and attention to detail in editing the book.
- To my students, current and former, at Montclair State University, who continually challenge me to think of training and education afresh.
- To the children I have been privileged to work with and learn from in the course of music therapy. You go unnamed but never forgotten.

Contents

Music Therapy Groupwork with Special Needs Children

Chapter 1

The Story of a Group: Unanswered Questions

This first chapter orients the reader to the purposes and content of the book. In my teaching and practice of music therapy over the past 28 years, I have found that most music therapy literature addresses individual therapy. However, in both public and private schools, economic constraints demand group therapy practice. Group work poses particular challenges in terms of initial assessment, selecting the group members, establishing goals and objectives, setting up the sessions, methodology and product and process evaluation. No matter what philosophy of helping the therapist adopts, there are overlapping concerns in all of the aforementioned areas. There is an ethical need for educators to train students for group work as well as individual work and therefore help beginning therapists meet the realistic demands of clinical practice today.

INTRODUCTION

The reader should feel free to indulge me as I write the first and only autobiographical chapter of this book. The name of this book, *Music Therapy Groupwork with Special Needs Children,* has personal significance. I began my journey in music therapy in the mid-seventies, a time when there were few books on the subject, a small number of training programs, very limited graduate studies in music therapy and little to no advertising of clinical positions. I had an undergraduate degree in English and enjoyed writing poetry and short stories. I was also a musician. My interest in the not so burgeoning field of poetry therapy turned to an interest in music therapy as I moved to Boston to work at a publishing firm and, in my free time, began to volunteer with two pioneering music therapists in the

Boston area, Donna Madden Chadwick and Beverley Wilson Parry, therapists whose work would quickly become the subject of the music therapy documentary, "The Music Child." Their work at a developmental center, based on the principles of Nordoff and Robbins, led me to study with Vera Moretti, a former student of Paul Nordoff.

Following my music therapy training, I was fortunate enough to work with several important models and, in some cases, mentors, all of whom had the end result of enriching my background, propelling me to return to graduate school and stimulating my subsequent work. The first of these mentors was Dr. Silvano Arieti, a prominent and unorthodox psychiatrist whose psychotherapeutic approach with schizophrenics (Arieti, 1955) and understanding of the link between creativity and schizophrenia (Arieti, 1976) greatly affected my work with mood-disordered and schizophrenic clients at The Creative Arts Rehabilitation Center. My interests in psychiatry led to clinical work and qualitative research on music therapy with the suicidal child, stimulated by my working association with psychiatrist Dr. Cynthia Pfeffer at New York Hospital, Cornell Medical Center. These experiences allowed me to develop my interests in group work within an analytic model and the development of a projective music therapy assessment tool with the disturbed child (Goodman, 1989).

Further along, graduate studies in special education and child psychology solidified my understanding of child development and its overlap with music therapy, an understanding that was deepened by clinical work and descriptive research with psychiatrist Dr. Judith Kestenberg who, fortunately for me, phoned me one day, drawing me into work at her therapeutic nursery, a working laboratory for the worlds of early musical development and musical attunement. Additional workshop training with Dr. Daniel Stern reinforced the interests I had in nonverbal attunement signals between mother and child, so important to nonverbal bonding through music. Finally, workshop training with Dr. Stanley Greenspan as well as my music therapy clinical work with several of the children he was seeing in treatment helped me bridge the gap between the developmental and psychoanalytic studies I had pursued and helped me gain a greater sense of perspective on sensory integration, an interest already stimulated by my graduate studies in neurology. Last but not least, the many years of teaching at Montclair State University I continue to enjoy today alongside clinical practice in psychiatric and school settings serve to remind me of the day-to-day reality of teaching and practicing group music therapy.

As I found myself getting increasingly excited about the field of music therapy, I also realized that I had to rely largely on myself to discover how to problem-solve the issues in doing music therapy. The leap from theoretical learning to applied practice looms large.

In presenting the process of a sample music therapy group to you in this first chapter, I offer my thinking process and therefore all the elements of how the group evolves: the initial composition of the group and its potential as a group, the assessment of the group members for intervention planning, the formulation of goals and objectives, the methods and materials that I use and the ongoing evaluation of the group. These are the elements of the chapters following this first group.

Now, flashback to September, 2000 to a working music therapy group at a large regional day school for multiply handicapped children. I am the music therapist there two days a week, simultaneously conducting music therapy and descriptive research in conjunction with my full-time university position at Montclair State University.

THE STORY OF A GROUP

THE SCHOOL

I have been working at this special education

school for six years, conducting six groups a day twice a week. It is a regional day school, receiving 31 sending districts throughout the State of New Jersey. The school has a wide variety of about 80 disabled children, ages 3–21. I am the first music therapist to set up school-wide programming. It did not start out this way. . . . I was initially hired to do individual and small group music therapy with six children who had music therapy on their IEP. After six months, the new principal advised me that "this program is disbanding." After some of the parents filed a lawsuit which included objection regarding the dissolution of the music therapy services, the principal called me back two days before school was to begin. She felt that all the children in the school should get music therapy, not just those selected on the IEP She offered me a fulltime job. I was only available two days a week since I was teaching in and coordinating the programs at Montclair State University full-time. Based on my recommendation, she hired an additional therapist another two days a week to work with the older students in the school. I tell this story not only to emphasize how important parent advocacy is but also to point out the possible political difficulties of some children receiving music therapy on the IEP and others not from the administrative point of view.

My personal and professional goals in taking this position are to maintain standards of practicing music therapy. That includes assessment, suggestion as to individual and group therapy placements, team conferencing time, records review time and inclusion in the IEP process. My first principal was very supportive of the music therapy program although, as you will see as my story unfolds, I have to struggle just to try to do my job properly. Unfortunately, she retired after four years. The next principal was disinterested in the program and despite several invitations to visit my music room, he never came. The current principal is minimally supportive of my efforts. She refers to me as a music teacher, probably because public school districts do not recognize the music therapy certification in New Jersey. A public school district maintains this school. By law, all music therapists working in the schools must have a school certification. My certification is in special education since I am a certified teacher of the handicapped in New York and New Jersey so I would more aptly, in this sense, be referred to as the special education teacher providing music. However, I am paid more than fairly as a music therapist and I think the constant efforts of music therapists to work with the politics of schools and state certification systems are difficult. My simple suggestion to others would be: do your job as well as possible, stick to your ethical and professional standards and try to get involved in state advocacy for creative arts therapy so your music therapy credentials are recognized.

In this school, transdisciplinary team members serve the facility from occupational therapy, physical therapy, music therapy, speech/language pathology, social work, psychology and special education. The administration of the school keeps changing and therefore my working space and assignments do as well. I have built a healthy respect for the work of music therapy with the special education teachers, other therapists and parents, to the extent where they are in the music room on a regular basis. I have to set up my meetings with other professionals informally; the extent to which professionals communicate with each other is not fixed by schedule and this, in my opinion, makes the implementation of goals more difficult. The only charge I have from the administration is to "provide music for the children." and share written session plans with the principal at the beginning of every week. My personal and professional goals exceed that simple directive. Whatever I learn from working with these children and the professionals in the school drives my teaching at the University level.

Now it is September again with the yellow school buses unloading at the front door, the leaves turning and a nip in the air. Even though many of the same children continue one year to the next, there are always those who come and go and there are always new classroom combinations, largely based on chronological age. I ask that I meet with the same six groups twice a week and that request is, thankfully, honored. Right now, I have my own music space which is a large classroom. I am pleased to tell you that everything I order is honored. As a result of this, I have a large and varied collection of instruments, a decent piano, sheet music and music posters on the walls.

The groups are chronologically ages 3–12, developmentally much younger and frequently medically fragile. They are, in effect, all the children from the sending districts who cannot be handled properly in the in-district self-contained classrooms. In that sense, they are very challenged children, requiring additional staff in each classroom (nurses, private aides, teacher assistant) and one-on-one programming much of the time. The notion of sending all the children as a group to "specials" of art, music and physical education is an educational norm. It remains a challenge for me to really conduct therapy with these children as a group and I have been compelled to find compromise solutions in order to do so. This group coming through the door of my music room is no exception.

THE GROUP

These six group members, chronologically ages 7–9, range in developmental age from preschool to early grade school, with a variety of physical and attentional difficulties and all are multiply handicapped. I have already been in their classroom so I have had a chance to meet them prior to their first music group. They are blessed with an experienced and lovely special education teacher who also happens to be a musician and uses music frequently during class activities.

Alexander, age 8, a tall olive-skinned child, rolls himself in on his wheelchair with a sweet smile on his face. He is cerebral palsied, not able to care for his physical needs independently and physically compromised to the extent that he has to struggle with his expressive language and also utilize augmentative communication. Yet he is progressing with early academic skills, including math and reading skills. According to his teacher, when challenged with more demanding tasks, Alexander reverts to regressive emotional behavior such as fake crying or ignoring the speaker. This issue was not addressed in his I.E.P. but could be addressed as a new goal for building self-esteem through music therapy since he seems very musical.

An aide wheels in *Simon,* age 9, a slight child with blonde hair and blue eyes. He is another physically compromised child, is wheelchair-bound, nonverbal and at an infant/toddler level in terms of developmental prowess. He uses picture exchange with verbal prompts and is beginning to make cause/effect connections.

Keisha, age 7, a petite and vivacious black girl, is eagerly pulling her assistant teacher by the hand as she enters the room laughing. She is visually compromised and impulsive in behavior, has weak oral motor control, an uneven gait pattern, and perseverative speech, reminiscent of a beginning talker.

Terrence, age 8, a muscular active black child with microcephaly, runs into the room in front of the other children. He is beginning preschool academic skills, such as identifying and sorting colors and shapes, attending to a simple story, preparing food, using simple computer operations, identifying numbers to 9 and counting. He speaks in 4–5 word sentences. His difficulty in controlling impulsive behavior remains a key behavioral issue.

Maria, age 9, a chubby strong looking child with black hair and dark eyes, pulls her Spanish-speaking aide along with her and plops into her seat with an air of finality. She is bilingual and understands one-step directions in both Spanish and English. She can approximate language and uses pictures for communication, especially for food-related activities. She can combine up to four signs/pictures to make requests but needs modeling first to help nudge her along. Since she likes music, she will use that sign as well as the sign for gym spontaneously and appropriately. Thus far, her medications have not solved any behavioral problems as far as mood swings and self-abusive and peer-abusive behaviors such as pinching, biting and slapping. She stares me down after she sits in the chair and then finally smiles at me.

Finally, *Linda,* age 9, comes in on her wheelchair. She is able to use simple signs and picture choices for communication and attempts some verbalizations for communication, all compromised by oral motor musculature issues, which result in excessive drooling. There is a need for hand-over-hand assistance on multiple tasks since her fine motor and gross motor skills are weak. At her highest functional level, she operates at an infant/toddler level.

ASSESSMENT

At this school I have been assigned back-to-back 45 minute groups with two preparation periods of 30 minutes each, one before the children arrive and one after the children leave. During my 30-minute lunch period, I struggle to take notes on the morning groups (three groups in the morning) while I eat my sandwich. After the children leave, I continue my note-taking on the afternoon groups (three groups in the afternoon). There is no downtime between classes. The notes are, at the beginning, based on generic types of developmental goals that I arrive at while I try to find the time upon arriving at school to read through IEPs. My efforts to read and educate myself about the six groups of children I am working with two days a week is, I think, minimal professionalism.

The possibility of assessment on an individual basis aside from group meeting times is impossible. Having done extensive literature reviews on assessment and having written an assessment myself (Goodman, 1989), I know that virtually all the literature on music therapy assessment is for individual students (see Chapter Two of this book) not group. This is not a school that will allow me to change the class schedule to accommodate individual assessment. With six groups of about six children in each group, individual assessment would take me a minimum of 36 clinical hours, or more than a week. Since my schedule is based around the classroom teacher taking a lunch break, I cannot break up the group. In a sense, my previous clinical work has spoiled me since, in virtually all previous jobs, I had free rein in conducting assessments and then setting up groups. With these children, I am going to have to assess on an ongoing basis, within the context of the group while using infant and early childhood milestones from the *Music Therapy Assessment Profile for Severely/Profoundly Handicapped, MTAP* (Michel and Rohrbacher, 1982). The concept of the MTAP, written during my own professional participation as a member of the two week summer of 1978 "Training Institute for Music Therapy with Severely/Profoundly Handicapped" in dusty Denton, Texas is simple: devise music tasks that reflect developmental milestones within the domains of cognition, fine motor, gross motor, social-emotional and speech-language development. I can extend this concept through the use of other developmental resources like the *HELP Activity Guide* (Furuno, 2005), which now includes developmental milestones for ages three-six (Vort, 1995), the estimated developmental age range for Alexander and Terrence.

The purpose of the music therapy assessment will be to determine the level of functioning in developmental domains of motor, language, cognition and communication in music and compare that to the stated current levels of functioning and goals of the IEP for compatibility. Children can perform differently in music and new expecations can be determined. I have thought a great deal about the issues involved in assessment and this group will push me to another level of consideration (see Chapter Two).

APPROPRIATENESS OF GROUP PLACEMENT

As I meet the children and work with them, I begin to think about their appropriateness and potential as a group. I started really trying to tease out what makes a group work about five years ago when I started my work at this school. The factors I consider are the following: 1) *The developmental level of the child;* 2) *The musicality of the child;* 3) *The sensory profile of the child;* and 4) *The practical consideration of the school setting.* As with other groups in the school, these children are *developmentally mixed.* Alexander and Terrence are on a preschool or beginning kindergarten level; Linda, Maria, Keisha and Simon are on an infant/toddler level. In this sense, they are all more like a family constellation, a heterogeneous sibling-like group. When I think about children beginning day care or preschool, I know that they do not relate to each other until they are generally past parallel

play, or about 2.5 years old. On a practical level, then, with all the aides and teachers in this room of six children (a personal aide for Keisha, a personal aide for Maria, a private nurse for Simon, an assistant teacher, a visiting speech pathologist and myself), the ratio is 1:1, more like a "Mommy and me" play group. In effect, am I practicing individual therapy within a group context?

Terrence, Keisha and Maria are quickly starting to show signs of *strong musical preferences* in the first few sessions. Terrence loves his Sesame Street Songs, Keisha adores her finger plays and Maria is most responsive to simple Spanish folk songs. They all have to learn to take turns in sharing musical materials with each other and sometimes this is hard for them. In a group where there are overriding musical preferences and the children simply cannot wait, this would be an impossible situation for the music therapist. Fortunately for me, these children are able to wait their turn. However, it is a stretch for them to attend to favorite materials of other children. They are, rightfully so at their developmental ages, musically egocentric. In terms of *sensory profile,* the children are very different and I find myself continually observing their reactions to stimuli. I love reading the work of Dr. Stanley Greenspan because he offers so many perspectives on this. He talks and writes about the response of the child to varied stimuli. When I talk, what does the child hear? When I sing or play instruments, what does the child hear? When I use visuals in my presentation, what does the child see? When I touch the child in a firm way, how does that feel? When I touch the child with a light fleeting touch, how does that feel? I notice that practically all of the children take time to react. Do they all have auditory processing delays? When I try to assist them with hand-over-hand movement activities, Alexander is very spastic, his arms flail and they are tight. Simon and Linda are floppy, like rag dolls. Maria is rooted to the ground and resistant to movement. Keisha and Terrence are small and tight in their bodies, moving dysrhymically in their seats, impulsively calling out. Since the children present such a mixed picture developmentally, musically and sensorily, I am going to have to work at different levels simultaneously. Sometimes

I feel like a juggling act but at the same time, it is intellectually stimulating to be noticing all these different levels and reactions all the time. The *practical limitations of the school* put me in the position of only taking this group as they exist in the assigned classroom. I see this as a rigid arrangement. I am scheduled to cover the teacher preparation periods and that leaves me no flexibility in grouping. If I had the option, I would place Alexander and Terrence in a separate dyad since they are closer to each other in terms of developmental age and would complement each other with different musical interest. The other children would either be on an individual basis or together in a type of infant stimulation model. This group, as it stands, will be quite challenging. The variables involved in determining individual or group placement have been ones I have been fortunate enough to act on in previous clinical settings (see Chapter 3) but not here. How then will I make this group "work"?

SETTING GOALS

Generic Goals

Phase One, Goal Setting

Until I have a chance to wade through all the IEP reports, my goals are relatively generic and relate to various uses of music throughout the session.

Through a variety of songs I want to:

- Increase and evaluate expressive/receptive language
- Increase and evaluate socialization
- Increase and evaluate vocal projection
- Decrease auditory processing time
- Increase consistent response to one and two-step directions

Through a variety of instrumental activities, I want to:

- Follow one step and two-step directions,

- Decrease impulsivity,
- Have the children recall and follow sequence of directions,
- Create a sense of rhythmic control.

Through movement, I want to:

- Decrease impulsivity,
- Increase response to one step and two step directions,
- Increase social interactions,
- Reinforce a sense of rhythmic control.

Reviewing the IEP

Setting goals for the music therapy session can be delimited to the simple expectation of the facility, in this case, "provide music for the children" or else live up to my own personal and professional expectations. As a therapist, I am not satisfied unless I can help the children progress developmentally. If I can fit into the team approach of the Individual Education Plan while using music to contribute a special context and meaning for completion of developmental goals, then I feel connected to the overall progress of the child. The federal mandate, IDEA, holds the special education teacher, occupational therapist, speech-language therapy, physical therapist, etc. responsible for writing observable measurable goals on the Individual Education Plan. Although, frankly, I am not a conformist, I decide to follow IEP goals as well as formulate music therapy goals and objectives as observable and measurable. It is not easy nor is it my natural bent. However, I think that music therapists will ultimately gain more recognition documenting the progress the children make than not. Therefore I am used to reviewing the goals of the IEP and seeing how they can be incorporated into my session planning. This is, in effect, a four-step process.

First, I *review the IEP goals and recent reports* (neurological, psychosocial, educational, psychological, occupational therapy, speech therapy, physical therapy) in a child's file. Second, after I have all this information on the children in a group, I create a table using the names of the children and *organizing the IEP goals into developmental domains* (social-emotional, cognitive, speech-language, fine motor, gross motor). Third, following the organization of IEP goals into the developmental grid, I *review goals to determine which are best addressed through music therapy* (see Chapter 4). In order to do this, I eliminate goals that are context-specific and cannot be addressed in music therapy, prioritize goals that focus on communication and socialization, especially in a child psychiatric group, where the cognitive goals and motor goals, relatively speaking, are of secondary concern, and, finally, prioritize a number of goals that can be handled in terms of methods and evaluation. Fourth, I *put the names of the child or children for whom the goal applies in parentheses so I get a clearer sense of overlapping needs.*

This is an admittedly tedious process but it assures that I am working on IEP goals through music therapy and therefore lends an even greater degree of credibility to the work. These goals remain uppermost in my mind whether I am working on premeditated musical experiences or spontaneous music making. As I do the assessment and the ongoing intervention, music therapy will reveal aspects of the child possibly not seen in these IEP goals and I will contribute that additional information to the team.

The Core Curriculum Content Standards for Students with Severe Disabilities

This year, not only do I review the IEP and relevant reports in the files of the children, but I am also asked to contribute goals for the IEP under the category of "Visual and Performing Arts." All the teachers and therapists in the school are being asked to adapt to a new template for writing IEP goals known as the "Core Curriculum Content Standards for Students with Severe Disabilities" (CCCSSSD) (2000).

One might see the CCCSSSD as trying to fit a square peg into around hole since CCCSSSD is an effort to modify and define educational standards for subject areas originally designated for the typically developing K-12 student in the State of New Jersey (Core Curriculum Standards, 1996). Educators and therapists working with special learners are expected to formulate IEP goals related to the subject areas of visual and performing

arts, comprehensive health and physical education, language arts literacy, mathematics, science, social studies and world language as well as areas that cross academic disciplines (termed "Cross-Content Indicators") such as career preparation, information technology, critical thinking, decision making, problem solving, self-management and safety principles. These goals will be evaluated on an annual basis as an alternate proficiency assessment (Appendix A, NJDE, 2000).

I realize there are always going to be changing trends in education and therapy so I try to understand the new process and adapt. I suggest you adapt also if your state suggests a specific format for IEP planning and you, as the music therapist, have to fit into that new template. The positives about using the new state template of the CCCSSSD include the following: 1) The therapists and teachers writing the IEP goals have to write the goals in terms of observable measurable behavior which will be evaluated during the school year. This mandate standardizes the way in which the goals are written across school districts and by therapists and educators working with special needs children; and 2) The Visual and Performing Arts are included in the CCCSSSD template, asking specialists to provide IEP goals.

I adapt to the new template as follows:

- First, I *review and organize the IEP goals* for each child as defined under CCCSSSD (see Table 1.1). The only difference here is that the CCCSSSD standards dictate and organize the content of the goals. Going through the CCCSSSD and the relevant goals for the children is a process that is helpful on many levels. I get a sense of how many of the standards are relevant to one or a number of children in the group. Further, I get a sense of how therapeutic goals have to stretch to fit into an educational framework. The list of standards and cumulative progress indicators in the entire CCCSSSD is exhaustive and only small portions of it are even being used to apply to the children in my group. I wonder about the appropriateness of the standards and see the teachers and therapists struggling to make the information regarding the childrens' needs fit the document. For example, I can see that the occupational therapy and physical therapy goals are under "Comprehensive Health and Physical Education" and speech /language pathology goals are under "Language and Literacy." Behavioral goals are under "Self-management," a cross-content indicator. All academic areas are introduced through multisensory strategies in the classroom and, admittedly, some of the ways in which the teacher chooses to relate the low-functioning skills of the children to the academic standards surprise me. As I read through, I can already imagine some of these standards being met in the context of music therapy and others not. This process feels similar to reviewing a more typical IEP.

- Second, I *prioritize those IEP goals, as defined under CCCSSD,* that are most relevant to music therapy (see Table 1.2). I can create music therapy objectives based on the CCCSSD standards I have just reviewed to fit into the context of the music therapy session. I decide that the language and literacy, cross-content indicators (i.e., critical thinking and self-management) and physical activity standards are most relevant to the typical emphases of a music therapy group session.
- Third, I *consider the overlapping needs of the children* in order to further prioritize and organize the working goals of the first few session (see Table 1.3). There are general overlaps in terms of the need to consider levels of expressive/receptive language, awareness of 1:1 correspondence, a sense of order in the session activities, behavioral standards for attending and turn-taking, and improvement in motor skills.
- Fourth, I opt to organize the prioritized IEP goals (from CCCSSSD) into *developmental domains,* my usual frame of reference (see Table 1.4).
- Fifth, I *place the overlapping goals within the framework of Visual and Performing Arts Goals for the IEP* and add goals that are not otherwise addressed (see Table 1.5).

Fortunately for me, my colleague and co-worker of the past six years, speech-language pathologist, Linda, is a consultant on the CCCSSSD. She has recognized, through our collaborative work together over the past six years, that children, even severely handicapped, develop through the music experience, create music and express aesthetic preferences. Therefore as I look more closely at the standards under Visual and Performing Arts (see Table 1.5). I quickly realize that they are compatible with what I am currently doing in music therapy and my efforts to create music therapy definitions for the Visual/Performing Arts IEP goals are satisfactory:

TABLE 1.1. CCCSSSD STANDARDS (IEP GOALS) FOR CHILDREN IN THE GROUP.

Standard 2. *Cross Content Indicator:* All students will use information technology and other tools.
Linda: Participate in ongoing evaluations for use of compensatory techniques and/or adaptive equipment in order to perform fine motor tasks.
Simon: Utilize a step-by-step switch to convey a message between school and home and vise versa, without perseveration on switch access or physical prompting.

Standard 2.1. *Comprehensive Health and PE:* All students will learn health promotion and disease prevention concepts and health enhancing behaviors
Maria: Reduce the instances of biting to her hands during school hours when given a verbal prompt "hands down" 4 out of 5 trials.

Standard 2.2. *Comprehensive Health and PE:* All students will learn health enhancing personal, interpersonal and life skills.

continued

TABLE 1.1. CCCSSSD STANDARDS (IEP GOALS) FOR CHILDREN IN THE GROUP–*Continued.*

Keisha: Substitute mouthing of objects by requesting an appropriate oral-motor device (i.e., a chewy "T") on 3 out of 5 occasions.

Linda: Demonstrate compliance when transitioning from a favored activity, given minimal physical assistance, after only 1 verbal prompt.

Simon: Remain dry when given the opportunity to use the potty before and during the school day, 4 out of 5 days.

Alexander: Demonstrate awareness of personal self-care needs at appropriate times on 3 out of 5 occasions with diminishing verbal prompts.

Standard 2.5. ***Comprehensive Health and PE:*** All students will learn and apply movement concepts and skills that foster participation in physical activities throughout life.

Maria: Demonstrate appropriate participation in a gross motor activity for a period of 10 minutes with good compliance and without complaint.

Keisha: Demonstrate improved supination during desktop activities as evidenced by the ability to independently execute 3 complete turns on a twist top object using her left hand. Demonstrate improved movement patterns to the left lower extremity incorporating appropriate flexion utilizing PNF patterning with carryover to ambulation as evidenced by improved heel strike and control.

Terrence: Participate in a reciprocal ball play activity for a period of 2 minutes with appropriate turn-taking on 4 out of 5 trials.

Linda: Demonstrate an improvement in flexibility and strength as evidence by a more upright posture while in a static standing position for a period of 1 minute and while ambulating as noted by maintaining a neutral position at the hips for 25 feet. Demonstrate transfers to and from her wheelchair and classroom chair with only contact guard on 4 out of 5 days. Willingly participate in formalized group gross motor activities demonstrating appropriate peer interaction 4 out of 5 trials.

Simon: Demonstrate bilateral hand use during classroom tabletop activities and/or music class without physical prompts on 3 out of 5 trials. Demonstrate appropriate gait patterns for ambulation within the gait trainer, with appropriate head righting and hands in a relaxed position for a period of 10 minutes. Tolerate passive range of motion to bilateral lower extremities and trunk without complaint. Demonstrate sitting on a slanted bench with hands at side for a period of 1 minute without a loss of balance or complaint. Demonstrate appropriate positioning of bilateral lower extremities when out of his classroom chair, with appropriate positioning aids to assist in passive range of motion.

Alexander: Spontaneously use bilateral hand skills in classroom activites. Demonstrate independent feeding skills by lifting a cup to drink from the tabletop and returning it without spillage. Demonstrate appropriate gait patterns using the gait trainer with the aid of his new orthotics and abduction positioner for a distance of 30 feet on 4 out of 5 occasions. Demonstrate improved posture, including trunk control with the use of his new seating system being applied to his current wheelchair frame. Demonstrate appropriate short sitting on a bench with appropriate support of his upper extremities to maintain an upright position without therapist's assistance for a period of 3 minutes. Demonstrate appropriate usage of upper extremities and trunk when engaged in ball play, throwing overhead/from the chest without loss of balance for a distance of 4 feet on 3 out of 5 trials.

Standard 3. ***Cross Content Indicator:*** All students will use critical thinking, decision-making, and problem-solving skills.

Terrence: Make appropriate choices from 4 pictures throughout the school and in the community on 3 out of 4 trials with verbal direction and gestural prompts.

Alexander: Make appropriate choices from up to 6 pictures or 3 verbal choices throughout the school and in the community on 4 out of 5 trials.

Standard 3.1. ***Language Arts Literary:*** All students will speak for a variety of real purposes and audiences.

Maria: Produce 3-word combinations through the use of pictures and/or manual signs when given verbal prompts, but without phrase modeling.

continued

TABLE 1.1. CCCSSSD STANDARDS (IEP GOALS) FOR CHILDREN IN THE GROUP–*Continued.*

Keisha: Spontaneously and consistently use short and appropriate verbal sentences/phrases within the school environment at least 5 times daily. Tolerate oral motor exercises to strengthen oral musculature for 2 minutes a minimum of 3 times weekly by a speech therapist. Correct answer given for activity-related "Wh" questions on 4 our of 5 trials. Follow a variety of simple 2-step directives with 1 repetition on 3 out of 5 trials.

Terrence: Respond to "Wh" questions with a short phrase or sentence without prompting on 3 out of 5 trials. Participate in oral motor exercises through imitation for a period of 2 minutes followed by proper lip closure for cup drinking/straw drinking a minimum of 3 times weekly.

Linda: Tolerate oral motor exercises to strength oral musculature for 2 minutes, a minimum of 3 times weekly by a speech therapist. Communicate wants, needs and preferences, given up to 5 picture choices and/or using an augmentative device with voice output throughout the school on 3 out of 5 trials when given verbal and gestural prompts. As a precursor to increasing picture vocabulary, match objects to pictures from a field of up to 5 objects/pictures (unfamiliar) when provided with a verbal prompt. Use an augmentative device with voice output to communicate events from school to home/home to school initiated by an adult with a verbal and gestural prompt.

Simon: Increase picture vocabulary to at least 10 pictures (including bathroom, angry, drink, eat, music, standing, and computer) as evidenced by appropriate usage throughout the day. Appropriately utilize combined pictures/messages on an augmentative device with verbal and gestural prompts that present a field of 4 throughout the school and school community on 3 out of 5 trials.

Alexander: Correctly answer routine-related questions with a short phrase or sentence and in a timely fashion without prompting on 4 out of 5 trials. Use expressive language to give peers simple directions during classroom activities with a verbal prompt on 3 out of 5 trials.

Standard 3.2. *Language Arts Literary:* All students will listen actively in a variety of situations, to information from a variety of sources.

Maria: Respond appropriately to an activity-related "who" question when given up to 6 picture choices on 3 out of 5 trials.

Terrence: Follow routine-related 3-step directions when given 2 additional prompts (verbal or gestural) on 2 out of 3 trials.

Linda: Listen to and comprehend a simple story as demonstrated by the ability to answer-related questions utilizing pictures or augmentative devices with verbal and gestural prompts on 3 out of 5 trials.

Alexander: Respond to "Wh" questions related to a story when given visual reminders on 3 out of 5 trials.

Standard 3.4. *Language Arts Literacy:* All students will read a variety of materials and texts with comprehension and critical analysis.

Terrence: Recognize name in printed form when given a choice of his and those of 2 other classmates on 2 out of 3 trials.

Alexander: Demonstrate reading comprehension of very simple material by answering simple questions correctly, 4 out of 5 attempts.

Standard 4. *Cross Content Indicator:* All students demonstrate management skills.

Maria: Work cooperatively on a familiar tabletop task without exhibiting aggressive behavior towards others for a period of 1 minute

Keisha: Work to complete a task independently for a 1-minute period of time, during 3 out of 5 activities. Refrain from grabbing/touching objects or people when 1 verbal prompt is provided on 3 out of 5 trials.

Terrence: Work to complete a familiar academically-related tabletop activity given only 2 redirections once during each school day. Follow a verbal directive without exhibiting inappropriate behavior (i.e., yelling, banging toys and/or hands, etc.) on 4 out of 5 occasions.

Linda: Attend to a simple assigned task for up to 1 minute with only 1 verbal redirection during 3 different periods of each school day.

Simon: Use a switch with picture to indicate when he is angry rather than exhibiting tantrum like behaviors given

continued

TABLE 1.1. CCCSSSD STANDARDS (IEP GOALS) FOR CHILDREN IN THE GROUP–*Continued.*

a physical prompt (1 hand held down) and verbal prompting.

Alexander: Follow directions and work appropriately with a variety of people, including unfamiliar adults or peers on familiar classroom activities on 4 out of 5 trials. Complete a task in a variety of settings without complaint, with 1 verbal reminder, 4 out of 5 trials. Verbally express his needs and wants in an appropriate manner and in a timely fashion, throughout the school with minimal prompts on 4 out of 5 trials.

Standard 4.1. *Math:* All students will develop to pose and solve mathematical problems in mathematics, other disciplines and everyday experiences.

Keisha: Demonstrate an understanding of 1:1 correspondence by responding to the directive, "give me one" or "give 1 to each person" on 4 out of 5 trials. Demonstrate accurate sorting of 3 types of objects with a tactile component (using varying textures for differentiation) on 4 out of 5 attempts.

Linda: Identify "what comes next" from a field of 2 familiar Mayer Johnson daily schedule pictures on 3 out of 5 trials.

Alexander: Demonstrate the ability to solve addition problems to 20, using real objects, 4 out of 5 attempts. Demonstrate the ability to solve subtraction problems to 20, using real objects, 4 of 5 attempts.

Standard 4.5. *Math:* All students will regularly and routinely use calculators, computers, manipulation and other mathematical tools to enhance mathematical thinking, understanding and power.

Maria: Routinely use measuring cups for dry and liquid measurements during cooking activities with verbal, gestural and physical prompting.

Standard 4.6. *Math:* All students will develop number sense and an ability to represent numbers in a variety of forms and use numbers in diverse situations.

Maria: Demonstrate 1:1 Correspondence up to 3 by giving the requested amount of objects to staff or peers on 3 out of 4 trials.

Terrence: Count up to 5 objects correctly using 1:1 correspondence on 4 out of 5 trials. Verbally relate address and phone number when requested.

Linda: Demonstrate comprehension of 1:1 correspondence by matching 1 object to each person in a group in a variety of settings throughout the school with 1 verbal prompt

Standard 4.9. *Math:* All students will develop an understanding of, and will use measurement to describe and analyze phenomena.

Simon: Choose the appropriate measuring utensil when presented with a choice of 2 during a cooking activity on 3 out of 5 trials.

Standard 4.11. *Math:* All students will develop understanding of patterns, relationships and functions and will use them to represent and explain real-world phenomena.

Terrence: Correctly answer the question, "What comes next?" 4 out of 5 times using the daily picture schedule.

Simon: Identify the "next" activity when presented with a choice of 2 after viewing a model daily picture schedule for his classroom routine on 3 out of 5 occasions.

Standard 4. *Cross Content Indicator:* All students will apply safety principles

Alexander: Follow safety directives throughout the school when prompted verbally once on 4 out of 5 trials showing appropriate self-restraint when directed.

Standard 5.6. *Science:* All students will gain an understanding of the structure, characteristics, and basic needs of organisms.

Maria: Demonstrate handwashing skills without physical prompting on 3 out of 4 trials (given verbal, visual, and gestural prompts)

continued

TABLE 1.1. CCCSSSD STANDARDS (IEP GOALS) FOR CHILDREN IN THE GROUP–*Continued.*

Terrence: Independently wash hands on 4 out of 5 occasions using a picture sequence as a reference.
Linda: Demonstrate increased independence with handwashing with only physical assistance for soap dispensing on 3 out of 5 occasions.

Standard 5.7. *Science:* All students will investigate the diversity of life.
Alexander: Demonstrate knowledge about pet care by answering simple questions accurately 5 out of 5 attempts. Demonstrate knowledge of plant care by answering simple questions accurately 4 out of 5 attempts.

Standard 5.9. *Science:* All students will gain an understanding of natural laws as they apply to motion, forces, and energy transformation.
Keisha: Make a choice from 3 verbal/visual options regarding temperature and/or weather during circle time on 4 out of 5 days.
Simon: Choose appropriate seasonal clothing when presented with 2 choices during circle time after the weather has been discussed.

Standard 5.12. *Science:* All students will develop an understanding of the environment as a system of interdependent components affected by human activity and natural phenomena.
Maria: Participate in recycling activities by crushing cans with adult supervision during vocational education given a verbal and gestural prompt.
Keisha: Choose appropriate clothing for the season/weather when presented with 2 articles, after the weather condition has been discussed, on 3 out of 5 trials.
Linda: Routinely demonstrate appropriate disposal of trash given only a gestural prompt.
Simon: Appropriately sort newspapers and aluminum cans that are properly labeled for recycling purposes on 3 out of 5 trials.

Standard 6.1. *Social Studies:* All students will learn democratic citizenship and how to participate in the constitutional system of government of the United States.
Maria: Attend during group activities to 2 other peer turns by sitting appropriately and not exhibiting aggressive behaviors toward herself or others, when given no more than 2 verbal prompts on 3 out of 4 occasions.
Keisha: Appropriately gain the attention of a staff person or peer by saying their name in place of pulling/grabbing them on 3 out of 5 occasions.
Linda: Demonstrate turn-taking during group activities in the classroom for 2 reciprocal sequences initiating her turn at the proper time, with only 1 verbal prompt.
Simon: Cease scratching, pinching or slapping of others when given physical and verbal prompts on 3 out of 5 occasions during the day.
Alexander: Demonstrate the use of good manners at appropriate times, without prompting 3 out of 5 given opportunities.

Standard 6.2. *Social Studies:* All students will learn democratic leadership through the humanities by studying literature, art history and philosophy and related fields.
Maria: Demonstrate the knowledge of what comes next on her daily school activity schedule, by making an appropriate choice from a field of 3 pictures presented after being shown a model schedule during circle time on 3 out of 5 trials.
Keisha: Follow a daily school schedule using pictures/objects by accurately stating what activity comes next on 4 out of 5 trials.
Linda: Identify her classmates when presented with a choice of 2 portrait photographs on 4 out of 5 trials.
Simon: Wait until the appropriate time and then activate a switch to say the Pledge of Allegiance during morning circle. Demonstrate compliance by participating in a presented activity, given physical and verbal prompting without exhibiting inappropriate behavior for a period of 10 minutes.
Alexander: Give a simple job description of community workers when requested, 3 out of 5 attempts.

TABLE 1.2. CCCSSSD GOALS FOR THE CHILDREN, PRIORITIZED FOR MUSIC THERAPY.

Maria

1. Reduce the instances of biting to her hands, given a verbal prompt, "hands down" 4/5 trials.
2. Participate in gross motor activity for a period of 10 minutes with compliance and without complaint.
3. Demonstrate 1:1 correspondence up to 3 by giving the requested amount of objects to staff or peers on 3 out of 4 trials.
4. Attend to 2 other peer turns by sitting appropriately and not exhibiting aggressive behaviors toward herself or others, when given no more than 2 verbal prompts, on 3 out of 4 occasions.
5. Demonstrate the knowledge of what comes next by making an appropriate choice from a field of 3 pictures presented after being shown a model schedule during 3 out of 5 trials.
6. Respond appropriately to an activity-related "Wh" question when given up to 6 picture choices on 3 out of 5 trials.
7. Produce 3-word combinations through the use of pictures and/or manual signs when given verbal prompts, but without phrase modeling.

Keisha

1. Spontaneously and consistently use short and appropriate verbal sentences/phrases at least 5 times daily.
2. Tolerate oral motor exercises to strengthen oral musculature for 2 minutes a minimum of 3 times weekly by a speech therapist.
3. Correctly answer activity-related "Wh" questions on 4 out of 5 trials.
4. Follow a variety of simple 2-step directives with one repetition on 3 out of 5 trials.
5. Work to complete a task independently for a 1-minute period of time during 3 out of 5 activities.
6. Refrain from grabbing/touching objects or people when 1 verbal prompt is provided on 3 out of 5 trials.
7. Demonstrate understanding of 1:1 correspondence by responding to the directive, "give me one" or "give 1 to each person" on 4 out of 5 trials.
8. Demonstrate accurate sorting of 3 types of objects with a tactile component on 4 out of 5 attempts.
9. Appropriately gain the attention of a staff person or peer by saying their name in place of pulling/grabbing them on 3 out of 5 occasions.
10. Follow a schedule using pictures/objects by accurately stating what activity comes next on 4 out of 5 trials.

Terrence

1. Participate in a reciprocal ball play activity for a period of 2 minutes with appropriate turn-taking on 4 out of 5 trials.
2. Make appropriate choices from four pictures on 3 out of 4 trials with verbal direction and gestural prompts.
3. Respond to "Wh" questions with a short phrase or sentence without prompting on 3 out of 5 trials.
4. Follow routine related 3-step directions when given 2 additional prompts (verbal or gestural) on 2 out of 3 trials.
5. Follow a verbal directive without exhibiting inappropriate behavior on 4 out of 5 occasions.
6. Count up to 5 objects correctly using one-to-one correspondence.
7. Relate address and phone number.
8. Answer the question, "What comes next" 4 out of 5 times using the daily picture schedule.

Linda

1. Demonstrate compliance when transitioning from a favored activity, given minimal physical assistance, after only 1 verbal prompt.
2. Willingly participate in formalized group gross motor activities demonstrating appropriate peer interaction on 3 out of 5 occasions.

continued

TABLE 1.2. CCCSSSD GOALS FOR THE CHILDREN, PRIORITIZED FOR MUSIC THERAPY—*Continued.*

3. Tolerate oral motor exercises to strengthen oral musculature for 2 minutes a minimum of 3 times weekly by a speech therapist.
4. Communicate wants, needs and preferences, given up to 5 picture choices and/or using an augmentative device with voice output on 3 to 5 trials when given verbal and gestural prompt.
5. As a precursor to increasing picture vocabulary, match objects to pictures from a field up to 5.
6. During vocal, instrumental and movement activity, attend to a simple task for up to 1 minute with only 1 verbal redirection.
7. Identify what comes next from a field of 2 familiar Mayer Johnson daily schedule pictures on 3 out of 5 trials.
8. Demonstrate comprehension of one-to-one correspondence by matching 1 object to each person with 1 verbal prompt.
9. Demonstrate turn taking during group activities for 2 reciprocal sequences for 2 reciprocal sequences initiating her turn at the proper time, with only 1 verbal prompt.
10. Identify her classmates when presented with a choice of 2 portrait photographs on 4 out of 5 trials.

Simon

1. Demonstrate bilateral hand use without physical prompts on 3 out of 5 trials.
2. Demonstrate appropriate reciprocal gait patterns for ambulation within the gait trainer, with appropriate head righting and hands in a relaxed position for a period of 10 minutes.
3. Tolerate passive range of motion to bilateral lower extremities and trunk without complaint.
4. Demonstrate appropriate positioning of bilateral lower extremities when out of his classroom chair, with appropriate positioning aids to assist in passive range of motion.
5. Increase picture vocabulary to at least 10 pictures (including music, standing).
6. Use a switch with picture to indicate when he is angry rather than exhibiting tantrum-like behavior; given a physical prompt (one hand held down) and verbal prompting.
7. Identify the "next" activity when presented with a choice of 2 after viewing a model daily picture schedule on 3 out of 5 occasions.
8. Cease scratching, pinching or slapping of others when given physical and verbal prompts on 3 out of 5 occasions during the day.
9. Demonstrate compliance by participating in a presented activity, given physical and verbal prompting, with out exhibiting inappropriate behavior for a period of 10 minutes.

Alexander

1. Follow directions and work appropriately with a variety of people, including unfamiliar adults or peers on familiar classroom activities on 4 out of 5 trials. Complete a task without complaint, with 1 verbal reminder, 4 out of 5 trials. Verbally express needs and wants in an appropriate manner and in a timely fashion, on 4 out of 5 trials.
2. Demonstrate reading comprehension of very simple material by answering simple questions correctly, 4 out of 5 attempts.
3. Respond to "Wh" questions given visual reminders on 3 out of 5 trials.
4. Correctly answer routine-related questions with a short phrase or sentence and in a timely fashion without prompting on 4 out of 5 trials. Use expressive language to give peers simple directions during classroom activities with a verbal prompt on 3 out of 5 trials.
5. Make appropriate choices from up to 6 pictures or 3 verbal choices on 4 out of 5 trials.
6. Spontaneously use bilateral hand skills.
7. Demonstrate appropriate gait patterns using the gait trainer with the aid of his new orthotics and abduction positioner for a distance of 30 feet on 4 out of 5 occasions. Demonstrate appropriate usage of upper extremities and trunk when engaged in ball play, throwing overhead/from the chest without loss of balance for a distance of 4 feet on 3 out of 5 trials.

TABLE 1.3. CONSIDER THE OVERLAPPING NEEDS OF THE CHILDREN IN ORDER TO
PRIORITIZE AND ORGANIZE THE WORKING GOALS OF THE FIRST FEW SESSIONS.

1. Children will use expressive language at appropriate developmental level:

   • Spontaneous and consistent short and appropriate verbal sentences (Keisha).
   • Response to activity-related "Wh" questions (Keisha).
   • Response to story-related "Wh" questions given visual reminders on 3 out of 5 trials (Alexander)
   • Give peers simple directions with a verbal prompt on 3 out of 5 trials (Alexander)
   • Answer routine-related questions with a short phrase or sentence and in a timely fashion without prompting on 4 out of 5 trials (Alexander).
   • Appropriately gain the attention of a staff person or peer by saying their name in place of pulling/grabbing them on 3 out of 5 occasions (Keisha).
   • Follow a music activity schedule using pictures and accurately stating what activity comes next on 4 out of 5 trials (Keisha), on 3 out of 5 choices (Linda; Simon).
   • Use a switch with picture to indicate when is he angry rather than exhibiting tantrum-like behavior, given a physical prompt (one hand held down) and verbal prompting (Simon).
   • Appropriate choices from up to 6 pictures or 3 verbal choices on 4 out of 5 trials (Alexander).
   • Spontaneous and consistent short and appropriate verbal sentences (Keisha).
   • Response to activity-related "Wh" questions (Keisha) with a short phrase or sentence without prompting on 3 out of 5 trials (Terrence).
   • Response to story-related "Wh" questions given visual reminders on 3 out of 5 trials (Alexander).
   • Give peers simple directions with a verbal prompt on 3 out of 5 trials (Alexander).
   • Communicate wants, needs and preferences, given up to 5 picture choices and/or using an augmentative device with voice output on 3 to 5 trials when given verbal and gestural prompt (Linda).

2. Children will use receptive language at appropriate developmental level:

   • Follow a variety of simple 2-step directives with 1 repetition on 3 out of 5 trials (Keisha).
   • Follow routine-related 3-step directions when given 2 additional prompts (verbal and gestural) on 2 out of 3 trials (Terrence).
   • Increase picture vocabulary to at least 10 pictures, including pictures for music and standing (Simon).
   • Follow directions and work appropriately with a variety of people on 4 out of 5 trials (Alexander).
   • Make appropriate choice from 4 pictures on 3 out of 4 trials with verbal direction and gestural prompts (Terrence).

3. Children will tolerate physical input introduced by speech-language therapist:

   • Tolerate oral motor exercises to strengthen oral musculature for 2 minutes (Keisha; Linda).

4. Children will participate in physical activity as specified:

   • Ten minutes with compliance and without complaint (Maria).
   • Appropriate peer interaction on 3 out of 5 occasions (Linda).
   • Demonstrate improved posture, including trunk control (Alexander).

5. During reciprocal ball play, children will participate as specified:

   • Appropriate usage of upper extremities and trunk when engaged in ball play, throwing overhead for a distance of 4 feet on 3 out of 5 trials (Alexander).
   • For a period of 2 minutes with appropriate turn-taking on 4 out of 5 trials (Terrence).

6. Demonstrate bilateral hand use spontaneously (Alexander) or without physical prompts on 3 out of 5 trials (Simon).

continued

TABLE 1.3. CONSIDER THE OVERLAPPING NEEDS OF THE CHILDREN IN ORDER TO
PRIORITIZE AND ORGANIZE THE WORKING GOALS OF THE FIRST FEW SESSIONS.

7. Tolerate physical input from physical therapist accordingly:

   • Passive range of motion to bilateral lower extremities and trunk without complaint (Simon).
   • Positioning of bilateral lower extremities and appropriate positioning aids to assist in passive range of motion (Simon).

8. Regulate gait patterns:

   • Using the gait trainer with the aid of orthotics and abduction positioner for a distance of 30 feet on 4 out of 5 occasions (Alexander).
   • Using the gait trainer, with appropriate head righting and hands in a relaxed position for a period of 10 minutes (Simon).

9. Demonstrate one-to-one correspondence accordingly:

   • Up to 3 by giving the request amount of objects to staff or peers on 3 out of 4 trials (Maria).
   • Count up to 5 objects correctly (Terrence).
   • Match objects to pictures from a field up to 5 (Linda).

10. Demonstrate comprehension of one-to-one correspondence by matching one object to each person with 1 verbal prompt (Linda).

11. Choose the type of activity that comes next:

   • Four out of 5 times using the daily picture schedule (Terrence).
   • Three out of 5 trials from a field of three pictures (Maria).

12. Demonstrate accurate sorting of 3 types of objects with tactile components on 4 out of 5 attempts (Keisha).

13. Attend without behavioral disruption:

   • Up to 1 minute with only verbal redirection.
   • Without biting to hands, given a verbal prompt, "hands down" 4 out of 5 trials (Maria).
   • By sitting appropriately during 2 other peer turns and not exhibiting aggressive behaviors toward herself or others, when given no more than 2 verbal prompts, on 3 out of 4 occasions (Maria).
   • Without grabbing/touching objects or people when 1 verbal prompt is provided on 3 out of 5 trials (Keisha).
   • Without exhibiting inappropriate behavior on 4 out of 5 occasions (Terrence) when following verbal directive.
   • Without scratching, pinching or slapping of others when given physical and verbal prompts on 3 out of 5 occasions (Simon).
   • By participating in a presented activity, given physical and verbal prompting, without exhibiting inappropriate behavior for a period of 10 minutes (Simon).
   • Complete a task without complaint with 1 verbal reminder 4 out of 5 trials (Alexander).
   • When transitioning from favored activity, given minimal physical assistance, after only 1 verbal prompt (Linda).

14. Take turns:

   • By sitting appropriately during 2 other peer turns and not exhibiting aggressive behaviors toward herself or others, when given no more than 2 verbal prompts, on 3 out of 4 occasions (Maria).
   • During group activities for 2 reciprocal sequences initiating her turn at the proper time, with only 1 verbal prompt (Linda).

TABLE 1.4. DEVELOPMENTAL DOMAINS FOR IEP GOALS.

SPEECH/LANGUAGE

1. Children will use expressive language at appropriate developmental level:

   • spontaneous and consistent short and appropriate verbal sentences (Keisha).
   • response to activity-related "Wh" questions (Keisha)
   • response to story-related "Wh" questions given visual reminders on 3 out of 5 trials (Alexander).
   • response to an activity related "Wh" question when given up to 6 picture choices on 3 out of 5 trials (Maria).
   • give peers simple directions with a verbal prompt on 3 out of 5 trials (Alexander).
   • answer routine-related questions with a short phrase or sentence and in a timely fashion without prompting on 4 out of 5 trials (Alexander).
   • appropriately gain the attention of a staff person or peer by saying their name in place of pulling/grabbing them on 3 out of 5 occasions (Keisha).
   • follow a music activity schedule using pictures and accurately stating what activity comes next on 4 out of 5 trials (Keisha), on 3 out of 5 choices (Linda; Simon).
   • use a switch with picture to indicate when is he angry rather than exhibiting tantrum-like behavior, given a physical prompt (one hand held down) and verbal prompting (Simon).
   • appropriate choices from up to 6 pictures or 3 verbal choices on 4 out of 5 trials (Alexander).
   • produce 3-word combinations through the use of pictures and/or manual signs when given verbal prompts, but without phrase modeling (Maria).

2. Children will use receptive language at appropriate developmental level:

   • make appropriate choice from 4 pictures on 3 out of 4 trials with verbal direction and gestural prompts (Terrence).
   • follow a variety of simple 2-step directives with one repetition on 3 out of 5 trials (Keisha).
   • follow routine-related 3-step directions when given 2 additional prompts (verbal and gestrual) on 2 out of 3 trials (Terrence).
   • increase picture vocabulary to at least 10 pictures including pictures for music and standing (Simon).
   • follow directions and work appropriately with a variety of people on 4 out of 5 trials (Alexander).

3. Children will tolerate physical input introduced by speech-language therapist:

   • tolerate oral motor exercises to strengthen oral musculature for 2 minutes (Keisha; Linda).

MOTOR

1. Children will participate in movement as specified:

   • 10 minutes with compliance and without complaint (Maria).
   • appropriate peer interaction on 3 out of 5 occasions (Linda).
   • demonstrate improved posture, including trunk (Alexander).

2. During reciprocal ball play, children will participate as specified:

   • appropriate usage of upper extremities and trunk when engaged in ball play, throwing overhead for a distance of 4 feet on 3 out of 5 trials (Alexander).
   • for a period of 2 minutes with appropriate turn-taking on 4 out of 5 trials (Terrence).

3. Demonstrate bilateral hand use spontaneously (Alexander) or without physical prompts on 3 out of 5 trials (Simon).

continued

TABLE 1.4. DEVELOPMENTAL DOMAINS FOR IEP GOALS–*Continued.*

4. Tolerate physical input from physical therapist accordingly:

   • passive range of motion to bilateral lower extremities and trunk without complaint (Simon).
   • positioning of bilateral lower extremities and appropriate positioning aids to assist in passive range of motion (Simon).

5. Regulate gait patterns:

   • using the gait trainer with the aid of orthotics and abduction positioner for a distance of 30 feet on 4 out of 5 occasions (Alexander).
   • using the gait trainer, with appropriate head righting and hands in a relaxed position for a period of 10 minutes (Simon).

COGNITIVE

1. Demonstrate one-to-one correspondence accordingly:

   • up to 3 by giving the requested amount of objects to staff or peers on 3 out of 4 trials (Maria).
   • count up to 5 objects correctly (Terrence).
   • match objects to pictures from a field up to 5 (Linda).

2. Demonstrate comprehension of one to one correspondence by matching 1 object to each person with 1 verbal prompt (Linda).

3. Choose the type of activity that comes next:

   • 4 out of 5 times using the daily picture schedule (Terrence).
   • 3 out of 5 trials from a field of 3 pictures (Maria).

4. Demonstrate accurate sorting of 3 types of objects with a tactile components on 4 out of 5 attempts (Keisha).

SOCIAL-EMOTIONAL

1. Attend without behavioral disruption:

   • up to 1 minute with only verbal redirection.
   • without biting to hands, given a verbal prompt, "hands down" 4 out of 5 trials (Maria).
   • by sitting appropriately during 2 other peer turns and not exhibiting aggressive behaviors toward herself or others, when given no more than 2 verbal prompts, on 3 out of 4 occasions (Maria).
   • without grabbing/touching objects or people when 1 verbal prompt is provided on 3 out of 5 trials (Keisha).
   • without exhibiting inappropriate behavior on 4 out of 5 occasions (Terrence) when following verbal directives.
   • without scratching, pinching or slapping of others when given physical and verbal prompts on 3 out of 5 occasions (Simon).
   • by participating in a presented activity, given physical and verbal prompting, without exhibiting inappropriate behavior for a period of 10 minutes (Simon).
   • complete a task without complaint with 1 verbal reminder 4 out of 5 trials (Alexander).
   • when transitioning from favored activity, given minimal physical assistance, after only 1 verbal prompt (Linda).

2. Take turns:

   • by sitting appropriately during 2 other peer turns and not exhibiting aggressive behaviors toward herself or others, when given no more than 2 verbal prompts, on 3 out of 4 occasions (Maria).
   • during group activities for 2 reciprocal sequences initiating her turn at the proper time, with only 1 verbal prompt (Linda).

TABLE 1.5. VISUAL/PERFORMING ARTS STANDARDS.

Now that all CCCSSSD goals have been organized and prioritized, fit them into the context of the Visual/Performing Arts Standards of CCCSSSD (see indicators in bold italicized typeface).

Visual Performing Arts

Standard 1.2–All students will refine perceptual, intellectual, physical, and technical skills through creating dance, music, theater, and/or visual arts.

Cumulative Progress Indicators

1. Create, produce, and perform works of dance, music, theater, or visual arts, individually and with others.

   Music Therapy Definition: Child will produce and perform music at appropriate developmental levels as indicated in CCCSSSD priorities for music therapy (see Table 1.2).

2. Express and communicate ideas and feelings through music and dance, visual arts, and theater arts.

   Music Therapy Definition: Child will increase use of emotional expression and communication by following CCCSSSD Language/Literacy goals (Cumulative Progress Indicators) as specified and also by initiating a minimum of one spontaneous musical experience in each session.

Standard 1.3–All students will utilize arts elements and arts media to produce artistic products and performances.

Cumulative Progress Indicators

1. Apply elements and media common to the arts to produce a work of art.

   Music Therapy Definition: Child will use the elements of music–melody, rhythm and harmony–to interactively work together on three out of four musical experiences in the music therapy session.

2. Demonstrate appropriate use of technology, tools, terminology, techniques, and/or media in the creation of dance, music, theater, or visual arts.

   Music Therapy Definitio: Child will use augmentative communication as necessary to be involved in making music in three out of four vocal or instrumental activities in music therapy.

Standard 1.4–All students will demonstrate knowledge of the process of critique.

Cumulative Progress Indicators

1. Communicate preferences for types of dance music, theater or visual arts.

   Music Therapy Definition: Child will use verbal and/or nonverbal means to select music preferences on three out of four occasions in the music therapy session.

2. Demonstrate/make a choice from among dance, music, theater or visual arts for leisure activities.

   Music Therapy Definition: Given four arts choices in the classroom (either through picture exchange or verbal suggestion), child will use verbal and/or nonverbal means to select listening materials for relaxation during rest time after lunch once during the week.

OBJECTIVES, METHODS, AND MATERIALS

On Objectives

I tend to link certain kinds of music activity with *categories of long-term goals and their related short-term musical objectives.* I teach the process of distinguishing between goals and objectives in several ways. The goals, in the language of the IEP, are long-term clinical goals without reference to music (note: unless they are goals specifically formulated for visual/performing arts or music therapy). The jump to formulating objectives requires the imagination of the therapist on two different levels. First, I have to think about how the goal can best be met. *Through what type of musical experience is the goal naturally embedded?* Then I have to think about the breakdown of the goal into a hierarchy of short-term objectives and stage these objectives in the language of the music therapy experience. *What can I realistically expect from these children in this session?*

Through what type of musical experience is the goal naturally embedded? I might start to answer this question by considering domains of development. When I consider vocal, instrumental, movement and listening experiences, they all involve the opportunity for conceptual development (cognition) and the sharing of musical experiences (social). Vocal experience seems most obviously connected to speech and language development, and instrumental and movement experience seem most related to gross and fine movement.

Let's start by looking at this particular group. The connection between goals of speech/language development and short-term objectives through vocal music seems very clear to me. In this particular group, the need for vocalizing vowels and consonants not only replicates an infant level of development for someone like Simon who has been asked to use augmentative communication or Maria who is expected to communicate through picture exchange or manual signing but also frees the oral-motor mechanism that Keisha and Linda have difficulty with. The opportunity for inclusion of simple sentences embedded in simple songs that the children like works well for

Terrence, Keisha and Alexander. The pairing of movement in finger plays, for example, with singing of simple lyrics, seems to provide the kind of sensory integration that helps Keisha and Terrence produce a greater amount of articulated language. In this group, the children most responsive to singing are Keisha, Terrence and Maria. As soon as I start any kind of song, they move in their seats, become animated and involved.

Instrumental music obviously involves movement, both gross and fine. However, it also involves many levels of cognition and socializing: not only the setting up and giving out of instruments, a functional way to introduce choice-making, color, shape, size, one-to-one correspondence and language infusion, but also turn-taking, following directions, fine and gross motor activity, and group awareness. In this group, Alexander, despite his motor restrictions, is bound and determined to use the instruments. His arms flail to find the means of control when playing the drum and, to the amazement of everyone in the room, he is successful in staying on the beat! This movement helps him coordinate his singing even though he is apraxic.

Finally, movement to music, similar to instrumental music, provides opportunity for following directions, turn-taking, fine and gross motor activity and group awareness. If the group is lethargic, I like to start with movement. I have a sense that it "wakes" the central nervous system. It helps the hyperactive children, like Terrence, Linda and Keisha, channel kinetic energy and calm down. On the other hand, it helps the hypoactive children, like Maria and Simon, become neurologically stimulated.

What can I realistically expect from the children in this beginning session? It seems obvious to me that I can't expect them to meet the behavioral demands of the annual IEP in the first session so I have to expect some baby step toward each goal. What type of baby step? This is what I consider educational guesswork. For example, if Linda is supposed to transition spontaneously from one activity to another without tantrumming, I can probably expect her to transition with prompting as well as the support of a transitional tune at least half the time in the session, right? On the other hand, if I see her beginning to transition without a support system, I wonder if this goal is applicable to music therapy. Is it not the enjoyment of music that helps children naturally move forward in situations that are otherwise more difficult for them? I will see.

It has been a learning process over the last few years to integrate different levels of expectation using the same materials. Sometimes, I think it is difficult for us to accept different expectations of response. It feels like a juggling act and it does not conform neatly to any kind of generic, middle-of-the-road session plan. But how could any group conform to similar expectations? That would be totally unnatural and unrealistic.

On Materials

In a sense, I "grew up" with the Nordoff-Robbins playsongs and the Herbert and Gail Levin orchestrations. I love using them, as well as the wealth of other materials that have been published in the music therapy literature over the years (see Chapter Six, "Materials"). Not only do I enjoy improvising on previously composed materials, from music therapy and music education, but also improvising from "scratch" based on what the children are doing in the session. I have also learned how to appreciate many types of music and most importantly, adapt it to the clinical needs of the children. In order to use music in a way that fits the functioning levels of the children, I have developed a kind of *hierarchy of expectations* that I refer to as *Continuum of Musical Response* (Goodman, 2002). I can create a hierarchy in both general and specific terms (i.e., for each musical experience) that makes sense for me in terms of *choosing materials that are flexible enough to invite different developmental levels of response and flexible enough for me to present on a different level methodologically. In terms of vocal activities, I expect the following general levels of participation:* 1) listening and watching (sensory intake); some affective reaction; vocal may be combined with movement and/or instrumental; 2) vocalization (may be delayed); 3) pitch approximation; phrase singing; 4) one word response; 5) more than one word song lyrics; and 6) song lyrics to convey feeling and thoughts.

In terms of movement activities, I expect the following general levels of participation: 1) listening while being physically manipulated to music (sensory intake); 2) watching while a visual is physically manipulated; 3) gross motor start and stop; 4) finger plays; 5) one-step directions; 6) multiple directions; 7) representational play; and 8) preacademic directives in the context of movement.

In terms of instrumental activities, I expect the following general level of participation: 1) Listening while instruments are being played (sensory intake can include visual, auditory, tactile, kinesthetic); 2) exploring instrument at beginning level (can be assisted or unassisted); 3) one-step directive (can include stop/start and can include "body percussion"); 4) two-step or multiply directive; 5) instruments as representational; and 6) instruments for preacademic directives.

I am always amazed when my students feel stumped about what materials to use for their clinical sessions with children. There is just so much music in this world to learn and create. I think the sense of "What can I do in music therapy? I can't think of what to do" is an anxiety reaction. It probably helps to think in terms of the overall structure of the session, goals and objectives, materials and then methods. I think of opening, "content" activities and closing. If the group is lower functioning, the group members generally require a great deal of structure. If the group is higher functioning, the group members tend to suggest what they like to do and I simply facilitate those suggestions.

On Format of Session

I think in terms of vocal, instrumental, movement and listening activities. If I can include all of these modes in the session, it provides opportunity for different preferences.

I see my plan in terms of a starting point only, not an ending point. I expect the children, no matter how low functioning, to spontaneously contribute elements to the session that will take it to "another place." I will happily follow them to that "other place" as long as I can keep the group intact and developmentally moving. As I continue to write in this chapter, I will present part of a session with this group, illustrating this balance between music planning and spontaneous music-making.

In a sense, it is easier for me personally to think about the *format of the session* and what kinds of music and music activity the children are responsive to first. Then I always manage to *incorporate* or *embed what I think of as musical objectives related to long-term clinical goals.* I really love the concept of always seeing all the developmental purpose in every musical experience, planned or spontaneous

On Methods

Special education teachers and allied therapists report using certain instructional/ therapeutic strategies with the children and these can possibly be replicated in the music therapy session. However, I feel very strongly that the music therapist has *music therapy strategies* that are unique to the work. Part of the music therapy strategy may consist of a "translation" of sorts from the classroom instruction to the music therapy context. For example:

- modeling
- infusing language
- keeping directions short, clear and concise
- different kinds of prompting
- positive reinforcement
- task analysis
- refocusing
- alternation of seated activities and physical activities
- extended response time
- multisensory strategies
- concrete "hands-on" instruction
- positioning and handling

Other strategies, however, revolve uniquely around music and need to be recognized as such. Why, for example, do we hold out for language at the end of a musical phrase? Why do we combine movement (either through dance movement or instrumental movement) with singing? Why do we set gait to rhythmic music? Why do we employ songs, movement or playing of instruments to help a child express feelings? How do we take our cues from the child in order to create musical experi-ence or adapt the musical experience we may have premediatated as an intervention?

The more we can identify strategies unique to music therapy, the more we can consider how these strategies transform the child within the context of the music session.

LINKING CLINICAL GOALS, MUSICAL OBJECTIVES, METHODS AND MATERIALS: A SAMPLE SESSION

Starting the Session

Opening Song

I like to start the session with an opening song and end with a closing song. When the group is lower functioning like this one, opening and closing songs provide a sense of structure that is comforting in their predictability. There are so many wonderful musical resources composed for therapy toward this end (see Chapter 6), For the opening song in my session today, I am going to use "Roll Call" from Book One of the Nordoff-Robbins Playsongs (1962). The beauty of this song lies in its freedom: the child can respond to the "Roll Call," "Where is (name), Oh, where is (name)" on any appropriate expressive language level (pictures, augmentative device, song lyrics). Children who are particularly demonstrative or, on the other hand, children who are shy and need to be encouraged to become more demonstrative, can jump up and act out out their response.

Goals and Objectives for Opening Song

With this group, I can anticipate and structure the following kinds of *goals and objectives* for my opening song:

Clinical Goal 1: Children will use expressive language at appropriate developmental level.

Objective 1a: During vocal activity, communicate using programmed touch talker with voice output on 1 of 3 trials when given verbal and gestural prompt (Linda; Simon).

Objective 1b: During vocal activity, produce 3-word combinations (Here I am) with manual signs when given verbal prompts (Maria).

Objective 1c: During vocal activity, use spontaneous and consistent short and appropriate verbal sentences (Keisha).

Objective 1d: During vocal activity, expect response to activity-related "Wh" questions (Keisha) with a short phrase or sentence without prompting on 1 out of 3 trials (Terrence).

Objective 1e: During vocal music, use full simple sentences (Here I am) in response to the question, Where is my friend (Name)? (Keisha).

Clinical Goal 2: Attend without behavioral disruption.

Objective 2a: During music therapy, without biting to hands, given a verbal prompt, 'hands down' 4 out of 5 trials (Maria).

Objecitve 2b: During music therapy, by sitting appropriately during 2 other peer turns and not exhibiting aggressive behaviors toward herself or others, when given no more than 2 verbal prompts, on 3 out of 4 occasions (Maria).

Objective 2c: During music therapy, without grabbing/touching objects or people when 1 verbal prompt is provided on 3 out of 5 trials (Keisha).

Objective 2d: During music therapy, without exhibiting inappropriate behavior on 4 out of 5 occasions (Terrence) when following verbal directive.

Objective 2e: During music therapy, without scratching, pinching or slapping of others when given physical and verbal prompts on 3 out of 5 occasions (Simon).

Objective 2f: During music therapy, by participating in a presented activity, given physical and verbal prompting, without exhibiting inappropriate behavior for a period of 10 minutes (Simon).

Objective 2g: During music therapy, complete a task without complaint with 1 verbal reminder 4 out of 5 trials (Alexander).

Objective 2h: During music, when transitioning from favored activity, 5 minimal physical assistances, after only 1 verbal prompt (Linda).

Methods for Opening Song

In terms of *methods,* I think about how I want to present this opening song and the modifications I need to make for various children. Some of the methods that I anticipate using in my opening song include 1) making sure the children are properly *positioned* to produce language; 2) using the teacher aide as a *model;* 3) *establishing eye contact* while singing to a particular child; 4) *pausing* after the sung question, "Where is my friend, (name)?" in order to allow time for delayed auditory processing and correct response in terms of gesture, touch talker or sung full sentence; and 5) *praising* each child after appropriate response.

When written out in a session plan by a beginning therapist, the methods for the opening would look like this:

Methods and Materials

1. Therapist uses aide in room as model if song is not familiar to demonstrate "Where is my friend, (name)" and the aide's response, "Here I am, here I am. I am here today."
2. Therapist establishes eye contact with each child as she sings.
3. Therapist pauses after question, "Where is my friend (name)?" anticipating correct response in terms of gesture (Maria), programmed touch talker (Linda, Simon) or sung full sentence (Terrence, Keisha, Alexander).
4. Repeat as necessary with modeling and prompting for response, providing musical bridges as necessary to allow time for auditory processing before the child responds.
5. Therapist positively and specifically reinforces correct response.

Material: "Roll Call" (Nordoff-Robbins, Book one, *Playsongs*).

Movement Activity

Movement

Following the opening song, I am comfortably

transitioning to a modified *movement activity,* one that the children can participate in while seated since half the group (Alexander, Linda, and Simon) is wheelchair-bound. I use the song "Clap your hands to the music," composed by the music therapist, Suzanne Nowickes-Sorel (Robbins, 1995). The lively beat continues the animated spirit of "Roll Call." When the directives in the song are modified by the therapist, they allow the children to do whatever sitting-down movements they are capable of, each movement repeated over a three-time rendition. For example, "Stamp your feet to the music, stamp, stamp; stamp your feet to the music, stamp, stamp; stamp your feet to the music, stamp, stamp" and then mobilize themselves to "Now get ready and stop." Following the "stop," the therapist sings to the children, "Hello to (name), hello to (name), hello to (name) and hello to (name)," and then returns to the movement portion of the song. As the children improve in their ability to process directions, I can modify the language of the song, including up to three sequential directions ("Clap your hands to the music, clap, clap; Stamp your feet to the music, stamp, stamp; Pat your knees to the music, pat, pat; Now get ready to stop").

For this group, I start with only one direction at a time and go through two renditions, the first rendition to "clap hands," the second rendition, "to stamp feet."

Goals and Objectives for Movement

In the group, I can anticipate and structure the following kinds of *goals and objectives:*

Clinical Goal 1: Children will use receptive language at appropriate developmental level.

Objective 1a: During vocal and movement activity, child will follow 2-step directive (Clap your hands, Stamp your feet) without resistance, 3 out of 5 trials (Keisha, Maria).
Objective 1b: During vocal and movement activity, child will follow 3-step directive (Clap your hands, Stamp your feet, Pat your knees) independently (Alexander) or given 2 prompts, 2 out of 3 trials (Terrence).
Objective 1c: During vocal and movement activ-

ity, select 1 picture from field of 2 (clap hands or stamp feet) in order to start song (Simon).

Clinical Goal 2: Demonstrate bilateral hand use spontaneously (Alexander) or without physical prompts on 3 out of 5 trials (Simon).

Objective 2a: Alexander will clap hands in midline, given modified tempo as necessary.
Objective 2b: Simon will initiate clapping hands without physical prompts on 3 out of 5 trials.

Methods for Movement

In terms of *methods* for this activity, I have to include an initial *verbal cue* for the children before even beginning the song, "Where are your hands?" After singing the initial verse, "Clap your hands to the music," I *pause,* taking my hands away from the keyboard, in order to clap two times with the children as a visual and auditory model. I establish *eye contact* as I continue the song and sing to each child. Following the second rendition of the song, using the motion to "stamp feet" and moving on to complete singing "Hello" to the remaining children and aides in the group. I close the song by extemporaneously singing, "Here we are in (*use sign for music*) Music." *Praise* for a job well-done.

Written in a session plan, the methods and materials would look like this:

Methods and Materials

1. Therapist begins song, issuing one direction, "Clap Your Hands," only. Verbal cuing as necessary (i.e., "Where are your hands?") before singing.
2. Therapist pauses after direction to clap 3 times with children. Aides assist if necessary.
3. Therapist sings the hello, continuing song, maintaining eye contact as she sings to the first 3 children.
4. Therapist continues song, issuing a different direction (stamp feet) only.
5. Therapist pauses after direction to stamp feet 3 times with children. Aides assist if necessary. Verbal cuing as necessary before singing,

"Where are your feet?"

6. Therapist sings hello, continuing song, maintaining eye contact as she sings to the next 2 children in the group and the teacher assistant.
7. Therapists sings song with 2 directions in sequence, "Clap your hands, stamp your feet," this time including the sign for music after singing, "Here we are in Music."
8. Repeat direction 3.
9. Therapist sings song with 3 directions in sequence, "Clap your hands (clap, clap, clap), 'stamp your feet' (stamp, stamp, stamp), 'pat your knees' in 'music' (sign)."
10. Repeat direction 6, ending with "here we are in music (sign)."
11. Specific positive reinforcement.

Material: "Clap Your Hands to the Music" written by Novickes-Sorel (Robbins, 1995).

Instrumental Activities

Instrumental/Rhythm Sticks

By now the children are excited and ready to use instruments. They enjoy using the rhythm sticks and the fact that every child can use them at the same time is very reinforcing for them as a group. In this activity I am using the tried and true Hap Palmer song, "Tap your sticks together" (Palmer, 1981). It's an easy song for embedding cognitive goals and following directions. At the same time, the goal of rhythmicity is vital for all music activities. As the children enjoy a sense of rhythm, they seem to center neurologically. Many of them will need hand over hand assistance to handle the sticks.

Goals and Objectives, Rhythm Sticks

My goals and objectives are:

Clinical Goal 1: Demonstrate one-to-one correspondence.

Objective 1a: Up to 3 by giving 2 rhythm sticks to other children in the group on 3 out of 4 trials (Maria).
Objective 1b: Count up to 4 objects (Terrence).

Clinical Goal 2: Attend without behavioral disruption.

Objective 2a: During music therapy, without biting to hands, given a verbal prompt, "hands down" 4 out of 5 trials (Maria).
Objecitve 2b: During music therapy, by sitting appropriately during 2 other peer turns and not exhibiting aggressive behaviors toward herself or others, when given no more than 2 verbal prompts, on 3 out of 4 occasions (Maria).
Objective 2c: During music therapy, without grabbing/touching objects or people when 1 verbal prompt is provided on 3 out of 5 trials (Keisha).
Objective 2d: During music therapy, without exhibiting inappropriate behavior on 4 out of 5 occasions (Terrence) when following verbal directive.
Objective 2e: During music therapy, without scratching, pinching or slapping of others when given physical and verbal prompts on 3 out of 5 occasions (Simon).
Objective 2f: During music therapy, by participating in a presented activity, given physical and verbal prompting, without exhibiting inappropriate behavior for a period of ten minutes (Simon).
Objective 2g: During music therapy, complete a task without complaint with 1 verbal reminder 4 out of 5 trials (Alexander).
Objective 2h: During music, when transitioning from favored activity, 5 minimal physical assistance, after only 1 verbal prompt (Linda) without physical prompts on 3 out of 5 trials (Simon).

Clinical Goal 3: Bilateral hand use spontaneously (Alexander) or without physical prompts on 3 out of 5 trials (Simon).

Objective 3a: Alexander will strike sticks in midline, given modified tempo as necessary.
Objective 3b: Simon will initiate striking sticks together without physical prompts on 3 out of 5 trials.

Methods, Rhythm Sticks

Methods for the rhythm stick activity include some *steps in preparation for the actual music-making.*

I hold out two pairs of sticks and ask Terrence to count them. Following this, he can keep one pair for himself and give another to Maria. She learns how to give out a pair of sticks, one pair at a time, to her friends in the group. It's great to get a sense of having different expectations for children while they are each participating at individual levels in the same group activity. Following this step, I *model* the song with the aides. I find that aides who were formerly emotionally uninvolved in other segments of the schoolday become very involved in music. In a sense, I think that it is therapeutic for them, too. I can have the aids model "Tap your sticks together with a one, two, three" as the original song lyrics are composed or, for a less ambitious or more ambitious undertaking, I can have them model simpler or more complex directives.

After the modeling of the rhythm stick pattern, I *face* the children, *sing acapella and have them join in with hand over hand assistance from aides as necessary.* For those children with physical limitations such as Alexander, Linda and Simon, *positioning and handling of the instruments* are critical. This is part of the methodology. By the time I finally get to the piano to play the song, I have the aides demonstrating in front of the children. The song, as composed, is rather dull harmonically, following the dutiful progression of many childrens' songs, I-IV-V. I add seventh chords and intermediate chords to enhance the harmony. If the children are able to follow the standard accompaniment and I want to repeat the song, I can change the accompaniment style, possibly syncopating it for a jazzier feeling. At the end of the activity, I ask Terrence to stand up, collect the sticks and put them away in the coffee can I hand him.

Written in the session plan, the methods would look like this:

Methods and Materials

1. Therapist will hold out 2 pairs of rhythm sticks, 1 in red and 1 in blue, and ask Terrence to count how many sticks she is holding.
2. Following successful response, therapist will ask Terrence to give 2 sticks to Maria and keep 2 for himself.
3. Ask Maria to give the 2 sticks to another child in the group. Repeat until all the sticks are given out and Maria has her own pair.
4. Therapist will model tapping of the sticks in the song with the aide up to the number 5. Adapt musically, i.e., tap your sticks together with a 1 (beat) etc.
5. Therapist will face children, sing acapella and have them join in on activity. Assist children physically as necessary.
6. Therapist will accompany at the piano, allowing the aide to demonstrate in front of the children.
7. At the end of the activity, ask Terrence to stand up, collect the sticks and put them away in the coffee can.

Material: "Tap your sticks together."

Instrumental, Drum/Cymbal

Now that the group is warmed up, we move on to a *second instrumental activity,* choice-making with the instruments and the use of the drum and cymbal. There are so many wonderful drum-cymbal songs composed for music therapy. My own introduction to these types of songs was the work of Nordoff and Robbins. Over the years, I have enjoyed orchestrating drum-cymbal pieces for music therapy with classical music but I still tend to start out with the Nordoff-Robbins songs. The one I am using today is from the second book of Playsongs (Nordoff and Robbins, 1962), "Let's Beat the Drum." I alternate this option with another from *Learning through Music* (Levin & Levin, 1998), "Mary is Sleeping," in order to use the cymbal. My *goals and objectives* include the following:

Goals and Objectives, Drum/Cymbal

Clinical Goal 1: Take turns consistently.

Clinical Objective 1a: In music, sit appropriately during 2 other peer turns and not exhibiting aggressive behaviors toward herself or others, when given no more than 2 verbal prompts, on 3 out of 4 occasions (Maria).
Clinical Objective 1b: In music, initiate turn at the proper time, with 1 verbal prompt, during group

activities for 2 reciprocal sequences (Linda).

Clinical Goal 2: Attend without behavioral disruption.

Objective 2a: During music therapy, without biting to hands, given a verbal prompt, "hands down" 4 out of 5 trials (Maria).

Objecitve 2b: During music therapy, by sitting appropriately during 2 other peer turns and not exhibiting aggressive behaviors toward herself or others, when given no more than 2 verbal prompts on 3 out of 4 occasions (Maria).

Objective 2c: During music therapy, without grabbing/touching objects or people when 1 verbal prompt is provided on 3 out of 5 trials (Keisha).

Objective 2d: During music therapy, without exhibiting inappropriate behavior on 4 out of 5 occasions (Terrence) when following verbal directives.

Objective 2e: During music therapy, without scratching, pinching or slapping of others when given physical and verbal prompts on 3 out of 5 occasions (Simon).

Objective 2f: During music therapy, by participating in a presented activity, given physical and verbal prompting, without exhibiting inappropriate behavior for a period of 10 minutes (Simon).

Objective 2g: During music therapy, complete a task without complaint with 1 verbal reminder 4 out of 5 trials (Alexander).

Objective 2h: During music, when transitioning from favored activity, 5 minimal physical assistance, after only 1 verbal prompt (Linda).

Clinical Goal 3: Children will use expressive language at appropriate developmental level.

Clinical objective 3a: Spontaneous and consistent short and appropriate verbal sentences (Keisha) such as "I want the cymbal" or "I want the drum."

Clinical objective 3b: Response to activity-related "Wh" questions such as "Which instrument do you want to play?" (Keisha) with a short phrase or sentence.

Clinical objective 3c: without prompting on 3 out of 5 trials (Terrence).

Methods: Drum/Cymbal

Methods for the drum/cymbal activity include *differentiated expectations* in asking the children for their selection of instrumental material, therapist *modeling* with aide, *specific praise* and/or *redirection* as necessary, *repetition* as necessary, *abbreviated/adapted directions* as necessary for children with slow auditory processing, *positioning/handling* as necessary for children with physical limitations (Linda, Alexander, Simon), *stated expectation* for "more" music and stated transition to next activity. As the music proceeds, I vary its presentation, playing off the melodies and harmonies to extend them for the children. It starts to feel a great deal like improvisation, a necessary skill in presenting any music to the children. Written in the session plan, the methods would look like this:

Method and Materials

1. Therapist asks child "Which instrument do you want to play?," anticipating a full sentence (Terrence, Keisha, Alexander), touching (Linda, Maria) or eye gazing (Simon) a preferred picture selection from a field of 2 kinds of drum photographs and a cymbal photograph.
2. Therapist provides selected drum or cymbal and selects appropriate song for selected instrument.
3. Therapist models appropriate playing of song with aide before giving the instrument to the child.
4. Therapist asks Alexander to repeat the directions to his friend before giving the instrument to the child.
5. Therapist then asks child to play, providing musical accompaniment.
6. Therapist asks child for striker to be passed to neighboring child.
7. Positive verbal reinforcement as appropriate.
8. Therapist repeats step 1 with next child, etc.
9. Therapist asks, 'Who wants more ?' anticipating sign from Maria, Linda or Simon.
   Materials: "Letss Beat the Drum" (Book 2, *Playsongs,* Nordoff Robbins) "Mary is Sleeping" (*Learning through music,* Levin, Herbert and Gail).

Closing

Good-Bye

Closing the session will use one of my favorite songs, "Good-bye," Nordoff-Robbins, Book 2 (1968) of the Playsongs. This song is simple enough to employ different levels of response on the part of the children. They can sing, sign or wave good-bye given their musical cue through the antiphonal nature of the song: "It's time to say Good-bye; It's time to say _____. Good-bye, _____, It's name to say _____." The children anticipate using a closing song. I can also use the closing song as an opportunity for the children to summarize what we did in the session so I can add that information to the song lyrics. The goals/objectives and methods would look like this in the session plan:

Goals/Objective/Methods: Good-bye

The goals, objectives, and methods here are similar to those of the opening activity, using the structure of a different song. **Closing**.

Clinical Goal 1: Children will use expressive language at appropriate developmental level:

Objective 1a: Communicate "Good-bye" using programmed touch talker with voice output on 1 of 3 trials when given verbal and gestural prompt (Linda; Simon)

Objective 1b: Produce 2-3-word combinations (Sing Good-bye) manual signs when given verbal prompts (Maria).

Objective 1c: In order to use spontaneous and consistent short and appropriate verbal sentences (Keisha).

Objective 1d: Response to activity related and summary-related (i.e., What did we do in music today?) "Wh" questions (Keisha) with a short phrase or sentence without prompting on 1 out of 3 trials (Terrence).

Objective 1e: Use use full simple sentences. "It's time to sing good-bye" in response to the question, "What time is it?" and in response to "What did we do in music today?" (Alexander).

Clinical Goal 2: Attend without behavioral disruption.

Objective 2a: During music therapy, without biting to hands, given a verbal prompt, "hands down" 4 out of 5 trials (Maria).

Objecitve 2b: During music therapy, by sitting appropriately during 2 other peer turns and not exhibiting aggressive behaviors toward herself or others, when given no more than 2 verbal prompts, on 3 out of 4 occasions (Maria).

Objective 2c: During music therapy, without grabbing/touching objects or people when 1 verbal prompt is provided on 3 out of 5 trials (Keisha).

Objective 2d: During music therapy, without exhibiting inappropriate behavior on 4 out of 5 occasions (Terrence) when following verbal directive.

Objective 2e: During music therapy, without scratching, pinching or slapping of others when given physical and verbal prompts on 3 out of 5 occasions (Simon).

Objective 2f: During music therapy, by participating in a presented activity, given physical and verbal prompting, without exhibiting inappropriate behavior for a period of 10 minutes (Simon).

Objective 2g: During music therapy, complete a task without complaint with 1 verbal reminder 4 out of 5 trials (Alexander).

Objective 2h: During music, when transitioning from favored activity, 5 minimal physical assistance, after only 1 verbal prompt (Linda).

Methods and Materials

1. Therapist uses aide in room as model if song is not familiar.
2. After modeling, therapist asks, "What time is it?"
3. Therapist establishes eye contact with each child as she sings to them.
4. Therapist adapts song for children who can provide sung sentence (Terrence, Alexander, Keisha) singing "What time is it right now?" and anticipating their sung response, "It's time to sing good-bye."
5. While singing and improvising, therapist asks

Terrence, Alexander and Keisha "What did we do in music today?," musically asking each child to recall one experience.

6. Therapist includes childrens' responses to "What did we do in music today?" in the good-bye song, improvising accordingly.

7. Therapist continues good-bye song with other children, one at a time (Simon, Maria, Linda) pausing before end of musical phrase, "It's time to sing _____?" and "(Name of child) can sing _____." anticipating correct response in terms of gesture, touch talker or sung full sentence.

8. Positively and specifically reinforce correct response.
Material: "Good-bye" (Nordoff-Robbins, Book one, *Playsongs*).

Final Session Plan

I have taken you through the session plan and I hope this explanation has been helpful. I include this as the type of detail that I suggest for the student or beginning therapist. For seasoned therapists who are able to internalize many of the methods and have a good sense of how the goals and objectives will be presented and incorporated into various premeditated as well as spontaneous musical experiences, the plan will not be as detailed.

It is important for me to remind the therapist that the notion of activity is often misunderstood. The word "activity," thought by many to be a rigid totally premeditated formulaic manner of conducting therapy with the group is, in fact, not that at all. Synonymous with the word "intervention" or "experience," *the term music activity is meant, in my opinion, to convey the concept of engaging in music. Whether the therapist engaged in music-making with the child(ren) on a premeditated or spontaneous basis, the importance of the musical experience or activity must be its capacity to adapt to the ongoing needs of the children.*

Transdisciplinary Work

During many of these sessions, I share music-making with the speech pathologist, Linda, the occupational therapist, Maureen and the physical therapist, Yvonne. They have found that they are more likely to elicit response from the children in the music therapy session as opposed to "pull-out" sessions. When Linda is in the room, we can share techniques used in both speech pathology and music therapy: choice of a particular picture for the child to convey a preference for a musical activity (i.e., vocal, instrumental, movement), choice of a picture for the child to convey a preference for a particular choice of song, instrument or dance, the use of a story board that accompanies a song selection as well as the use of instruments that promote oral-motor musculature (i.e., the reed horn). When Maureen and/or Yvonne are in the room, I am always assured of appropriate positioning and handling techniques for the musical task at hand. Maureen is particularly adept at sensory integration techniques, such as proprioceptive input (i.e., sensory input to the joints) to stimulate reactions during musical activities. Rather than just planning our goals together as an interdisciplinary treatment team, I feel so fortunate to be planning and conducting transdisciplinary work; work that crosses disciplines during music therapy. In the session today, Yvonne is helping Alexander and Simon with positioning and handling.

EVALUATION

Objective Evaluation

I use both objective and subjective evaluation in my notes. The objective evaluation is a simple record of whether or not the child is able to reach the objective and, if so, on what level. Here I look for varying degress of success with each child achieving his/her goal and the use of fewer and fewer prompts as the sessions move along. I also look for patterns of response. If, for example, a child is not able to meet the majority of the goals, then I may be overestimating the developmental levels of the child. Conversely, if the child is able to meet the majority of the goals consistently, then I may be underestimating the developmental levels of the child. I start to create a checklist with a Code: a check plus for "consistently observed," a check for "observed when cued–physical, verbal, visual," a check minus for "inconsistently observed" and NO for "not observed." In order to use my limited time for evaluation while behaviors are fresh in my mind, I create a grid that looks something like this (see Table 1.6). This is just a starting point for evaluation and I am not sure I am even comfortable with it. I know that the administration wants accountability and that means data collection.

Subjective Evaluation

For me the observation of group dynamics and the questions that I ask myself during the session are more helpful in planning treatment and yet I can also appreciate the need for documentation of

what the child was able to "accomplish" in terms of clinical objectives during the session.

During my breaks, I add comments about group process and try to analyze what did or did not "work" in the group. Highlights of the sessions are included in my notes. When I look back over the subjective notes, I see that I am relating to the children on many levels, some of which could be considered countertransferential. I also find myself very aware, moment to moment, of what methods are working with the children and which need to be spontaneously adapted in the session. Along with these observations, I connect theory and application, probably a natural process for an academic but a process I like to encourage in my students as well.

TABLE 1.6. OBJECTIVE EVALUATION.

Objective Evaluation

Regional Day School

Class Number 6

Student Evaluations

Date of this evaluation

CODE

√+   Consistently Observed

√   Observed When Cued (Physical, Verbal, Visual)

√-   Inconsistently Observed

NO Not Observed

NA Not applicable

Objectives	Keisha	Terrence	Maria	Simon	Alexander	Linda
Communicate using programmed touch talker with voice output on 1 of 3 trials when given verbal and gestural prompt (Linda; Simon): Hello, Good-bye.				√		√
Produce 3-word combinations (Here I am; Sing Good-bye) with manual signs when given verbal prompts (Maria).			√			

continued

TABLE 1.6. OBJECTIVE EVALUATION–*Continued.*

Objectives	Keisha	Terrence	Maria	Simon	Alexander	Linda
Use spontaneous and consistent short and appropriate verbal sentences (Keisha) and response to activity-related "Wh" questions (Keisha) with a short phrase or sentence without prompting on 1 out of 3 trials (Terrence).	√√	√				
Attend to musical tasks without biting to hands, given a verbal prompt "hands down" 4 out of 5 trials (Maria).			√+			
Attend to musical tasks by sitting appropriately during 2 other peer turns and not exhibiting aggressive behaviors toward herself or others, when given no more than 2 verbal prompts, on 3 out of 4 occasions (Maria).			√+			
Attend to musical tasks without grabbing/touching objects or people when 1 verbal prompt is provided on 3 out of 5 trials (Keisha).	√+					
Attend to musical tasks without exhibiting inappropriate behavior on 4 out of 5 occasions (Terrence) when following verbal directive.		√+				
Attend to musical tasks without scratching, pinching or slapping of others when given physical and verbal prompts on 3 out of 5 occasions (Simon).				√-		
Attend to musical tasks by participating in a presented activity, given physical and verbal prompting, without exhibiting inappropriate behavior for a period of 10 minutes (Simon).				√-		

continued

TABLE 1.6. OBJECTIVE EVALUATION–*Continued.*

Objectives	Keisha	Terrence	Maria	Simon	Alexander	Linda
Complete a task without complaint with 1 verbal reminder 4 out of 5 trials (Alexander).					√	
Attend to musical task when transitioning from favored activity, 5 minimal physical assistances, after only 1 verbal prompt (Linda).						√
Follow 2-step directive (Clap your hands, Stamp your feet) without resistance, 3 out of 5 trials (Keisha, Maria).	√		√			
Follow 3-step directive (Clap your hands, Stamp your feet, Pat your knees independently) (Alexander) or given 2 prompts, 2 out of 3 trials (Terrence).		√			√	
Select 1 picture from field of 2 (clap hands or stamp feet) in order to start song (Simon).				√		
During instrumental and movement activity, demonstrate bilateral hand use spontaneously (Alexander) by striking sticks in midline given modified tempo.					√	
Initiate striking sticks together without physical prompts on 3 out of 5 trials (Simon).				√		
Clap hands in midline, given modified tempo as necessary, in context of song (Alexander).					√	
Initiate clapping hands on 1 out of 3 trials (Simon) in context of song.				√-		
Give 2 rhythm sticks to other children in the group on 3 out of 4 trials (Maria).			√			

continued

TABLE 1.6. OBJECTIVE EVALUATION–*Continued.*

Objectives	Keisha	Terrence	Maria	Simon	Alexander	Linda
Count up to 4 objects (Terrence).		√				
Sit appropriately during 2 other peer turns and avoid exhibiting aggressive behaviors toward herself or others, when given no more than 2 verbal prompts, on 3 out of 4 occasions (Maria).			√			
Initiate turn at the proper time, with 1 verbal prompt, during group activities for 2 reciprocal sequences (Linda).						√
Communicate wants, needs and preferences (i.e., choice of instrument), given up to 5 picture choices and/or using an augmentative device with voice output on 3 to 5 trials when given verbal and gestural prompt (Linda).						√-
Produce 3-word combinations through the use of pictures and/or manual signs when given verbal prompts, but without phrase modeling (Maria).			√			

ANECDOTAL NOTES:

Subjective Evaluation

Opening the group today is comfortable. Even though it is just the second session, the children seem very "up" as they enter the room. Terrence, Maria, Keisha and Alexander are smiling. Simon has so much physical limitation in his facial muscles because of his low tone that it is hard for me to figure out how he is feeling. Linda, in her wheelchair, is drooling and moving arhythmically in the chair. She seems restless and discomforted. Everyone is able to respond to the "Hello" song, either through augmentative device, sign or singing. They seem to have an instinctive sense of when to enter the song and I don't think I will have to prompt as the sessions progress.

As I move into the clapping song, I notice that Keisha and Terrence lose eye contact with me and start clapping impulsively. I do not want to interrupt their enthusiasm for the music and so I choose not to "correct" them. I think there is a grey area between judging impulsivity and enthusiasm here. During the last rendition of the song, where I combine three different steps, I notice that the uninterrupted clapping has turned into intentional rhythmic clapping. I wonder about the processing time that these children need to decode the pattern I have been introducing. Clearly, they process "correctly" after the repetitions in the song. Likewise, Alexander is having some difficulty bringing his flailing hands to midline in order to physically grasp the beat. Again, I do not 'correct' him. By the end of the song, he "catches up." Maria is only clapping once each time on her own even though her aide keeps assisting her with the second two beats. Here again, I wonder about processing time. If I had Maria on an individual basis, I could have her clapping only one beat. The transition from opening and clapping to the use of the rhythm sticks works well due to my singing a little tune I spontaneously compose while walking over toward the instruments in the room, "Watch me, watch me, I am looking for the rhythm sticks." This seems to keep Linda from getting upset and helps her visually track me moving toward another corner of the room. I return quickly, even walking to the pulse of my singing voice, as the children watch me with the can of sticks. Some of my

students in training at the university express a need to "keep the activities going so the children do not 'act out'" but I think transitions are always a welcome comfort to children rather than back-to-back activities which seems robot-like.

There is a brief moment of anxious anticipation as the children wait for their turn to select rhythm sticks. Again, I try to keep the momentum stable while talking through what is happening in the room. It works. As we move into the song, I notice the aides automatically trying to do hand-over-hand assistance with the children. The only gentle way I can encourage autonomy is to say, "Let's let the children try it on their own first," rather than singling out one particular offender. It works. Granted, the children are all physically limited in one way or another but it is helpful for me to see how they naturally approach using these materials. At one point, Terrence playfully tries to play one of his sticks with Keisha. The visual-motor match is not quite right at first and then it improves. Again, I don't feel a need to change this. It is a great effort at befriending and sharing each other's musical energy. After a while, laughing, they return to playing their own sticks.

After we put the rhythm sticks away, I again transition with my little song but by this time, the stimulation has been too much for Linda and she starts crying. We are about a half-hour into a 45-minute session, a session time that easily leads to sensory overload for some of these children. I suggest that one of the aides take Linda out for a brief reprieve and she ends up going to the nurse for a nap. I wonder about the balancing act for children who are overly reactive to stimuli, other children who need to channel their hyperactivity, and finally children who are underreactive. This remains one of the great challenges in doing group work.

Bringing out the drums and the standing cymbal is an exciting moment for the children and Maria begins to spontaneously clap her hands in anticipation. I wonder how she can clap her hands several times here but only clapped once before.

Again, the children are able to wait their turns while I demonstrate with the aide and then offer instrumental preference cards to the first child, Maria. In her excitement, she is spontaneously pointing to herself and I take advantage of this moment by acknowledging her communication, "Oh, look everyone, Maria wants music (sign)!"

I am trying to involve the other children even though they are waiting. "Maria, do you want (this), or (this)?" and I show her the cards. She chooses the cymbal. After the preliminary modeling, she plays. Her playing is so loud that Simon begins to shake.

How do I monitor this level of excitement? Again, the issue of balancing the sensory input in the session is apparent. Fortunately, Simon is able to contain his reaction to the cymbal "crash" and self-regulate. I can see that this issue of "self-regulation," the first milestone Stanley Greenspan writes about, is such a fundamental issue. If Maria was truly able to follow the dynamics in the song I was playing, she would be self-regulating . . . but she is not there yet. The same thing happens after Terrence and Keisha play. I think about the stated goals in the IEP that I have set up for this activity. They don't seem to reflect much humanistic feeling for the developmental goals. Why didn't the clinicians who set up this plan think about self-regulation as preparatory for any of the behavioral regulating? The music is a perfect way to help with regulation.

By the time I get to Alexander, he is hyperventilating in his excitement. He chooses both the drum and the cymbal so I change the orchestration in "Mary is sleeping" in order for him to basic beat the melody and play the cymbal at the end of the piece. He tries to acclimate his flailing arms to the dynamics of the piece and is partially successful. I can tell that in his mind he knows what he has to do physically, but he is not successful in keeping his body under control. I admire his fortitude and the other teachers and aides in the classroom are amazed at this. It is hard to believe that this is a child who the teacher says "complains" in the classroom when he is so highly motivated in music.

As we arrive at the end of the music time, I can tell that the group is still largely attentive and I am truly impressed. In terms of assessment, when I compare the functioning levels stated in the Individual Education Plans with the functioning levels I see in the music activities, the levels are similar, with the exception of behavioral issues. In

the music, the emotional relatedness of the children is overwhelmingly positive, something that I did not expect based on my reading of the behavioral goals for the children. I do think the drive to engage in music channels the energy of the children in such a positive way that they simply do not need to be distracted in negative ways. Even though the children are limited in their functioning, their enthusiasm is going to override their functioning level and allow them to start facilitating the session on their own level. Relatively speaking, this is going to be a workable group.

THE CHANGING GROUP

We meet twice a week for 45 minutes at a time. The weeks are passing and the group is developing a sense of anticipation, comfort level with the structure of the session, support for each other and familiarity with a repertoire of preferential materials. They progress toward previously stated developmental goals and share more of their personalities through music. Spontaneous contributions to the music-making allow me to provide more challenge and necessary creative freedoms to group members.

Anticipation

Maria passes by in the hall en route to another classroom and begins to walk into my classroom. She is still nonverbal with differentiated verbal sounds only in addition to her use of simple sign and picture exchange. She points to the drum and then points to herself. This music room draws her attention and she has to be redirected to leave the music room until it is her turn for session. Other members of the group see me in the hallway on my way to lunch and ask, "Time for music now?" Members of the group have made an emotional connection with the events going on in the music room and they want to be there. When it is finally their turn to enter as a group, they enter with anticipation and excitement yet able to focus and be attentive. Even the opening chords of the various greeting songs, particularly, "Clap your Hands" (Nowickes-Sorel in Robbins, 1995), presented prior to any song lyric, are an auditory cue for the children to raise their hands and get ready to clap.

Comfort Level with the Structure of the Session

Greeting songs continue to open the session, largely from the material of *Greetings and Good-byes* (Robbins, 1995). Through these openings, a sense of group awareness and communication is developing, with the children watching each other and waiting for their turns in the opening.

As the group gains a comfort level with the possible format of the session, I introduce a series of laminated picture exchange cards, one for movement, one for vocal, one for listening and one for instrumental. Each card is a simple drawing of a child either dancing, singing, listening or playing instruments. The cards are backed with Velcro in order to stick to a board that helps the group visually organize the time and the selected sequence of activity. The selection of which kind of activity the group wants to proceed with following the opening, following the first activity, etc. is a democratic process and binds the members together despite their low functioning level. As the children begin to find their own favorite music materials, I create card choices for use of those as well. This picture selection process allows more decision-making on the parts of Maria, Simon and Linda, the nonverbal members of the group.

Preferred Materials/Progress Toward Developmental Goals

The session methods and materials balance two developmental levels, sensorimotor learning and concrete learning, analogous to the first two Piagetian cognitive stages. Even the children like Keisha, Alexander and Terrence who are firmly rooted in concrete learning need the sensory integration techniques of multisensory input in order to spark their auditory processing, visual-motor processing and motor planning abilities.

We are using many songs to stimulate *vocalizing* as well as antiphonal and/or "fill in the blank" songs that focus on the here and now activity level

in the classroom (see Chapter 6, Materials). A simple song from Sesame Street like "Sing After Me" (Moss and Raposo, 1998, p. 62), involves simple imitation of vocal patterns either initiated by the therapist or by the child. Terrence, in particular, adores this song. His ability to imitate and/or originate long streams of vowel/consonant melodic sequences is growing rapidly. Now Keisha has joined in this repartee and is beginning to socialize more with Terrence as a result of the interplay of the vocalizations–watching him more, laughing with him, and anticipating her turn to imitate. Even though these particular vocalization goals are not included in their IEP the process of having so much fun vocalizing appears to free the children up for further language response later in the session that is developmentally challenging. For a child of sensorimotor level, like Maria, Simon and Linda, the listening and watching level with some affective reaction is a start. At one point, these children surprise me by approximating the beginning vowel sounds.

For a child at the concrete level, like Keisha and Terrence, songs like "I Have a Hat" (Nordoff-Robbins, 1968) might incorporate the existence of one- three words or a simple sentence (I have a ____,), the function of the word (I'll go for a ___, for a ___ in my ____). For a child at the representational play level, like Alexander, the words in this song, "I Have a Hat" (Nordoff and Robbins, 1968) can go further, "Outside its raining, raining on my hat" (throw off the hat, pretending it's wet). In order to stimulate visual as well as auditory cues, I work with the speech pathologist, Linda, to incorporate songboards into the session. Some of these songboards can be prepared through published collections of visual aids (Coleman and Brunk, 2001) but others need to be created for traditional folk songs and music therapy songs. Making the songboard is a simple arts and crafts chore and after the "pieces" of the song story are Velcro-mounted to a brightly colored oak tag file folder, the children enjoy giving me the pictures as we refer to them in song.

The cultural backgrounds of the children are beginning to play a part in the selection of materials. Maria and Alexander are both Latin-American and this leads to the use of folk songs such as the "Mexican Hat Dance," "Jamaican Farewell," "La Cucaracha," "La Colores," "Estrellita," "La Golondrina," "La Paloma," "El Choclo," "Adios Muchachos," "A Media Luz," "Chiapanecas," and "Cielito Lindo" (Ay-ay-ay-ay) all unearthed from a collection of Latin-American songs, which incorporate simple vocalizations in chorus, and rhythmic instrumental responses to close musical phrases. The beauty of this cultural connection is such that Maria and Alexander, although on different developmental levels, share obvious pleasure in *relating together in their cultural rhythms.* Similarly, Terrence and Keisha favor movement and the use of orchestrated and improved rhythm arrangements to African rhythms as well as the development of simple raps, some of these sparked by Sesame Street songs such as "New Way to Walk" (Moss and Raposo, 1992, p. 116): "I've got a new way to walk, walk, walk" extemporaneously transformed to "a new way to talk, talk, talk" and the previously mentioned "Sing After Me" (Moss and Raposo, 1992, p. 62).

The cultural rhythms introduce *movement* possibilities. In order to have hands-on contact with the children while moving to music, I use CDs with Latin rhythms and CDs with African-American rhythms. For example, I help the children with simple choreographed patterns, imitating a two-step sequence at a time in the African song "Pata Pata" (Stewart, G., 1991). Within the context of planning these sequences, I work with Yvonne, the physical therapist, to incorporate lower trunk movement for children like Simon and Linda. To further stimulate movement, Yvonne and I use the parachute to help all the children with gross motor arm movement as the parachute moves up and down. The "wind" of the parachute excites Maria, Linda and Simon and they giggle when I add the motion of a rolling plastic ball to the movement of the parachute. In order for the ball to move to the other side of the group, the children have to extend their arms. They can also follow patterned rhythms (Abramson, 1997) or toss and catch a beanbag to another child accompanied by a beanbag song.

The children have started with instrumental exploration using such instrumental textures as the zither, omnichord, multi-textured percussion instruments such as the ocean drum and the uli-uli (Hawaiian multi-tufted shakers), and autoharp to accompany music therapy and folk songs. Now they can follow simple orchestraions, many based on the work of Nordoff-Robbins, 1972, 1977, 1979; Herbert and Gail Levin, 1977, 1997a, 1997b; and Ritholz and Robbins, 1999, 2003. Whereas the instrumental textures have been stimulating on a tactile level, other instruments are stimulating on a motoric level. The use of the reed horns develop oral-motor musculature; the use of the drums and cymbal are developing bilateral beating and midline crossing; the use of the tone-bells and xylophone pitches are promoting whole arm and visual-motor skills. There is a sense of emotional mastery in following these simple orchestrations that continues to focus on the children. None of the children act out negatively in these sessions. All the behavioral goals regarding negative "self-stimulating" or abuse toward peers is totally absent. These were never issues to begin with in the music therapy session. I have moved on to helping these children find emotional expression through the music, at whatever level they can.

Support for Each Other

It is mid-March with the winter almost gone but the air still chilly and grey outside. We are working on a Nordoff-Robbins song from the fifth book of playsongs (Nordoff and Robbins, 1980c), "Let's Make Some Music." With some adaptation, I can use this song for one or two-step direction depending upon the cognitive level of the child, taking turns waiting recall of instrumental sequence from Alexander, and picture choice from Maria, Simon and Linda as to which instrument they choose to solo on in the song.

Terrence chooses the Tambourine and, within his solo, has some difficulty controlling his rhythmic impulse. Alexander calls out, "You can do it. Stop!" and Terrence is able to stop at the end of the musical phrase. Now it is Keisha's turn to play her reed horn. She purses her lips and plays loudly, something she was not able to do a few weeks ago. Linda is watching closely. Linda now attempts to use the reed horn as well. She is still drooling; it is difficult for her to create a tight embouchure with her lips. She approximates the sound and Simon laughs. We finish the piece with Alexander playing the drum and Simon assisted on the zither.

The next picture choice of the group members is a visual songboard for the Aaron Copland arrangement of "Bought me a Cat." This arrangement allows the lowest functioning children, Maria, Simon and Linda, to choose the next animal to sing about in our adapted version and imitate animal sounds. The arrangement allows the higher functioning children, Terrence, Keisha and Alexander to sing simple song lyrics (e.g., "I bought me a cat. The cat pleased me. I fed my cat under yonder tree.") some of which require change in order to simplify (e.g., "yonder tree" can be changed to "a big oak tree") and imagine. The children watch each other and clap at the end of the song. This is a song that holds further potential for orchestration as the weeks pass. Following the song, I can ask Terrence, Keisha and Alexander about the sequence of the animals in the song. I notice that the children take shared pleasure in watching and listening to each other, as do the aides. We can use the same kinds of goals for similar songs such as "Down on Grandpa's Farm" and "Going to the Zoo" (Raffi).

As we move into the closing, I introduce another song. It is adapted from a music education songbook but seems totally appropriate for music therapy, "I can do it." I syncopate the rhythms of the song: "I can do it. I can do it, if I just stick to it. I can do it; I can do it, if I try" (repeat). With this song, I ask children to show me what they did in the session. This involves picture exchange, signing or verbal response. Remarkably enough, the children *can* do it.

Sharing of Personalities

Despite their developmental and different sensory profiles, I have managed to work with this group this year. It is not an ideal group, "not a group meant to be a group," but it seems to have progressed from my first impressions of a "mommy and me" type of protocol. I have a sense of Maria's fortitude, Terrence's excitement,

Keisha's sense of humor, Alexander's burgeoning leadership and growing self-esteem in the group, Simon's ability to cope with his physical discomfort and Linda's determination to try new things. This is all quite gratifying as a therapist. There are other groups in the school that have moved through more identifiable group dynamics. They are, to be honest, "more favorite" groups. These I save for other vignettes throughout the book. This group, a challenging one to be sure, "worked."

SUMMARY: UNANSWERED QUESTIONS

Conducting this group as well as countless others always raises unanswered questions. Whenever I feel myself "tuning out" to a group so to speak, I know that I am up against a challenge and I am not sure how to handle it. I don't believe in boredom. No group is ever boring. No group is ever stagnant. Only the therapist who handles the group is stagnant in his or her resistance to confronting and solving problems.

What kind of group works? How do I determine this in order to form groups that have growth potential? What do I do if the group has limited growth potential? How do I know if a child is ready for a group?

How can I conduct assessment with a group? I have not read anything about this in music therapy.

How do I set up goals for these music therapy sessions? I don't want to set up goals unless they are meaningful. What is the uniqueness of the music therapy session that leads to different emphases in goals?

How do I know how much structure to introduce? My natural bent is to balance structure and freedom. There are so many ways I could go in setting up the session. What kind of methods and materials should I select? Especially if all the children are operating on so many levels?

How do I evaluate my efforts and the efforts of the children? I see many things happening that go beyond the IEP goals and objectives. Are they just as valid as reaching the IEP goals? What is the unique contribution of music in these children's lives?

I ask the reader to follow me as I try to answer these questions in the rest of the book.

STUDY GUIDE QUESTIONS

1. In your own words, describe the members of the group depicted in this opening chapter.
2. If you were presented with these children, what might your thoughts be?
3. How does the therapist organize goals for this group? Describe the process.
4. How does the therapist provide a format for each session? Describe the process.
5. How does the therapist select materials for each session? Describe the process.
6. What kinds of changes happen in the group over the academic year?
7. What kind of unanswered questions do you have after reading about this music therapy group?

Chapter 2

In the Beginning: Assessment

INTRODUCTION

There is a great deal of emphasis on assessment in the music therapy literature. However, assessment varies widely depending on one's clinical orientation, the population and the demands of the workplace. This chapter provides an initial review of literature regarding music therapy assessment, issues concerning the choice of assessment, clinical examples of published assessment tools with individual children and the role of assessment in group music therapy with children. As the clinician considers the decision regarding the child's placement in individual or group therapy (see Chapter 3), the individual assessment is an important step in establishing treatment intervention.

OVERVIEW AND REVIEW OF LITERATURE

WHAT IS ASSESSMENT AND HOW DOES IT RELATE TO EVALUATION

Assessment is the process by which the therapist strategically observes the child, and, based on that assessment session or sessions, makes clinical recommendations in terms of services and/or treatment planning. As such, it is an important segment of the clinical standards (AMTA, 2006) for training and education of music therapists. Generic standards for assessment are detailed in the clinical standards for training and education of music therapists as follows:

TABLE 2.1. AMTA CLINICAL STANDARDS, ASSESSMENT.

2.0 Standard II—Assessment

A client will be assessed by a Music Therapist prior to the delivery of music therapy services.

2.1. The music therapy assessment will include the general categories of psychological, cognitive, communicative, social, and physiological functioning focusing on the client's needs and strengths. The assessment will also determine the client's responses to music, music skills and musical preferences. Consideration may be given to a client's spirituality and cultural background.

2.2. All music therapy assessment methods will be appropriate for the client's chronological age, diagnoses, functioning level, spirituality and cultural background. The methods may include, but need not be limited to, observation during music or other situations, interview, verbal and nonverbal interaction, and testing. Information may also be obtained from other disciplines or sources such as the medical and social history.

2.3. The assessment will recognize variations in performance which may result from diagnoses, medications, adaptive devices, positioning, involvement in other therapies, psychosocial conditions, seizure disorders, and current health status. In addition, the assessment will identify the availability of family and other support systems, and their role in the care of the client.

---

continued

TABLE 2.1. AMTA CLINCIAL STANDARDS, ASSESSMENT–*Continued.*

2.4. All interpretations of test results will be based on appropriate norms or criterion referenced data.

2.5. The music therapy assessment procedures and results will become a part of the client's file.

2.6. The results, conclusions, and implications of the music therapy assessment will become the basis for the client's music therapy program and will be communicated to others involved with provision of services to the client. When appropriate, the results will be communicated to the client.

2.7. When assessment indicates the client's need for other services, the Music Therapist will make an appropriate referral.

2.8. The music therapy assessment should be individualized according to the student's level of functioning.

REVIEW OF MUSIC THERAPY LITERATURE ON ASSESSMENT

Rationale for Assessment

Review of literature on music therapy assessment emphasizes assessment of the individual child. Reasons for conducting assessment may include the need to gather information about a patient's strengths and weaknesses for the purposes of program planning (Cohen and Gericke, 1972) as well as the overriding needs for accountability, justification of services and professional credibility (Isenberg-Grzeda, 1988), and rationale common to multiple fields of education and therapy (Wolery, Gessler, Werts and Holcombe, 1994). It is probably for these reasons that the inclusion of music therapy assessment in the AMTA Standards of Clinical Practice (2006), following patient referral and acceptance, is dictated.

In specific settings the assessment model is required to establish medical reimbursement for services (Scalenghe and Murphy, 2000) as well as eligibility for music therapy on the individual education plan (Coleman and Brunk,1999).

Types of Published Assessment for Children

In a relatively recent review of music therapy assessment tools, Wilson and Smith (2000) found that 49 percent (16) of the 41 assessment instruments being used by therapists working with children throughout the country were "named" assessment tools. These "named" assessments were used for the following purposes: 1) to compare with data gained from other assessment measures (39%); 2) for baseline or pretest (29%); 3) to determine eligibility for services (12%); 4) to determine psychometric properties of the assessment (7%); 5) to determine suitability of the instrument for the given population (7%); and 6) toward identification of musical preference. Both musical and nonmusical elements were assessed and various populations were included in the assessments with mental retardation (44%) and emotionally disturbed children (22%) as the most frequent recipients of the assessments. The named "music therapy" assessment tools cited in the Wilson study included the following:

- Primary Measures of Music Audition (Gordon, 1979)
- Continuous Response Digital Interface (Robinson, 1988)
- "Toney Listens to Music" (software) (Williams and Fox, 1983)
- Checklist of Communicative Responses/Acts Score Sheet (Edgarton, 1994)
- Cohen Music Therapy Assessment Tool (Cohen, 1986)
- Instrument Timbre Preference Test (Gordon,

1984)
- Music/Activity Therapy Intake Assessment for Psychiatric Patients (Braswell et al., 1986)
- Music Aptitude Profile (Gordon, 1965)
- Music Therapy Assessment Tool for Emotionally Disturbed Children (Goodman, 1989)
- Music Therapy Physiological Measures Test (Sutton, 1984)
- Musical Perception Assessment of Cognitive Development (Rider, 1981)
- Seashore Measures of Musical Talents–Rhythmic Subtest (Seashore, 1919)
- Songwriting Assessment of Hopelessness (Goldstein, 1990)
- Test of Rhythmic Responsiveness (Kaplan, 1977)
- Walker Test (Walker, 1987)

What is striking about this list is that, with the exception of the Goodman (1989) and the Rider (1981) assessments, none of the others are specifically music therapy and/or specifically designated for use with children with special needs. Furthermore, the list is not inclusive.

The few published music therapy assessments written for children are briefly described below and include the following:

1) Nordoff -Robbins Scales (Nordoff and Robbins, 1977, 2007)

Based on their pioneering work at the University of Pennsylvania and their familiarity with the assessment of the autistic child from Dr. Bernard Rutterberg (Ruttenberg, Dratman, Fraknoi and Wenar, July, 1966), Paul Nordoff and Clive Robbins developed two scales for individual assessment.

The first scale entitled "Child-Therapists Relationship in Musical Activity" (Nordoff and Robbins, 1977, p. 182), details ten levels of participation on the part of the child, ranging from "Total obliviousness" (Level One) to "Establishment of functional independence in groupwork" (Level Ten). These levels of participation are equated to qualities of resistiveness. Children described within these levels conform to

descriptive rating scales. The scale was revised in 2007 (Nordoff and Robbins, 2007) to eliminate the tenth rating and merge the first three ratings. Level 10 was eliminated due to the emphasis of the levels on individual work; nevertheless the original mention of Level 10 remains implicit and provides the therapist working with the group with an idea of when the child will be ready to move from individual to groupwork.

The second scale, entitled "Musical Communicativeness" (Nordoff and Robbins, 1977, p. 196) spells out ten levels of musical communicativeness, ranging from "No communicative responsiveness" (Level 1) to "Commitment to musical objectives in groupwork" (Level 10). Children are described within these levels for various modes of musical behavior: instrumental, vocal and body movement. Descriptions of musical behaviors conform to descriptive rating scales and therefore achieve a rating total. Similar to the first scale, the second scale was also revised (2007) to reflect the emphasis on individual therapy and the redundancy of the first three levels. Therefore, the tenth level was eliminated and the first three merged.

The scales are both quantitative and qualitative and, in their original form, rely upon videotaped analysis of the music therapy session to invite a measure of both objectivity and subjectivity.

2) MTA-ED or Music Therapy Assessment for Emotionally Disturbed Children (Goodman, 1989)

Based on several years of both in-patient and out-patient psychiatric music therapy work conducted at New York Hospital, the MTA-ED (Goodman, 1989) is open-ended and outlines basic musical elements that the child may express. The interpretation of how, why, and when the child musically communicates may be viewed in context of the child's pathology. Areas of description include the following: natural response choice, musical preference, musical responsiveness (rhythm, dynamics, articulation, tone quality, melodic line/phrasing, pulse, physical disposition of instrument, appropriateness of expressive quality), verbal associations, nonverbal reactions and client/therapist interaction. A final segment of the assessment format details discussion and recommendations for treatment. I developed this tool as a projective means of viewing musical response for the disturbed child.

3) The Musical-Perception Assessment of Cognitive Development (M-PACS)

Written for a normed population (Rider, 1981), the M-PACS outlines 15 musical tasks which conform to Piagetian tasks for school-aged children. Although it was written for a normed population, it was later field-tested by Jones (1986) as an adapted tool for mentally retarded children.

4) Cleveland Music School Assessment of Infants and Toddlers (Libertore and Layman, 1999)

Written for developmentally delayed infants and toddlers, this assessment is based on developmental age norms in five developmental areas and requires a yes/no response. Scoring creates a quantitative tool.

5) Auditory-Motor Perception Test (Heimlich, 1975)

Created by a para-verbal therapist, this little-known perception test consists of rhythmic imitation tasks which are then scored to predict neurologic impairment.

6) Improvisation Assessment Profiles (Bruscia, 1987)

Written for a wide variety of ages and diagnoses, the IAPs are based on musical analysis and interpretation of client behavior during improvisations. Six profiles, each containing subscales of musical descriptors, relate to the following areas of behavior: Integration, Variability, Tension, Coingruence, Salience and Autonomy. Interpretation of musical behavior is related, in effect, to aspects of personality.

7) Music Therapy Assessment for the Diagnosis of Autism and Communication Disorders in Children (Wigram, 2000)

Wigram devised this assessment to include aspects of the Bruscia IAPs (Bruscia, 1987) he considers most relevant to the diagnosis of autism and communication disorders. Musical behaviors of the improvisation are scored for further analysis.

8) Special Education Music Therapy Assessment Process, commonly referred to as the SEMTAP (Coleman and Brunk, 1999)

Created for the specific purpose of establishing music therapy eligibility on the Individual Education Plan, or IEP, the SEMTAP outlines the systematic collection of information from related therapists and teachers as well as the observation and interviewing necessary to form a picture of the child who will be assessed for music therapy. Given this information as well as the goals and objectives of the IEP, the music therapist prepares a music therapy session to prove or disprove the efficacy of music therapy in furthering the goals of the IEP through music therapy.

9) Psychiatric Music Therapy Questionnaire, commonly referred to as the PMTQ (Cassity and Cassity, 1998)

This is essentially a verbal interview intended to collect information related to symptoms for the disturbed child. The information will presumably be used to form a music therapy intervention program. There is no music used in the assessment.

10) Music Psychotherapy Assessment (Loewy, 2000)

Loewy created a music psychotherapy assessment tool initially used with both children and adults in a medical setting. Her assessment is exploratory in nature and qualitative in terms of report. It relates to the following areas of inquiry: Awareness of self, other and of the moment; thematic expression: listening, performing; collaboration; relationship: concentration; range of affect; investment/motivation; use of structure; integration; self-esteem: risk-taking and independence.

11) Music Therapy Assessment Profile for Severely/Profoundly Handicapped (Michel and Rohrbacher, 1982)

Now out-of-print, the MTAP serves as a developmental checklist model. Milestones of development up to 36 months of age are listed within their various domains (social-emotional, fine motor, gross motor, cognitive, communication).

Music tasks for each milestone are suggested as assessment tasks. The practitioner can start wherever it is functionally appropriate for the child to perform. Following the assessment tasks, the therapist can check off the current levels of performance as a beginning guideline for setting goals and objectives.

Issue of Assessing both Nonmusic and Music Behaviors

The issue of assessing both nonmusic and music behaviors, contained in music therapy literature reviews (Wilson & Smith, 2000) is worthy of further study. Most music therapists, whether they use a formal or informal tool, assess both nonmusic and music behaviors (Cassity, 1985). In his review of 66 clinical training facilities for psychiatric music therapy, Cassity (1985) finds that 83 percent of the clinical training directors surveyed assess both nonmusic and music behaviors; 17 percent assess nonmusic behavior only; 1 percent assess music behavior only. In the Chase (2004) survey of therapists working with developmentally delayed children, 35 percent of the therapists assessed music behaviors compared to 95 percent assessing nonmusic behaviors.

In assessing both nonmusic and music behaviors, however, music therapists may be compartmentalizing these two areas. As shown in the literature (Lathom-Radocy, 2002), music therapists have a tendency to evaluate nonmusic skills within the context of musical activities, with the well-proven and certainly valuable assumption that children may perform nonmusic skills differently within the context of musical activities. For example, it is valuable to assess a particular child on social skills, auditory skills, motor skills and visual skills in the *context* of a drum set activity

(Gladfelter, 2002) and, further, it is valuable to do a "Musical Skills Assessment" (Gladfelter, 2002) but *do the musical behaviors themselves carry diagnostic value?* Apart from looking at the way in which the client behaves in the music therapy activities versus other environments, what does the observed *musical behavior* mean?

Assessment of Music Behaviors

Several theorists, music therapists as well as nonmusic therapists, consider musical behavior as indicative of normalcy vs. pathology, considerations which effect not only assessment but, of course, intervention strategies aimed at changing the course of musical behavior which may be indicative of pathology. The history of this inquiry begins early in the music therapy-related literature as researchers relate musical preference and thematic choice to personality (Cattell, 1953, 1954; Yingling, 1965) and music therapists begin to explore projective response to listening (Crocker, 1955; Bean and Moore, 1964).

A key inquiry regarding music behavior is in the area of rhythmic response. Starting in the seventies, Nordoff and Robbins present the idea of expanding and relating musical expression as it relates to increasing interrelatedness with others (1977) and therefore greater personal and interpersonal growth. More specifically, Nordoff and Robbins present categories of drumming and related diagnostic implications (1971). In a comparable sense, rhythmicity is investigated by Migliore (1991), Stein (1977), Steinberg, Raith, Rossnagl and Eben (1985), Perilli (1995) and Gibbons (1983) as follows. Migliore (1991) finds a relationship between marked depression and decreased rhythmic competency; Stein (1977), links tempo error with diagnosed mania; Perilli (1995), similarly to Stein, writes about a sense of subjective tempo with and without psychiatric disorder; Gibbons (1983), relates needs for structure to various success rates on rhythmic imitation tasks in preadolescents and adolescents, ages 11–15. Finally, Heimlich (1975) presents an auditory-motor percussion test (rhythmic imitation tasks) with the hypothesis that the presence of "structual alteration" in the responses of children may indicate pathology.

Sample assessment tools based on changes in musical behavior include the IAPs (Bruscia, 1987), Nordoff and Robbins (2007) and Goodman (1989).

Assessment of Nonmusic Behaviors

Assessment of nonmusic behaviors will vary depending upon the population. In the Cassity survey of informal (nonpublished) child psychiatric music therapy assessments (1985), common areas of concerns overlap developmental areas of interpersonal, behavior, cognitive, motor and receptive/expressive language areas. More specifically, the interpersonal behavior of children is most commonly assessed (31%) as it presents in disruptive or socially inappropriate behavior, withdrawal and lack of cooperation in sharing. Cognitive issues present a second most frequent problem with children (17%) in the Cassity study (1985) and include difficulty following directions, lack of directionality and spatial concepts and low self-esteem, the latter issue, of course, being directly related to interpersonal behavior. Finally, another second most frequent type of problems assessed with children (17%) is considered by Cassity to be physical: motor coordination, physical communication and expressive language.

In the Goodman (1989) music therapy assessment tool with emotionally disturbed children (MTA-ED), a tool for inpatient and outpatient psychiatric population, nonmusic behaviors presented include changes in positioning of music equipment and the content and theme of verbal association to music.

In the Michel and Rohrbacher (1982) tool with young (0–3 years) *multiply handicapped* children, all developmental milestones are considered within the context of musical tasks: speech/language, cognition, fine motor, gross motor, social-emotional.

In the Chase survey (2004) of assessment with *developmentally delayed* children, 95 surveys yield the following information regarding most frequently assessed areas: Motor (95%); Communication (83%); Social (79%); Cognitive (64%); Music (35%).

Finally, Rider (1981) delimits his assessment to assess Piagetian developmental cognitive tasks such as mental imagery, seriation, class inclusion and conservation. When the M-PACD was used with retarded students (Jones, 1986), the procedures had to be adapted and the validity of the tool with this population was debatable. This is an assessment-specific rather than a global assessment.

ISSUES CONCERNING CHOICE OF ASSESSMENT TOOL

In reviewing assessment tools and deciding which one may suit the music therapy situation, the therapist should consider the nature of the assessment tool in terms of purpose, client prerequisites, philosophy, time to administer, methodology and efficacy in the setting.

PURPOSE OF THE ASSESSMENT

According to Bruscia (1988) the purpose of the assessment may be diagnostic, interpretive, descriptive or prescriptive:

- In the diagnostic assessment, the therapist works through music to "detect, define, explain and classify the client's pathology" (Bruscia, 1988, p. 5).
- In the interpretive assessment, client problems are presented within the context of a "particular theory, construct or body of knowledge" (Brusica, 1988, p. 5)
- In the descriptive assessment, the effort to understand the client is presented only in reference to the client.
- In the prescriptive assessment, the therapist works to provide an intervention plan, which may involve placement, service needs, appropriate programming and methodology.

How does the therapist decide which of these assessment purposes is appropriate?

The therapist may start out with singular purposes. For example, the purpose, most typically, of assessment is to provide an intervention plan and, for this reason, in the context of the school, it is almost always *prescriptive*. Another example of singular purpose is the therapist working with short stay hospital patients and conducting assessment for the purpose of *diagnosis* only (Goodman, 1989). In this type of scenario the therapists might find consistency in the behaviors, exhibited in the music therapy assessment, that reflect on certain diagnosis. This is particularly interesting if the behaviors are musical.

On the other hand, the therapist may start out with singular purpose and end up with overlapping purposes. Here is an example of that scenario: In the course of using the assessment in order to set up *prescriptive* goals and intervention, the therapist selects an assessment tool that ascribes to a particular model. The results of the assessment, then, are *interpretive* in the context of the assessment tool model. Further, the therapist is able to provide information that is *diagnostic*, since it casts light on the diagnosis and affirms or contradicts other professional reports.

What if the purpose of the assessment is to provide eligibility information for music therapy on the Individual Education Plan?

In the case of IEP assessment, the purpose of assessment deviates from a more typical music therapy assessment. Aside from the fact that the assessment may yield prescriptive, interpretive and diagnostic information, the school districts requesting eligibility information for music therapy may have varying criteria for approval of services. Is it necessary, as the SEMTAP model (1999) suggests, to "prove" that the child's functioning behavior in the music therapy assessment session (i.e., based on tasks set up through goals already set on the Individual Education Plan) is *higher* than behavior in other contexts of functioning in order to receive services on the IEP?

Could there be other reasons for suggesting services ? In my assessment reports over the last 15 years, I provide varying rationale for recommendations regarding music therapy on the IEP. In *Case Study One,* the child's motivation and atten-

tion serve as prognostic indications for potential growth. In *Case Study Two,* the child's performance in individual vs. ongoing groupwork does not differ; due to the need for modeling from other children in a group and less "performance pressure," group therapy is recommended.

Case Study One

Music Therapy Recommendations:
1. Stephen's developmental skills do not differ in the music therapy session from those indicated in recent reports reviewed by this therapist.
2. Nonetheless, Stephen's motivation for and attention to musical activities make him an appropriate candidate for individual music therapy.
3. Music therapy goals should emphasize vocal communication and interactional music-making. These goals will help Sam develop further speech and language and invite interactional play for a child who appears to be self-absorbed. (Goodman, 1998)

Case Study Two

Music Therapy Recommendations:
Carolyn's increased alertness with the use of music has been cited by her teacher and related therapists. However, her performance in individual music therapy is not significantly higher than in other context and it is for this reason that the following recommendations are made:
1. Continued small group music therapy twice a week, affording Carolyn the advantage of ongoing musical stimulation without constant performance pressure.
2. Use of live and record music therapy strategies in the classroom.
3. Use of music therapy strategies in speech therapy through integrated programming.
4. Use of music therapy strategies in occupational therapy through integrated programming. (Goodman, 1998)

If one compares the eligibility assessment of occupational therapy, speech therapy, physical therapy, et al. for services on the child's Individual Education Plan, it is clear that the child needs these services because their functioning in fine motor skills, speech/language, gross motor, and so forth is delayed. Since music therapy can support *multiple* IEP goals through an alternative means of therapy, is that not enough of a rationale to provide services? This remains an unanswered question in the literature.

Further, the issues of eligibility for music therapy on the IEP continue to baffle school administrators, parents and music therapists. According to the federal statutes of the Individual with Disabilities Education Act, known as the IDEA, music therapy is not specifically mentioned as a related service. However, in a letter dated June 9, 2000 from the then Director of Special Education, United States Department of Education, Richard Warlick to Andrea Farbman, Executive Director of the American Music Therapy Association, the following is stated:

> If the IEP team determines that music therapy is an appropriate related service for a child, the team's determination must be reflected in the child's IEP, and the service must be provided at public expense and at no cost to the parents. However, let me emphasize that there is nothing in this clarification or in any statements in the discussion of comments and changes to the final regulations or in notes previously included in these regulations that would require that every disabled child receive music therapy as a related service regardless of the IEP team's determination as to whether the service is appropriate for the individual disabled child.
> We continue to support our prior position that for some children, art, music, or dance therapy is to be identified in their IEPs as a related service if the IEP team, which includes the child's parents, determines that the particular therapy would be necessary for the child to benefit from special education and to receive FAPE.
> In the past, much confusion has arisen when a request is made for a child to receive a related service not specifically identified in the statutory list of example of related services. It has been the Department's longstanding interpretation that ". . . (A)s under prior law, the list of related services is not exhaustive and may include other developmental, corrective, or supportive services (such as artistic and cultural programs, art, music, and dance therapy), if they are required to assist a child with a disability to benefit from special education in order for the child to receive FAPE (Fair

and Appropriate Services).
Analysis of Comments and Changes, published as Attachment 1 to the final Part B regulations, 64 Federal Register at 12548 (3/12/99).

These notes of clarification may be presented to any school administrator who seeks guidence regarding the unstated mandate of the term "related services." If a music therapy evaluation suggests music therapy on the IEP, the recommendation should also include the delivery of treatment (individual or small group) and number of times per week.

DEVELOPMENTAL PREREQUISITES FOR USE OF THE ASSESSMENT

Various music therapy assessments imply or specifically state developmental levels appropriate for use of certain tools. The *Music Therapy Assessment Profile for Severely/Profoundly Handicapped, MTAP* (Michel and Rohrbacher,1982), follows a developmental framework of birth-three years. Bruscia's *Improvisatory Assessment Profiles* (1987) or IAPs (utilized by Wigram, 2000, for the autistic child) suggest a beginning developmental age of two years. Goodman's *Assessment for Emotionally Disturbed Children, MTA-ED* (1989) invites representational thinking and verbal association, typically no earlier than a developmental two and a half years.

In all cases, the therapist must consider the developmental behaviors of the child and the developmental tasks of the assessment. In cases when there is a broad range of developmental tasks presented in the assessment, it makes sense to start the assessment at the reported current functioning level of the child. In this way, the child "works his/her way" toward more challenging tasks.

In order to estimate the beginning level of the child's functioning, it is useful to review the following information available on the child: Individual Education Plan, reports from therapists (occupational therapy, speech pathology, physical therapy), teachers (special education teacher, learning disabilities teaching consultant), psychologists and physicians (neurologist, psychiatrist). In cases where information is not accessible to the therapist or where there is limited time to review this information, the therapist will find it helpful to observe the child in the classroom in order to establish a beginning level of functioning. Of course, this informal evaluation of a starting point is dependent upon the therapist being experienced with different aspects of development: social, speech-language, cognition, fine and gross motor.

PHILOSOPHICAL ORIENTATION AND NATURE OF THE ASSESSMENT

Philosophical orientations generally dictate the nature of the assessment:

- *Behavioral:* includes observable behaviors. Measurement of these behaviors may be organized in terms of checklist, duration, frequency and/or rating scales (numerical or descriptive rating scales). The behavioral assessment can be global assessment, assessment-specific or a functional assessment, a specific assessment of a "problem" behavior (Griggs-Drane & Wheeler, 1997). In the music therapy literature the measurement of these behaviors is well described by Hanser (1999). The behavioral assessment is more likely to be quantitative and is frequently used with lower-functioning children, especially severely-profoundly retarded or severe conduct disordered children. These children are in greater need of structure.
- *Psychodynamic:* may include observable behavior but this behavior is in the context of interpretation. The behaviors, nonmusical and musical, are frequently viewed as symbolic or projective, representing other themes, motivations, or indicative of pathology (Goodman, 1989; Bruscia, 1987; Wigram, 2000). Frequently, there may be a psycho-analytic model as the basis for this assessment. The psychodynamic assessment is more likely to be qualitative and is frequently used with children who are verbal,

capable of representational play and emotionally disturbed. These children can tolerate less structure in their sessions.
- *Humanistic/Client-Centered:* may include observable behavior but this behavior is in the developing context of the patient's self-actualization needs. The humanistic model is more likely to be qualitative but may also include musical scoring and analyses of the child's response to particular improvisations (Nordoff and Robbins, 1977, 2007) which will then be repeated within an appropriate context of the session. It is used with both the preverbal and verbal child.
- *Developmental:* will include observable behavior but these behaviors will be in the context of a developmental model (i.e., Piaget, Greenspan, Freudian).The achievement of developmental tasks can be checked off or deliniated with a yes/no response (Libertore and Layman, 1999). The nature of the developmental tasks can be further described if the therapist so desires. Hence, the assessment can be both objective and subjective, both quantitative and qualitative. Further it can be global (Libertore and Layman, 1999) or assessment-specific (Rider, 1981). The overall practice of approaching assessment from a developmental perspective is advocated for children
- (Lathom-Radocy, 2002) as well as any music therapy population (Michel and Pinson, 2005).
- *Eclectic:* it is, of course, possible to combine approaches depending on the client. Dr. Stanley Greenspan, for example, combines the use of developmental and psychodynamic models in his assessment and intervention with children (see Chapter 3). Although this is not music therapy assessment, it paves the way for an eclectic music therapy model.

The question of philosophical orientation and the nature of the assessment are as much related to the purpose of the assessment as to the developmental readiness of the child and the orientation of the facility. In cases where the philosophical direction of the therapist and that of the facility vary drastically, there will obviously be problems. The rest of the staff needs to decode the assessment of the music therapist in subsequent team meetings and therefore everyone must have an understanding of the philosophy employed in the assessment.

SCOPE OF THE ASSESSMENT

In most cases, the child the therapist is assessing in music therapy will receive a global assessment, that is, an assessment covering multiple domains of behavior: social, communication, motor, and cognition. In other cases, however, the child may be referred to the music therapist for a specific purpose that relates to only one domain or area of development. It appears that this child would require an assessment specific to the referred problem. For example, the child is referred for communication delay and the therapist feels it necessary only to assess the extent of the communication delay in the music therapy evaluation. This, however, is a simplistic solution because all other domains impact upon communication. The issue of specific assessment, therefore, can be debatable.

METHODOLOGY

The issue of methodology is related to the philosophy of the therapist and, consequently, the purpose of the assessment. For example, the clinician trained with the behavioral model may be comfortable following through with a premeditated musical activity, writing down behavioral data and quantifying the results. The clinician comfortable with the psychodynamic or humanistic model may be more comfortable with an exploratory direction in the assessment session all the time, however, keeping in mind the purposes of the assessment. Finally, the clinician comfortable with the developmental model may prepare specific developmental tasks but meander forwards or backwards depending on the inclination of the child. Hopefully, the case study material in this chapter will begin to demonstrate the demands of

various types of assessment.

Further, in a very practical sense, methodology is related not only to philosophy but to the musical training of the therapist in connection with that philosophy. Is the therapist comfortable only following previously prepared materials or can the therapist improvise as well as follow tunes by ear?

The need for the therapist to balance previously designated musical tasks set forth in a given assessment tool with a degree of spontaneous flexibility in reacting to a child's response will define the difference between a novice and an experienced therapist.

TIME TO ADMINISTER ASSESSMENT

The practical issue is clear here. Does the facility offer you sufficient time to administer an assessment or portion of an assessment? If the answer is no, you may be compelled to develop an assessment for observation of group behavior and/or observation of the child within the group. This is, unfortunately, a common problem for many clinicians and one unaddressed by the music therapy literature.

Other key questions related to time include the following: How much time do you need to prepare for the music therapy session and how much time (i.e., how many sessions) to administer it? Is this a one-session assessment? Is this going to take more than one session? At what point might you want to repeat the assessment?

NEEDS EXPRESSED BY MUSIC THERAPISTS IN USING AN ASSESSMENT TOOL

In the most recently published survey of desired feature of an assessment tool (Chase, 2004), therapists cited the following needs from an assessment: 1) Easy to use (23%); 2) Comprehensive (19%); 3) Adaptable (13%). As the reader is introduced to the use of three sample published assessment tools, these aspects of usability can be subjectively evaluated.

CLINICAL EXAMPLES OF PUBLISHED ASSESSMENT TOOLS

It is common knowledge in the music therapy profession that many therapists create their own manner of generic assessment tools. In fact, Cole (2002) provides guidelines for doing this. Nevertheless, these assessment tools may follow a previously suggested format based on published assessment tools. It is for this reason that sample published or previously published assessments are presented, described further in terms of procedure and as a means of illustration include clinical examples.

Humanistic: The Nordoff-Robbins Scales (2007)–Overview

Introduced in the late sixties (1966) and early seventies (1973) while Nordoff and Robbins were working at the University of Pennsylvania with autistic children and recently revised (Nordoff and Robbins, 2007) the Nordoff-Robbins Scales (see Table 2.2) are based on clinical work with 52 children with diagnoses of multiple nature (i.e., autistic, schizophrenia, severely disturbed, retarded, blind, cerebral palsy) and behavior presenting with scatter skills.

As previously mentioned in this chapter, the current edition of the first scale entitled "Child-Therapists Relationship in Musical Activity" (see Table 2.2) details seven levels of the child's participation, ranging from "Unresponsive nonacceptance" (Level 1) to "Stability and confidence in interpersonal musical relationship" (Level 7). These levels of participation are then equated to qualities of resistiveness. The original Level 10, "Establishment of functioning independence in groupwork" (Nordoff and Robbins, 1977, p. 186) is now implicit in a child having reached the top step (step seven) of the relatedness scale. All the levels of the scales are described in terms of observable interpersonal behaviors (Nordoff and Robbins, 2007).

The second scale, entitled "Musical Communicativeness" (see Table 2.3), details seven levels of musical communicativeness, ranging from Level 1, "No musically communicative responses" to Level 7, "Musical intelligence and skills freely functioning and competently, personably communicable; Enthusiasm for musical creativity." The former Level 10 (Nordoff and Robbins, 1977) "Commitment to musical objectives in groupwork" is now implied with a child having reached the top step, step seven of the musical communicativeness scale. Children are described within these levels for various modes of musical behavior: instrumental, vocal and body movement. Similar to descriptive statements for the definition of scale levels in the "Child-Therapists Relationship in Musical Activity" scale, the "Musical Communicativeness" levels within each category modality are carefully described in terms of observable behavior. In effect, a behaviorist could view the descriptions as a series of descriptive rating scales.

The scales are both quantitative and qualitative in their appeal.

TABLE 2.2. SCALE 1. CHILD-THERAPIST RELATIONSHIP IN
COACTIVE MUSICAL EXPERIENCE RATING FORM.

Child:_____ DOB:_____ Date:_____ Session:_____

Therapist:_____ Rater:_____ Rating Date:_____

P	R	LEVELS OF PARTICIPATION	QUALITIES OF RESISTIVENESS
(7) _____/_____		Stability and confidence in interpersonal musical relationship.	Through identification with a sense of accomplishment and well-being resists own regressive tendencies.
(6) _____/_____		Mutuality and co-creativity in the expressive mobility of music.	a) Crisis-toward resolution. b) No resistiveness.
(5) _____/_____		Assertive coactivity. Working relationship. Self-confident purposefulness.	Perseverative compulsiveness. Assertive inflexibility. Contest.
(4) _____/_____		Activity relationship developing.	Perversity and/or manipulativeness.
(3) _____/_____		Limited responsive activity.	Evasive defensiveness.
(2) _____/_____		Wary ambivalence. Tentative acceptance.	Anxious uncertainty. Tendency toward rejection.
(1) _____/_____		Unresponsive nonacceptance.	Apparent obliviousness. Active rejection. Panic/rage reaction when pressed.

Reprinted with permission from Nordoff, P. and Robbins, C. (2007), *Creative Music Therapy: A Guide to Fostering Clinical Musicianship.* Gilsum, NH: Barcelona.

TABLE 2.3. SCALE II. MUSICAL COMMUNICATIVENESS RATING FORM.

Child:_____ DOB:_____ Date:_____ Session:_____

Therapist:_____ Rater:_____ Rating Date:_____

LEVELS OF COMMUNICATIVENESS	MODES OF ACTIVITY			RATING TOTALS
	Instrumental	Vocal	Body movement	
(7) Musical intelligence and skills freely functioning and competently, personably communicable. Enthusiasm for musical creativity.	_____	_____	_____	_____
(6) Participating communicative responsiveness firmly established. Growing musical self-confidence. Independence in using rhythmic, melodic, or expressive components.	_____	_____	_____	_____
(5) Sustaining of directed response impulses setting up musical communication. Musical motivation appearing. Involvement increasing.	_____ _____	_____ _____	_____ _____	_____ _____
(4) Musical awareness awakening. Intermittent musical perception and intentionality manifesting.	_____	_____	_____	_____
(3) Evoked responses (ii): more sustained and musically related.	_____	_____	_____	_____
(2) Evoked responses (i): fragmentary, fleeting.	_____	_____	Nonactive	_____
(1) No musically communicative responses.				

Reprinted with permission from Nordoff, P. and Robbins, C. (2007), *Creative Music Therapy: A Guide to Fostering Clinical Musicianship*. Gilsum, NH: Barcelona.

Gathering Preliminary Information

Nordoff and Robbins do not suggest gathering any preliminary information on the child coming to music therapy. Indeed, some practitioners believe that review of records can be the basis of negative or positive bias on the part of the therapist preparing to meet the child in therapy.

Administering the Assessment

Certainly the basis of the Nordoff-Robbins

approach is meeting the emotional state of the child through a matching musical improvisational approach. As such, there are no specific "activities" previously considered in administering what is essentially an ongoing assessment or rating scale.

Scoring

In both Scales One and Two, there are levels indicated for the child's performance in the session. The behaviors that define these levels are clearly outlined in the work of Nordoff and Robbins (2007). The therapist can use the scales as a simple checklist, checking off the behavior levels that are indicated in a session. If, on the other hand, the therapist chooses to rate the child with numbers, ten points are to be distributed on the rating scale over as many levels of behavior as are recognized in the child's response. The more prevalent the behavior(s) ascribed to a level, the higher the number of points will be allotted to that level.

If the rater is using the 10-point system, rating totals on each level of scale one and two are to be entered on a running tally sheet with dates of entry.

Case Examples

Scale One

Nordoff and Robbins describe an eleven-year-old learned disabled child, Martha, self-protection in her responses. This insecurity, reflected in her need to develop musical confidence, shows up in tentative singing and drumbeating, leading to an initial scoring of Level (3) in participation *Limited Responsive Activity,* and in resistiveness *evasive defensiveness.*

With further experience and musical support, her confidence increases and she begins to enter into the Level (4) *Activity Relationship.* Elements of expressive decisiveness in her drumbeating, although inconsistent, suggest that she may reach Level (5), *Self-confident purposefulness.* However, resistence to some of the activity suggested in the song "Marcie is Going to Sing" shows Level (4) resistiveness: Perversity and/or Manipulation. As Martha moves into another song, "Marcie's

Beating that Cymbal," animation improves and there is a brief musical dialogue which suggests *Assertive Coactivity,* Level (5) response.

In reflecting on the scoring, Nordoff and Robbins suggest that the initial Level (3) scores are to be expected in response to new experience. More importantly, the Level (4) scores, consistent in a second session, are leading her toward Level (5) where familiarity and musical comfort will reign. A suggested rating of the second session for Martha, using a ten-point system, would include the following : Level (3) *Limited Responsive Activity,* 2 points, *Evasive Defensiveness,* 1/2 point, Level (4) *Activity Relationship Developing,* 6 points, *Perversity and or Manipulation,* 1/2 point; Level (5) *Self-confident Purposefulness,* 1 point (Nordoff and Robbins, 2007).

Scale Two

Nordoff and Robbins (2007) describe a four-year-old nonverbal child, Lisa, who displays many autistic-like behaviors. As she begins her second session she is softly humming and her pitches are reflective of the music being sung and played for her. In brief response to the music, she runs a few steps and her sounds take on more excitement and musical inflection. Up to this point, her communicativeness is scoring in Nonactive (N), Vocal (V), Levels (2) and (3) and Body Movement (B), Levels (1) and (2).

Lisa's attraction to the cymbal leads her into rapid and firm beating. As the therapist improvises to this playing, Lisa pauses and then resumes rapid beating. As her playing becomes more ordered with the musical support of the improvisation, she adapts to the fast tempo of the improvisation and stops abruptly on an accented chord that concludes the melodic-rhythmic phrase.

According to Scale Two, communicativeness moves through levels 1/2, 1/3, 1/4 and, for a brief moment, 1/5, When Lisa withdraws from activity, the therapist decides to sing "Good-bye." In response to her name being sung in the song, Lisa makes a short, excited tonal cry and impulsively moves through the center of the room. These responses score in N, V/2 and B/2.

When moving away from the simple checklist

manner of evaluation, Nordoff and Robbins score Lisa in the following manner: "Using the 10-point system, an appropriate distribution of scores for Lisa K.'s second session would probably be 1/2 point in I/2, 1 in I/3, 11/2 in I/4, 1/2 in I/5; 1 in V/2, 1 in V/3; 1 in B/1, 1/2 in B/2, 3 in N. The Rating Totals would then be: Level (1), 4 points; Level (2), 2 points; Level (3), 2 points; Level (4), 11/2 points; Level (5), 1/2 point. In this rating, the scoring identifies the main levels of Lisa K.'s present response and also indicates the developmental thrust of her involvement" (Nordoff and Robbins, 2007). Although most of Lisa's responses are divided between noncommunicative and evoked response levels, the momentary intention responses in her cymbal playing as well as the more musically connected vocal responses of Level (3) suggest a higher prognosis.

BEHAVIORAL: SEMTAP

Overview

Published in 1989, the *SEMTAP: Special Education Music Therapy Assessment Process* (Coleman and Brunk, 1999) was written to answer the need for a methodical music therapy assessment process, particularly in determining eligibility for children who are being assessed for individual music therapy service on the Individual Education Plan.

The decision-making piece of the assessment focuses on the child's ability to make progress toward the goals of the IEP with or without music therapy. For this reason, the SEMTAP is criterion–referenced, describing performance in terms of specific behaviors and/or skills. Presumably, the child who can make significantly better progress toward stated IEP goals through music therapy (than without) is the child who will be recommended for direct service music therapy on the IEP. Direct service, in this case, is provided by a music therapist scheduled to meet with a particular child each week and work toward completion of stated IEP goals and objectives. Progress toward these goals and objectives is reviewed at annual IEP meetings. Educational enrichment through music therapy is provided for all children

receiving music therapy from a therapist hired for the school. In this case, music therapy services are not indicated on the IEP. They are, in effect, supplementary to the program for the children. According to SEMTAP, assessment for these children can be used as a baseline treatment planning model but it is not legally necessary.

Gathering Preliminary Information

Coleman and Brunk (1999) suggest each of the following steps in preparing for the assessment: 1) carefully review Individual Education Plan; 2) interview with members of the IEP team regarding progress or lack or progress toward stated goals and objectives; 3) target a specific number of IEP objectives on which the assessment will be based; 4) observe the child working on targeted IEP objectives in a nonmusical setting; 5) plan music therapy assessment session to address targeted objectives; and 6) if any of the targeted objectives involve ability to function within a group, consider conducting part of the assessment within the context of a group music therapy activity.

Administering the Assessment

After appropriate preparation for the music therapy assessment, the therapist will find a quiet space for the actual assessment. The session is documented through the use of notes, audio recording or videotape.

Scoring

No scoring system is described. The final report should include the following elements: 1) purpose of assessment; 2) outline of procedures; 3)relevant information from files reviewed; 4) information from interviews; 5) summary of classroom observation; 6) description of music therapy assessment setting and student alertness on that particular day; 7) detailed description of assessment session with performance on targeted objectives; 8) comparison of performance toward IEP skills with and without music therapy intervention; 9) recommendations for or against music therapy service on IEP; and 10) suggestions.

Case Example

No case examples are included in *SEMTAP*. For purposes of illustration, Goodman provides a case example below:

Case Example (K. Goodman, 1996–2002)

Name: Carolyn

D.O.B.: 04-01-92

Date of Assessment: 4-18-99

Reason for Referral:
Request from mother to determine appropriateness of individual music therapy on the IEP.

Background History:
Carolyn, currently 7 years of age, is multiply disabled, visually impaired, hearing impaired and nonambulatory. She operates at an infant level of development and is on seizure medication, dependent on full-time caretakers for activities of daily living
Carolyn received individual music therapy on the IEP once a week during the years AY 95–06 and 96–97; this was arranged without formal music therapy assessment. Following those years, she received group music therapy as a component of educational enrichment twice weekly during the years 97–98 and 98–99.

Report of Response to Music from Therapists and Mother:
According to interviews with therapists and mother, Carolyn's motivation to respond to the simplest of tasks is highest with reinforcements of food and music. This information is based on interview with the physical therapist, occupational therapist, speech therapist, mother and special education teacher of the last 3 years.

Current Goals in accordance with the IEP:
1. Look, move or reach toward a sound source.
2. Roll a ball.
3. Reach for desired object from choice of two.
4. Increase range of motion to trunk and lower extremities.
5. Increase tonal range and use of vowels and consonants in vocalization.
6. Grasp and release of objects.
7. Follow one-step requests.
8. Increase tactile exploration.

Progress Toward Goals in Music Therapy Assessment:
Carolyn has progressed in several areas but this progress is inconsistent and does not appear to relate to individual vs. group therapy. Her vocalization of sound is increasingly reliable, as is her increased tactile exploration. Her reaching for instruments is infrequent. Her vocalization is generally low-pitched and limited to one vowel, but she has, on two recent occasions, increased her tonal range. She will, on occasion, reach for the ball and release it. There is no increase of range of motion unless she is physically assisted. Her alertness in music is evident for several minutes at a time and then she appears to "need a break" from listening. Based on observation of her progress in other educational settings within the school (occupational therapy, physical therapy, speech therapy, classroom), her progress in music therapy does not differ from her progress in areas of other therapy or education.

Recommendations:
Carolyn's increased alertness with the use of music has been cited by her teacher and related therapists. However, her performance in individual music therapy is not significantly higher than in other context and it is for this reason that the following recommendation is made:

1. Continued small group music therapy twice a week, affording Carolyn the advantage of ongoing musical stimulation without constant performance pressure.
2. Use of live and record music therapy strategies in the classroom.
3. Use of music therapy strategies in speech therapy through integrated programming.
4. Use of music therapy strategies in occupational therapy through integrated programming.

Discussion of Case Example

This case example, while it does not follow the exact format dictated by Coleman and Brunk, is a brief example of the basis of SEMTAP intake. Here, according to the rater, the child does not warrant individual music therapy on the IEP. The therapist hired in Carolyn's school can continue to provide group programming and continue to work with consult services.

Discussion of Adaptability, Ease of Procedure, Comprehensive Scope

The SEMTAP, relying upon the appropriateness of stated IEP goals and objectives as a basis for decision-making, may be short-sighted. The statement of the goals and objectives, presumably comprehensive in scope, varies greatly depending upon the expertise of the evaluators in the child's home district. There may be problems with the IEP goals and objectives: 1) Too vague or too specific; 2) Developmentally inappropriate (too high or too low). These issues are not addressed by Coleman and Brunk. Furthermore, the issues of sensory profile are not mentioned in SEMTAP. Yet these issues impact greatly on the preparation of musical assessment material.

While the SEMTAP is relatively systematic and therefore provides ease of procedure in terms of data collection, observation, targeting objectives and devising music therapy tasks, it may ignore the process-oriented nature of a potential music therapy assessment session. If the therapist is busy administering specific activities and proceeding step-by-step with a premeditated plan, what happens when the child 'meanders' into a plan of his/her own making ?

Finally, in terms of adaptability, the SEMTAP seems clearcut and almost common-sense. Surely, any child with an IEP can be assessed using the SEMTAP process. Somehow a process which is so straightforward begs a closer look.

PSYCHODYNAMIC: THE GOODMAN MUSIC THERAPY ASSESSMENT TOOL FOR EMOTIONALLY DISTURBED CHILDREN

Overview

Introduced in the late eighties, the MAT-ED (Goodman, 1989) is based on individual short-term clinical work I conducted with latency age (3–12) inpatient (14 boys, 4 girls) and outpatient (3 girls, 3 boys) children at New York Hospital Cornell Medical Center. Inpatient children presented with diagnoses that included organic personality syndrome, adjustment disorder, socialized aggressive disorder, dysthmic disorder, major depression, conduct disorder, atypical psychosis, attention deficit, separation anxiety, and oppositional disorder. All were suicidal. Outpatient children presented with diagnoses including conduct disorder, pervasive developmental disorder, elected mutism and oppositional disorder.

Coming from a clinical background of long-term psychodynamic work in an outpatient creative arts center, I was not used to short-term work. Influenced by my training in Nordoff-Robbins methodology and my interest in psychoanalytic theory, I sought to create an exploratory psychodynamic assessment tool that could shed a different perspective on the children and provide an immediate purpose for short-term clinical work.

As such, the MAT-ED is based on the behaviors observed in all children seen over a two year period, each averaging a three month stay and receiving individual music therapy once a week.

Choice and preference for certain music materials as well as multiple aspects of musical responsiveness are detailed in the assessment. These are all to be considered by the assessing therapist as representative of the child's personality. Further verbal and nonverbal associations add additional material to consider in the context of musical activity. All this information provides a detailed picture of the child's musical expression and the child's developing relationship with the therapist. There is no format given for what happens in the session; this remains open-ended. The purpose of this assessment is to portray a musical picture of the child's personality, albeit pathology and/or potential health.

The Goodman Music Therapy Assessment Tool for Emotionally Disturbed Children, MTA-ED, is shown below in Table 2.4.

TABLE 2.4. MAT-ED (GOODMAN, 1989).

I. Natural Response Choice (include description of developmental response)

___A. **Percussive:** Immediate response is physically rhythmic. This child must express self by somehow beating or clapping.

Describe:

___B. **Vocal:** Immediate response is respiratory, evidenced by heavy breathing. This child will inevitably express self vocally, react primarily to songful music and the therapist's voice by singing, humming, whistling.

Describe:

___C. **Movement:** The child is physically energized by rhythm and must interpret the music through whole body movement.

Describe:

___D. **Listening:** Child listens intently to select music rather than actively express a musical response.

Describe:

___E. **Instrumental**

1. Keyboard

    a. piano
    b. xylophone
    c. resonator bells

Describe:

2. Wind

    a. Reed horn
    b. recorder
    c. other

Describe:

3. Percussive

    a. drum
    b. cymbal

Describe:

4. Strings

    a. autoharp
    b. guitar
    c. violin
    d. other

Describe:

continued

TABLE 2.4. MAT-ED (GOODMAN, 1989)–*Continued.*

5. Vocal

 a. soprano
 b. alto
 c. tenor
 d. bass

Describe:

___F. **Composition**

Describe:

___G. **No Clear Choice**

1. Child works with a variety of materials (previously described)

2. Child relies on therapist to choose material and then engages with therapist

3. Child is passive, chooses material and asks therapist to perform it.

Describe:

___H. **Negative Choice**

1. Child is strongly opposed to using _____.

Describe:

___I. **Natural Response Choice changes** when _____.

Describe:

II. Musical Preference

___A. **Tolerance:** Child is tolerant of music as an accompaniment (action songs, dances) but does not express any preference for the music itself.

Describe:

___B. **Particular Attraction:** Child is attracted to music as an entity in itself:

1. Child is dependent on material conventionally popular with peers

 a. Pre-school, nursery tunes, lullabies
 b. Latency: children's folk songs
 c. Adolescent rock and roll, popular, Broadway

Describe:

2. Child is dependent on material that appears developmentally regressive:

Describe:

continued

TABLE 2.4. MAT-ED (GOODMAN, 1989)—*Continued.*

3. Child is attracted to music apart from the convention of peers:

    a. classical
    b. religious
    c. jazz/blues
    d. other

Describe:

4. Child needs the security and predictability of:

    a. heavily accented rhymes
    b. I-IV-V harmonies
    c. Step-wise melodic intervals
    d. The repetition of the melody

Describe:

5. Child is bored by simplicity and prefers:

    a. Dissonance in chord structures
    b. Syncopated rhythms
    c. Larger melodic intervals
    d. Modes other than major and minor

Describe:

6. Child associates music preferences with _____

Describe.

III. Musical Responsiveness (note changes in)

___A. **Control of Rhythm** (movement, speech, percussion instruments)

1. *Chaotic:* Beating is confused and wild, completely unrelated to the piano. Child cannot discriminate different rhythms.

Describe:

2. *Compulsive:* Beating is unrelated to therapist's improvisation. The beating maintains an obsessive unchanging quality. Child finds significance in constant repetition of a particular pattern and is unable to beat anything else.

Describe:

3. *Forced:* Child uses the drum as an aggressive tool to outplay in volume and noise over the piano. Drum is used to disrupt or dominate. Child takes opportunity for unchecked activity to bring into play unformed physical and emotional impulses.

Describe:

4. *Evasive:* Child is fearful of the music and avoids contact with instruments. The union of the musical excitement with her own impulses is overpowered so she avoids playing in rhythm with the piano.

Describe:

continued

TABLE 2.4. MAT-ED (GOODMAN, 1989)–*Continued.*

5. *Disorder:* Child tries to relate but cannot. The problem is physical or perceptual in origin not emotional.

Describe:

6. *Sporadic:* Sporadic beating is indicative of a short attention span or preoccupation with fantasies.

Describe:

7. *Playful:* Child treats the sessions as a game and the therapist cannot really tell what potential there is since the music reveals nothing about the child's mental or emotional level.

Describe:

8. *Stable:* Child is able to follow the piano by beating consistent 2/4, 3/4 or 4/4 pattern.

Describe:

9. *Creative:* Child initiates original patterns. Follows therapist with changes in tempo, dynamics, rhythm.

Describe:

10. *Melodic:* Child initiates melodic rhythm.

Describe:

11. *Control of Rhythm* changes when:

    a. child is given a model and becomes dependent on imitation.
    b. Child reacts negatively to synchronous beating from the therapist and changes pattern to avoid contact.
    c. Child has distracting mental associations.
    d. Child is trying too hard.
    e. Child responds positively to introduction of familiar tune.
    f. Child appears more comfortable with therapist and tunes into music.
    g. Child uses change in musical pattern to symbolically express a spontaneous emotion.

Describe:

___B. **Control of Dynamics**

1. Child is dependent on exaggerated loudness.

Describe:

2. Child is dependent on exaggerated softness.

Describe:

3. Child is responsive to an interplay of dynamic changes.
    a. tolerates
    b. imitates
    c. initiates

Describe:

continued

TABLE 2.4. MAT-ED (GOODMAN, 1989)–*Continued.*

4. Control of dynamics changes when.

Describe:

___C. **Control of Articulation**

1. Child lacks the ability to produce physical movement of the body, which would result in control of durations of sound.

Describe:

2. Child uses fine motor coordinator or gross motor coordination to produce desired sound durations on the:

    a. recorder (tongue)
    b. violin (bow arm)
    c. hand drum (hands)
    d. piano (fingers)
    e. other

Describe:

3. Control of articulation changes when:

Describe:

___D. **Control of Tone Quality**

1. Child is aware of tone quality appropriate to instrument and strives to achieve this.

Describe:

2. Child only wishes to get a sound out of the instrument and is not particular as to timbre:

Describe:

3. Child associates a timbre to the instrument that is inappropriate:

Describe:

4. Control of tone quality changes when:

    a. therapist models
    b. emotional quality of musical exchange changes
    c. Child changes instrument from _____ to _____.

Describe:

___E. **Control of Melodic Line/Phrasing**

1. Child correctly elucidates patterns of melodic tension and release.

Describe:

2. Child's patterns are consistently tense.

Describe:

continued

TABLE 2.4. MAT-ED (GOODMAN, 1989)–*Continued.*

3. Child's patterns are consistently unfocused.

Describe:

4. Control of phrasing changes when:

Describe:

___F. **Control of Steadiness of Pulse** (detail context: motor, instrumental, speech)

1. Child cannot maintain steady tempo:

    a. races ahead
    b. slows down

Describe:

2. Child maintains tempo and sense of pulse.

Describe:

3. Child's sense of pulse and tempo changes when:

Describe:

___G. **Physical Disposition of Instrument**

1. Child uses instrument in most physically efficient method of tone production.

Describe:

2. Child prevents efficient tone production

    a. slouching
    b. holds instrument too acutely or obtusely
    c. inserting too much of the instrument in hand or mouth

Describe:

3. Child avoids contact:

    a. positioning equipment away from therapist
    b. rejecting instrument after a matter of seconds
    c. exploring instrument in developmentally regressive manner.

Describe:

4. Child employs instrument in representational play.

Describe:

___H. **Appropriateness of Expressive Quality**

1. Child chooses musical material appropriate to own mood:

Describe:

continued

TABLE 2.4. MAT-ED (GOODMAN, 1989)–*Continued.*

2. Child is able to match the mood of the music with own musical response:

    a. vocal
    b. instrumental
    c. movement
    d. listening

Describe:

3. Child chooses material contrary to own mood.

Describe:

4. Child's musical responsiveness proves contrary to that of the composer's mood.

Describe:

5. Child's total musical affect (vocal, instrumental, movement) is in synchony.

Describe:

6. Child's musical behavior is contradictory.

Describe:

IV. Verbal Associations

___A. **During musical experiences**

Describe:

___B. **After musical experiences**

Describe:

___C. **Song Lyric**

1. Nature of:

    a. Thematic content

Describe:

    b. Changes in (and changes in accompanying musical elements)

Describe:

    c. Cohesiveness of mental associations changes when

Describe:

___D. **Storytelling/Musical Drama**

1. Nature of:

    a. Thematic content

Describe:

continued

TABLE 2.4. MAT-ED (GOODMAN, 1989)–*Continued.*

b. Changes in (and changes in accompanying elements)

Describe:

c. Cohesiveness of mental association changes when __

Describe:

V. Nonverbal reaction

___A. **Before musical experience**

Describe:

___B. **During musical experience**

Describe:

___C. **After musical experience**

Describe:

VI. Client/Therapist Interaction

___A. **Mutually Responsive:** Client is consistently able to give and take with therapist in session.

Describe:

___B. **Selective:** Client is responsive to therapist on selective level.

Describe:

___C. **Oppositional:** Client is oppositional throughout most of the session.

Describe:

VII. Discussion/Recommendations

Originally presented in *The Arts in Psychotherapy,* Spring, 1989.
Version above has been modified (Goodman, 2005).

Gathering Preliminary Information

In this particular psychiatric setting, the therapist was given initial information regarding tentative diagnosis, presenting problems and social history. This was reviewed prior to meeting with the child.

Administering the Assessment

There are no specific guidelines for administering this assessment.

Scoring

There is no system of scoring for this assessment.

Case Example

MAT-ED (K. Goodman, 1981–1984)

Colleen

Age at time of intake: Eleven years old

Tentative diagnosis: Borderline Personality Disorder (based on fluctuation in behavior, decompensation when anxious, potential for psychotic thoughts and impaired intellectual functioning)

Reason for inpatient admission: Suicidal Ideation; History of behavioral and academic issues (lability, tantrums when stressed, attentional difficulties, impaired reality testing at times of escalation, anxiety and fear; cognitive difficulty in math and temporal relationships).

Social History: Parents recently divorced.

Session One: Colleen's entry into her first music therapy session was guarded, but only momentarily. She told the music therapist: "I don't know you and I never had music here before." After selecting and singing her first song, "Coming Round the Mountain" from a songbook of American folk tunes, Colleen warmed up to the therapist. Her natural tendency was to nasalize the timbre and lower the register of her voice, giving it a restrictive and childlike sound. Already she referred to her parents in contrasting terms. Her mother's piano had claws for feet and her father was the parent who had given her a beloved flute and drum set.

Colleen's reference to the flute and drum led into a drum duet with the music therapist. Given a standing Orff drum, Colleen initiated a drum pattern to imaginary parades and then began to attempt rather sophisticated roll techniques. When one of these rolls became technically difficult and, therefore, out of rhythm, Colleen stopped playing and verbally associated to embarrassing situations in the past. This seems to have led to a shorter attention span in subsequent musical work. As described in this first session, one had the impression that Colleen was quite talkative and used this tactic defensively in order to stop the musical performance when it became threatening.

Back on the unit, Colleen boasted about her music therapy session and sang loudly in a provocative fashion. As if to undo all the praise she had received in the music session, she antagonized her peers and the ward staff with her singing.

Session Two: Colleen's second session was held at the piano. Her song choices continued to stay within the realm of the separation theme: "Somewhere Over the Rainbow" and "The Rainbow Connection" were emotional magical connections to escape for her. She appeared to choose this material to suit her depressed mood and made a concerted musically sensitive effort to match the mood of the music with her response. Sensing the restricitve quality in Colleen's voice, the music therapist engaged Colleen in free vocal warmups. Singing with the music therapist, Colleen's voice opened up in a bell-like tone and another soprano register. She responded to this unexpected voice with a dismay and blamed the therapist: "Don't make me do that. You sound like a stupid woman–like my father's girlfriend."

Colleen continued on, vocally maintaining her tempo and sense of pulse. At a moment when she was slightly ahead of the rubato the music therapist offered her, she stopped and said she was "afraid of losing the beat." This reaction was consistent with the first session when Colleen lost control of the drum beating rhythm. Likewise, Colleen reported difficulty when other voices or instruments (i.e., like that of the music therapist) joined in and distracted her rhythmic momentum.

Session Three: The fear of losing control became an obvious theme in Colleen's music therapysession and one of which she was keenly aware. She needed to be reminded that music-making was a place where she could make mistakes, correct them and go on. The therapist modeled this behavior for her. Colleen remained highly structured.

She came prepared to session in the sense that she told the music therapist exactly what she now wanted to work on. Her selection of songs from "Annie," the story of an orphaned child who finds foster parents, reflected the theme of separation anxiety and the wish for happy reunion. The concerted effort of her singing could only lead one to velieve that she felt orphaned. Further, Colleen explained, after singing "Tomorrow" and "Maybe" ("their one mistake was giving up on me") that she believed her successful reenactment of certain Broadway roles like "Annie" would earn her the love and admiration she never received from her mother.

In line with her fantasy, her singing voice had to be "just so"–more like a child (i.e., orphan Annie) than the preadolescent she was. She grew more sensitive to the therapist's intervention while modeling the singing role of "Annie" in a more grownup voice. She asked, "Is this a kind of therapy where you judge how I feel by how I sing?" In response to her anxiety, the music therapist tried to help Colleen clarify the issues she was bringing up in session: What did the child's voice sound like to her? The adult voice? Could these ever merge? If so, then how would she feel? What might happen? Would that be so bad? Good?

Session Four: Colleen's fourth session was held in the auditorium of the hospital. She was going to be videotaped and so, for her, this was a test of her performance. Distraught about the continuation of a vocal warm-up, she complained that her voice was hoarse from a cold she had the week before. Grudgingly, she consented to sing. Her

performance anxiety made the singing more difficult and her goals more perfectionistic. She stopped singing in the middle of "Tomorrow," complaining that the accompaniment register was too high. Given more vocal support from the therapist, her voice lost its nasal quality, became more relaxed and more open. She thought about the song after singing it and compared the orphanage in "Annie" to the locked ward of the inpatient child psychiatric unit with the "birds and rainbow outside." A brief playback on the camera was initially a pleasure for Colleen to see. Then she denied the fact that she had done well and, in holding her ears to listen more closely to the vocal warm-up, stated, "This way I get the crap that's underneath."

TABLE 2.5. USE OF MAT-ED ITEMS, COLLEEN.

I. Natural Response Choice (include description of developmental response)

___B. **Vocal:** Immediate response is respiratory, evidenced by heavy breathing. This child will inevitably express self vocally, react primarily to songful music and the therapist's voice by singing, humming, whistling.

Describe: Child prefers vocal and dramatic activity

___I. **Natural Response Choice Changes** when _____.

Describe: Therapist introduces drum activity in response to Colleen's free associations about the drum

II. Musical Preference

___B. **Particular Attraction:** Child is attracted to music as an entity in itself:

1. Child is dependent on material conventionally popular with peers

a. Preschool, nursey tunes, lullabies
b, Latency: children's folk songs
c. Adolescent rock and roll, popular, Broadway

Describe: Comfortable with folk songs as well as Broadway.

6. Child associates music preferences with _____.

Describe: Her father's silly girlfriend. Avoidance of developing sexuality in her voice?

III. Musical Responsiveness (note changes in)

___A. **Control of Rhythm** (movement, speech, percussion instruments)

8. Stable: Child is able to follow the piano by beating consistent 2/4, 3/4 or 4/4 pattern.

Describe:

continued

TABLE 2.5. USE OF MAT-ED ITEMS, COLLEEN–*Continued.*

11. Control of Rhythm changes when:

b. Child reacts negatively to synchronous beating from the therapist and changes pattern to avoid contact.
c. Child has distracting mental associations.
d. Child is trying too hard.

Describe: All of above have happened in various musical scenarios with Colleen.

___B. **Control of Dynamics**

3. Child is responsive to an interplay of dynamic changes:

a. tolerates
b. imitates
c. initiates

Describe: See above

4. Control of dynamics changes when:

Describe: Trying to arrest feelings during songs.

___C. **Control of Articulation**

3. Control of articulation changes when:

Describe: Difficulty in controlling drum rolls leads to stopping.

___ D. **Control of Tone Quality**

3. Child associates a timbre to the instrument that is inappropriate:

Describe: Developmentally regressive nasal voice.

4. Control of tone quality changes when:

b. emotional quality of musical exchange changes

Describe: She begins to relax and her voice opens up. This appears to be frightening for her.

___E. **Control of Melodic Line/Phrasing**

4. Control of phrasing changes when:

Describe: She becomes more aware of her changing voice.

___F. **Control of Steadiness of Pulse** (detail context: motor, instrumental, speech)

1. Child cannot maintain steady tempo:

a. races ahead
b. slows down

Describe: May be trying to resist synchronous contact with therapist sometimes.

continued

TABLE 2.5. USE OF MAT-ED ITEMS, COLLEEN–*Continued.*

2. Child maintains tempo and sense of pulse.

Describe: Most of the time.

3. Child's sense of pulse and tempo changes when

Describe: She gets out of syncrony with therapist

___G. **Physical Disposition of Instrument**

4. Child employs instrument in representational play.

Describe: Free associates to "Coming around the Mountain"

___H. **Appropriateness of Expressive Quality**

1. Child chooses musical material appropriate to own mood;

Describe: Anxious, depressed yet ambivalent about capacity to have meaningful relationships with others.

6. Child's musical behavior is contradictory:

Describe: Difficulty with control issues leads her to stop and go with her voice as well as percussive instruments.

IV. **Verbal Associations**

___ A. **During Musical Experiences**

Describe: Resists going into another register of the voice.

___B. **After Musical Experiences**

Describe: Says she "gets the crap that's underneath."

___C. **Song Lyric**

1. Nature of

a. Thematic content

Describe: Abandonment issues (Annie); separation (Coming Around the Mountain).

c. Cohesiveness of mental associations changes when:

Describe: She free associates to song lyrics to excess (i.e., Coming Around the Mountain).

___D. **Storytelling/Musical Drama**

1. Nature of

a. Thematic content

Describe: Annie is the story of a child who is orphaned and hopes to be taken in and loved again

b. Changes in (and changes in accompanying elements)

Describe: NA

continued

TABLE 2.5. USE OF MAT-ED ITEMS, COLLEEN–*Continued.*

c. Cohesiveness of mental association changes when:

Describe: Colleen gets angry, anxious, scared in the music.

V. Nonverbal reaction

___ A. **Before Musical Experience**

Describe: Generally eager to come to music and get involved. Interested and motivated.

___B. **During Musical Experience**

Describe: Restrictive, if she has musically allowed herself to lag behind or get ahead, i.e., with the voice.

___ C. **After Musical Experience**

Describe: Tends to be reflective about her physical and psychological process.

IV. Client/Therapist Interaction

___ B. **Selective:** Client is responsive to therapist on selective level.

Describe: Colleen's capacity to relate to the therapist reflects her mixed feelings about her relationships with her parents and her ego strength. When she finds herself getting too close to the therapist either musically or verbally, she appears to stop herself from enjoying these moments, as though to protect herself from the potential of abandonment.

VII. Discussion/Recommendations

The issues that emerged in Colleen's singing, choice of the material, musical behaviors and verbal associations are helpful to her primary therapist insofar as they expand on initial observations. Her primary emotions expressed through music focus on longing, a sense of child-like vulnerability rather than rage. Her intention to use music making to initally please her mother needs to be channeled into a tool toward her own sense of self-esteem. Her use of a baby voice appears to indicate a need for regressive behavior in order to be loved. She needs to recognize the purpose of her regressive behavior and the positive value of age-appropriate behavior. Her fantasy of being a Dorothy (*Wizard of Oz*) or Annie clarifies her feelings that she is abandoned and searching for a nurturing mother. The repetition of singing these songs and musically acting them out with dance, gestures and facial expression is cathartic and helps her talk out her accompanying feelings. The structure of the music and permission to be fanciful within selected character roles appears to help Colleen avoid any tendency toward psychotic, acting-out behavior. Her attempt to be perfect (fear if failure) speels inevitable failure–a self-fulfilling prophecy. She needs to learn to accept mistakes in the course of learning (i.e., making music) and begin to distinguish between good and bad.

These issues can be explored in individual therapy. Further, individual music therapy once/weekly is highly recommended.

Discussion of Adaptability, Ease of Procedure, Comprehensive Scope

This is an assessment that is highly inferential and interpretive and therefore relies on the specialized training of the music therapist in the psychoanalytic tradition. It is recommended for verbal clients, clients who are capable of representational play and symbolic thinking as a basis for projective music-making and thematic choices.

Adaptability is limited given the nature of the music therapy client who would benefit from the MAP-ED. The procedure is open-ended and requires skills on the part of the therapist in following the process-oriented behavior of the client.

As mentioned in the overview of the MAP-ED, Goodman observed children over a two-year period for the musical behaviors included in this assessment. It is considered comprehensive in scope but that does not mean that the clinician may not discover additional material to include. The purpose of this assessment is to share a unique perspective on the disturbed child that will help other music therapists and therapists understand the child's behavior, its underlying meaning and eventual therapeutic goals.

DEVELOPMENTAL: THE MUSIC THERAPY ASSESSMENT PROFILE FOR SEVERELY/PROFOUNDLY HANDICAPPED PERSONS

Overview

Written as part of a training grant to supply materials in music therapy for severely/profoundly handicapped persons held at Texas Woman's University, Denton, Texas, this assessment profile is edited by Michel and Rohrbacher (1982). Probably underutilized at the time of its publication, it is no longer in publication. It represents a developmental checklist for children ages birth–27 months (note: some sections span up to 36 months). Although it was originally developed as part of a grant for SVR, the developmental milestones represent normal development and therefore can be used with any population up to the developmental age of 27 months old.

The primary developmental areas represented include gross motor, fine/perceptual motor skills, communication, cognition and social-emotional. The developmental checklist is accompanied with simple music therapy tasks suggested for music therapy assessment purposes. It certainly is a model that can be replicated and fine-tuned. For a more comprehensive list of developmental milestones the reader is directed to a resource entitled H.E.L.P., Hawaii Early Learning Profile, (Furuno, et al., 1997).

Gathering Preliminary Information

The therapist is advised to review information about the child from previous and currrent medical records, educational records (classroom teacher; physical education; other) and therapy reports (physical therapy, occupational therapy, speech therapy, arts therapies, psychology, social work). Previous assessments may suggest a preliminary treatment plan. The parents and members of the educational/therapeutic team can be interviewed for further information on the status of the child. Finally, information regarding the child's prior experiences with music (recreational, educational, therapeutic) can be requested.

Administering the Assessment

Specific musical tasks are suggested in the assessment to assess each milestone. However these are described as "sample assessment procedure" (1982, p. 2) and the therapist is advised "to be aware of and to make note of any special techniques, devices or procedures used in the assessment" (1982, p. 2).

Scoring

There is no quantifiable scoring. Items are evaluated with a P (pass), F (Fail) or PF (Pass-Fail for tentative or uncertain task completion) and O (omit when item must be ommitted for whatever reason).

Case Example

MTAP (K. Goodman, 1992–1998)

Music Therapy Evaluation:

Name: Stephen

D.O.B.: April 1, 1988

Evaluation Date: May 27, 1996

Reason for Referral:
It was suggested by Dr. Treman, the examining psychologist, that Stephen appears to be motivated by musical activities and might benefit from music therapy (December 16, 1995). The request for a music therapy evaluation was made by Stephen's social worker, Mrs. Berger, to determine the appropriateness of music therapy. Stephen is visually impaired, developmentally delayed and unable to ambulate independently.

Goals of Music Therapy Evaluation:
1. Using musical activities designed by the therapist in accordance with the goals of Stephen's Individual Education Plan, establish developmental levels within the areas of social-emotional behavior, communication behavior, cognitive behavior and motor behavior.
2. Compare results of music therapy evaluation to other evaluations.
3. Make recommendations as to the efficacy of music therapy.

Assessment Instrument Being Utilized:
The Music Therapy Assessment Profile (MTAP) for Severely/Profoundly Handicapped Persons (1982, Michel and Rohrbacher) was utilized to establish Stephen's developmental level within the music therapy session.

*Music Therapy Observations Related
to Developmental Functioning:*

Communication: In terms of nonverbal communication, Stephen lifted his head and reached out his hands to seek out the reappearance of preferred instruments such as the tambourine, omnichord, casio keyboard, autoharp and reed horn. Further, he communicated pleasure by laughing at the sensation of the reed horn which he physically directed the therapist to blow into his ear.
Vocally, Stephen appropriately "sang" on the "h" sound within the tonality of a song which included the stimulation of two-tone chimes in harmony. His vocal range is limited and infrequently stimulated but is musically related. Stephen's

mother reports that he sings the "hallelujah" in "Michael, Row the Boat Ashore." This was not observed.

Cognition: Stephen's level of attention for a 45-minute intake was excellent. He remained alert, focused on the activity at hand and responsive, albeit on limited levels. No self-stimulating behaviors were observed and the initial disstraction of his fingers in his mouth decreased as the session progressed.
In terms of explorations, Stephen sought out the varied function of various instruments quite appropriately (i.e., turning up and down volume buttons, manipulating and repeating manipulation to produce different sounds; plucking, resting on and strumming the strings of the autoharp; shaking the tambourine with two hands) and was able to manipulate new instruments appropriately after initial modeling from the therapist (i.e., afuche, tone chimes). Use of his most familiar instrument, the tambourine, was appropriate and musical although not in accordance with the given tempo of the music.
Auditory discrimination appears to be excellent. Stephen oriented to front, back and side-to-side when instruments were moved and paused to listen when the therapist changed the instrumental sounds/timbres on the casio keyboard.

Social: Stephen was compliant and expressed pleasure while using preferred instruments. He also expressed appropriate anxiety when he could not manipulate the keyboard because the therapist had turned it off. In this instance, he persisted in looking for a way to turn the casio back on.
When Stephen's mother left the room, he wailed and appeared to physically search for her. When she returned, he appeared pleased.

Motor: Seated on the floor, Stephen did not reach to roll the ball back to the therapist. No large motor activity was attempted in this intake.
Stephen's pincer grasp was excellent and he easily manipulated all instruments. Drooling was observed and although Stephen was interested in the reed horn, an instrument often used with children developing oral-motor musculature, he accepted it into his mouth, but would not attempt to blow it.

Conclusions:
1. Stephen's developmental skills do not differ in

the music therapy session from those indicated in recent reports reviewed by this therapist.

2. Nonetheless, Stephen's motivation for and attention to musical activities make him an appropriate candidate for individual music therapy.

3. Music therapy goals should emphasize vocal communication and interactional music-making. These goals will help Stephen develop further speech and language and invite interactional play for a child who appears to be self-absorbed

Recommendations:

1. Individual music therapy with a music therapist accredited by the American Music Therapy Association is recommended at least once a week. Ideallly, this would be done by an accredited music therapist at Stephen's school. If not, the music therapist employed by the district should communicate with Stephen's teachers on a regular basis.

2. The infusion of music into Stephen's daily curriculum is recommended. Songs sung to Stephen can be used by the classroom teacher to mark transitions, accompany here and now play and structure requests. Similarly, songs sung to Stephen by the occupational and physical therapists can rhythmically accompany movement. Instrumental activities should allow Stephen's initial exploration followed by efforts to antiphonally interact with him musically, invite imitation and finally movement. Instrumental activities should allow Stephen's initial exploration followed by efforts to antiphonally interact with him musically, invite imitation and, finally, follow Stephen's creative play. (Goodman, 1998)

Discussion of Case Example Using the MTAP

Use of Milestones in MTAP

This particular case example utilizes the following milestones included in the MTAP (1982):

- *Fine Motor, item #58: Uses neat pincer grasp with a small musical instrument. (Attract the child's attention to a small bell or finger cymbal within reach. Pass if the child picks up the instrument using thumb and forefinger opposition.) 6-8 months.*
- *Fine Motor, item #61: Releases musical instrument, voluntarily. (After shaking a maraca, demonstrate for the child how to place the maraca on the table.*

Pass if the child voluntarily sets it down and releases it without dropping.) 12–15 months.
- *Fine Motor, item #62: Two hand (grasps) coordination activities (Present a tambourine to the child and encourage grasping and shaking with both hands; pass if the child is able to shake it at least three times with symmetrical arm movements.) 16–19 months.*
- *Communication, item #84: Imitates words inexactly. (Pass if child is heard to use or imitate any words during assessment.) 9–11 months.*
- *Communication, item #86: Uses gestures and other movements to communicate. (Pass if child uses head, hand, or body to reach for, ask for, or reject objects such as rhythm instruments, etc.) 12–15 months.*
- *Cognitive, item #29: Uses more than one rhythm instrument appropriately (Pass if the child is independently able to perform on at least two contrasting rhythm instruments and produce their most characteristic sound.) 12–15 months.*
- *Cognitive, item #133: Attempts to activate cassette tape recorder (without demonstration of how to push the buttons, place a cassette in front of the child). (Pass if the child locates the buttons and pushes down at least one.) 20–27 months. (Note: The assessor liberally interpreted this item in the actual report to include activation of a casio keyboard.)*
- *Social-Emotional, item #164: Initiates musical play. (Pass if child tries to draw adult into musical play by initiating sounds with instruments, record-player, singing or other musical behavior.) 12–15 months.*

Permission to reprint the MTAP milestone originally published by N.A.M.T. (1982) per Dr. Donald Michel and Dr. Michael Rohrbacher.

Discussion of Adaptability, Ease of Procedure, Comprehensive Scope

Perceived attributes of any assessment, according to the respondents in the Chase survey (2004) included adaptability, ease of procedure and comprehensive scope. In the clinical example presented by Goodman (1998), the MTAP was used not only to suggest an intervention plan but also to suggest eligibility for music therapy on the Individual Education Plan. In this particular case, the referring district did decide, on the basis of the report, to put music therapy on the IEP and follow the recommendations of the assessing therapist. Rather than using the checklist procedure suggested by the authors of the MTAP, Goodman wove the information into a narrative report of her own invention. This suggests that the MTAP can be used *adaptively* to collect information.

In terms of *ease of procedure,* the therapist is provided with guidelines but left free to pursue methods and materials that are appropriate to the session with the individual child. In the case of "Stephen," visually impaired, developmentally delayed and nonambulatory, methods and materials relied heavily on tactile cues and sensory exploration. Further, the primary caretaker, the mother, was included in the session due to the child's separation anxiety. The strategy of including the primary caretaker(s) in the session is one suggested by the work of Dr. Stanley Greenspan (Greenspan, 1992), Since preliminary information included clear descriptions of multiple sensory challenges and, further, suggested a highest functioning developmental age of 15–20 months, materials for those developmental tasks were anticipated.

In terms of *comprehensive scope,* the MTAP includes representative tasks in developmental milestones up to the age of 36 months. Developmental milestones are not comprehensive compared to other models of developmental milestones (Furano, 2005) that may be important in the reporting of the assessment. Further, descriptions of learning styles and sensory limitations are not included in the context of a simple checklist.

THE ROLE OF ASSESSMENT IN GROUP MUSIC THERAPY WITH CHILDREN

ASSESSING THE CHILD IN THE GROUP

At this time, there is no assessment for children in the music therapy group. Nor is there a model in place for assessment of the child music therapy group as a separate entity. Simply put, the therapist who wishes to assess a child in the context of a group must plan carefully in order to gather information on one child who is part of an ongoing group. Part of this preparation may involve a teacher or another therapist willing to sit outside of the group and take notes while the group is ongoing and the music therapist is engaged in running the group. The music activities as well as the methodology should be strategically geared toward evaluation of developmental areas relevant to the assessment of the child. As a general guideline, the music activities can include listening, movement, instrumental and vocal possibilities with methods geared to the varying needs of all the children in the group.

Some of the key differences between assessment of the child in individual music therapy and the child in group music therapy, both negative and positive, include the following:

- Other children may serve as a positive role model (positive)
- Attention given to other children may provide a time-out for the child who is typically feeling overly pressured, put "on the spot" or has slow processing time (positive).
- Other children may serve as a negative role model (negative).
- The child is subject to being distracted by other children (negative).
- The child must share the attention of the therapist (negative/positive).
- The child must share the instruments in the session (negative/positive).
- The child is subject to other sensory input in the room (negative/positive).
- The therapist must balance the needs of all the children in the group while, at the same time, working to assess a particular child (negative/positive).
- The therapist may have more difficulty using an exploratory or tangential approach if needs of different children in the group need to be handled (negative).
- The therapist must share her music-making with all the children in the group (negative/positive).
- The therapist will gain a working perspective on the child in relation to other group members as opposed to being alone with her (positive/negative).

ASSESSING THE PROGRESS
OF THE GROUP

There has been much written about the progress of the group, most notably by Dr. Irving Yalom (1985). Specific levels of group progress in music therapy in terms of adolescent groups (Joseph, 1989), adults (Sandness, 1991) or children (Friedlander, 1994) can be considered. This process, however, would not look at the particular developmental functioning of the child in the group but, rather, at the holistic progress or lack of progress of the group. At what level is the group, as a separate entity, functioning? Is it possible to assess the group as a whole and, if so, how does that impact on the assessment of particular children in the group? These are all important questions to be considered in subsequent work with groups.

SUMMARY

It is up to the individual therapist to determine the appropriateness of their skills as a music therapist to provide appropriate assessment for a child. This chapter provides different alternatives for the therapist to consider. There is no one right way for the therapist to administer music therapy assessment and, in fact, it is suggested that the therapist consider and try different routes toward the same ends, namely to determine the strengths and weaknesses of the child and the appropriate intervention plan in music therapy. In terms of eligibility for music therapy on the IEP, any assessment can logically be used as long as the recommendations emphasize the child's unique response to music as a means towards therapeutic goals.

This chapter leads the clinician into decision-making regarding the child's appropriateness for individual or group therapy. Regardless of that decision, the initial, periodic or ongoing assessment of the child will elucidate strengths and weaknesses and pave the way for an ongoing intervention plan that makes sense.

STUDY GUIDE QUESTIONS

1. Define assessment. What are some of the reasons a music therapist would do an assessment?
2. In the practice of music therapy, what kinds of information do music therapists assess? Please detail nonmusic areas commonly described as well as music areas commonly described.
3. What music therapy tools have been published for children? Name these and briefly describe them.
4. What factors should the music therapist take into account when choosing an assessment?
5. Briefly describe the Nordoff-Robbins Scales. What is their philosophical basis, how are they used in music therapy and how are they scored?
6. Briefly describe the MTA-ED developed by Goodman. What is its philosopohical basis and how can it be used in music therapy?
7. Briefly describe the MTAP developed by Michel and Rohrbacker. What is its philosophical basis and how can it be used in music therapy?
8. Briefly describe the SEMTAP developed by Coleman and Brunk. What information collection does it require and how is it administered?
9. Is SEMTAP the only assessment that can be used to determine music therapy eligibility on the IEP plan? Explain.
10. Are there any assessments for group music therapy? How would a music therapist conduct assessment within the group?

Chapter 3

Decision Making: Individual or Group Placement in Music Therapy with Children?

INTRODUCTION

The question of individual or group placement in music therapy with children remains a critical issue and one largely absent from the music therapy literature. Accounts of children moving from individual work to group and visa versa (Hibben, 1991; Tyler, 2002) exist as does the general rationale that children with social issues in groups benefit from group music therapy (Nicholls, 2002) or need to move to a group if their needs are not being met in individual therapy (Oldfield, 2006). However, a specific and carefully considered rationale for initial individual vs. group music therapy placement for the child is nonexistent. Further, the rationale for the constellation of the group members in the music therapy group requires definition.

The music therapist may include the recommendation for individual or group therapy within the context of the music therapy assessment, as outlined in Chapter 2. However, the questions the therapist can consider when recommending individual or group therapy are not outlined in the assessment. Therefore, a separate chapter on the nature of groupwork with children, the nature of group music therapy with children and the therapist's thought process in considering critical factors related to the recommendation of initial individual or group music therapy assignment (Goodman, 2002) is presented here:

- What is the nature of the group in both special education and psychiatry? How does music therapy groupwork fit into the special education or psychiatric setting?

- What particular considerations regarding the child play a part in helping the therapist decide if the goals for the child are compatible with the goals for the group? What factors should the therapist consider in arriving at a recommendation for individual or group music therapy?

First, this chapter includes an *introduction to the nature of groupwork and the requirements for a child entering specific types of groups.* This information, based on a review of relevant literature, is extremely useful for the field of music therapy as it presents a theoretical structure for the formation of music therapy groupwork and helps prepare the music therapist for the understanding of how music therapy fits into groupwork in the special education and psychiatric settings.

Second, in considering music therapy as a unique type of groupwork, the answer to the question: *What factors should the therapist consider in arriving at a recommendation for individual or group music therapy? is as follows: 1) The developmental level of the child; 2) The musicality of the child; 3) The sensory profile of the child; 4) Practical considerations of the school setting.*

These factors are based largely on years of clinical experience, as well as review of relevant psychological, allied therapies and psychiatric literature (Goodman, 2002). Each of these factors must consider the readiness of the child for the work of the group, namely the abilities to join in musical interaction, contribute to social, communicative and cognitive problem-solving and engage in activity while aware of others. If the child is not ready for the groupwork, the child can begin in the individual session and hopefully "grow into" the group session. The child must be ready to musically contribute, developmentally engage with others and tolerate the sensory impact of the group session. When practical considerations of the school setting delimit the possibility of the individual session, the therapist must learn how to cope. Even in this situation, the therapist will emerge with new skills and awareness after reviewing this chapter.

THE NATURE OF GROUP THERAPY FOR CHILDREN

THE NATURE OF GROUP PSYCHOTHERAPY IN THE CHILD PSYCHIATRIC MILIEU

When one looks at the evolution of group therapy with children, it is instructive to consider the origins of group in the adult setting first.

Group therapy, starting with the days of the asylum, began with the model known as *Activity Therapy* (Montgomery, 2002). *Activity therapy,* as the term implies, involves the clients in activity and is used to engage even the most vulnerable patients in activities such as cooking, exercise, craft, artwork and music-making.

Psychodynamic groups, which have greater relevance for personality disordered clients where interpersonal difficulties have led to chronic depression and/or anxiety, promote lasting personality change through nondirective free association. The three commonly known models of psychodynamic group structure include: 1) *Interpersonal group therapy,* 2) *Tavistock,* and 3) *group analytical.* They are differentiated from each other in terms of theoretical underpinnings.

Interpersonal group therapy, aiming to provide a corrective emotional experience through the curative factors (Yalom, 1985) operating within the group, encourages transfer of emotional and cognitive connections in the here and now group to be generalized to behavior outside of the group. Examples of interpersonal group therapy in the child music therapy group are demonstrated in

Chapter 7, "Methods."

The *Tavistock model,* developed by Bion (1961) focuses on the assumptive behavior that impedes personal development, namely *dependency, fight or flight* and *pairing.* Tavistock has not yet taken a role in the literature of group music therapy although the concepts make sense in the context of a higher functioning child group. In particular the concept of "fight or flight" is of interest to the music therapist because this concept respects the need of the client to become, in effect, dysfunctional when their defenses or physiological homeostasis (Berger, 2002) is threatened. Music therapy can pave the way for these clients to channel their projective work. Music therapy can also help bring the client into a comfortable physical state, a state of regulation (see Greenspan and Wieder, 1998).

Finally, in the *group analytic* model, Foulkes' interpretation of Freudian concepts transferred to group behavior, the clients engage in four therapeutic processes: mirroring, exchange, social integration and activation of the collective unconscious (note: with the first three of these related to Yalom curative factors).

Theoretically, the model of activity therapy appears to best suit groupwork with children in music therapy. The rationale here would be as follows:

1. Making music constitutes activity which can be viewed as both work and play;
2. Activity therapy engages clients functioning on multiple levels, frequently the case with music therapy groups;
3. Activity therapy is brought into the literature of group therapy appropriate for children (see Slavson and Schiffer, 1975).

Theoretically, the psychodynamic approaches used with adults could be workable with higher functioning children, namely those with chronic personality difficulties that lead to depression and/or anxiety. There is practically no literature on this type of work with children in music therapy groups with the one exception of the reference both Friedlander and Hibben make to the impact of Garland, Jones & Kolodney (1976), theoreticians basing their work on the *group analytic model,* in interpreting the stages of their groupwork.

In forthcoming case vignettes (see Chapter 7, "Methods"), suggestions (Goodman, 1996–2002) are provided in terms of facilitating group process in both the child psychiatric and the special education group. These suggestions rely largely on the curative factors cited by Yalom: Interpersonal learning, catharsis, group cohesiveness, self-understanding, development of socializing techniques, existential factors, universality, instillation of hope, altruism, corrective family reenactment, guidance, identification/imitative behavior. In this sense, then, the suggestions are within the framework of Interpersonal Group Therapy.

The Nature of Child Group Therapy

The nature of group psychotherapies for children, work starting in the 1930s and originally described by Slavson and Schiffer (1975), pioneers in the field, is focused on the child psychiatric population and embraced within a psychoanalytic and psychodynamic framework.

Historically, the nature of group psychotherapy changed according to the needs of the inpatient child psychiatric setting. Group psychotherapy with children originally began in an outpatient child psychiatric setting (Slavson, 1943). This work was translated to an inpatient setting with more severely involved children (Rosenthal and Nagelberg, 1956). Original child psychotherapy groups, with an emphasis on psychoanalytic theory, were possible in the middle to late twentieth century child psychiatric units and were run primarily by psychiatrists and then social workers. Within the last two decades, however, long-term hospitalization is of the past. Current practice generally involves the duration of the child psychiatric hospitalization from one month (Goodman, 1982) to three months (Friedlander, 1994). Following the hospitalization, the child is generally referred to an outside day or residential special education school. This short-term child psychiatric stay results in psychiatric assessment and diagnosis, as well as psychotherapeutic and psychopharmacological treatment. Short-term therapy emphasizes activity therapy and play therapy, formats originally defined in longer-term treatment, but now intended primarily for diagnosis, ongoing recommenda-

tion and emotional stabilization. In many child psychiatric milieus, short-term treatment is influenced by the development of cognitive and behavioral therapies.

Therefore, the emphasis is on problem-solving (i.e., cognitive therapy) and behavioral change in the "here and now" (behavioral therapy). These groups are run by a variety of staff: child psychiatrists, child psychiatric residents, activity therapists (also known as recreational therapists), and social workers.

Slavson and Schiffer (1975) detail the two types of group psychotherapy historically assigned to the nonpsychotic disturbed child. The types of groups have remained a constant although they are short-term. These two types are: 1) *activity group therapy* for latency-aged (5–12) children, and 2) *play therapy for prelatency* (3–5) children. The nature of a group, three or more persons, implies developmental readiness since it involves "intellectual/emotional interaction (which) occurs among individuals in their relations with one another" (Slavson and Schiffer, 1975, p. 464). The primary group is considered the family constellation, the first group encountered in one's life.

The *intellectual and emotional readiness* for a beginning level group starts with the *prelatency child, the child who is now developing representational play* or the ability to use objects of play to represent unconscious and subconscious thoughts and feelings. Therefore, the concept of play therapy makes sense and was particularly popular in the seventies after being introduced by Virginia Axline (1969).

Intellectual and emotional readiness with the latency-aged child, on the other hand, involves activity. The latency-aged child is school age and learns through directed activity, activity that also directs itself toward motoric action. Therefore, activity group therapy is developmentally congruent for the school-age child. It involves following directions, problem solving, social interaction and product-oriented work. Further, *both the play and activity therapy groups, by virtue of being groups, involve group dynamics and group process,* namely what evolves in the group as children interact with each other, with the given materials and with the therapist. In other words, "the corrective modality is experiential, flowing from significant activities and interactions in a group" (Slavson and Schiffer, 1975, p. 463).

Prerequisites for Joining the Play Therapy or Activity Therapy Group in the Child Psychiatric Setting: Considerations in Grouping

As previously, explained, both play and activity group therapy presuppose the developmental readiness of the prelatency (developmental ages 3–5) or latency (developmental ages 5–12) child, as presented in Freud's psychosexual theory of child development (Freud, 1932).

According to Slavson and Schiffer (1975), *the members of the group will present varying temperaments, behavioral patterns and diagnoses to insure a psychological balance and therapeutic effectiveness.* This is viewed as a *heterogeneous* group rather than a *homogeneous* group. Ideally, the children are of the same age or close in age.

Slavson and Schiffer (1975) further specify that children might be grouped into the identity of an *instigator, neutralizer, or neuter.* The instigator can be *positive,* psychologically and/or socially beneficial, or *negative,* promoting disharmony, hyperactivity, rancor and hostility. The *neutralizer,* a child who is more reasonable and less impulsive, can be a calming influence in the group. Finally, the *neuter* is the child with a floating or weak identity, a child who will be influenced by stronger personalities. Although these various roles may not be apparent to the clinician who is in the position of choosing various children to form a group, they should be considered in terms of possible tempermental directions. Heterogeneity assures a mix of roles within the group.

In summary, then, the prerequisites for joining the psychotherapy group in the child psychiatric setting suggest developmental age-appropriateness. Customarily children seen in child psychiatric treatment are ages 5–12, although they can be as young as 2 and as old as 14 (Friedlander, 1994). Their primary diagnosis is one of emotional disturbance, which can be referred to as SED, Seriously Emotionally Disturbed. These children can manifest disturbed behavior in overly-aggressive as well as withdrawn and self-destructive, or even suicidal behavior

(Goodman, 1982; Goodman, 1989). Children in psychiatric treatment can include such diagnoses as autism, conduct disorder, schizophrenia, borderline personality, mood disorders, severe learning disabilities, etc. While these children may have secondary issues in learning and certainly primary issues in ego organization and relatedness, they are generally developmentally functioning in terms of their chronological age and therefore meet the developmental guidelines previously suggested by Slavson and Schiffer. It is recommended that the specific constellation of the group be heterogeneous in terms of temperament, behavioral pattern and diagnosis while the ages should be relatively homogeneous.

THE CHILD PSYCHIATRIC GROUP MUSIC THERAPY SETTING

The ideas regarding group psychotherapy, originally presented by Slavson and Schiffer (1975) and previously described in this chapter, translate into music group psychotherapy described by Friedlander (1994) as activity therapy with children within a psychodynamic framework. Although both Friedlander (1994) and Goodman (1989) describe psychodynamic work in the context of the inpatient and outpatient child psychiatric milieu, there is no reason that psychodynamic work cannot be applied to other population groups. The developmental prerequisites for this kind of work, however, would have to be maintained with any population. In short, the child must be capable of interacting within a group, capable of representational play, cognitive insight and ideally, the ability to engage in verbal process.

Developmental Stages Within Music Therapy Groupwork, Psychiatric Setting

Friedlander (1994) tracks her group process with children on an in-patient psychiatric ward in terms of group developmental stages originally introduced into group therapy literature (note: for classroom groups) by Garland et al. (1976) and then into the music therapy literature by Hibben (1991a, 1991b).

The Garland et al. (1976) stages of group activity originally conceived in reference to groups of children, many of them disadvantaged and handicapped, ages 9–16, in social clubs. include the following:

1. Pre-Affiliation Stage, a stage where children do not easily share ideas, a period of approach/avoidance, ambivalence regarding the extent of personal involvement in the group, and a need to explore while maintaining a sense of distance.
2. Power and Control, a stage where they are sub-groups within the group vying for power and control both for protection and aggression.
3. Intimacy, a stage where children become more involved in activity and will take emotional risks by taking turns, assuming leadership roles and taking on more responsibility while defining against intimacy.
4. Differentiation-cohesion, a stage where power problems decrease as children gain freer expression, accepting individual differences in the group.
5. Separation, a stage where the group terminates (based on the school calendar) and therefore may either regress to an earlier developmental stage or choose to return to previous activity and relationships.

Friedlander (1994) describes the first three of these phases as they manifest themselves in the *child psychiatric music therapy group*. *Pre-affiliation* is marked by the child's exploration of musical materials where the child must have enough ego strength to avoid open conflict and hostility. *Power and Control* involve challenging the authority of the therapist and competing for attention, both verbally and nonverbally through the music; *Intimacy,* after several weeks of intensive work, relies on familiarity, structure and music to help members work toward a common musical goal as they listen to and support each other. Prior to the work of Friedlander, Hibben (1991a) suggests a theoretical model that also utilizes the stages presented by Garland. However, Hibben uses a *correlation* between levels of activity setting initially

proposed by Vinter (1974) and the aforementioned stages of group activity initially presented by Garland (1976).

Accordingly, Hibben suggests that activity-setting dimensions (Vinter, 1974) governing rules (Prescription), control (Control), the amount of physical movement in the activity (Physical movement), the level of ability needed to do the activity (Competence), the degree to which the activity requires or provokes interaction (Interaction) and the rewards (Rewards, extrinsic or intrinsic) become increasingly demanding as the stages of the Garland group progresses. Hibben subsequently applies this model to her clinical work (1991b).

It is possible that some models of music therapy group process with adolescents (Joseph and Freed, 1989) and adults (Apprey and Apprey, 1975; Doyle and Ficken, 1981; Morgenstern, 1982; Plach, 1980; Wood et al., 1974) as summarized in the work of Sandness (1991) can be applied to groupwork with children (see Chapter 7).

Balance Between Music-making and Verbal Process in the Psychiatric Group

The issue of insight as a factor in music group psychotherapy is one alluded to in the work of Dr. Barbara Grinnel. Grinnel (1980) finds that children *"retreated" to the use of music for emotional expression when talking became personally threatening.* This interplay between the use of nonverbal and verbal therapy helped many severely ill children in her clinical work. Although both Grinnel and Goodman (1989) write about individual children in their work on child psychiatry, the same phenomena can be observed in group work in the child psychiatric setting (Goodman, 1982).

Joining the Music Psychotherapy Group in the Child Psychiatric Setting

According to Friedlander (1994), the music therapist uses age and developmental functioning level in the areas of cognition and motor and social skills as primary indicators for grouping, assigning three to six children to a group that meets for one hour five days a week. The group is heterogeneous in terms of mixed diagnoses, gender and culture but homogeneous in terms of functioning level. Only children with the most severe psychopathology (i.e., psychotic, inappropriately aggressive, extreme confusion and agitation) are excluded as group participants. These guidelines concur with the original recommendations put forth by Slavson (1975).

Other music therapists (Knak and Grogan, 2002) find that the diversity of the group including children with different needs, ages and genders optimizes success by encouraging separate ego identity. Recently published casework, representing itself as psychodynamic, alludes to the reasons for referring a child to group by describing the purpose of the group: Carter and Oldfield (2002) represent the possibility of the child music therapy group as a vehicle for psychiatric assessment; Stewart, (2002), writes about the changing relatedness or attunement of the autistic child through musical improvisation in music therapy group; Knak and Grogan (2002) discuss the importance of the heterogeneity of group members; Sutton (2002) highlights the importance of psychological containment through music and Tyler (2002) compares the groupwork stages in music therapy to Winnicott's stages of the development of play.

In summary, heterogeneity in terms of mixed diagnoses, gender and culture is sought after in the group constellation; on the other hand, homogeneity vs. heterogeneity in terms of functioning levels of the children remains an open issue in the limited literature available. There are no prerequisites per se to enter the group unless the child is excluded because of severe pathology.

THE NATURE OF GROUP THERAPY WITH THE MULTIPLY HANDICAPPED, DEVELOPMENTAL DELAYED OR AUTISTIC CHILD

Direct Instruction

Since the onset of mandatory special education in the United States (1975 Public Law 94-142), the effort to appropriately provide for children has expanded tremendously. Much of the early educa-tional work was provided by individual "direct instruction" (DI), as children were grouped largely by chronological age in the classroom and therapies were achieved on a "pull-out" one-to-one basis.

Activity-Based Instruction

More recently, groupwork in the special education sector (Brickner, et al., 1998), *namely work with developmentally delayed, multiply handicapped and autistic children,* is an area of focus, structured around a cognitive-affective developmental framework. The modus operandi of this group work is to *embed developmental skills within the context of ongoing activities throughout the classroom day as opposed to direct instruction and "pull out" therapy sessions.* Activity-based instruction is commonly referred to as *ABI* (note: not to be confused with *ABA*).

It is possible that the use of both play and activity group therapy in the psychiatric milieu influenced the current use of activity-based instruction (ABI) in the special education classroom for multiply handicapped, developmentally delayed or autistic children. This has been a positive move for special education, one that balances structure with freedom for the developing child. *Activity-based intervention,* contrary to *direct instruction,* provides a naturalistic setting for the educator as well as the therapist to work toward developmental goals (Bricker, Pretti-Frontczak and McComas, 1998). The naturalistic teaching approach includes the following features: novel materials, encouragement of the child to join the activity/play with peers, invitations to the child to make choice, incidental strategies, comments and questions intended to encourage a response from the child, encouragement of the child to expand on his or her communication attempts, and encouragement of the child to interact with peers. It begins in preschool settings, but extends to settings with school-age children.

Activity-based instruction, embedding developmental skills within the context of activity, encourages therapists who formerly did "pull-out" work, to work within the context of ongoing activity within the class. This modeling affords the special educator teacher the advantage of observing therapeutic techniques such as language infusion and stimulation, proper physical positioning and handling, and appropriate physical stimulation. *When the therapists and teachers join the children in the music room, they are similarly involved in observing and participating in activity-based planning.*

In the course of ABI, the developmental goals of the Individual Education Plan are embedded (Daugherty, Grisham-Brown, and Hemmeter, 2001) in the activities themselves. Although Pretti-Frontczak and Bricker (2001) report that teachers are more likely to embed individual education goals in activity-based instruction in *one-on-one situations* with delayed children as compared to group, this format can be used with children on both an individual and group basis and many special educators (Fox and Hanline, 1993; Kohler, Anthony, Steighner, and Hoyson, 1997; Kohler, Strain, Hoyson, and Jamieson, 1998; Losardo and Bricker, 1994) and related therapies report significant success rates using activity-based instruction and planning in the naturalistic setting.

The grouping for higher functioning special learners is an issue in and of itself since inclusion remains a vital concern for these children. Higher functioning special learners will join a typically functioning group of children and will have to adjust to the larger classroom setting supplemented by resource room activity and personal aides.

Prerequisites for Joining the Activity-Based Planning Group in the Special Education Setting

Since activity-based intervention in the special education setting is either individual or group based, there do not appear to be prescribed prerequisites for participation (Heward, 2003). It is noted that, in the group setting, lower functioning children will imitate the higher functioning behavior of their peers (Venn et al., 1993). In terms of classroom placement, various special education schools place the children in different ways. Some administrators place children in homogeneous classroom groups; these children are developmentally at similar levels and may even have similar temperaments. Other administrators place children in classes based on their chronological ages. The result of this can be a great disparity in developmental ages, producing a heterogeneous classroom.

In summary, one can see that prerequisites for joining the group in the special education setting are perhaps nonexistent. The provision of an activity-based instructional or therapeutic (note: in the special education school setting, these terms are used in an overlapping manner) approach in the naturalistic setting encourages the teacher or therapist to embed goals in activities that are comfortable and appropriate for the children. In the classroom, this can take place while the children are physically together in a group and yet developmentally apart. A group, in this framework, is considered a number of children rather than a number of children ready to interact with each other dynamically. Further, the rationale for grouping does not appear to be consistently well-defined and varies widely depending on the philosophy of the administration and the school. Frankly, it is easiest for the administration of a special education school to group children by chronological age rather than developmental functioning.

THE SPECIAL EDUCATION GROUP MUSIC THERAPY SETTING

Review of Literature

The literature base regarding *group* music therapy for children in the special education setting, in general, is limited in scope and will be briefly presented here. There is numerous mention of ongoing group work with different populations within special education as well as related strategies (Adamak and Darrow, 2005). Included in these accounts is an emphasis on developmental needs with the cerebral palsied (Ford, 1984), behavioral contingencies with the learning disabled (Steele, 1984), sensory needs of the autistic child (Nelson, Anderson, Gonzales, 1984), "Mommy and Me" groups with preschoolers (Oldfield, 2006), behavioral levels of music therapy expectations for children labeled as "severely behaviorally handicapped" (Presti, 1984) and advantages of inclusion for atypically developing preschool children enjoying music therapy along with typical learners (Gunsberg, 1991). These approaches and orientations will be covered in Chapter 7, "Methods for Group Gherapy." Yet, clinical descriptions of actual sessions are sparse and, in terms of this specific chapter, the rationale for referral to group rather than individual is lacking. Historically, clinicians who have done a great deal groupwork include Nordoff and Robbins (1971, 1977, 1983) and Purvis and Samet (1976).

Nordoff-Robbins (1971, 1983) Groupwork

In the 1970s, music therapy groups in the Philadelphia, Pennsylvania school system started by Nordoff and Robbins (1971), provided original compositional materials, strove for unique definition and appeared to have some overlap with music education in the school setting. Nordoff and Robbins started the group music therapy compositions for children with their volumes of songs, resonator bell arrangements and plays. Pioneers in the field of improvisational music therapy, Nordoff and Robbins reported the use of both spontaneous and planned musical activity in their humanistically-oriented groupwork, yet their writing (Nordoff and Robbins, 1971, 1977) presented individual case material. Robbins, trained as a special educator, and Nordoff, trained as a composer, contributed a wealth of material and practical suggestions in terms of programming for the group. Their suggestions regarding group music therapy are brilliantly presented in their classic book on the subject, *Music Therapy in Special Education* (1983) but unfortunately, there are no case studies of groupwork included in the book.

Purvis and Samet Developmental Therapy Levels (1976) in Group

Purvis and Samet (1976) developed a system of music therapy in the special education system that grouped children by developmental functioning ages in the areas of behavior, communication, socialization and academics. Music therapy groups and sessions are organized in terms of the following levels:

1. *Responding to the environment with pleasure:* The child at this stage is minimally or nonresponsive to the environment and requires stimulation and arousal to satisfy their basic needs. The use of structure, routine, body contact, touch and physical intervention is suggested.
2. *Respond to the environment with success:* The child's skills are limited; therefore the musical environment must be structured so the child can develop and test her skills and abilities within a familiar routine setting in order to experience success.
3. *Learning skills for successful group participation:* Child learns to apply individual skills to group procedures.
4. *Investing in group processes:* The music therapy session is structured in a manner that invites group planning and problem solving.
5. *Applying individual/group skills in new situations:* The child is no longer a part of the music therapy group and is encouraged to use musical skills in a traditional setting.

Presti (1984) Behavioral Levels for Group

Presti presented a behavioral system of four hierarchical levels, with severely disturbed children in a school setting (Presti, 1984). The four levels are based on music tasks that require varying degrees of behavioral control in terms of motor, verbal, and social behaviors. The behaviors of the children in the music therapy groups were recorded and involved reinforcement and consequences.

Activity-Based Instruction

Numerous clinical examples of activity group therapy, previously unpublished, are now presented throughout the latter part of this book (Goodman, 1982, 1992, 1996) and illustrate the use of embedded developmental goals in the music therapy group. This method, in all probability, is routinely provided in the music therapy room but not identified as ABI. Although ABI is purported to present itself in the classroom and in the naturalistic setting of the child moving through the school day, it can be utilized in both a planned and spontaneous manner in the music therapy room.

Since group music therapy typically takes place in a designated time and place, it can be activity-based but it is not typically infused in the naturalistic setting of the child moving through the school day. Goodman (1982) has taken advantage of a university model special education program for preschool autistic spectrum children to infuse music therapy into the school day curriculum. Hopefully, case examples of activity based planning in this book (Goodman, 1996) will provide the impetus for other music therapists to utilize and write about this approach.

Prerequisites for Joining the Music Therapy Group in the Special Education Music Therapy Setting

The prerequisites for joining the music therapy group indicated in the Purvis/Samet model (1976) are based on functional behaviors yet, by their very definition, do not necessarily correspond to group behavior. It is not until level three of the model (*Learning skills for successful group participation*) that the child is operative in the group. Before that stage, it appears that the children are operating on a one-to-one level within a group setting.

Within the Nordoff-Robbins model, a scale of interpersonal and musical relatedness (Nordoff and Robbins, 1977) shows music co-activity within the group as the highest rung of the ladder. This demonstrates that Nordoff and Robbins recognized the relationship between interpersonal connectedness and musical sharing as a goal for the child in music therapy.

This apparent emphasis in music therapy on the ability to socialize through music therapy in a group is further supported by the work of Steele (1984) who writes "although the five boys and one girl ranged in age from 7–11, their levels of social maturity were similar and they shared a common preference for musical activity" (1984, p. 6).

In summary, the limited information base regarding the constellation of the music therapy group in the special education setting suggests that social maturity and interest in musical activity can form the basis for functional levels. There are no prerequisites per se for entering the group. Functional levels do not suggest interactive levels.

FACTORS IN THE CONSIDERATION OF GROUP OR INDIVIDUAL MUSIC THERAPY IN BOTH THE CHILD PSYCHIATRIC AND SPECIAL EDUCATION SETTING

OVERVIEW

Since the music therapy group is generally held at a predesignated time and place in the special education or psychiatric setting, it becomes a more formal structure. The structure of the group is generally activity-based, whether there are pre-planned activities (closer to the model of activity therapy) or spontaneously planned activities (note: more akin to the model of play therapy) and, of course, the activities are musical activities with developmental goals embedded in the activities themselves. Although children referred for music therapy present from varying diagnoses, those most commonly referred are much lower functioning than typically developing children. For this reason, many case examples in this chapter introduce children who have a variety of developmental and sensory challenges.

When practical considerations in the organization of the groups are not an issue, the therapist is at liberty to form the groups. Previous considerations in the activity-therapy group model presented by Slavson and Schiffer (1975) include the developmental readiness of the child as well as the heterogeneous presentation of varying temperaments. Should one carry these considerations forth to the formation of the music therapy group, they will be presented here as two factors to be considered: 1) the developmental level of the child; (Goodman, 2002) and 2) the sensory profile and/or temperament of the child (Goodman, 2002).

Since music therapy uniquely involves the emphasis on music as a therapeutic modality, the factor of musicality (Goodman, 2002) should also be considered.

In summary, then, the therapist should consider four factors in deciding the individual or group placement of the child in music therapy: 1) The developmental age; 2) The sensory profile and/or temperament of the child; 3) Musicality; 4) Practical considerations. These factors will be defined and discussed in this chapter within the context of case study examples.

DEVELOPMENTAL AGE

The "developmental level" and "developmental behaviors" are terms commonly used, discussed and written about in the fields of child psychology, developmental psychology, school psychology, abnormal psychology, child psychiatry, education, special education, occupational therapy physical therapy, speech-language therapy, and, most pertinent to this writing, the fields of creative arts therapy.

Child development is, from a generic perspective (Furuno et al., 1979), divided into the following domains: 1) social-emotional development; 2) speech-language development; 3) gross motor development; 4) fine motor development; 5) cognitive development. Within each one of these areas, the child reaches certain milestones at more or less predictable ages.

There are several developmental scales which have contributed to the *Hawaii Early Learning Profile* (Furuno et al., 1997), an excellent guide to functional development in children birth through three years of age. Much critical development takes place in the first three years of life and many children referred for music therapy fall into these years developmentally.

Contrary to the chronological age of the child, the age as defined by the birthday, the developmental ages are considered from the perspective of developmental behaviors (i.e., social-emotional, motor, communication, cognitive, musical). In short, the behaviors of the special needs child generally place him in a range of development that is lower than the chronological age.

Developmental areas have, of course, received different theoretical emphases as foremost theorists have approached development from unique perspectives. For example, Dr. Anna Freud, the daughter of Dr. Sigmund Freud, and a noted analyst in her own right, emphasized social-emotional development in children from a psycho-sexual perspective while Jean Piaget (1929, 1952, 1954, 1964) emphasized the development of cognition from the perspective of his stated sensorimotor, preoperational, concrete operational and formal operational periods.

The task of modern day theorists is to expand upon their particular training as educators, therapists, psychologists, psychiatrists, etc. in order to reinterpret foremost theories of child development (Greenspan, 1992; Greenspan & Wieder, 1998), consider them in other contexts (i.e., musical development) and apply them to therapeutic scenarios. What models of development can further aid the music therapist in this process ?

In the case of music therapy, the developmental model presented by Briggs (1991) integrates musical research with accepted models of child development, presenting a useful model for psychological interpretation of musical behaviors. This interpretation can be used as a starting point for what might be called musical developmental age.

Another developmental model that fits in well with music therapy is that described by Dr. Stanley Greenspan (1992). Greenspan presents developmental ages through an integrative cognitive-affective-communicative-sensory picture.

In an effort to pave the way for understanding child development from two unique developmental perspectives that lend themselves to the goals of music therapy, the work of both Briggs (1973) and Greenspan (1992; Greenspan & Wieder, 1998) will be presented here.

Musical Developmental Age

In her work on musical development, Briggs (1991) provides a clear literature review of previous work in this field and places her interpretation of musical behaviors within the context of such theorists as the aforementioned Freud and Piaget. Other theorists who have extended the work of Freud (1966) are included: Stern (1985); Mahler, Pine and Bergman (1975). Similarly, theorists who have extended the work of Piaget are included:

Rosen (1977) and Kegan (1982).

Phases of Musical Development

According to Briggs, phases of musical development in early childhood include the following (1991, p. 10):

Age	Phase
0–9 months	Reflex Phase
9–18 months	Intention Phase
18–36 months	Control Phase
36–72 months	Integration Phase

These phases are further delineated by musical behaviors that include the broad categories of *auditory, vocal/tonal, rhythmic behaviors,* and, in the case of the Integration Phase, *cognitive* behaviors.

What makes this information valuable to the practicing music therapist is the *possibility of identifying musical behaviors in special needs children and "placing" that child in the context of an identifiable "musical developmental phase."*

Reflex Phase

The musical behaviors in the *Reflex Phase,* alluding to sensory exploration on the part of the child, include the most beginning levels of auditory awareness, vocal/tonal exploration and uncontrolled motor rhythms in moving to music with separate body parts.

Control Phase

Musical behavior in the *Control Phase* leads the child to a more focused exploration, hence the word *control.* In the *Control Phase,* the child begins to listen, sing and move with more intention and, ultimately, with more peer interaction.

Integration Phase

In the *Integration Phase,* the child is able to reach a beginning sense of coordination in singing, playing and moving to music. Following the *Integration Phase,* or at around the age of six years, the child can begin study of an instrument and has reached elementary school age, the age of formal music-making instruction.

Musical Behaviors Consistent with a Group

Notably, it is at the *Control Phase* of musical development and ideally at the *Integration Phase* of musical development that the child begins to develop behaviors consistent with a group: *the beginning ability to listen, sing, play and move to music within the context of other children and the growing awareness that the group is working together to select and make music* (see Table 3.1).

TABLE 3.1.

Age	Musical Milestones
Reflex Phase	
Auditory	
0-6 months	Is learning to hear
2 weeks	Stops moving in presence of sound; demonstrates interactional synchrony to sound
2 months	Has fixed attention when sung to
3 months	Becomes calm when quiet music is played; prefers high pitches
3–5 months	Makes involuntary/reflexive responses to music
3–4 months	Distinguishes between two tone qualities; distinguishes between two pitches; discriminates different temporal groups
5 months	Recognizes a melodic pattern transposed

continued

TABLE 3.1–*Continued.*

| 6–8 months | Searches for music source |
| 7.5 months | Attends to moderately discrepant auditory stimuli |

Vocal/Tonal

Birth	Cries as a newborn (at 60 decibels); makes 5 to 12 reflexive, repeated sounds; increases the decivel level and duration of cries as distress increases
2–6 months	Exhibits vocal contagion; shows vocal circular reactions; participates in mutual imitation; matches discrete pitches with 60% accuracy; has no tonal center
4 months	Vocalizes pitches up to an octave higher than at birth; increases the variety of sounds produced
6–12 months	Increases vocalization; has continued, elaborated circular reactions.

Rhythmic

Birth	Exhibits reflexive motor rhythms of crying, sucking
2 weeks	Demonstrates interactional synchrony to sound
2–3 months	Rocks
3–6 months	Discriminates rhythm pattern change
6 months	Moves to music with whole body

Intention Phase

Auditory

| 9–12 months | Localizes sound source using eyes, head; localizes using horizontal and vertical planes |
| 12 months | Moves to music with separate body parts |

Vocal/Tonal

| 9 months | Uses sound to express dislike of music; has no tonal center; is unable to control pitches; plays with range-glides, shrieks |
| 10–18 months | Recognizes familiar songs; makes sing-song,musical babble; uses first syllables, vowels and consonants |

Rhythmic

| 10–14 months | Is learning to walk |
| 12 months | Moves to music with separate body parts; exhibits uncontrolled motor rhythms of bouncing, pulling |

Control Phase

Auditory

| 24 months | Listens to music quietly for several minutes; has more accurate pitch perception |

Vocal/Tonal

18 months	Shifts from vocalizing sound blends to singing recognizable pitches and pitch contours; remembers lyrics more consistently than melody or rhythm; sings short phrases and bits of songs; uses intervals of major 2nd and 3rd, minor 3rd, perfect 4th and 5th
24 months	Continues to make improvements in pitch accuracy (vocal/tonal); has a 4 to 5 step singing range (vocal/tonal)
24–36 months	Demonstrates a large increase in amount of singing (vocal/tonal)

continued

TABLE 3.1–*Continued.*

Rhythmic

18 months	Prefers to move to music with a partner/other (rhythmic), exhibits perseverative rhythms of pounding and banging (rhythmic)
24 months	Shows increase in variety of movements to music (rhythmic)
24–36 months	Demonstrates large increase in rhythmic/motor control (rhythmic)

Integration Phase

Auditory

36 months	Can discriminate "loud"
36–72 months	Shows improvement in pitch perception
60 months	Recognizes familiar songs consistently; can discriminate "soft"
72 months	Shows large increase in listening skills; can discriminate intervals of 4th and 6th
36 months	Sings spontaneous songs; can sing melodic outline/contour of song with words and rhythm; can do learned movement to music; shows large increase in rhythm synchrony
48 months	Sings spontaneous songs with the following features: 1–5 seconds long, 1–3 short phrases, 2 to 4 notes per phrase, whole steps or monotonal, descending intervals, especially descending minor 3rds, nonsense syllables and vowel sounds, inverted melodic pattern, shifts tonality from phrase to phrase; can sing with lyrics, melody, rhythm, phrasing, and pulse; can sing with better melodic rhythm than melodic intervals; can sing descending intervals easier than ascending.

Vocal/Tonal

36–72 months	Shows large growth in song repertoire; can sing lyrcis consistently
60–72 months	Sings in major and minor tonality; sings entire songs with accurate pitch contour

Rhythmic

36–72 months	Has coordinated motor patterns; shows steady improvement in eye-hand coordination, and speed and range of movement over the three years; can learn duple and triple rhythms
48–60 months	Has increasingly stable motor patterns
60 months	Shows improvement in rhythmic synchrony; can use visual cues to organize rhythmic behaviors

Cognitive

60 months	(Best age to begin training): Conserves musical elements with much inconsistency; can understand musical concepts but cannot describe or demonstrate them; confuses high and low with up and down and with loud and soft
72 months	Can begin to demonstrate musical concepts; can recognize high and low pitches as isolated pitches; shows some progress in conservation, beginning with tonal conservation, followed by rhythmic conservation (neither stabilize until age 9–12)

Briggs, C. (1991). A Model for Understanding Musical Development (in) *Music Therapy,* Volume 10, No. 1, pp. 1–21. Pages 10–17. Reprinted with permission from Dr. Cynthia Briggs.

Cognitive Affective Development: Greenspan

Dr. Stanley Greenspan's developmental structural approach, referred to as Developmental Individual Difference Relationship-Based (DIR), recognizes the unevenness of developmental levels and subsumes cognitive, psychodynamic, behavioral and relational perspectives on child development in his objective descriptions of his young clients. In effect, he provides a biopsychosocial model of psychiatry which meshes beau-

tifully with all the potential impact of music therapy. Originally writing for the professional reader
(1992), Greenspan extends his writing (1995,
1998) to include the lay audience, particularly the
parents of the children he sees in private practice.

The Six Milestones

In his presentation of six developmental milestones (see Table 3.2), Greenspan describes development from the perspective of emotional interaction. This is emotional interaction that helps the
child develop cognitive, social, emotional, language and motor skills. Greenspan's first milestone, *Self-Regulation and Interest in the World,* essentially describes the capacity of the child to regulate
the self physiologically. This is a key item for
music therapy since music has the capacity to help
the child experience a state of stimulation or seda-
tion which might not be readily available to the
child with a problematic sensory profile.
Experiencing a regulatory state is possibly the first
impetus for a child to want to repeat that state of
physiological regulation in order to learn and
attend. Greenspan's explanations regarding the
sensory profile of the child and the impact of the
profile on the child in the course of physiological
regulation and the capacity to learn is invaluable
for the music therapist.

The second milestone, that of *Intimacy,* is the
necessary nonverbal attunement that one hopes
will happen between child and primary caretaker.
It is the nonverbal attunement written about by
Dr. Daniel Stern (1977, 1985) and so many other
psychoanalytic theorists versed in attachment-sep-
aration theory. In the music therapy process, this
is a bonding between therapist and child through
the musical experience within the context of individual therapy, the bonding that is essential, for
example, in order to move forward developmentally with the autistic child.

The third milestone, *Two-Way Communication,*
builds on the bonding between child and therapist
in order to dialogue nonverbally.as well as
through antiphonal musical vocalization, a process
well-known to music therapists working with the
child just starting to develop speech and language.

The fourth milestone, *Complex Communication,*

invites imitation of the behavior the parent or the
therapist models. The child is hungry to learn and
will imitate behavior in an intentional way while
anticipating feedback. Verbal communication
increases as does emotional awareness even
though the child is still learning at a concrete level.
The beginning explorations of cause and effect as
well as the imitative behavior of learning to play
simple instruments and sing simple songs lends
toward exchanges and learning at these levels in
the music therapy session.

At the fifth milestone, *Emotional Ideas,* the child
is busy with pretend drama, also referred to in the
developmental literature as representational play.
At this point in music therapy, projective work is
possible since there is a conscious, subconscious or
unconscious need to project emotions into play.
As the child pretends, the child is also growing
cognitively and is able to engage in more rule-
bound games and movement experiences with
multiple directions. Multiple ideas can be
expressed in play or, obviously, through music
therapy experiences.

Milestone six, *Emotional Thinking,* establishs the
child's capacity for more sophisticated pretend
play and communication, response to many more
directives, but, most importantly, the capacity to
begin to problem-solve through the course of pretend play, and in the context of music therapy,
through the course of musical pretend play and
musical drama.

In terms of intervention with the special needs
child, the Greenspan nomenclature includes the
use of "floor time," simply a 20–30 minute period
when the parent, teacher, therapist, or aide, etc.
gets down on the floor with the child, interacting
and playing in such a way as to spur developmental growth. The closing of "circles" with the child
means that the child is responding appropriately
enough with the nonverbal or verbal exchange
that a sense of closure is reached. This play is
achieved on a one-to-one level: *It is not until your
child can open and close circles of communication most of
the time (that) it is important to facilitate interaction
between him and other children, starting with one other
child. He will then be more ready to enter a group*
(Greenspan, 1998, p. 428).

This sense of reciprocal play, a prerequisite for

groupwork, appears to be reached in Milestone 4, *Complex Communication.* It is important to note, however, that a child who is entering the stage of complex communication may still have significant weaknesses in previous stages of development and therefore may appear inappropriate for group-work. This recognition of the uneven process in development serves to remind the therapist that *while a child may reach the top rungs of a developmental hierarchy, the child's footing on the bottom rungs may be shaky.*

In work with preschool, autistic spectrum disordered children, Goodman (1996, 1998) finds that the *"floor time" approach does not translate well in the group music therapy setting.* In order to intensively interact with the child of lower developmental age,

it is necessary to pair each child with an aide who is trained in the six milestones and intervention strategies. Nevertheless, the six milestones represent a means toward interaction in any naturalistic setting, interventions based on consideration of the child's developmental level and biological sensory profile regardless of diagnosis. Their emphasis on a cognitive affective framework is compatible with the work of music therapy as well as a relationship-based therapy. Furthermore, music therapy with its many avenues for nonverbal attunement and the expression of feelings and ideas is an ideal modality for floor time leading toward groupwork. The milestones are presented in Table 3.2 and presented in music therapy case examples following in this chapter.

TABLE 3.2. THE SIX MILESTONES.

Milestone I: Self-Regulation and Interest in the World

1. Shows interest in different sensation for 3+ seconds
2. Remains calm and focused for 2+minutes
3. Recovers from distress within 20 minutes with help from you
4. Shows interest in you

Milestone 2: Intimacy

1. Responds to your overtures (i.e., smile, frown, reach, vocalization)
2. Responds to your overtures with obvious pleasure
3. Responds to your overtures with curiosity and assertive interest
4. Anticipates an object that was shown and then removed
5. Becomes displeased when you are unresponsive during play for 30 sec. +
6. Protests and grows angry when frustrated
7. Recovers from distress within 15 minutes with your help

Milestone 3: Two-Way Communication

1. Responds to your gestures with intentional gestures (i.e., reaches out in response to your outstretched arms, returns your vocalization or look)
2. Initiates interactions with you (i.e., reaches for your nose or hair or for a toy; raises arms to be picked up)
3. Demonstrates the following emotions:
   • Closeness
   • Pleasure and excitement
   • Assertive curiosity
   • Protest or anger
   • Fear
4. Recovers from distress within 10 minutes by being involved in social interactions

---

continued

TABLE 3.2. THE SIX MILESTONES–*Continued.*

Milestone 4: Complex Communication

1. Closes 10 or more circles of communication in a row (i.e., takes you by hand, walks you to refrigerator, points, vocalizes, responds to your questions with more noises and gestures, and continues gestural exchange until you open door and get what he wants)
2. Imitates your behavior in an intentional way (i.e., puts on Daddy's hat, then parades around house waiting for admiration
3. Closes 10 or more circles using
   • Vocalization or words
   • Facial expressions
   • Reciprocal touching or holding
   • Movement in space (roughhousing)
   • Large motor activity (chasing games, climbing games)
   • Communication across space (i.e., can close 10 circles with you from across the room)
4. Closes 3 or more circles in a row while feeling the following emotions:
   • Closeness
   • Pleasure and excitement
   • Assertive curiosity
   • Fear
   • Anger
   • Limit setting
5. Uses imitation to deal with and recover from distress (i.e., bangs on floor and yells after being yelled at)

Milestone 5: Emotional Ideas

1. Creates pretend dramas with two or more ideas (i.e., trucks crash, then pick up rocks, dolls hug, then have a tea party; ideas need not be related)
2. Uses words, pictures, gestures to convey two or more ideas at a time (i.e., No sleep, play); ideas need not be related
3. Communicate wishes, intentions and feelings using:
   • Words
   • Multiple gestures in a row
   • Touch (i.e., lots of hugging or rough-housing)
4. Plays simple motor games with rules (i.e., taking turns throwing ball)
5. Uses pretend play or words to communicate the following emotions while expressing two or more ideas:
   • Closeness
   • Pleasure and excitement
   • Assertive curiosity
   • Fear
   • Anger
   • Limit setting
6. Uses pretend play to recover from and deal with distress (i.e., plays out eating the cookie she couldn't really have)

Milestone 6: Emotional Thinking

1. In pretend play, two or more ideas are logically tied together, even if the ideas themselves are unrealistic (i.e., the car is visiting the moon and gets there by flying fast)
2. Builds on adult pretend play idea (i.e., child is cooking soup, adult asks what is in it, child answers, "rocks and dirt")

continued

TABLE 3.2. THE SIX MILESTONES–*Continued.*

3. In speech, connects ideas logically; ideas are grounded in reality (No go sleep; want to watch television)
4. Closes two or more verbal circles of communication (i.e., "Want to go outside"; adult asks, Why?; "To play")
5. Communicates logically, connecting two or more ideas, about intensions, wishes needs, or feelings, using
   - Words
   - Multiple gestures in a row (i.e., pretending to be an angry dog)
   - Touch (i.e., lots of hugging as part of a pretend drama in which child is the daddy)
6. Play spatial and motor games with rules (i.e., taking turns going down a slide)
7. Uses pretend play or words to communicate two or more logically connected ideas dealing with the following emotions:
   - Closeness (i.e., doll gets hurt and Mommy fixes it)
   - Pleasure and excitement (i.e., says bathroom words, such as "doody" and laughs)
   - Assertive curiosity (i.e., good soldiers search for missing princess)
   - Fear (i.e., monster scares baby doll)
   - Anger (i.e., good soldiers fight bad ones)
   - Limit setting (i.e., soldiers can hit only bad guys because of the rules)
8. Uses pretend play that has a logical sequence of ideas to recover from distress, often suggesting a way of coping with the distress (i.e., the child becomes the teacher, bossing the class)

From Greenspan, S. and Wieder, S. (1998), *Intellectual and Emotional Growth.* Reading, MA: Perseus, pp. 92–97. Reprinted with permission from Dr. Stanley I. Greenspan.

The Task of the Music Therapist Regarding Child Development

After reviewing two unique theories of child development (Briggs, 1991; Greenspan and Wieder, 1998) as well as standard references for tracking developmental milestones (Furano et al., 1979), *it is the task of the music therapist to review the individual education plan and reports from therapists, educators and physicians as well as observe and identify behaviors that clarify developmental ages.* There may be cases where the child's behavior is developmentally higher or even lower in the music therapy session. Reference to this possibility is reviewed in Chapter 2 on assessment.

It is of critical importance to work with the child at the appropriate developmental level. Setting goals for the child that are developmentally too low or too high interrupt the possibility of progress. Understanding the developmental level(s) allows the therapist to decide if groupwork is developmentally appropriate for the child.

In cases where groupwork is not developmentally appropriate for the child and groupwork is mandated by the administration of the school setting, the therapist is still at an advantage in understanding the limitations of the groupwork.

QUESTIONS RELATED TO CHILD DEVELOPMENT AND INDIVIDUAL VS. GROUP PLACEMENT

How do developmental ages affect deciding whether a child receives individual or group music therapy?

In the discussion of interactive levels in music therapy, Goodman (2002) presents the following possibilities: 1) No group interaction or awareness; one-on-one awareness developing; 2) Beginning awareness of each other or parallel play; and 3) interactive awareness leads to interactive play. According to the Slavson and Schiffer definition of group work, only interactive awareness leading to interactive play, level three of the proposed scenario, really constitutes a group.

According to Goodman (2002), the formation of a group with children that act at developmental levels of behavior lower than prelatency lead to severe restrictions in the possibility of group cohesion and is only physically possible when the therapist models intervention with one child while aides assist in one-on-one attention with other children in the group. In other words, the effort to form a music therapy group that does not meet developmental prerequisites is a forced effort and redefines the traditional definition of group. Further, Goodman (2002) found that some disparity in developmental ages was acceptable in group music therapy but that a significant disparity was not. Therefore, the question of homogeneity vs. heterogeneity in group special education placement can be confusing and can depend upon the extent of the differences.

Common sense dictates that children are only able to really participate in a group when they are developmentally ready. This reference to "developmentally ready" means the cognitive, social, communicative awareness of a child who is minimally at a toddler level and ideally at a preschooler level, the developmental age of a nursery school child, a child who begins to enjoy and engage in group activities. The infant relies on 1:1 awareness; the toddler relies on parallel play; the preschooler is able to interact using representational play; the latency age child can enjoy the "rules of games." With this in mind, one can conclude that a child who is developmentally at an infant level will not get much out of a group. Nevertheless, we find severely handicapped children in the classroom as well as in the music therapy session. These groups present severe restrictions in the possibility of group cohesion which call for additional help in group achieved with the therapist modeling and collaborative planning with other therapists and aides (note: see practical considerations). Following are case examples in which the therapist is in the process of determining developmental appropriateness for music therapy group using both the Briggs and the Greenspan models to determine developmental readiness.

Case Example One: Abby (Goodman, 1996–2002)

Abby, chronologically eight years old, is a multiply disabled child. Her visual perception is inconsistent due to cortical blindness; she is prone to seizures and has a left side motor weakness, particularly noted in the use of her left hand, which makes bilateral tasks more challenging. She is unable to model verbal, gestural or motor responses secondary to apraxia and inconsistent use of visual information. Auditory processing delays are also noted. Abby has a good attention span, is eager to learn and enjoys a happy disposition and sense of humor.

Functionally, her academic, social and communication skills place her at a preschool level and her social skills are such that she enjoys contributing within a group. Socially, she demonstrates representational play, shares toys, waits her turn and waits her turn cooperatively yet she is known to become easily overwhelmed. Linguistically and conceptually, she can follow two-step directions, respond to yes/no and "Wh" questions, talk about events in her life and sing simple songs despite auditory processing delays. Motorically, she walks and runs with confidence. Although her developmental skills are inconsistent and uneven due to multiple neurological and sensory issues, she is at a *beginning* level of *interactive awareness leading to interactive play.*

In terms of aforementioned theoretical models, Abby is entering the developmental stage of what Greenspan calls *complex communication* with inconsistent behavior in earlier stages of *two-way communication.* Within the context of the musical developmental stages, Abby is also entering what Briggs calls *Control.*

In music therapy the somewhat shy and easily overwhelmed demeanor that Abby initially presents become more relaxed as she volunteers to lead a song, try a drum-piano improvisation and vocally and motorically improvise with her friends within the context of such songs as "New Way to Walk" and "Sing After Me" from Sesame Street. Her difficulties in sustaining attention and attending to other students' responses appear to decrease once in the group. She is comfortable in the group. Furthermore, her more assertive classmates act as role models for her (Goodman, 1996).

Case Example Two: Terrence (Goodman, 1996–2002)

Terrence, a multiply disabled seven-year-old

boy, functions at or around the age of two-three with some scatter skills (i.e., Motor) closer to five years old. He is a friendly child who enjoys being in a music therapy group. His temperament is best described as easily excitable, outgoing and impulsive; this is a style of being that requires encouragement as well as auditory direction to persevere on a task. When he wants to "tune out," Terrence may cover his ears, close his eyes or drop his head so he faces the floor. In terms of language, his lowest developmental area (closer to 18–24 months), Terrence is echolalic, has a short attention span, a weak understanding of directions and limited vocabulary. Here, according to Greenspan, he is firmly at the *Two-Way Communication* level with inconsistencies in the ability to cope with regulation but with many imitative behaviors indicative of *Compex Communication.* According to Briggs, however, he is between *Intention* and *Control.* His functioning levels in music appear to be higher than in the classroom.

In music, Terrence may be in a "grey" area to determine the efficacy of individual vs. group placement. His social and motor strengths place him in a group. However, his difficulty in understanding directions and expressing himself seem to contraindicate the group placement. Interestingly enough, Terrence's musicality and neurological makeup help him learn song lyrics easily. In order to avoid the rote use of language in the song, the therapist improvises on simple concepts and structures the songs in such a way as to promote spontaneous language. The group experience is a successful one for Terrence.

Case Example Three: Edward (Nordoff and Robbins, 1977)

In their landmark book, *Creative Music Therapy* (Nordoff and Robbins, 1977), Paul Nordoff and Clive Robbins present the story of "Edward," a five-year-old autistic child referred for individual music therapy. Edward becomes musically engaged through song at a level where he "converses" with Paul Nordoff through vocal/piano improvisation. This series of "dialogues" demonstrates Edward's speech-language development through the acquisition of increasingly sophisticat-

ed tonal vocalization and babbling exchanges with the therapist. Edward increases his repertoire as well as duration of vowel/consonant exchanges. Musically engaged, Edward is aware of the ongoing tonality and musical "attunement" which deepens the emotional relationship in therapy.

Clearly Edward is, according to the Greenspan framework, in the stage of *Two-Way Communication.* According to the Briggs framework, Edward is in the Intention Phase. Although he may musically be beyond *Intention,* his communicative/affective place is lower. He relishes the attention of the two music therapists as he emotionally and musically connects. Individual therapy is right for him.

Case Example Four: Ari (Goodman, 1992–1998)

Ari, a seven-year-old boy diagnosed with autism, is part of a model classroom for autistic spectrum disordered children. He does not show a pronounced response to music and so it is debatable whether or not this modality is appropriate for him. In terms of development, he is entering his highest level at Greenspan's milestone 5, *Emotional Ideas.* Earlier levels are problematic in their scope. For example, Ari's ability to achieve *regulation* is variable. In some cases, he is very distractable, around the room and focusing for no longer than 30 seconds; at other times, he is focused on an interactive communication for about a minute or two. In terms of *intimacy,* Ari is in and out of relating due to attention rather than emotional withdrawal. The area of *two-way communication* is present but quite limited in terms of duration. The development of *complex communication* again is present but limited in terms of frequency and duration.

Watching Ari wander around the room with minimal and affectless participation if any during music activities is like watching a disengaged child who, despite his evaluation of entering the *Emotional Ideas* phase, is clearly inappropriate for group. His earlier developmental stages need to be strengthened in intensive one-on-one work, not even necessarily in music therapy. He is visually very sophisticated and particularly enjoys mechanical things.

What if the children in a class are developmentally ready for group but varied in terms of their developmental ages?

Great disparities in developmental ages of children in the group can make planning difficult. Difficult, of course, does not mean impossible. One can imagine having a party for a child where cousins and siblings of different ages join the child's friends. In order to make the activities of the party work, one would need to work on multiple levels of activities and assign different children different roles. This is what happens when children of disparate developmental ages try to participate in a music therapy group. It is possible but not preferred.

Case Example One (Goodman, 1996–2002)

Assigned to work with children by previous classroom arrangement, the therapist encounters many groups where the children, all multiply handicapped, are extremely different in terms of developmental, sensory and musical needs. By virtue of their involved sensory profiles, all the children have difficulties in the area of self-regulation which impacts on subsequent stages of consistency in intimacy and two way communication. Their highest levels of functions based on the Greenspan model deviate between complex communication, emotional ideas and emotional thinking.

In terms of the Briggs musical development model, the range is between that of late stage intention, middle stage control and early to late stages of integration, in short a developmental age range of one to five years.

The positives of the group are the following: Beth, Gabriel, Ben, Mason, and Richard all enjoy a social disposition and like each other; they are close to each other in terms of musical levels and have varying musical interests which they share with each other. Beth delights in singing, Gabriel loves to play the drums, Ben enjoys leading the instrumental ensembles and Richard adores leading musical drama. They are socially mature

enough to be sympathetic to the peers who are developmentally younger, namely Carl and Marcus. They seem to have a sense that Dora is aware of the group even though her actual participation is limited; they try to physically support her.

The challenge of the group is incorporating two members who really do not fit, namely Carl and Marcus. Their developmental levels are significantly lower than their other classmates and they need constant attention to attend. The therapist (Goodman, 1996) works with diligence to handle the varying cases:

- Beth, age nine, is extremely social, in some cases, inappropriately so. Her language, motor abilities, social skills and cognition are at or about that of a three-year-old, well into the stage of *emotional thinking*. Her greatest delight is in singing and dancing at the beginning stages of *integration*.
- Gabriel, age ten, is quiet and reserved most of the time, with lovely explosions of gleee when he plays the drum. He speaks infrequently with 2–3 word phrases, evidences low motor tone and poor motor planning, needs frequent prompting to complete simple tasks and is inconsistent in nonverbal gesturing to indicate *complex communication.* Musically, Gabriel is at a higher level, entering the stage of *integration,* 24–36 months
- Richard, age eight, uses poorly enunciated simple sentences for communication, compromised by his moderate hearing loss, auditory processing delays and verbal apraxia. He has a flair for the dramatic and loves to be in the limelight, acting out songs with the puppets. This takes on the flavor of *emotional ideas* moving toward *emotional thinking.* His pretend play scenarios, expedited through musical accompaniment from the therapist, reveal a higher level of thinking and sense of humor than his limited communication.
- Carl, age 9, is nonverbal, using vocalization and differential cries to communicate his pleasure, displeasure and basic needs. He enjoys clapping dysrhythmically to the music, exploring the instruments in a senso-

ry fashion and watching the other children. He is prone to assaultive behavior and sits with his aide somewhat apart from the rest of the group. At the beginning of two-way communication in terms of the Greenspan model and at the beginning of intention in terms of the Briggs model, Carl bounces in his seat to the music and expresses great pleasure when his favorite Sesame Street song, "C is for Cookie" is performed for him.

- Dora, age 11, is nonverbal but able to make choices regarding instruments and songs based on a picture exchange system developed with the speech therapist. She is quadriplegic and therefore severely physically compromised. For this reason, it is difficult to ascertain her levels of development. Her greatest pleasure in the group is listening to classical music.

- Marcus, age 11, is classified as trainable mentally retarded. Of all the children in the group, he is the least responsive to the music. He is inappropriately self-stimulative in the session, screams frequently and is either restrained or removed from the group. Since he shows little regard for the music, it is not even fair to ascertain his level of musical development. In terms of the Greenspan model, he is having great difficulty with *regulation, intimacy,* and *two-way communication.*

- Ben, age 12, is a higher functioning child in the group, enjoying a leadership role in "conducting" simple music therapy orchestrations and leading songs. He is a vital force in suggesting activities and helping the lower functioning children in his class. In terms of development, he is in the highest stages, namely *emotional thinking* and musical *integration.*

- Mason, age 8, is another leader in the group, despite his inconsistent behavioral functioning. At the levels of *emotional thinking* and musical *integration,* he greatly enjoys singing simple rap songs, playing and clapping complex rhythmic imitation and free dancing to his selected rock music.

SENSORY PROFILE

An Explanation Regarding Sensory Profile

The necessity to understand the sensory profile of group members is of the utmost importance since each therapy session, particularly one of music therapy, creates a sensory environment which demands appropriate tolerance and processing of sensations by all group members.

In describing and understanding the sensory profile of a child, it is absolutely necessary for the music therapist to understand the sensitivities observed in various children, the different ways that children process types of sensory input and, finally, the terms used to describe various sensory profiles. This information will help the therapist observe the child's reactions to sensory input in the music therapy session, appropriately recommend individual or group therapy, and, of course, plan music therapy strategies (see Chapter 7).

When referring the child to a group, the therapist must consider the sensory input of the music therapy session in terms of auditory (instruments, singing, talking), visual (instruments, set-up of the room, persons in the room), touch (cuing, movement games, physical stimulation from the instruments), and movement (movement activities, dances and games) from the perspective of a special needs child with a challenging biological profile. In some cases, the child will be visually or hearing impaired. In many cases, the sensory profile as well as sensory processing of the special needs child will be aberrant. One population where sensory profiles are notably complex is that of the autistic child (Nelson, Anderson and Gonzales, 1984).

In addition to the five senses of seeing, hearing, touching, smelling and tasting, the child has the body senses. Body senses include the vestibular system, sensitive to gravity, movement and influencing muscle tone, balance and arousal and the proprioceptive system, providing an awareness of movement and the position of the body in space, thereby influencing motor control and body schema.

Children can be under or overreactive depending on sensory thresholds. The global effect of these sensory temperaments soon evidences itself in the music therapy session. It is the goal of the music therapist to help the child modulate either up or down depending upon their global sensory picture. This constitutes an effort to return the child to an optimum level of arousal. If the child is underreactive, hyporeactive, he is underresponsive and has sensory regulation problems. Therefore, the therapist will use music and music activities to stimulate the child. If the child is overreactive, or hyperreactive, he experiences overload or sensory shutdown. In this case, the therapist will use music and music activities to calm the child. A further complication evolves when the child is hyporeactive in one sensory system and hyperreactive in another. Sensory defensiveness, the tendency to react negatively or with alarm to sensory input that is usually considered harmless or nonirritating, is a common issue in overreactive or hyperreactive children. This may include oversensitivity to light or unexpected touch, sudden movement or over-reaction to unstable surface, high frequency noises, excesses of noise or visual stimuli and certain smells. It can range from mild to severe. In either case, the effect of the therapy or the modulation effort is toward physiological integration, often referred to as "sensory integration."

Sensory integration, a theory and remediation approach developed by A. Jean Ayres (1979) as standard training for occupational therapists, is characterized by the ability to take in, sort out and connect information from the environment. It is easiest to remember the meaning of this term as one defines the words "sensory," pertaining to our senses (hearing, sight, smell, touch, taste, perception of motion/movement and gravity) and integration, the process of making whole, unifying, allowing the brain to use the information that the senses take in. The topics of sensory integration and sensory profiling are found in the music therapy literature (Berger, 2002; Joseph, 1984; Nelson, Anderson and Gonzales, 1984; Goodman, July, 2002), topics of obvious concern to the music therapist since music holds the ability to appeal to the child at a simultaneous level through multiple senses, thereby helping the child "integrate," or to

put it another way, neurologically connect.

Processing of various sensations is equally important in the therapy setting. Various amounts of time are needed for children to achieve *auditory processing, cognitive processing, emotional processing and visual and spacial processing.* The understanding and observation of these processing profiles within the group assist the therapist to plan carefully and accommodate various children within the group in different ways.

Temperament Related to Sensory Profile

Temperament is a topic first introduced in the literature by Thomas and Chess (1977) and later emphasized by Brazelton (1974) and Greenspan (1995, 1998) in parenting books. Temperament is certainly related to sensory profile insofar as the disposition of a child, for example, relaxed and easygoing vs. tense and anxious, can show up in the reactions to the sensory world around him.

Thomas and Chess (1977, pp. 21–22) cite nine categories of temperament:

1. *Activity level:* proportion of active and inactive periods. Mobility during bathing, eating, playing, dressing and handling, information regarding sleep-wake cycle, reaching, crawling and walking.
2. *Rhythmicity (Regularity):* predictability or unpredictability in time of any function.
3. *Approach or Withdrawal:* nature of initial response to a new stimulus., positive or negative.
4. *Adaptability:* responses to new or altered situations.
5. *Threshold of Responsiveness:* intensity level of stimulation necessary to evoke response (i.e., concerning reactions to sensory stimuli, enviornmental objects, and social contacts).
6. *Intensity of Reaction:* energy level of response.
7. *Quality of Mood:* amount of pleasant, joyful and friendly behavior vs. unpleasant, cying and unfriendly behavior.
8. *Distractibility:* effectiveness of extraenous environmental stimuli in interfering with or in altering the direction of the ongoing behavior.

9) *Attention Span and Persistence:* length of time activity is pursued by the child; continuation of activity despite obstacles.

It appears that the traits labeled as *Approach* or *Withdrawal, Adaptability, Threshold of responsiveness* and *Distractability* are directly related to the sensory profile.

The Task of the Music Therapist Regarding Sensory Profile

After reviewing the Individual Education Plan and the reports contributed by the teacher, the therapists and the physicians who work with the child, it is critical for the music therapist to take note of the child's responses to sensory input both in and out of the music room. There may be different kinds of responses depending upon the environment. Where the sensory profiles are extreme, the music therapist must be careful not to place the child in a group setting that is contraindicated by a child of an opposite sensory profile.

On rare occasion, there may be children who have such extreme auditory sensitivity that they may be contraindicated for music therapy entirely.

In detailing the ideal prerequisites for forming the group in terms of sensory profile, Goodman (2002) finds that heterogeneous sensory profiles appear to provide the most success provided they are not extreme. Traits of temperament are directly related to sensory profile.

In general, the heterogeneity of the group is important in providing both stimulative and calming forces. The child can be observed at play in the classroom to establish what kind of children she functions well with.

The following questions relate to the recommendation of individual or group therapy when considering the issue or sensory profile.

QUESTIONS RELATED TO SENSORY PROFILE AND INDIVIDUAL OR GROUP PLACEMENT

Why is the nature of this child's sensory profile important?

The nature of the child's sensory profile informs the therapist of the child's capacity for sensory intake, processing abilities and, above all, capacity to adapt to the music therapy environment. If a child is developmentally able to join a group in terms of social age, the therapist must also consider the tolerance of the child for group sensory input before recommending the group placement.

Case Example One: Melinda (Goodman, 1996–2002)

Melinda is chronologically seven years old and developmentally disabled. She does not use verbal language but can use manual signs to spontaneously indicate "more," "my turn," and "I want." Her inquisitive nature leads her to independently seek out activities, generally in a very impulsive manner. The sensory profile includes poor auditory processing skills, short attention span, lack of visual focus, tactile defensiveness and hyperactivity. The therapist must decide which deficit is more pronounced and to what degree Melinda can learn through her stronger, albeit still problematic, senses.

Although her lack of visual focus limits the use of a picture communication system for learning language, Melinda learns successfully with visual prompting and modeling.

In music, Melinda enjoys exploring the use of instruments, sufficiently enough that her tactile defensiveness is decreasing. Severe auditory processing delays and impulsivity make it difficult, but not impossible to establish her level of musicality. This profile requires much adaptation on the part of the teacher and therapist. Successful strategies include the use of modeling, increasing tactile input slowly, emphasis on visual presentation of stimuli, gestural prompts and a high degree of structure to help channel her hyperactivity. Developmentally, she is at or about 18 months of age on a cognitive level, too young for a group. Furthermore, her sensory profile is so problematic that she is best served with an individual session where she can receive intensive attention.

Through what senses does the child learn most effectively?

An understanding of the learning style on the part of

the child helps the therapist effectively plan the music therapy session in a way that appeals to different children in different ways. The learning style also affects the variety of activities offered in the session, which can offer instrumental, vocal, movement and listening activity.

Case Example One: George (Goodman, 1996–2002)

George, age 12 years old, is blind, hyperreactive and multiply handicapped. In music, he listens intently for cues to play his favourite instrument, the tambourine. For a child whose original goals include tolerating tactile input for one minute without withdrawal, increasing awareness of movement, start/stop, in activity and spontaneously using bilateral hand use in 2 out of 3 sessions, he is doing extremely well.

Clearly, his favored sense is that of the auditory, despite the processing delay inherent in his response. The gap between musical direction and response is getting smaller as George anticipates the musical structure of his songs and his motor planning.

He requires less and less physical prompting from the occupational therapist who sits behind him in group.

Ideally, he should be in an individual session but this was not practically possible in the school (see practical considerations) and, on the other hand, would create more performance pressure for him. He appears to be listening to the other children as the group progresses.

If the child is hyporeactive, how will this affect the individual or group referral?

The hyporeactive child requires multisensory inputs and can also benefit from the transdisciplinary planning with an occupational therapist, physical therapist and speech therapist. If the child is developmentally and musically appropriate for the group and the additional support of an aide is possible for sensory stimulation, this child can function well in a group. On the other hand, if the child is developmentally unsuited for a group but musically inclined, the individual session can be a good recommendation. There are occasions, however where the child is so

underresponsive in the individual session that the therapist can spend a thirty minute session trying to stimulate her and possibly get only a few minutes of reaction time.

Case Example One: Carolyn (Goodman, 1996–2002)

Carolyn, age 11 years old, is cortically blind, has hearing losses, cerebral palsy, and signficant delays in all areas of development. She is functioning at an infant level.

In order to enhance sensory processing, the therapist is attempting to help Carolyn consistently localize to a sound source in music with carryover to the classroom. Further, the goal is for Carolyn to increase functional hand use by reaching for and grasping an object other than food without prompting.

Carolyn sits in the wheelchair and appears quite sluggish. It takes ongoing proprioceptive input from the occupational therapist for Carolyn to attain minimal attention to the music therapy effort. Following this input, Carolyn raises the trunk of her body, lifts her head and appears to be listening and localizing the sound of the musical instruments. Sufficiently stimulated by the sound of the tambourine, she reaches out for it and briefly holds it, allowing herself to be led through physical exploration of the instrument.

This is an extreme example of hyporeactivity and this child appears to be best suited for individual music therapy. However, the work involved in getting her to respond is so sustained that performance pressure becomes an issue (also see Chapter 2, Assessment example). If she has an individual session, it should be no longer than 20 minutes.

If appropriate for a group, an extremely hyporeactive child requires ongoing stimulation, and for that reason, would detract from the ongoing process of groupwork. This is the same issue with an extremely hyperreactive child.

If the child is hyperreactive, how will this affect the individual or group referral?

The hyperreactive child has difficulty sorting out stimuli and is easily overwhelmed. In responding to so many stimuli in the environment and having difficulty with focus, this kind of child may become a serious distraction in the group. If, however, the child is developmentally and musically appropriate for the group and not hyperreactive to the point of being a serious disruption, the group placement is appropriate. *In some case, the reactivity of the child in the group can have a stimulative effect on other children and, in this way, be a positive force.*

Case Example One: Jared (Goodman, 1996–2002)

Jared, chronologically ten years old, is very social and very musically inclined. He is delayed in all areas and functions at approximately a four to five-year-old level. His frustration tolerance is very low and his moods variable, going from extremely happy to extremely upset, crying or tantrumming. Issues in the classroom with appropriate self-help skills, particularly inconsistency with toilet-training, seem at odds with Jared's abilities to follow directions, beginning reading, prewriting, classification and use of longer sentences in communication. His difficulty in sorting out stimuli and his tendency to be easily overwhelmed are the earmarks of hyperreactivity.

Perhaps his emerging ability to identify his emotions and discuss them will help him gain autonomy.

Jared has difficulty waiting his turn, particularly in music where he anticipates singing a treasured song, playing a favorite instrument or listening to a particular piece. His highly charged enthusiasm for specific musical experiences makes him a challenge in the group and yet, at the same time, a stimulant in the group.

If the child has processing delays, how will this affect the individual or group referral?

Processing delays require anticipation on the part of the therapist to wait for responses and feed information in an appropriate manner and rate of speed. *Should processing delays be severe, the wait time can be a distraction for other children and should be taken into account when recommending the child to group placement.*

Case Example One: Arthur (Goodman, 1996–2002)

Arthur comes to the music room smiling and enthusiastic. He is eight years old and his participation is compromised by visual impairment, some degree of paralysis on his right side, seizure episodes, poor motor planning, auditory processing delays and apraxia.

Despite these obstacles, Arthur loves a Hap Palmer song, "Sammy" (Palmer, (1981) which allows him to act out a variety of animals. In order to act out the song, Arthur approximates the lyrics and, without cuing, deciphers the words and actions associated with such animals as the snake, the monkey, the bear, the dog, and so forth.

Initially, Arthur takes time to decode the language of the song. His peers, also hindered by auditory processing, are patient. With further practice, the auditory processing speed is improving. Arthur is so proud of himself.

Is the child able to accommodate to the sensory impact of a group?

Observing the child in the classroom is a good indication of how the child accomodates to the sensory impact of a group. Keeping in mind the visual, spacial, auditory attributes of the classroom, the sound level of activity, the reaction to visitors entering the room, and the reactions to the kinds of sensory activities planned in the classroom, the music therapist can observe the child's tolerance for sensory input, learning style and processing time. This information is also critical in establishing the time frame of the session.

Case Example One: Evan (Goodman, 1996–2002)

Evan, 12 years old, is an enigma to many of the therapists and teachers. He demonstrates strength in receptive language through use of a communication book and response to pictures presented for nonverbal communication. In music, the therapist sings Evan's favorite song, "Do, Re, Mi," reportedly a song picked out on the piano at home. Evan laughs as he holds his hands over his ears and looks mischievously at the therapist. Yet, this sense of pleasure and possibly humor is confounded by his tantrum behavior when imposed upon to perform tasks or activities. Evan exhibits multiple self-stimulatory behaviors including mouthing and biting his fingers, rocking, and on occasion, banging his head against a surface.

This kind of behavior is indicative of a low sensory threshold, one that Evan needs to control. When he wants to play the drums, he "plays" by striking each drumhead and putting his hand atop to feel the vibrations.

When his classmate, Gabriel, in the group plays the drum directly and loudly, Evan tried to physically retreat from the group.

As time goes on, Gabriel modulates his playing to a more intermediate level of dynamics which Evan can tolerate more easily. Evan, in return, lets go of his need to control the sound by playing the drum appropriately and musically with the sticks, albeit for brief moments of time.

MUSICALITY OF THE CHILD

An Explanation of Musicality

A traditional definition of musicality, simply defined as the child's propensity for making music and emotionally being attached to that process, is generally recognized by the formal music-making tasks of school-age children (Shuter-Dyson, 1982); tasks such as dancing, playing an instrument, singing, composition, or music analysis. This definition goes awry in the field of music therapy since musicality in the special needs child is one that may be recognized at a more primitive or nascent level. For example, musical behaviors in their earliest stages are expressed through rhythmicity, movement, vocalization and listening: the changes in the sucking(Wolff, 1968) or breathing pattern of the infant can signal a musicality; the changes in the movement patterns (Kestenberg, 1965) of the baby can signal a musical propensity; the changes in the beginning vocalizations (Papousek and Papousek, 1981) or cries (Fridman, 1973) of the baby can signal a musical ability, and so forth.

The Context of Musicality with the Special Needs Child

When one recognizes and considers very early musical behaviors, they are naturally placed in the context of child development as well. Therefore, it is the responsibility of the music therapist to link musical behavior, from birth forward, to a developmental and psychological context. This additional context allows the therapist to understand the musicality of the child from a global perspective.

In recognizing musicality as related to musical development and musical development as an additional perspective on child development, Ostwald (1973) is one of the first theorists to detail musical behavior in early life, ages 0–5 years. His literature review is based on the then burgeoning field of psychology of music authors (Revesz, 1954, Shuter, 1968 and Farnsworth, 1969). Musical behaviors in their earliest stages are expressed through rhythmicity, movement, vocalization and listening.

Beginning with Ostwald, other psychiatrists (Noy, 1968; Stern, 1985; Kestenberg, 1965; Wolff, 1968), music educators (Fridman, 1973), music therapists (Briggs, 1991) and psychologists (Condon, 1974) explore musical behavior within a developmental and psychological context. For example, Wolff (1968) and Condon (1974) consider the physiological origins of rhythmicity (i.e., sucking patterns, breathing patterns; movement patterns) in the infant; Fridman (1973) relates the discriminating musical cries of the infant to different emotional states; Papousek and Papousek (1981) relate changing vocalizations of the infant to evolving communication; Stern (1977, 1985) and Spitz (1965) explore the musical cuing that goes on between mother and child, inciting emotional bonding and Noy (1968) and McDonald (1973) consider the ability of music to carry the child through psycho-sexual developmental transitions.

Ostwald (1973) goes on to explore the topic of early musical talent which could be indicated by absolute pitch, but more interestingly, "a high emotional value to acoustical experience per se" (Pike, 1967; Noy, 1968; Ostwald, 1968, p. 369). This sense of intense pleasure through music is what Paul Nordoff (Nordoff and Robbins, 1977) describes as the "music child": You don't need to say "Follow me and imitate me on the drum. You play 'dah-dah-dah'; he plays 'dah-dah-dah.'" He is the music child (Film, "The Music Child"). In their pioneering music therapy work, Paul Nordoff and Clive Robbins (Nordoff and Robbins, 1977), describe children who are drawn to music, children who delight in jumping to music, babbling to music, drumming to music, singing to music, and playing a variety of instruments. While this musicality may show up in a relatively obscure fashion with some children due to their handicapping conditions, it becomes clear to the observing therapist. Again, it is this intense sense of pleasure through music-making that is a key to musicality in the special needs child.

The Task of the Music Therapist Regarding the Child's Musicality

In observing musicality in the special needs child, the therapist must keep in mind that each type of child, depending on his physical, sensory, emotional and communication profile presents musicality differently. It is the unique perspective of the music therapist that sees the musicality in the special needs child and knows how to extend it.

In general, *children in a group who can work toward group sharing of different musical preferences seem to have the best potential for benefiting from the group.* One might also say that the children in this kind of group have *heterogeneous* preferences or *preferences* that work in conjunction with each other to keep the group active and productive. There are many case studies illustrating a child appropriately starting in individual music therapy and then moving on to group therapy. This transition to a group indicates developmental growth and adaptation as well as sensory tolerance of the musical environment.

QUESTIONS RELATED TO MUSICALITY AND INDIVIDUAL VS. GROUP PLACEMENT

It is the child's particular musicality that leads the therapist to consider the following questions in deciding the appropriateness of individual or group music therapy placement.

What is the presentation of and quality of this child's musicality?

In every case study one presents, *the presentation of and quality of the child's musicality is particular to the rationale for receiving music therapy.* Not only does the very presentation of *musical behavior indicate a readiness for music therapy but it also leads the therapist to recognize what the child responds to in music* and what the child enjoys (i.e., vocal, instrumental, movement, listening). The quality of the child's musicality helps one perceive what Paul Nordoff, in his lectures, (1998) alluded to as the musical soul of the child.

Case Example One: Gabriel (Goodman, 1996–2002)

Gabriel, a delightful 12-year-old, is diagnosed as Downs Syndrome and moderately retarded. Functioning at a preschool level, he requires physical prompting and frequent help to complete simple tasks, demonstrates sensitivity to different food textures and frequently distracts himself with self-stimulatory behaviors. Less spontaneous speech and more difficulty with auditory processing, short attention span and one-to-one instruction for academic tasks are issues stated in his individual education plan.

Gabriel's mother reports her son's great interest in and enjoyment with music. In the music therapy session, Gabriel is surprisingly animated. He is able to improvise beautifully on the drum and the cymbal while the therapist accompanies his playing. Following these experiences, there is a noted increase in his spontaneous, albeit simple, communication and his affect. The musical directives he successfully follows in terms of rhythmic imitation are complex and of greater duration than verbal directions often given to him in class. This is an example of "the music child," music bringing out the best in the child.

Will the pronounced musicality of the child be enhanced and directed in the group or, on the contrary, will the therapist be in the position where she cannot appropriately address the musical level /needs of the child in a group?

In cases where the musicality of the child is so intensely or idiosyncratically expressed, the therapist may have a difficult time asking the child to compromise or merge his musical interests with the group. Furthermore, *an intensely musical child who has a clear and pronounced amount of material to share with the therapist, may move more quickly through individual music therapy than group music therapy.* Finally, there is the issue of the child who is able to verbally *free-associate in the music therapy sessions and may not feel as comfortable doing this in a group setting.*

Goodman (2002) describes the importance of children with heterogeneous preferences (i.e., listening, movement, vocal, instrument), assuming, again, that these preferences do not "overtake" the group in their intensity. *Group sharing of different preferences is key.*

Case Example One: Stanley (Goodman, 1977)

Stanley, a vibrant looking nine-year-old boy diagnosed with moderate retardation and serious hyperactivity issues, is drumming on every surface possible with his hands and musically babbling to himself. *He is using vocalization and beginning instrumental playing as a means of stimulation, behaviors normally attributed to a child at a beginning toddler level.*

In the case of Stanley, there is a toddler level of musical behavior which is confounded by his extreme hyperactivity. *Developmentally, he is not ready to take advantage of a group.* Furthermore, he demonstrates a *musical capacity that is so intense and*

driven that one wonders how he would be contained in a group. Within the context of the individual session, his hyperactivity is addressed by setting up instuments throughout a large space, providing him with a challenging orchestration and watching him motor-plan well enough to get from one instrument to another within the timing of a given piece of music. Eventually, he joins a group.

Case Example Two: Colleen (Goodman, 1981–1984)

Colleen is a tall, rather ungainly pre-adolescent 11-year-old girl, diagnosed with borderline personality disorder. She comes to the inpatient child psychiatric hospital setting as a suicidal child who is emotionally vulnerable in her dysfunctional family environment. Since Colleen loves to act, sing and dance (Goodman, ref), she selects repertoire for her session, songs from the musical, "Annie." The themes in the songs are reminiscent of Colleen's life: looking for love, reflecting on emotional abandonment, wondering if she will find caretakers. As she sings, Colleen becomes emotionally caught up in her songs and her voice starts to feel "strangled," to the point where she has to stop singing. Later, she free-associates about her feelings of abandonment. *Colleen is using the act of musical drama to project her innermost feelings. Her vocal restriction is a projective sign of distress but it does not stop the therapist from understanding her emotional investment in the song, "Maybe."*

In the case of the emotionally disturbed child, a child who is not necessarily developmentally delayed but, rather, is regressed or deviant in terms of social-emotional development, we look for the *musical behavior as a primary source of expression, albeit disturbed.* By the word "disturbed" we mean to allow for the possibility of irregular musical behaviors.

In the case of Colleen, there is a directed need to project the theme of abandonment through the music of "Annie." Though it is possible that this could be done in a group, it is questionable whether her verbal process would be free. It is also open to question if she would have a difficult time sharing the musical material she so needs to express. Since Colleen was only in the inpatient child psychiatry unit for 6–8 weeks, *she did not progress to the point where her ego could tolerate being in a music therapy group.*

Case Example Three: Mickey (Goodman, 1981–1984)

Mickey is wandering the hospital floor, appearing disoriented, with blunt affect, infrequent eye contact and lack of communication. He is diagnosed as a "conduct disordered" preadolescent. At the age of 12, he set fire to his parents' home and tried to kill himself. He has now been on the inpatient child psychiatric unit for three weeks and has not talked to anyone. The child psychiatry intern assigned to conduct verbal therapy with Mickey is bewildered. The music therapist asks Mickey to help move the piano. After Mickey helps with the move, he spontaneously sits down at the piano with the therapist. They open a music book and the therapist asks him to choose which song he might like her to sing to him. At first, he points to a page of music with a woman sitting at the piano with a young boy. Then, Mickey begins to use words, sparingly. "This one." "That one." Before the half-hour is over, Mickey and the music therapist are singing together and Mickey is shyly smiling. The psychiatrist rushes over after the child goes to dinner, "What did you do?"

Mickey is not threatened by singing and this opportunity to do so, supported by the therapist playing the piano, helps him begin to communicate choices. His singing reflects an obvious love of music. This is his first reported "opening" with a therapist and it is open to question whether he will be comfortable enough to really talk. His short-term stay does not allow the therapist to answer that question.

In the case of Mickey, we see a child who is so threatened emotionally that all his emotional reserves have shut down to the point of becoming "mute" He is regressed emotionally and communicatively even though he is perfectly capable cognitively and motorically. Because of Mickey's severe emotional regression, he will achieve more in individual treatment.

Case Example Four: Bruce (Goodman, 1992–1998)

Bruce, a freckle-faced nine year old diagnosed with autistic spectrum disorder, loves to sing to himself and has already been assigned to a music therapy group by the principal of the special education school. After singing a "Hello" song with the music therapist in group, Bruce becomes very upset. He does not like the opening pitch of the song: "Don't sing it there, sing it here." As he proceeds to start the song a third higher, the therapist begins to realize *he is on his own musical wavelength.* As the group progresses over the next several weeks, Bruce's preferences in terms of vocal key signatures, rhythms, types of songs and types of instruments he uses become more pronounced. Further, he really wants to learn how to play the piano. *For reasons which the therapist might call idiosyncratic musical tastes, he is unable to enjoy the group.* The therapist takes him aside for a period of individual music therapy over the next year. Following this period, he is able to enjoy both individual and group music therapy. He is now able to satisfy his musical needs and learn, on a one-to-one basis, how to deviate from previously rigid musical preferences.

In the case of Bruce, *there is an idiosyncratic musical preference that does not allow him to share in the group choices.* Within the individual session, the therapist is able to help him take "baby steps" in the direction of bending these preferences. Some methods used are drum/piano improvisation that necessitate his adaptive rhythmic responses, simple duets at the piano that are initially predictable, and eventually, less predictable and the use of songs that deviate from one key to another. *Brian rejoins the group a year after he starts individual therapy.*

The autistic child may demonstrate a specific sensory profile that discriminates sounds in a seemingly resistive manner. Yet, it is this very rigidity that can also be viewed as musical sensitivity for enjoying certain kinds of sound that may be utilized to "unstop" the musicality of the child.

Is the child high functioning enough in terms of cognition, social-emotional and communication development, all of which may show up in musical behaviors, to engage with other children in a group?

In this chapter, the topic of child development is explored. *The child who is developmentally at an infant or toddler level is not ordinarily expected to socially or communicatively engage in a group.* According to Briggs (1991), these infant and toddler developmental behaviors correspond to identifiable musical developmental behaviors as well. According to Greenspan (1998), the child can become "stuck" developmentally if there is a difficulty in emotionally relating. The work of Greenspan figures into both a cognitive-stucturalist and psychoanalytic perspective.

Case Example One: Rene (Goodman, 1977)

Rene, 6 years old, is olive-colored, dimpled, microcephalic, blind and smiling. These things do not, however, monopolize one's attention. *What is immediately noticed is that he has latched onto a set of keys and is playfully tossing them around on the floor.* Each time they land on the ground with an audible thud, he laughs with squeals of delight. He continues this behavior as a means of self-stimulation and amusement. It means that *he is using an auditory stimulus as a primary source of stimulation and learning,* developmentally a nine-month-old behavior (Furuno, 2005).

The developmentally young or delayed child is showing the first inklings of musicality, *early signs of musicality.* This behavior is observed in babies when they are preoccupied with sound sources and begin to babble and move to music with their entire body. Similarly, musical behavior in toddlers is observed when they make up songs, with words or without, to accompany their play. With preschoolers, musicality is observed in the way they attend to music, their eagerness to sing a song and their joy in moving to music in a rhythmic fashion. Many of the special needs children music therapists work with are developmentally much younger than their chronological years and so it makes imminent sense to look for developmental-

ly younger musical behaviors. In the case of Rene, we find a child who is developmentally at or around the age of nine months, stimulated by sound sources and developmentally *unable to engage socially in a group.*

Case Example Two: Dora (Goodman, 1996–2002)

Dora, a fourteen-year-old adolescent, is quadriplegic, strapped into her wheelchair almost all the time, mouth drooling, eyes wild, and frequently subject to germs that land her in the hospital. Reportedly, Dora loves the music from "Titanic." As the therapist (Goodman, 1996–2002) sings the love song, "My Heart will Go On," Dora's body posture and breathing become excited and then stabilize. *Dora is able to regulate her body and breathing due to the emotional satisfaction of hearing one of her favorite songs.* Although there are certainly augmentative devices that allow the motorically impaired child to cognitively respond, these devices do not indicate Dora is beyond an infant level of intellectual development.

The motorically impaired child will have difficulty moving, singing and playing in the normal way of a typically developing child. However, it is the child's apparent emotional investment in listening to music that can be the basis for uncovering inherent musicality. *Dora, like Rene, is developmentally at or around the age of twelve months and therefore requires individual treatment.*

PRACTICAL CONSIDERATIONS OF THE SCHOOL SETTING

The Limitations of the School Setting in Terms of Grouping and Scheduling

Strict scheduling and previously grouped classes are the reality many therapists have to cope with in the school setting. The settings that may offer the greatest latitude in scheduling both individual and group sessions are model programs run in a university setting, new programs under the direction of the entering therapist, psychiatric hospital settings, outpatient clinical settings and special education schools where the individual music therapy has already been arranged as part of the Individual Education Plan. The settings that offer the least latitude are special education schools in the private and public sector that offer music therapy services for each class in the school, almost always not on the IEP, and have a strict structure in terms of scheduling and class grouping.

Obviously, in situations where all children are put into groups, the therapist must either develop coping strategies to make those groups work or implore the principle to consider alternative options. Realistic scenarios of placement and scheduling as well as coping strategies for the music therapist are discussed here.

The Task of the Music Therapist in Handling Practical Limitations

Although music therapy has been an established profession since the 1950s, there may still be misunderstanding regarding its goals and practice. In many cases, the music therapist is not free to establish the schedule and selection of children for individual and group music therapy.

Practical considerations of the school setting or hospital setting may disrupt the therapist's previously considered thought process and for assessment and decision-making regarding individual or group placement. The practical considerations often imposed on the therapist will compel the therapist to reconsider the therapeutic and professional approach. Common issues include grouping by classroom rather than clinical music therapy considerations (i.e., development, sensory profile, musicality) in forming the groups, no option for individual music therapy, misunderstandings about the nature and goals of music therapy, strict scheduling times that may be inappropriate for the attention span of group members, too many sessions in the school day to allow the therapist sufficient planning or evaluation time, insufficient help in the music therapy room, and sound distractions from other parts of the school.

QUESTIONS RELATED TO PRACTICAL CONSIDERATIONS OF THE SCHOOL SETTING AND INDIVIDUAL OR GROUP PLACEMENT

Why is the school setting up music therapy this way?

While the initial reaction of the therapist may be negative, the administrative response must be understood in context of the educational system as follows:

1. *Many classroom groupings do not necessarily constitute a working group for the special education teacher.* Therefore, the teacher will have both individual and group lesson plans, frequently employing teacher assistants and teacher aides to support her lesson plans. For example, *different "stations" in the classroom make one-on-one work viable. This kind of flexibililty is not really possible in the music therapy group* unless it is structured that way in the music room. Furthermore this structure might be contraindicated in music for two reasons: a) the staff are not trained to provide music therapy for the children; b) different musical experiences going on in the room could be overly stimulating.
2. Music, art and physical education area, considered "specialty" areas in the school and, in some hospital settings, recreational therapy, constitute social experiences for children and, for this reason, the developmental and sensory contraindications of grouping are often quickly forgotton by administrators. Furthermore, *some educators do not understand the differences in these areas between therapy, adaptive education and education.*

How do I cope, overall, with the limitations imposed by this school setting?

Although the initial impulse of the music therapist in response to an inappropriate schedule is often defensive, it is important to educate both peers and administrators as to the efficacy and rationale for music therapy. This is accomplished through in-service presentations, shared professional literature, frequent professional dialogue and cooperative efforts to show professionals in the workplace what the job of the music therapist is. There are occasions where therapists start out in working situations that are difficult to cope with, and through careful working through of the issues, are able to change their situation.

Either short-term or long-term, the therapist may have to redefine the working concept of the "group" as a group of disparate children who are in need of one on one attention within the group. This requires efforts to program group activities with different expectations of participation level, care in sensory input, use of higher functioning children to lead the group, and training personal aides and teacher assistants to model music therapy strategies (i.e., positioning and handling, praise, cuing, hand-over-hand assistance, etc.) demonstrated by the therapist.

How do I cope with strict scheduling of groups when a child cannot effectively operate within a group yet and, further, the time frame set for their music therapy session is inappropriate?

Many school settings consider art, music and physical education "special periods" which allow the primary special education teacher to take what is called a "preparation" period. This generally means that the teacher will not join the group in music therapy. Furthermore, *the entire group of children must be taken as a group for the average 50-minute music therapy session time.* This precludes therapist-decision making about whether or not children should meet as a group. The therapist cannot "break up" the time into smaller segments since, by law, the children are under therapist educational supervision for that 50 minutes while the teacher is on "prep."

One possible alternative to this problem is to work with an understanding teacher who will *allow part of the class to remain in her classroom part of the time while the aide supervises them.* It is the rare teacher who will go along with this arrangement.

Another possible alternative to this problem is to *provide group activities with a number of aides and*

therapists in the classroom following your lead in order to allow each child to get as much one-on-one attention as possible. The importance of collaboration is pursued in Chapter 7 where much attention is given to interdisciplinary, and more relevantly, transdisciplinary work. Fortunately, the collaborative effort is one that most therapists enjoy (Stewart, 2002). The word "alternative" rather than solution is used here because ideally the therapist should be allowed to work with the children in a way that makes sense educationally. If the therapist has an understanding principal, she can meet with the administrator, *explain the decision-making process and ask to have the music therapy session scheduled when it does not coincide with a preparation period.*

Case Example One (Goodman, 1996–2002)

Presented with a preschool handicapped group of 8 children functioning at 9–18 month levels, the therapist is perplexed and annoyed (Goodman, 1996). Advised by the principal that she is to service each class with a 50-minute period of music therapy twice a week irregardless of their functioning levels, she is told that this schedule allows the teacher to take a preparation period while the children are in music, art or physical education.

In order to cope with the situation, the therapist prevails upon the support of the teacher assistant to bring four children at a time for a 25-minute music therapy session which involves personal aides modeling the efforts of the music therapist in providing sensory stimulation through music activity. While the four children are in the music room, the teacher takes her preparation period in the library and the teacher assistant involves the other four children in alternative activities within the classroom.

How do I cope with groups that do not easily work well in music therapy?

At the beginning of the year, children are grouped together in classes, and, more often than not, travel to art, music and physical education in their groups. In some cases, the therapist may even choose to join together seemingly disparate groups of children and strategically plan in anticipating the challenges of this grouping (Sutton,

2002). In any event, rationale for grouping can vary widely. In some schools, the children are grouped merely by chronological age (Goodman, 1996–2002); in other schools, children are grouped according to developmental ages (Goodman, 1992–1998); in the unusually progressive schools, children may be grouped together by developmental age as well as sensory profile (Goodman, 1992–1998). In other settings, music therapists may start out considering a homogeneous grouping in terms of gender, age and diagnosis; this effort often proves disadvantageous (Kank and Grogan, 2002) since heterogeneity, as previously pointed out, adds to the successful dynamic and individual identification of group member. Although musicality, sensory profile and developmental levels are core considerations in composing the group, one may frequently be put in the position where these aspects are at odds with each other.

In the "Methods" section of this book, Chapter 7, there are multiple suggestions on how to cope with groups that do not easily work well in music therapy. Further, it is important to remember that no matter what the composition of the group is, groups evolve, hence the name of this book!

However, here are sample strategies in coping with common music therapy group issues:

- In groups where there are combinations of extreme sensory profiles, the materials used must attempt to modulate toward a moderate level of sensory stimulation.
- In groups wherever developmental levels co-exist and the variation is extreme, the therapist can use one activity with different degrees of developmental expectation for each child.
- In groups where there are extremes of musical interest, the therapist can appeal to different children at different times in the group and help them all to eventually tolerate, if not appreciate, each other's preferences.

Case Example One

Presented with a group of latency-age children with mixed developmental and sensory profiles of extreme variety, the therapist (Goodman, 1996–2002) is unable to convince the principal to change the schedule or grouping. All the children are multiply handicapped, nonverbal and functioning with scattered levels from infant to preschool level. The therapist has to find a way of working with the following group members:

- Margaret is autistic-like, follows one-step directions with prompting and has little effect in music. Her primary problem is spitting on the instrument
- Carolyn is extremely hyporeactive and needs constant stimulation for moments of participation.
- Simon is able to follow one-step directions in using the drum, enjoys exploring the keyboard and has begun to show more awareness of peers.
- Mally, hyperreactive, shows her pleasure in listening to music by body movement and spontaneous vocalization.
- Edmund, resistive to following directions while laughing to himself, is probably the highest functioning member of the group in terms of cognition and the lowest functioning in terms of behavioral resistance.
- Darren, cerebral palsied, is able to utilize picture exchange to communicate which adapted instrument he wants to play.
- Arthur, blind and hyperreactive, enjoys playing the tambourine and is able to communicate gesturally with the therapist.

Through a carefully constucted session involving movement, vocal, instrumental and listening activity at various developmental levels (see Chapter 7 on Methods), the therapist is able to employ the help of the aides, teacher assistant, and occupational therapist to reach each child at an appropriate level of stimulation.

How critical is the decision to have an individual vs. group session?

If a child cannot adapt to the group setting and has the potential of benefiting from music therapy, the therapist should make every effort to insure that there is a possibility of individual therapy. In some cases, this may only be possible by alerting the parents to the possibility of an outside private practitioner.

Case Example One: Ellen (Goodman, 1986–1992)

Ellen, diagnosed autistic at an early age, attends a special education school where there is no music therapist. Even when her family moves to a school where group music therapy is provided to each classroom, the situation is not satisfactory. Ellen is nonverbal, has intermittent attention span, inappropriate self-stimulating behaviors and the tendency to wander the room while music activity is ongoing. Yet, her parents report her consistent listening to music at home, vocalizing to herself, singing songs to herself and playing with musical toys.

Once referred for individual therapy, Ellen is able to quickly bond with the therapist, establish gestural and then beginning word communication, indicate musical choices and follow simple directions. She continues to attend private music therapy through adolescence.

Can a child who would initially benefit from individual music therapy adapt to group therapy if the individual session is not possible?

There are many cases where the child learns to acclimate to music therapy group and it is for this reason that every attempt should be made to help the child adapt.

Case Example One: Mason (Goodman, 1996–2002)

Mason is a good-looking African-American boy from the home of a single mother in a family that moves frequently. He has been asked to leave four special education schools for inappropriate behavior and is considered emotionally disturbed. On an academic functioning level, he is mild to moderately retarded. On a musical level, he is easily engaged and, once engaged, became appropriately social in the group.

Mason's typical behavior is to hide under a desk in the classroom and cry whenever a transition to an art, music or physical education period is announced. The teacher's initial tactic is to punish him with a "time-out" for not listening. In this way, Mason is initiating an invitation for and receiving negative reinforcement. The therapist (Goodman, 1996) changes this pattern by beginning with a "hide and seek" game. Entering the classroom, she playfully says, "Where is Mason? He is not in music. I guess he is not here today." Mason pops his head up from under the desk, laughs mischievously, and hides again. The therapist says, "Oh, you are here. Let's count to three and go to music. Everyone is waiting for you."

As time goes on, Mason develops longer periods of tolerance for waiting his turn in the session and his favorite music activites, especially a song called "Hand Jive" (Sclesa, 1983, Volume 4) become his rewards as he works through the session with the other children. His higher functioning level allows him to eventually lead other children in musical activity, tolerate, and understand their preferences.

Can a child who would initially benefit from group music therapy adapt to individual therapy if the group therapy seems contraindicated?

There are numerous examples of children who join groups, appear to have the developmental, musical, sensory prerequisites and cannot adapt to the group. In those cases, *the music therapist can refer the child for individual therapy, and assuming the child progresses sufficiently in individual therapy, he can rejoin the group.*

Case Example One: Beverley (Tyler, 2002)

Tyler (2002) cites the example of an eight-year-old girl, Beverley, from the home of a dysfunctional family, diagnosed with learning difficulties, who is not able to manage her inappropriately impulsive and aggressive behavior in the group. Once Beverley is able to receive the undivided attention of the therapist, she is able to act out her conflicts and project her anger through instrumental playing and dramatic play. In retrospect, one might hypothesize that Beverley did not have the developmental ego stability to withstand sharing the therapist in the group.

SUMMARY

This chapter serves to help the therapist establish the goals and nature of the particular music therapy group. The goals and nature are, to some extent, defined by the setting and the diagnoses of the children. For this reason, the description of the group in both the child psychiatric milieu and the special education setting are discussed.

The next task of the therapist is to carefully consider which children are most appropriate for the group. This determination is based on careful observation of the children in respect to the following factors (Goodman, 2002): 1) *Developmental level;* 2) *Sensory profile;* and 3) *Musicality.*

Given that the developmental level of the child is sufficiently intact to interact with other children, the child is a candidate for group music therapy. The nature of the sensory profile and the musicality of the child are always issues that impact the functioning of the group and must be planned for by the therapist. In general, *extremes in sensory profile and musicality do not lend themselves well to group interaction.*

However, the variety of sensory profiles, musical interests, and developmental strengths and weaknesses add to the *heterogeneity* of the group and ultimately lead toward success.

Finally the *practical considerations* and limitations of the school or unit setting must be dealt with. To the extent that previous structures are flexible, the therapist can undertake individual and groupwork that makes sense educationally and clinically. In situations where there is no flexibility in changing the group limitations, the therapist can, with a flexible attitude and on a short-term or long-term basis, redefine the nature of a "group," adapt strategies as necessary and try to educate peers and administrators.

STUDY GUIDE QUESTIONS

1. Describe the nature of the group in the child psychiatric setting. What are the prerequisites for inclusion?
2. Describe the nature of the group in the child special education setting. What are the pre-requisites for inclusion?
3. Describe the nature of the music therapy group in the child psychiatric setting. What are the prerequisites for inclusion?
4. Describe the nature of the music therapy group in the child special education setting. What are the prerequisites for inclusion?
5. Goodman describes four factors to be considered in recommending a child for individual or group music therapy. Name these factors and describe why they are important variables in making such a recommendation.
6. Describe five children from your current clinical work. After analyzing them in terms of developmental level (i.e., Greenspan model; Briggs model), sensory profile and musicality, decide what recommendation, individual or group therapy, you would make for each child.
7. Would any of the five children be compatible in a group? Why or why not?
8. Are there any practical considerations that would prevent you from providing individual or group therapy for any of the five children? If yes, please describe what the practical considerations are and how you will cope with the situation.

Chapter 4

Starting Out: Goal Planning in Music Therapy

INTRODUCTION

In order to come up with a group plan, the therapist takes into account the prioritized needs of the children and then decides on group goals. This may sound deceptively simple. It is not. Given the clinical orientation of the therapist, the perspective of the music therapist in terms of priority and best use of the time for the music therapy group, the group plan can differ dramatically.

The seasoned therapist knows that in order to work effectively with a child individually or as part of a group, it is necessary to help the child physiologically regulate, form a bond with the therapist, being to communicate verbally and nonverbally and enjoy making music toward developmental ends. Simple. So why does the therapist have to even set more goals beyond this? The answer to this question concerns the necessary accountability of working within a school system or a psychiatric hospital, not to mention other settings which have not been introduced in this book. Suffice it to say that the clinical orientation of the therapist may be purist or eclectic. In any event, it is reasonable for a facility to request documentation of progress the children are making and the more observable the progress, the clearer-cut it is.

The primary thrust of this chapter is to outline the organization of goals given the constraints of following the Individual Education Plan for the child in the school setting. Further, the organization of goals within the child psychiatric plan for the child in the hospital setting are reviewed. Within these confines, there are many liberties the therapist can take. Questions of the value of the music itself and how the music is best utilized to address certain issues in the group are privy to the therapist's discretion, even as one works for the

developmental goals of the IEP or therapeutic purpose of the hospital treatment plan. If, through the course of the music therapy, the therapist discovers that the particular goal or goals of the school or hospital setting are subject to question then the therapist should, by all means, take the initiative to challenge the appropriateness of those goals.

For the purpose of defined terms in this chapter, group goals are long-term, observable changes in behavior, generally set on an annual basis according to the school calendar or, in the case of the child psychiatric hospitalization, the duration of the stay. Goals can be organized based on different levels of behavior. The questions that seem to dominate decision-making in the preparation of group priorities are the following: 1) Which goals are best achieved through music therapy?; and 2) Which goals overlap amongst the children, despite different levels of achievement toward those goals?

Through the careful review of records, discussion with other clinicians and teachers, observation and assessment, the individual goals of the child can be ascertained. Following that, the formation of group goals begins. In this chapter, the creation of the group "grid" is a practical tool for analyzing, organizing, prioritizing and setting group music therapy goals, which, in the school setting, have been spelled out in the Individual Education Plan, and in the hospital treatment plan, are defined as well. The specificity and appropriateness of the goals will vary from one school district to another and from one hospital setting to another.

Four clinical examples in this chapter will present sample groups of children in the preschool intervention, latency-age special education and inpatient child psychiatric contexts and the thought process the therapist goes through to set initial group goals. Although the clinical examples present goals that encompass all developmental domains, it is important that the therapist remember it is not necessary to "do it all." The adage, "Quality rather than Quantity" is key. As necessary, prioritize the purpose of the group in order to restrict the number of goals (and short-term objectives) you, as the therapist, can address in the sessions and evaluate in the session.

It is critical for the music therapist to keep in mind that, as the music therapy group becomes more cohesive and higher functioning, the children themselves will contribute to a sense of flexible group goals, goals that the therapist will come to reflect on and goals that may not have been initially included in therapy plans.

DEFINING GOALS, CHALLENGES OF GOAL PLANNING, RATIONALE FOR GOAL SETTING

THE DEFINITION OF A GOAL

A goal must be defined in context of the type of music therapy group, its clinical orientation, the functioning level of the children and the expectations of the therapeutic facility.

In the music therapy literature, a goal has been defined as "a broad statement of the desired outcome of treatment" (Davis, Gfeller, 1999, p. 281) or "very general statements about what the student should learn, usually distinguishable by the lack of overall behavioral responses that are directly measurable and therefore subject to a variety of interpretations" (Jellison, 1983, p. 18) versus objectives which are "very specific statements about what the student should be able to do, distinguishable by the inclusion of overt behavioral responses that are measurable and therefore subject to limited interpretations" (Jellison, 1983, p. 18). This remains true in the child psychiatric setting but is changing in the educational setting. In the school setting, if the music therapist chooses to have long-term goals that are compatible with the goals of the Individual Education Plan, those goals

would be observable and measurable.

Music Therapy Goals which Conform to IEP Mandates: Individual Example

The current mandate for writing goals in the Individual Education Plan, Federal law, IDEA, under content of IEP, requires that the IEP include "A statement of measurable annual goals, including benchmarks of short-term objectives (Sec. 300.347(a)(2)." Nevertheless, music therapists will find variability in the specifics or lack of specifics found in IEP goals.

In order to write a music therapy goal that conforms to the IEP mandate, the therapist can use the clinical language of the IEP goals.

Case Example: Maria (Goodman, K., 1996–2002)

This example of IEP goals, clinical goals for the session, is taken from Chapter 1.

Maria (Goodman, K., 1996–2002)
1. Reduce the instances of biting to her hands, given a verbal prompt, "hands down"4/5 trials.
2. Participate in gross motor activity for a period of 10 minutes with compliance and without complaint.
3. Demonstrate 1:1 correspondence up to three by giving the requested amount of objects to staff or peers on 3 out of 4 trials.
4. Attend to 2 other peer turns by sitting appropriately and not exhibiting aggressive behaviors toward herself or others, when given no more than 2 verbal prompts, on 3 out of 4 occasions.
5. Demonstrate the knowledge of what comes next by making an appropriate choice from a field of 3 pictures presented after being shown a model schedule during 3 out of 5 trials.
6. Respond appropriately to an activity-related "Wh" question when given up to 6 picture choices on 3 out of 5 trials.
7. Produce 3-word combinations through the use of pictures and/or manual signs when given verbal prompts, but without phrase modeling.

Were they to be written, contrary to the federal

mandate, in broader terms, they would be written as follows:

1. Maria will reduce biting to her hands.
2. Maria will participate in gross motor activity.
3. Maria will demonstrate 1:1 correspondence.
4. Maria will demonstrate choice-making.
5. Maria will indicate which activity comes next.

Similarly, were they to be written in the broadest terms possible, they could be construed as follows:

1. Maria will increase appropriate behavior.
2. Maria will increase gross motor activity.
3. Maria will increase cognitive understanding.

Music Therapy Goals for the Group

Since the IEP is written for the individual child, there is no federal definition, of course, of how to constitute goals for the group. In order to include specific IEP goals for children in the group, the following procedure is suggested:

1. Review all goals for group members after organizing them into a developmental grid.
2. Prioritize areas of developmental concern most relevant to music therapy and most relevant to group members.
3. Create broad categories of goal-setting with *specific* IEP goals and music therapy objectives underneath.
4. Handle "stumbling blocks" that frequently involve lack of specificity in IEP goals or IEP goals that are so specific that they do not allow the therapist to create overlapping goals easily.

Case examples in this chapter will demonstrate this method.

The School Setting

In many school settings the music therapy group is considered educational therapy, therapy that enhances the child's potential to learn. The clinical orientation may be predetermined or left to the philosophy of the individual therapist. The functioning level of the children is mixed and the expectation of the facility is to meet the goals and objectives of the Individual Education Plan in terms of observable behavior. If one works in a school setting the academic year generally runs ten months and the Individual Education Plan is reviewed annually. This calendar sets up the long-term goal as one that is temporally defined by the academic year and descriptively defined by the individual education plan goals. In the school setting then, goals as long-term and indicate outcome expectations in selected domains of the child's development. On the other hand, objectives (see Chapter 5) are steps toward the goal, steps that change as the child progresses throughout the academic year.

The Child Psychiatric Setting

If the child is in a short-term hospital setting, the type of music therapy group is considered therapeutic and there is an emphasis on psychosocial interaction. Again, the clinical orientation may be predetermined or left to the philosophy of the individual therapist. The functioning level of the children is mixed and the expectation of the facility is to meet the goals and objectives of the hospital treatment plan in an observable fashion. Here, the goal can be as short as a few weeks and as long as a few months. Therefore, the temporal nature of the *goal* is relative to its therapeutic or educational setting. The short-term hospital goals will overlap with the clinical goals of the treating psychologist, psychiatrist, social worker, and so forth.

The likelihood of a third level of psychotherapy, that of insight therapy with reconstructive therapy is unlikely in music therapy groupwork with children since most groups are conducted on an annual basis and the possibility of insight therapy with reconstructive therapy would be delimited to children who require personality redefinition. Insight music therapy with reconstructive goals occurs when music therapy techniques are utilized to elicit unconscious material, which is then worked with in an effort to promote reorganization of the personality.

Clinic

If the child is part of an outpatient music therapy or creative arts therapy clinic, the type of music therapy group may be educational or therapeutic. The clinical orientation in a clinic may be predetermined by an overall philosophy. A good example of this would be the Nordoff-Robbins clinics set up in New York, London and Sydney. The functioning level of the children is likely to be mixed and the expectations of the therapeutic facility may either be egocentric, or on the other hand, work in tandem with a school district. Nevertheless, the music therapy goals, if set in conjunction with the school setting, will convey a greater understanding of music therapy, an understanding which is integral to the growth of the field and, possibly, institutional support of outpatient therapy. In terms of time, the group goals will be set for the projected duration of the group.

CHALLENGES OF GOAL PLANNING

Challenges of goal planning frequently relate to the following issues:

1. The clinical orientation of the therapist
2. The clinical orientation of the facility
3. The anticipated outcomes of the facility.
4. The appropriateness and review of initial goal planning, whether it is set by a treatment team in a hospital or a educational/therapeutic team from a school district.
5. Relationship of clinical goal to musical objective.
6. The changing needs of the child in music therapy.
7. Music therapist initiating new goals not found on the Individual Education Plan or the hospital treatment plan.

All of these issues can be considered in relationship to the individual child and then to the needs of the individual child, as she becomes part of a group.

Relationship of Clinical Orientation to Goal Setting for the Group

The actuality is *that the goal-setting need not define the therapist's way of working. It simply provides ends to the means. It is also critical to realize that, as the child changes, the goals can change.* In the chapter on methods (see Chapter 6), case examples demonstrate various clinical orientations and clarify the relationship between goal-setting, methods, materials and evaluation.

Behavioral

Goal-setting has been approached in the music therapy literature differently depending upon clinical orientation. As cited in Chapter 2, there is a very limited description of group music therapy with children in the literature; therefore, most of the information cited on goals and objectives belongs to the clinical work with individual children.

In the limited behavioral groupwork studies reviewed, goals and objectives are observable, quantifiable (Hanser, 1999; Standley, 1996a) and may proceed based on anticipated levels of cognitive functioning (Presti, 1984). However, the terms *goal* and *objective* may in used in different ways. For example, Standley (1996b) refers to a series of developmentally appropriate learning *objectives* for preschoolers and does not delineate if these are long-term or short-term. Presti refers to clinical goal areas and delineates behavior within the context of the music therapy session as *objectives* for multiply handicapped children. Level I target behavior to increase motor on-task behavior is defined as playing one's instrument when verbally cued or physically prompted by the music therapist (p. 121, Presti, 1984); at Level II the expectation is increased to anticipate that the child will play the instrument only when cued (Presti, 1984, p. 122). Then the Level III goal of increasing cooperative behaviors with a partner is defined as follows: a) sharing instruments without verbal or motor off-task behaviors; b) taking turns and c) completing the entire musical task (Presti, 1984, p. 123; Jellison, 1983).

Humanistic/Psychodynamic

In humanistic and psychodynamic literature, *goals tend to evolve and surface* based on what the group members are doing in various phases of treatment (Pavlicevic, 2003): the work is exploratory. This is one way to approach goal-setting. After detailing the dynamic process of the music therapy sessions of an adolescent Nordoff-Robbins-based music therapy group at an outpatient clinic, Aigen (1997, pp. 48–51), reflects on the role of music in accomplishing clinical goals: facilitating transitions, meeting individual and group needs, working with physical expressions, increasing emotional self-awareness and enhancing interpersonal relating.

Goals may also be connected to psychodynamic treatment factors. In her work with emotionally disturbed children, Friedlander (1994) reflects on treatment *objectives* that are linked to the curative factors originated by Yalom: group cohesion, universality, identification, enhancement of interpersonal learning and social coping skills. "Patients meet these objectives by attending music psychotherapy groups willingly and demonstrating increased positive interrelatedness and an ability to problem-solve" (Friedlander, p. 94, 1994). These "objectives" are reflected in identified behaviors related to the five-stage model (Garland, Jones, Kolodney, 1976) that Friedlander utilizes.

The Clinical Orientation of the Facility

It is probably reasonable to assume that in order to be understood, the therapist must "speak" the same language as the administration as well as other therapists and educators in the facility. However, the defined goals can be framed in behavioral, humanistic or psychodynamic language and not necessarily impact on methodology. To put it another way, *goals can be written in the terminology of the facility but the manner in which the goals are achieved is up to the training and clinical orientation of the therapist.*

The Anticipated Outcomes of the Facility

In order to receive additional funding from the state as well as school districts, it is wise to assume that children should progress toward their stated goals on the Individual Education Plan. This, then, is the anticipated outcome of the facility. How the child arrives at success is based on the prowess of the therapist.

In situations where no Individual Education Plan is immediately relevant (i.e., medical hospitalizations, emergency psychiatric hospitalization, private practice, outpatient clinic), the therapist may choose not to set goals, but, rather, to work within the process of the group, assuming it is a group that can direct itself and set its own goals. This would, however, be an unusual situation. The hospital itself may have a treatment plan or directive for the therapist to follow. In situations of private practice or outpatient clinic, it is wise for the therapist to join hands with the teachers and therapists at the child's school in order to create an integrative treatment program for the child(ren).

The Appropriateness and Review of Initial Goal Planning

Although goals, objectives, and strategies are included in the Individual Education Plan, it behooves the therapist to review the goals in a critical fashion, particularly as the therapist develops a working relationship with the child within the group. Hanser (1999) provides valuable criteria for the selection and evaluation of goals, which suggest the following questions:

- What is the *value* of the goal insofar as its achievement impacting on related behaviors and generalizing to other environments?
- If the targeted goal is truly a *primary* concern, was it a possible reason for *referral* to music therapy or one reached by *team consensus*.
- Is the goal at the appropriate developmental level for the child?

- If the goal is *appropriate developmentally,* is there a *liklihood of success?*
- How will the progress toward the goal be *observed and evaluated?*
- Is this a goal *suited to the modality of music therapy?*

Although these criteria are indeed basic, it is amazing how frequently teachers and therapists come up with goals that are problematic in terms of functionality, likelihood of transfer to other environments throughout the day, developmental appropriateness, prospect of being concretely evaluated and the likelihood of success. The end result may be a frustration on the part of the teacher, therapist, child and administrator. Therefore, the effort to review the basic questions and "rework" goals is generally instructive.

Further, *the language of the goal is critical.* In order to easily observe the completion of a goal, it makes sense to use a verb. For example, "Respond to 'Wh' questions with a short phrase or sentence without prompting on 35 trials" includes the following components: 1) observable behavior (respond to "Wh" questions with a short phrase or sentence) 2) qualitative and/or quantitative definition involving response (without prompting on 35 trials). The musical equivalent of the clinical language goal adds the context of the musical activity and might be: Within the context of a song, respond to "Wh" questions with a short phrase or sentence without prompting on 35 trials.

Relationship of Clinical Goal to Musical Objective

Assuming the therapist is working in the common language of the IEP or a child psychiatric hospitalization plan, the goals appear unrelated to the context of music. This can be problematic for the music therapist because, as a music therapist, one frequently works for *musical* goals, understanding their purpose in furthering the development of the child. A suggested compromise is to stage the language of the short-term objective, which is a means to the end goal in terms of the behavior seen in the context of the music activity, be it preplanned or improvisational, or the musi-

cal behavior in the session. Examples of this will be found in Chapter 5.

The specificity or lack of specificity of the goals will affect the writing of the objectives. If the IEP are broad and overlap several children, each broad goal statement leads to writing one objective for several children at a time (see Case Example One and Case Example Four, Chapter 5). If the IEP goals are specific and overlap fewer children, each specific goal statement can lead to one objective for one child. A reasonable shortcut involves the writing of one objective that encompasses different levels of specificity (see Case Example Two and Case Example Three, Chapter 5) toward the goal. In some cases, the terminal objective may actually be the IEP goal in the context of music activity (Case Example Three, Chapter 5).

REVIEW OF THE INDIVIDUAL EDUCATION PLAN

When reviewing the Individual Education Plan, it is important to remember that these are initially created by therapists and teachers from the child's home district who generally see the child on a one-time basis for intake. Subsequently, the IEP, is revised annually by the educational team serving the child. In these contexts, the Individual Education Plan may be viewed as a document "under construction."

In some states, there may be particular recommendations or trends by the Department of Education for the construction of the IEP. For example, in the State of Massachusetts, there is currently a trend to condense goals that encompass subsets of objectives (i.e., increase use of activities of daily living skills). On the other hand, the State of New Jersey has produced a document known as the "Core Curriculum Content Standards" which is used for all students in the state as well as a version called "Core Curriculum Content Standards for Students with Severe Disabilities" (June, 2000) used as a template for the IEP with multiply handicapped children. The New Jersey template specifically includes Visual/Performing Arts goals (see Chapter 1). The common denominator in all IEPs is the notion of accountability.

Although the annual meeting is considered the formal arena for reconstruction of IEP goals, objectives, methodology and services, based on additional input from the special education professionals at the school as well as the parents, one need not wait until June to reevaluate and question the stated goals of the IEP. Clinicians working in the child's school can suggest modification of some of the stated goals and objectives, relaying this information to the key representative of the child study team, frequently the school district social worker.

Music Therapist Initiating New Goals not Found on the Individual Education Plan or the Hospital Treatment Plan

Using the IEP goals of the team does not preclude the therapist from adding goals specifically related to music whether this is part of the IEP template (see IEP template for the State of New Jersey which includes Visual/Performing Arts), the hospital treatment plan, or not. The music therapy context is unique and it is quite possible that the music therapist will be in a position to suggest alteration of existing goals or additional goals based on the behavior of the child. This information needs to be brought to the attention of the child study team or hospital treatment team, and whenever possible, integrated into the plan.

RATIONALE FOR GOAL SETTING

One of the most concrete reasons to set observable goals is to quantify the amount of progress a child makes. The end result of this will validate the modality of music therapy and respond to the goals of the Individual Education Plan, a plan that dictates funding of supplementary services.

In the context of the inpatient child psychiatric setting, the results of the treatment plan will further demonstrate the efficacy of music therapy and can also prove evaluative (Goodman, 1989) in context of the music therapy assessment. Assessment information can prove valuable for

other professionals who will work with the child when the child is discharged from the hospital.

GOAL SETTING IN THE GROUP: CREATING THE DEVELOPMENTAL GRID

The developmental grid represents a means of organization for both the individual child and the group in therapy or special education. For purposes of this chapter, the focus is the organization of goals for the group.

An example of the grid is shown in Table 4.1. The grid includes the respective names of the children longitudinally and the goals pertaining to four developmental areas horizontally. In this way it is easier to see the goal areas that overlap in the session as well as the goal areas that are most germane to music therapy.

All Individual Education Plan goals are initially indicated on the grid in order to then analyze their relevance to the music therapy session.

Step 1 A: Review of Team Information

When working within a school setting, it is important to review all the Individual Education Plans of the children the therapist will be working with. Further, it is vital to review this information and evaluate it with the therapeutic/educational team one is working with. This may include the following: 1) Special education teacher; 2) Speech language pathologist; 3) Occupational therapist; 4) Physical therapist; 5) School psychologist or Learning Disabilities Teaching Consultant. The purpose of all this networking is to gain varied perspectives on the goals that have been set by district personnel on the IEP.

Step 1 B: Organization of Ideas within the Developmental Grid

It is generally easiest to use the four developmental areas of communication, motor (gross and fine), cognition and social-emotional behavior, commonly referred to as learning *domains,* in constructing a developmental grid. In situations where the IEP is constructed within other frames of reference (i.e., Curriculum Content Standards), it is up to the music therapist to either use those frames of reference, or transfer the information into the developmental area that seems most appropriate. For purposes of clarification, developmental areas are simplistically defined here.

COMMUNICATION: This area can include, but is not delimited to the following items: nonverbal communication (i.e., eye contact, body posture, facial expression), specific articulation goals, specific levels of receptive language, specific levels of expressive language, quantity and quality of language.

MOTOR: This area can include, but is not delimited to the following items: specific levels of gross motor behavior, specific levels of fine motor behavior; quality and quantity of gross and fine motor behaviors.

COGNITION: This area can include, but is not delimited to the following items: ability to follow directions, learning style, sensory issues that impact on learning, level of learning, specific cognitive stages related to theories of development and psychodynamic psychology, preacademic and academic skills that can be incorporated through music.

SOCIAL-EMOTIONAL: This area can include, but is not delimited to the following items: developmental levels of relatedness, quality and quantity of relatedness, impulse control, themes of relatedness, ability to effectively participate in group.

Step 2: Evaluating Group Priorities

Which goals overlap between children in the group?

1. Review goals to see if any are written in a similar fashion.
2. Review goals of seemingly disparate nature that relate to the same goal area (i.e., receptive language, expressive language, paying attention, participation, and so on) but under different conditions or levels of achievement.
3. In doing so, look for key words such as "partic-

ipate," "demonstrate," "awareness of," "identify," and so forth.
4. Review goals that overlap between developmental areas (most do) and delimit their inclusion in the session plan by deciding which developmental area they fit best.

Step 3: Evaluation Priorities for Group Music Therapy Goals

Which goals are best addressed through music therapy?

1. Review goals to determine which are best addressed through music.
2. Eliminate goals that are context specific and cannot be addressed in music therapy.
3. Prioritize goals that focus on communication and socialization, especially in the case of a child psychiatric group, where the cognitive goals and motor goals, relatively speaking, are of secondary concern.
4. Prioritize a number of goals that can be handled in terms of methods and evaluation.

Step 4: Considering Stumbling Blocks

Even after the therapist decides on overlapping goals that appear to be best addressed through music therapy, there are invariably inconsistencies. *Clearly, not every child in the group has the same goals.* Therefore, it becomes necessary for the therapist to design activities that, in effect, "juggle" the varying needs of different children in the group. The skilled therapist is able to design and/or spontaneously develop musical activity that addresses different goals at the same time. Further, she must be able to evaluate the ongoing goals at the same time. The difficulty of this is obvious. Therefore, the therapist must be cautioned: *Do not design an activity meant to evaluate more goals than you can observe. It is fine to work on only one or two goals at a time.* Think quality observation and evaluation rather than quantity. This same rule applies to the therapist who *is handling several groups a day and has limited time for note taking.*

CASE EXAMPLES: CREATING DEVELOP-MENTAL GRID AND ESTABLISHING GROUP MUSIC THERAPY GOALS

Case Example One: Developmentally Delayed Preschoolers

The Group

This group is composed of six preschoolers who are developmentally delayed. They attend school out-of-district in a small model special education program. Chronologically 3–4 years old, their average functioning level is a developmental age of 2.5. There is a scatter of skills in all domains: motor, language, social, and communication with a transdisciplinary team of physical therapy, occupational therapy, play therapy, music therapy, special education and speech/language pathology all contributing to the session plans and meeting weekly to conference the children.

The clinical orientation of this facility is strongly geared to "Gentle Teaching" (McGee, 1991) and "Floortime" (Greenspan, 1998). These approaches engage a humanistic philosophy as well as developmental premise and psychodynamic awareness.

Despite this, there is a strong sense of order in the classroom, necessary for children who do not yet have the internal mechanisms to govern their own environment or effectively problem solve their communication and learning. The goals present the sense of developmental progress expected from the children. *They are specific and observable although not defined quantitatively (i.e., child will succeed at given task x# of times over x# of days, etc.) as seen in other Individual Education Plans.* Ultimately, in order to measure success for the various school districts, this school may have to impose numbers. Music therapy plays a large part in the school day. All the therapists and teachers have been taught how to infuse music into the day. There are transitional songs, songs used for the opening of the day, lunchtime, rest time, music time, of course, and finally, leaving to go home. The recognition of the importance of music in the child's day helps the music therapist feel a sense of belonging and acceptance in adopting and adapting IEP goals to the music therapy program. Other related personnel can in effect, reinforce these goals.

Table 4.1 represents the creation of the developmental grid for this group, the first step toward establishing group music therapy goals.

Step One: Creating the Developmental Grid

TABLE 4.1. DEVELOPMENTALLY DELAYED PRESCHOOLERS.

Name of Child	Cognition	Language	Social	Motor
Joseph	1) Decentured symbolic play across objects	1) Request help 2) Increase comments upon actions	1) Attending 2) Taking turns	1) Foam Boards 2) Increase equilibrium in walking
Amanda	1) Functional Play	1) Single word approximation to request and to comment on existence, non-recurrence.	1) Attending 2) Maintaining eye contact 3) Making interactive bids toward others.	1) Manipulating objects (stack), turn, open, close)

continued

TABLE 4.1. DEVELOPMENTALLY DELAYED PRESCHOOLERS–*Continued.*

Name of Child	Cognition	Language	Social	Motor
Tommy	1) Sequential play	1) Following one-step directions 2) Three word combinations (objects + attribution + action+	1) Control impulsive behavior 2) Decrease shoving	1) Sort by color 2) Use form boards 3) Mark/crayons 4) Tactile exploration
Samantha	1) Shapes and colors 2) Classification 3) Body Knowledge 4) Pattern imitation 5) Memory	1) Comprehension of "Wh" questions 2) Directives 3) Sequencing and retelling stories 4) Increasing grammatical complexity	1) Increasing attention 2) Decreasing tantrums	1) Scissor skills 2) Imitation 3) Motor planning
Paula	1) One-to-one correspondence 2) Classification 3) Memory 4) Number recognition	1) Topic maintenance 2) Sequencing and retelling stories 3) Memory of verbal information	1) Mastery 2) Motivation 3) Attention 4) Reducing extraneous talk	
Lawrence	1) Matching 2) Classification by one feature 3) One-to-one correspondence 4) Pattern imitation	1) Adjective +noun verb use 2) Word retrieval 3) Increasing grammatical complexity 4) Sequencing and retelling stories 5) comprehension of "Wh" questions	1) Sharing	1) Cutting

Step Two: Evaluating Group Priorities

The developmental grid shown for this group, Table 4.1, is based on IEP goals.

In evaluating group priorities, the therapist first poses the question, *what goals overlap for these children?* The answers follow here:

Related social goals: Include the following: 1) *attending* (Paula, Samantha, Amanda, Joseph); 2) *decreasing impulsivity* (covering the areas of extraneous talk, Paula; tantrumming, Samantha, shov-

ing, Tommy, impulsive behavior, Tommy) and 3) *taking turns/sharing* (Joseph, Lawrence)

Related communication goals: Include the following: 1) Comprehension of "Wh" questions (Samantha, Lawrence); 2) Sequencing and retelling stories (Paula, Lawrence, Samantha). 3) Increasing grammatical complexity (Samantha, Lawrence) as well as related expressive language goals, which could conceivably come under the same goal area. (Increase comments on actions, Joseph, three-word combination sentences,

Tommy).

Related cognitive goals: Include the following: 1) Classification (Paula, Samantha, and Lawrence); 2) Pattern imitation (Samantha, Lawrence); 3) Correspondence (Paula, Lawrence). These are specific skills in reference to three children, possibly from the same school district with overlapping styles of IEP goals. The other three children in the group define their cognitive goals in terms of developing and contrasting levels of play, namely functional (Amanda), decentered (Joseph) and sequential (Tommy). While these are not related cognitive goals, they each refer to a defined level of play which needs to be recognized and enhanced and could possibly be contained under the goal of "reinforce and increase developmental level of play."

Related motor goals: In this developmental grid only reference goal more than once, in reference to the "use of foam boards." Motor goals are, relatively speaking, the most underdeveloped part of the grid.

In response to the second question, *Which goals are best addressed through music therapy?* the therapist may reach the following conclusions:

1. The only twice mentioned motor goal is not applicable to a music therapy session;
2. *Correspondence and Classification* are cognitive goals that can both be addressed not only in the selection of instruments and the recognition of instrument families but also in song material detailing these concepts;
3. *Pattern imitation* can be reinforced in both vocal and instrumental activities;
4. *Functional, symbolic and sequential play* can all be addressed through instrumental and vocal activity;
5. *Attending* is a basic goal for music therapy;
6. Decreasing impulsivity is easily accomplished through the temporal nature of music activity;
7. *Taking turns and sharing* is a functional prerequisite in all group instrumental activity.

Note: If the therapist chooses to delimit the above goals, then the social goals (see number 5, 6, 7) will take precedence.

Step Three: Deciding on Group Goals

Accordingly, the group goals established for the first clinical example are as follows:

Cognitive goals include the following:
1. Increase ability to classify (Paula, Samantha, Lawrence)
2. Increase ability for pattern imitation (Samantha, Lawrence)
3. Increase ability for one-to-one correspondence (Paula, Lawrence)
4. Establish appropriate level of learning, (i.e.,
   • Functional (Amanda)
   • Decentered (Joseph)
   • Sequential (Tommy)

Communication goals include the following:
1. Increase comprehension of "Wh" questions (Samantha, Lawrence)
2. Increase ability to sequence and retell stories (Paula, Lawrence, Samantha)
3. Increase grammatical complexity (Samantha, Lawrence), comments on actions (Joseph) and three-word combination sentences (Tommy).

Social goals include the following:
1. Increase attending skills (Paula, Samantha, Amanda, Joseph)
2. Decrease impulsivity in reference to extraneous talk (Paula), tantrumming (Samantha), shoving and impulsive behavior (Tommy)
3. Increase ability to take turns (Joseph) and share (Lawrence)

Motor Goals–to be clarified by occupational and physical therapists in classroom, working in tandem with sending district professionals.

Step Four: Handling Stumbling Blocks

The IEP goals for these children do not indicate measurable behavior as a annual goal. Therefore, it will be helpful to do a preassessment of functional skills in the first few sessions in order to evaluate the degrees of change at the middle and end of the school year. There is one member of the group, Amanda, who is clearly lowest functioning. She can, however, be a part of all activities but with limited expectations on the part of the therapist. In designing and carrying out activities, the therapist must provide varying degrees of expectation. This way of working will be illustrated in Chapter 5, "Methods."

Case Example Two: Preschool Autistic Spectrum Disorder (Goodman, K., 1992–1998)

The Group

This case concerns a group of five boys, chronologically ages three and four, attending the same school cited in case example one. These boys are functioning developmentally at a higher level, closer to 3 years or above. However, they all share the diagnosis of autistic spectrum disorder. As such, they have significant deficits in relatedness. The fact that Andrew is beginning to read and Theo and Jacob are creative in terms of creating drama does not discount their social issues. Here again, then, the goals are presented in observable fashion but are not quantifiable. Since this is an older case study, it is likely that current practice at that time did not mandate quantifiable goals for the IEP as it does now. The means of reaching these goals will be largely creative since the boys have strengths in music, drama and art.

Table 4.2 represents the creation of the developmental grid for this group, the first step toward establishing group music therapy goals.

Step One: Creating the Develomental Grid

TABLE 4.2. PRESCHOOL AUTISTIC SPECTRUM DISORDER GROUP.

Name	Cognition	Language	Fine and Gross Motor	Social
Jonathan	1. Practice following nonroutine directions 2. Practice problem solving. 3. Practice acting out stories with friends. 4. Practice generalizing size concepts. 5. Practice recalling and sequencing past events.	1. Practice using language to plan and describe. 2. Practice responding contingently. 3. Practice using "ing." 4. Practice using past tense.	1. Practice cutting curved shapes 2. Practice printing first name. 3. Practice responding to directions in games. 4. Practice participating in rule-based games. 5. Practice skipping. 6. Practice catching a ball.	1. Practice participating with peer in routine. 2. Practice sharing and turn-taking. 3. Practice increasing length of interactions with peers. 4. Practice conforming to game rules.
Andrew	1. Practice solving problems. 2. Practice decentered play. 3. Practice categorizing. 4. Practice reading.	1. Practice responding to directions. 2. Practice commenting. 3. Practice use of recurrence.	1. Practice modulation with glue. 2. Practice coloring in defined space. 3. Practice responding to directions in games.	1. Practice joint regard. 2. Practice responding to peers.

continued

TABLE 4.2. PRESCHOOL AUTISTIC SPECTRUM DISORDER GROUP–*Continued.*

Name	Cognition	Language	Fine and Gross Motor	Social
Theo	1. Practice recalling events. 2. Practice problem solving. 3. Practice acting out stories with friends. 4. Practice adding new components in play. 5. Practice sound/letter correspond.	1. Practice using language to plan and describe. 2. Practice using "and" and "because." 3. Practice responding contingently.	1. Practrice cutting complex shapes. 2. Practice copying complex shapes. 3. Practice printing name. 4. Practice responding to directions in games. 5. Practice participation in rule-based games. 6. Practice balancing on one foot.	1. Practice participating with peer in routine. 2. Practice sharing and turn-taking. 3. Practice increasing length of interactions with peers. 4. Practice responding to others with words.
Jacob	1. Practice discriminating labels and shapes. 2. Practice grouping by attributes. 3. Practice completing sequences. 4. Practice adding new components in play.	1. Practice informing. 2. Practice narrating events. 3. Practice staying on topic. 4. Practice asking what and where questions.	1. Practice copying simple shapes. 2. Practice cutting paper in two. 3. Practice responding to directions in games. 4. Practice galloping.	1. Practice participating with peer in routine. 2. Practice sharing. 3. Practice increasing length of interactions.
Mark	1. Practice finishing activity. 2. Practice quantitaative concepts. scripts. 4. Practice decentered play. 5. Practice sequencing concepts.	1. Practice responding to what and where. 2. Practice responding to topics. 3. Practice causality. 4. Practice connecting thoughts.	1. Practice modulation with glue. 2. Practice coloring. 3. Practice cutting. 4. Practice copying shapes 5. Practice responding to directions in games. 6. Practice alternating feet on staircase.	1. Practice joint regard. 2. Practice responding to peers. to peers.

Step Two: *Evaluating Group Priorities*

The grid shown for this group, Table 4.2, is a collection of goals derived from IEPs.

In evaluating group priorities, the therapist first poses the question, *what goals overlap for these children?* The answers follow here. Note that due to various levels of goal achievement expected for different children in the group, the general heading for each goal will only hold definition and meaning if it includes the specific goal expectations for various children in the group. Further objectives (see Chapter 5) will proceed accordingly.

Related social goals include the following:

1. Participate in peer interaction
   • In routine (Jonathan, Theo, Jacob)
   • Sharing and taking turns (Jonathan, Theo, Jacob)
   • Increasing length of interaction (Jonathan, Theo, Jacob)
   • Responding (Andrew, Mark)
   • Initiating (Mark)
   • With words (Theo)
   • By conforming to game rules (Jonathan)
   • With joint regard (Andrew, Mark)
   • Decentered play (Andrew, Mark)
2. Complete activity (Mark)

Related communication goals include the following:

1. Extend expressive language:
   • Plan and describe (Jonathan; Theo)
   • Respond contingently (Jonathan, Theo, Mark)
   • "Ing" (Jonathan)
   • Past tense (Jonathan)
   • Respond to directions (Andrew)
   • Commenting (Andrew)
   • Recurrence (Andrew)
   • Causality
   • "And" and "because" (Theo)
   • Informing (Jacob)
   • Narrate events (Jacob)
   • Stay on topic and complete sentences (Jacob)
   • Practice connecting (Mark)
   • Ask what and where questions (Jacob)
   • Respond to what/where

Related cognitive goals include the following:

1. Extend ideas
   • Nonroutine directions (Jonathan)
   • Problem solving (Jonathan, Andrew, Theo)
   • Acting out stories (Jonathan, Theo)
   • Add new components in play (Theo, Jacob)
   • Changes in scripts (Gabriel)
2. Increase ability to discriminate and classify information:
   • Discriminate labels and shapes (Jacob)

   • Grouping by attributes (Jacob)
   • Generalizing size concepts (Jonathan)
   • Categorizing (Andrew)
3. Increase memory and sequential ability:
   • Recall (Theo, Jonathan) and sequence past events (Jonathan)
   • Complete sequences (Jacob)

Related motor goals include the following:

1. Respond to directions in games, (Jonathan, Andrew, Theo, Jacob, Mark)
2. Increase motor skills by:
   • Galloping (Jacob)
   • Balancing on one foot (Theo)
   • Skipping (Jonathan)
   • Catching a ball (Jonathan)
   • Alternating feet (Mark)

In response to the second question, *which goals are best addressed through music therapy?* the therapist may reach the following conclusions:

1. *Social:* Peer interaction and the motivation to complete activity are necessary components of any group music therapy activity that can be structured by the therapist.
2. *Expressive Language:* Any aspect of expressive language can be addressed in the course of conversation with a child as the therapist models the appropriate level of language. In music, the song is an ideal way to introduce interactive levels of language.
3. *Cognition A:* Extending ideas is a logical process when children are pursuing song-writing, musical drama, instrumental "stories" and movement drama.
4. *Cognition B:* Discriminating and classifying are easily accomplished when selecting and describing types of and families of instruments, whether they are being played or listened to.
5. *Memory and sequential ability* are interrelated with the extension of ideas.
6. *Motor A:* Responding to directions is a natural part of any movement, instrumental or interactive song activity whether it be precomposed or improvised.
7. *Motor B:* incorporating various movements in

any activity directive is easily accomplished and aided by temporal organization.

Note: If the therapist chooses to delimit the number of goals, then the social and expressive language goals will take precedence.

Step Three: Deciding on Group Goals

Accordingly, the group goals established for the second clinical example are as follows:

Social goals include the following:

1. Participate in peer interaction:
   • In routine (Jonathan, Theo, Jacob)
   • Sharing and taking turns (Jonathan, Theo, Jacob)
   • Increasing length of interaction (Jonathan, Theo, Jacob)
   • Responding (Andrew, Mark)
   • Initiating (Mark)
   • With words (Theo)
   • By conforming to game rules (Jonathan)
   • With joint regard (Andrew, Mark)
   • Decentered play (Andrew, Mark)
2. Complete activity (Mark)

Communication goals include the following:

1. Extend expressive language in the following manner
   • Plan and describe (Jonathan, Theo)
   • Respond contingently (Jonathan, Theo, Mark)
   • "Ing" (Jonathan)
   • Past tense (Jonathan)
   • Respond to directions (Andrew)
   • Commenting (Andrew)
   • Recurrence (Andrew)
   • Causality
   • "And" and "because" (Theo)
   • Informing (Jacob)
   • Narrate events (Jacob)
   • Stay on topic and complete sentences (Jacob)
   • Practice connecting (Mark)
   • Ask what and where questions (Jacob)
   • Respond to what and where questions (Mark)

Cognitive goals include the following:

1. Extend ideas by
   • Nonroutine directions (Jonathan)
   • Problem solving (Jonathan, Andrew, Theo)
   • Acting out stories (Jonathan, Theo)
   • Add new components in play (Theo, Jacob)
   • Changes in scripts (Mark)
2. Increase ability to discriminate and classify information:
   • Discriminate labels and shapes (Jacob)
   • Grouping by attributes (Jacob)
   • Generalizing size concepts (Jonathan)
   • Categorizing (Andrew)
3. Increase memory and sequential ability:
   • Recall (Theo, Jonathan) and sequence past events (Jonathan)
   • Complete sequences (Jacob)

Motor goals include the following:

1. Respond to directions in games, (Jonathan, Andrew, Theo, Jacob, Mark)
2. Increase motor skills by:
   • Galloping (Jacob)
   • Balancing on one foot (Theo)
   • Skipping (Jonathan)
   • Catching a ball (Jonathan)
   • Alternating feet (Mark)

Step Four: Handling Stumbling Blocks

In this group, it appears that there are two different levels of functioning or, in effect, two subgroups within the group: 1) Jonathan, Theo, Jacob; 2) Andrew and Mark. Each level must be dealt with. Although the goals are different they are all subsumed under the same general content areas. The higher functioning children, particularly in terms of relatedness, Jonathan, Theo and Jacob can therefore serve as models and possibly facilitators for the lower functioning children, Andrew and Mark.

As in the first case example, these IEP goals are not measurable and therefore will benefit from preassessment of baseline functioning in order to gain a comparative picture of how the children progress in mid-year and end of year reports. Although the group goals are *organized* under general terms (i.e., increase motor skills), the group goals include the detail of functioning levels for each child under the general term goal. As emphasized earlier in the book, the therapist should only plan to track behavior that can be observed and evaluated. There are so many detailed goals for this group that even the most seasonsed of therapists would have difficulty including all these goals in any one music therapy session.

Case Example Three: Multiply Handicapped Latency-Age Children (Goodman, K., 1996–2002)

The Group

This group of five latency-age children ranges in age from 10 to 13 years old. They attend a regional day school, which receives 31 sending districts throughout the state of New Jersey. The school has a wide variety of disabled children, ages 3–21. The goals in the IEP's for this group of multiply handicapped children are written from a variety of school districts and from different professionals within each school districts. The goals in the IEPs lack a uniform level of specificity. One example of this is the specificity of Dora's cognition goals compared to the vagueness of her language, social and motor goals. More information will be needed to clarify the expectation of the

school district that is sending her to our school. In other situations, there are goal areas which go unaddressed, such as Patrick's needs in social and/or motor realms.

The facility itself makes no effort to define any type of clinical orientation. Transdisciplinary team members serve the facility from occupational therapy, physical therapy, music therapy, speech/language pathology, social work, psychology and special education. The extent to which professionals communicate with each other is not fixed by schedule. This makes the implementation of goals more difficult.

Developmentally, these group members range from preschool to early grade school, with a variety of physical and attentional difficulties. Dora has a nurse to assist her since she is medically fragile and quadriplegic; Jared is extremely hyperactive and demanding and therefore consumes a great deal of the teacher aide's attention; Richard relies on a great deal of attention from the therapist and can be passive-aggressive when he does not get this attention; he is apraxic. Evan is a Rett's child and although he loves music, he is often distracted by his sensory preoccupations. It is not a group that works easily and therefore will require a great deal of structure from the therapist. Table 4.3 represents the creation of the developmental grid for this group, the first step toward establishing group music therapy goals.

Step One: Creating the Develomental Grid

TABLE 4.3. MULTIPLY HANDICAPPED LATENCY-AGE GROUP.

Name of Child	Cognition	Language	Social	Motor
Dora	1. Identify all 26 manuscript letters and their sounds (D) 2. Identify eleven color words (D). 3. Identify 12 words frequently seen on signs and 13 other sight words (D). 4. Identify numerals	1. Expand her receptive vocabulary (D). 2. Improve response to yes/no questions (D). 3. Develop the use of computer skills for communication (D). 4. Develop the use of augmentative device	1. Demonstrate an interest in group activities (D). 2. Enjoy attention from peers and adults (D).	1. Child will increase developmentally progressive fine/gross motor behaviors. 2. Develop gestures to communicate her needs and wants (D).

continued

TABLE 4.3. MULTIPLY HANDICAPPED LATENCY-AGE GROUP–*Continued.*

Name of Child	Cognition	Language	Social	Motor
	to five (D). 5. Demonstrate an understanding of quantitative concepts such as more/less, empty/full, and many/one (D).	for communication (D).		
Jared	1. Listen and respond to simple questions correctly across school environments (J). 2. Recognize and count numbers up to 30 (J). 3. Respond correctly when asked his address and phone number (J).	1. Expand his vocabulary as indicated by the correct use of temporal terms in response to simple questions, with verbal prompts, 3 out of 5 trials (J). 2. Read and combine a sight word vocabulary of 25 words (J).	1. Complete a simple 10-minutes classroom activity with minimal verbal prompting 4 out of 5 trials (J). 2. Behave appropriately during classroom activities, as measured by appropriate volume of verbalizations, reduction of inappropriate behaviors and attention-seeking noises (J). 3. Demonstrate increased awareness of his emotional states by spontaneously verbalizing his feelings (J). 4. Demonstrate increased frustration tolerance by maintaining appropriate behaviors in challenging circumstances (J).	1. Attend to verbal directions and modify movement to participate in variations of gross motor activities (J). 2. Choose between three recreational activities and engage in the chosen activity independently for 15 minutes (J).
Evan	1. Develop 1 to 1 correspondence for counting objects used during classroom activities, correctly counting on 3/5 occasions (E).	1. Use technology based materials for the expansion of vocabulary, language concepts, and listening skills for a 20 minute period on a one to one basis (E). 2. Expand his use of pictures and a low-tech augmentative device with voice output for communication and interaction (E). 3. Demonstrate understanding of verbal messages given	1. Use technology based materials for the expansion of vocabulary, language concepts, and listening skills for a 20 minute period on a one to one basis (E). 2. Expand his use of pictures and a low-tech augmentative device with voice output for communication and interaction (E). 3. Demonstrate understanding of verbal messages given only once by responding	1. Participate in group gross motor activities with minimal verbal redirection on 3/5 occasions (E).

continued

TABLE 4.3. MULTIPLY HANDICAPPED LATENCY-AGE GROUP–*Continued.*

Name of Child	Cognition	Language	Social	Motor
		only once by responding appropriately through pictures or action during one activity per day (E). 4. Read 10 sight words with comprehension (E).	appropriately through pictures or action during one activity per day (E). 4. Read 10 sight words with comprehension (E).	
Richard	1. Use whole numbers to count groups of objects within the context of everyday tasks (R). 2. Find correct monetary amounts from coins presented in order to "purchase" snack daily (R). 3. Verbally communicate home address including street, town, state, and country when asked (R).	1. Intelligibly verbalize wants, needs, and feelings given only one chance for self correction (R). 2. Spontaneously verbalize wants, needs, and feelings to appropriate staff (R). 3. Demonstrate comprehension of verbal information through appropriate verbal responses on 4/5 opportunities (R). 4. Demonstrate pre-readiness reading skills by recognizing up to 35 words presented in a variety of ways and environments (R).	1. Complete seatwork independently on 3/5 days given only verbal instructions (R). 2. Improve classroom sitting posture with verbal prompting 3/5 times on increased attention to task (R). 3. Participate in group activities with a maximum of 2 verbal redirections (R).	
Patrick	1. Use whole numbers to count groups of objects within the context of everyday tasks (P) 2. Find correct monetary amounts from coins presented in order to "purchase" snack daily (P). 3. Verbally communicate home address including street, town, state, and country when asked (P).	1. Verbalize wants and needs clearly and intelligibly by repeating a 4-word phrase (P). 2. Demonstrate comprehension and retention of auditory input during group activity by responding appropriately, given adequate processing time (P). 3. Demonstrate pre-readiness skills by recognizing up to 40 words presented in a variety of ways and environments (P).		

Step Two: Evaluating Group Priorities

The grid shown for this group, Table 4.3, is a collection of goals derived from IEPs.

In evaluating group priorities, the therapist first poses the question, *what goals overlap for these children?* The answers follow here:

Related social goals include the following:
1. Participation in activity with:
   • A maximum of two verbal redirections (Richard)
   • ten-minute period with minimal verbal prompting, 4 out of 5 trials (Jared)
   • in gross motor/balance activity with verbal prompts only (Patrick)
   • with minimal verbal prompting and decreased behavioral response at least once during session (Jared)
   • interest (Dora)
   • for up to 1/2 hour during each school day with prompting and redirection (Evan)
   • Demonstrate awareness of the need for help by appropriately accessing pictures or gesturing on 3/5 (session) days (Evan)
   • of emotional states by spontaneously verbalizing feelings (Jared)
   • of increased frustration tolerance by maintaining appropriate behaviors when challenged (Jared)
   • attention from peers and adults (Dora)
2. Practice "appropriate" behavior as defined below:
   • appropriate volume of verbalizations, reduction of inappropriate behaviors and attention-seeking noises (Jared)
   • appropriateness in challenging circumstances (Jared)
3. Initiate parallel play with a classmate once during each school day (Evan)

Related communication goals include the following:

1. Use of augmentative device
   • develop for communication (Dora)
   • expand use of low-tech augmentative device with voice output for communication and interaction (Evan)
2. Receptive vocabulary

   • expand (Dora)
   • Improve response to yes/no questions (Dora)
   • responding appropriately through pictures or action during one activity per day (Evan)
   • Demonstrate comprehension of verbal information through appropriate verbal responses on 4/5 opportunities (Richard)
3. Expressive communication
   • Spontaneously verbalize wants, needs, and feelings to appropriate staff (Richard)
   • Verbalize wants and needs clearly and intelligibly by repeating a 4-word phrase (Patrick)
   • Demonstrate comprehension and retention of auditory input during group activity by responding appropriately, given adequate processing time (Patrick)
   • Intelligibly verbalize wants, needs, and feelings given only one chance for self-correction (Richard)
   • Correct use of temporal terms in response to simple questions, with verbal prompts, 3 out of 5 trials (Dora)
   • Use of sight words (Richard)
   • Demonstrate prereadiness reading skills by recognizing up to 35 words presented in a variety of ways and environments (Richard)
   • Demonstrate prereadiness skills by recognizing up to 40 words presented in a variety of ways and environments (Patrick)

Related cognitive goals include the following:

1. Preacademic:
   • Identify 11 color words (Dora)
   • Identify 12 words frequently seen on signs and 13 others sight words (Dora)
   • Identify numerals to 5 (Dora)
   • Identify all 26 manuscript letters and their sounds (Dora)
   • Use whole numbers to count groups of objects within the context of everyday tasks (Richard)
   • Find correct monetary amounts from coins presented in order to "purchase" snack daily (Richard)
2. Verbally communicate home address including street, town, state, and country when asked (Richard, Patrick)

Related motor goals. Motor goals are, relatively speaking, the most underdeveloped part of the grid.

1. Increase developmentally progressive fine/gross motor behaviors (Dora)
2. Develop gestures to communicate needs and wants (Dora)
3. Modify movement to participate in variations of gross motor activities (Jared)
4. Participate in group gross motor activities with minimal verbal redirection on 3/5 occasions (Evan)

In response to the second question, *which goals are best addressed through music therapy?* the therapist may reach the following conclusions:

1. All social goals are relevant to music therapy group.
2. The majority of the communication goals are relevant to music therapy group and may also be couched in the manner that the therapist gives direction and receives feedback from the child. The goal of recognizing sight words may be better suited to the cognitive category and is not immediately relevant to music therapy.
3. All cognitive goals are preacademic. Although they can be approached through song, vocal and instrumental activities, they can also be approached in functional ways such as choosing the color of an instrument, counting instruments to give out to classmates, using theme-related pictures with simple words to decide on musical activities and making simple instruments in order to hold an instrument sale before lunchtime.
4. There are important social goals missing from these IEPs that may be added to the list. These include expression of feelings leading to simple problem-solving skills for those children with attentional difficulties.
5. Many of the aforementioned goals in the original grid are out of context, developmentally inappropriate, redundant or vague
   Note: With a group this large and the goals so disparate, it will probably be necessary, at least in beginning stages, to delimit goals to social and communication.

Step Three: Deciding on Group Goals

Accordingly, the group goals established for the third clinical example are as follows:

Social goals include the following:

1. Increase participation in activity:
   • a maximum of two verbal redirections (Richard)
   • ten-minute period with minimal verbal prompting, 4 out of 5 trials (Jared)
   • in gross motor/balance activity with verbal prompts only (Patrick)
   • With minimal verbal prompting and decreased behavioral response at least once during session (Jared)
   • interest (Dora)
   • for up to 1/2 hour during each school day with prompting and redirection (Evan)
   • participate in group gross motor activities with minimal verbal redirection on 3/5 occasions (Evan)
2. Increase awareness:
   • of the need for help by appropriately accessing pictures or gesturing on 3/5 session days (Evan)
   • of emotional states by spontaneously verbalizing feelings (Jared)
   • of increased frustration tolerance by maintaining appropriate behaviors when challenged (Jared)
   • attention from peers and adults (Dora)
3. Practice "appropriate" behavior as defined below:
   • appropriate volume of verbalizations, reduction of inappropriate behaviors and attention-seeking noises (Jared)
   • appropriateness in challenging circumstances (Jared)
4. Initiate parallel play with a classmate once during each school day (Evan)

Communication goals include the following:

1. Use of augmentative device
   • expand use of low-tech augmentative device with voice output for communication and

interaction (Evan, Dora)
2. Increase receptive vocabulary at appropriate developmental level
   • Improve response to yes/no questions (Dora)
   • Responding appropriately through pictures or action during one activity per day (Evan)
   • Demonstrate comprehension of verbal information through appropriate verbal responses on 4/5 opportunities (Richard)
3. Increase expressive communication at appropriate developmental level
   • Spontaneously verbalize wants, needs, and feelings to appropriate staff (Richard)
   • Verbalize wants and needs clearly and intelligibly by repeating a 4-word phrase (Patrick)
   • Demonstrate comprehension and retention of auditory input during group activity by responding appropriately, given adequate processing time (Patrick)
   • Intelligibly verbalize wants, needs, and feelings given only one chance for self correction (Richard)
   • Correct use of temporal terms in response to simple questions, with verbal prompts, 3 out of 5 trials (Jared)
   • Develop gestures to communicate needs and wants (Dora)

Cognitive goals include the following:

1. Increase preacademic skills at appropriate developmental level
   • Identify all 26 manuscript letters and their sounds (Dora)
   • Identify 11 color words (Dora)
   • Identify 12 words frequently seen on signs and 13 others sight words (Dora)
   • Identify numerals to 5 (Dora)
   • Use whole numbers to count groups of objects within the context of everyday tasks (Richard)
   • Find correct monetary amounts from coins presented in order to "purchase" snack daily (Richard)
   • Verbally communicate home address including street, town, state, and country when asked (Richard, Patrick)

Motor goals include the following (note: Motor goals are, relatively speaking, the most underdeveloped part of the grid).

1. Modify movement to participate in variations of gross motor activities (Jared)

Step Four: Handling Stumbing Blocks

The goals in the IEPs related to preacademic skills can be included in music therapy sessions but not to the exclusion of communication and socializations, key elements of the group's potential to help the children. There are children in the group who will need aides physically assisting them. This can be handled in the methods section of planning. It is mentioned here because it makes the "juggling" act of setting and observing goals more difficult.

As in the second case study, the therapist can organize the goal areas under various umbrella terms (i.e., increase expressive communication as developmentally appropriate) but this goal is not to exclude the specifics for each child. In this case study, we note the inconsistency of IEP goals in terms of measurable outcomes. However, compared to case study examples one, two and four, these IEP goals are the most specific in terms of looking for certain outcomes; perhaps because it is one of the more recent examples (Goodman, 1996–2002). Again, this problem can be counteracted by taking baseline information on current functioning levels related to goals and comparing this information to mid-year and end of year outcomes.

Case Example Four: Latency-age Child Psychiatric Group (Inpatient School Setting) (Goodman, K., 1981–1984)

The Group

This group of four latency-age children, ages 9–12, all brought to a private psychiatric hospital because of attempted suicide or consistent suicidal ideation, are diagnosed with various psychiatric disturbances: conduct disorder (Alan), clinical depression (Betsy), schizophrenic (Debbie) and bipolar disorder, manic phase (Edgar).

Since these children are temporarily housed in the hospital (several weeks to three months), their education is handled by the special education teacher in the unit classroom. She, in effect, prioritizes their goals based on their clinical needs and their emergency entrance into the hospital. The task, then, of the in-patient psychiatric unit staff, therapists, doctors and teachers, is to emotionally stabilize the child so that they may leave the hospital in due time and return to their homes or residential settings, as necessary.

In this case, then, the educational and clinical goals overlap well and it is easy for the therapist to derive a treatment plan from these goals. Since the stay is a short one, it is likely that the composition of the group will change quickly, adding another challenge to the changing constellation of group goals. Table 4.4 represents the creation of the developmental grid for this group, the first step toward establishing group music therapy goals.

Step One: Creating the Develomental Grid

TABLE 4.4. LATENCY-AGE CHILD PSYCHIATRIC GROUP.

Name of Child	Social	Communication	Cognitive	Motor
Alan	1. Increase peer interaction. 2. Reduce suicidal ideation. 3. Reduce impulsivity. 4. Increase aware-ess of mood.	1. Use of first person pronouns.	1. Increase ability to problem solve.	1. Reduce self-stimulating habits.
Betsy	1. Increase peer interaction. 2. Reduce suicidal ideation. 3. Increase positive affect. 4. Increase aware-ness of mood.	1. Thought completion.	1. Increase ability to problem solve.	1. Increase participation in movement.
Debbie	1. Increase peer interaction. 2. Reduce suicidal ideation. 3. Reduce rigidity in play patterns. 4. Increase aware-ness of mood.	1. Decrease irrelevant communication.	1. Increase ability to problem solve.	1. Increase flexibility in movement.
Edgar	1. Increase peer interaction. 2. Reduce suicidal ideation. 3. Increase aware-ness of mood. 4. Decrease impulsivity.	1. Decrease ideas of flight.	1. Increase ability to problem solve.	1. Decrease impulsivity in movement.

Step Two: Evaluating Group Priorities

The grid shown above is a collection of goals derived from IEPs.

In evaluating group priorities, the therapist poses the question, *what goals overlap for these children?* The answers follow here:

Related social goals include the following:

1. Increase peer interaction (Edgar, Debbie, Betsy, Alan)
2. Reduce suicidal ideation (Edgar, Debbie, Betsy, Alan)
3. Increase awareness of mood (Edgar, Debbie, Betsy, Alan)
4. Decrease impulsivity (Edgar, Alan)
5. Reduce rigidity in play patterns (Debbie)
6. Increase positive affect (Betsy)

Related communication goals include the following:

1. Use of first person pronouns (Alan)
2. Thought completion (Betsy)
3. Decrease irrelevant communication (Debbie)
4. Decrease ideas of flight (Edgar)

Related cognitive goals include the following:

1. Increase ability to problem solve (Edgar, Debbie, Betsy, Alan)

Related motor goals include the following:

1. Reduce self-stimulating habits (Alan)
2. Increase participation in movement (Betsy)
3. Increase flexibility in movement (Debbie)
4. Decrease impulsivity in movement (Edgar)

In response to the second question, *"Which goals are best addressed through music therapy?"* The therapist may reach the following conclusions:

All goals relate to psychiatric disturbance and dysfunctional temperament. They are all easily and healthfully approached in music therapy.

Step Three: Deciding on Group Goals

Accordingly, the group goals established for the

fourth clinical example are as follows:

Social Goals

1. Increase peer interaction (Edgar, Debbie, Betsy, Alan)
2. Reduce suicidal ideation (Edgar, Debbie, Betsy, Alan)
3. Increase awareness of mood (Edgar, Debbie, Betsy, Alan)
4. Decrease impulsivity (Edgar, Alan)
5. Reduce rigidity in play patterns (Debbie)
6. Increase positive affect (Betsy)

Communication Goals

1. Use of first person pronouns (Alan)
2. Thought completion (Betsy)
3. Decrease irrelevant communication (Debbie)
4. Decrease ideas of flight (Edgar)

Cognitive Goal

1. Increase ability to problem solve (Edgar, Debbie, Betsy, Alan)

Motor Goals

1. Reduce self-stimulating habits (Alan)
2. Increase participation in movement (Betsy)
3. Increase flexibility in movement (Debbie)
4. Decrease impulsivity in movement (Edgar)

Step Four: Handling Stumbling Blocks

Due to the relatively rapid turnover in the group composition, goals will have to be reevaluated on a week-to-week basis. In this regard, some of the goals may be viewed as evaluative rather than treatment goals (see Goodman, 1989). Since goals are stated in relative terms of "increase" and "decrease," no concrete changes can be reported unless the therapist uses the first session to record baseline data.

A further stumbling block of this group is the wide variety of disturbance. Even though the children are not far apart in age, they demonstrate extremes in terms of their mood (i.e., manic, depressed) and their cognitive organization (rigidity, disorganized impulsive).

SUMMARY

These four case studies illustrate the working process of reviewing the Individual Education Plans or hospital treatment plans of group members and organizing and prioritizing the materials. As a practical consideration, this process takes a great deal of time. It is ongoing time since the therapist will, of course, update material on an ongoing basis. The only way that the therapist can "save" time, as it were, is to delimit goals. Hopefully, the goals focused on in the session will be the most meaningful in the work. In the next chapter, the analysis of goals leads the therapist to short-term musical objectives.

STUDY GUIDE QUESTIONS

1. How are IEP goals written?
2. How would you suggest music therapy goals be written?
3. What is a long-term goal given the context of the academic school year?
4. What is a developmental grid?
5. How is a developmental grid used to organize IEP information?
6. What are some of the possible shortcomings of goals on the IEP?
7. What steps should the music therapist go through to organize music therapy goals in the group setting?
8. Using a group of 4–6 children from your clinical setting, organize the IEP goals in the same process demonstrated in this chapter.

Chapter 5

Watching During Music Group: Objectives in Group Music Therapy

INTRODUCTION

RELATIONSHIP OF CLINICAL GOAL TO MUSICAL OBJECTIVE

In the last chapter, the process involved in reviewing, organizing and prioritizing goals of children assigned to a group music therapy session is presented. The long-term clinical goal is often achieved through what one might think of as baby steps, or a series of preliminary successes leading to the achievement of the goal. These preliminary successes are referred to as short-term objectives. For purposes of the music therapy session, it makes sense *to stage the language of the short-term objectives in terms of behavior in the context of the music therapy session and/or musical behavior in the session.*

Music therapy objectives proceed on two levels: 1)The musical experience supports changing non-music behavior; 2) The changes in the *musical* behavior of the child are intrinsically related to developmental gains. In formulating music therapy objectives, the music therapist clarifies what should be observed in the music therapy session, in terms of nonmusical and musical behaviors. This chapter gives examples of how music therapy objectives may be derived and written for the group.

DEFINING OBJECTIVES, CHALLENGES IN WRITING OBJECTIVES, RATIONALE FOR OBJECTIVES

For purposes of the education or hospital plan and for purposes of "translation" into the music therapy plan, the objectives constitute a series of steps which are short-term and lead to the achievement of the long-term goal. Short-term is a relative expression since one of the short-term objectives could take three months to achieve with the group meeting the therapist twice a week for 40-minute sessions. Some initial and commonplace suggestions for defining short-term objectives are indicated below.

THE DEFINITION OF SHORT-TERM OBJECTIVE, NOT NECESSARILY RELATED TO MUSIC THERAPY

The articulation of steps, which ultimately lead to clinical goal completion, can be defined as objectives.

Coleman (2002) gives us the acronym 'SMART," standing for "specific, measurable, attainable, realistic, time frame" to remind us of the pieces of any objective. Objectives rely on techniques such as shaping, successive approximation, fading, generalization, and, in general, successive levels of expectation (reached by task analysis). *Although these are behavioral terms, they can be reconsidered in terms of different language: working at the functional level of the child in the musical experience is to work at their present level in order to help them achieve successively higher gains* (shaping). *As the child gains independence in more challenging musical experiences and related developmental gains, the need for support decreases* (fading of prompts) *and the likelihood of the child's developmental gains transfer* (generalization) *to other settings.*

THE DEFINITION OF SHORT-TERM OBJECTIVE, RELATED TO MUSIC THERAPY

Quantitative Criteria

• The number of times a task is completed in the music activity
• The amount of time it takes, duration, to complete the task in the music activity.
• The percentage of time a task is completed during the suggested musical experience.
• The degrees of prompting during the music experience

Clinical Example, Nonmusic Behavior in Music Therapy Session

Clinical Goal 1: Children will sign the words "more" and "music"

Music Therapy Objective 1a: Child (Lori, Jared) will sign the word "more" on *one out of three trials* during the session when she/he wants more use of an instrument or a song.

Clinical Example, Nonmusic Behavior Prompted by Music

Music Therapy Objective 1b: Child (Lori, Jared) will sign the word "more" to the music on one out of three trials during the session in the musical context of an activity song (i.e., What do you say when you want more?).

Clinical Example, Musical Behavior in Music Therapy Session

Clinical Goal 1: Children will regulate activity levels accordingly on 3 out of 5 trials.
Music Therapy Objective 1a: Child (Lori, Jared) will decelerate or accelerate drum playing to match tempo of therapist in improvisation of varying tempo, 70–120, 3 out of 5 trials.

CHALLENGES IN WRITING OBJECTIVES

Challenges in writing musical objectives can be related to the following issues:

1. Practical considerations in tracking observable objectives.
2. Realistic anticipation of what the child(ren) can accomplish on a short-term basis.
3. Appropriate functional expectation for the number, duration and nature of prompts and cues.
4. Appropriate embedding of clinical short-term objective in musical task.
5. Clinical understanding of why the musical task easily embodies the clinical short-term objective.

Practical Considerations in Tracking Observable Objectives

The gap between setting observable quantifiable objectives and being able to keep track of what is really happening over the sessions is truly difficult and will be further discussed in the chapter on evaluation. *It may be these difficulties that form some of the resistance to formulating observable objectives, particularly in the process of music therapy which one hopes will be inherently artistic, creative and therefore spontaneous to a great extent.* So, as discussed earlier in this book, the therapist may not feel the necessity to set observable goals or objectives, particularly those that have the degree of specificity set in the IEP.

However, if the therapist can find a reasonable way of setting goals and objectives and tracking progress towards these, the work itself gains additional credibility. Suffice it to say then that *setting objectives is meaningless unless the therapist can keep track of responses.* Some suggestions, based on long-term clinical experience are:

1. Create an easy to use checklist chart to keep track of observable behaviors (see Chapter 8, Evaluation for sample checklist examples) with a code of graphics for various levels of participation and participation when prompted.
2. Do not set more objectives for a given session than you can reasonably keep track of.
3. Do not attempt to set up quantifiable information that will be impossible to keep track of.
4. Use the adjunct personnel in the room (i.e., teachers' aides, special education teacher, nurs-

ing aides, additional therapists, student interns, and so forth to help you keep track of what is happening. They can use the checklist and/or tell the therapist what they observed.

5. Consider notating information every other week, particularly if your group schedule is daunting.

6. Consider notating information when there is noteworthy change in behavior that conforms to progress or regression.

7. Make sure you have a wrist watch that is easy to read if you are keeping track of duration of time.

Observing and tracking progress or lack of progress is, admittedly, another task in running the group. Considering the fact that the therapist has to prepare the room for the group, premeditate the necessary instruments, music, props, and such consider the focus of the session before the children enter the room, it is easily understandable that this additional responsibility can feel daunting. However, it is also obvious that unless there is a concrete sense of where the group is going, the validity of the work is limited. *No matter what the clinical orientation of the therapist is, there must be a sense of direction toward helping each child in the group progress toward physical and mental growth.* The *objectives appear to be based on behavioral philosophy because they are stated in terms of observable behavior, however, the working philosophy of the therapist need not be behavioral.*

Realistic Anticipation of what the Child(ren) can Accomplish on a Short-Term Basis

Current Functioning Level

One of the points made in the last chapter was the criteria the music therapist needs to use in establishing goals. The same, of course, is true with objectives. One important criterion of any goal or objective is that it needs to be realistic–not too high, not too low. There are different ways to approach this realistic expectation of what the child(ren) can do in the group in progressing toward their goals. One suggested way is to start at

the highest level of functional behavior observed and work upward. If the child satisfies the minimal expectation, strive for more in the same session. Conversely, if the child does not satisfy the minimal expectation, aid the child with physical and/or verbal prompts, thereby taking a step backwards. Try to get a sense of the child's working pace in the session and the group's pace in working together with new materials or new expectations.

Case Example (Goodman, K., 1992–1998)

Howard is in a group of other moderately retarded children. He has a tendency to go off on verbal tangents, drawing attention to himself and away from interaction and participation with the group. The IEP goal related to this behavior calls for eliminating this behavior completely by the end of the year. In order to provide Howard with an experience that is appropriately attention-getting but also allows him to move toward completion of his goal, the therapist decides to use opening song material that allows Howard as well as the other children in the group to sing about themselves. The first week, the objective is for Howard to appropriately participate in this experience. The second week the objective is for Howard to not only participate in this experience but also tolerate listening to the other four children in the group without interrupting more than once. The third week the objective is for Howard to participate in the opening and also tolerate listening to the other four children without interrupting at all. As Howard's tolerance for listening to and engaging with the other children improves, his behavior can generalize to other experiences within music and, eventually, outside of the music room.

Appropriate Functional Expectations for the Number, Duration, and Nature of Prompts and Cues

This issue returns the therapist to the first issue, that of expectation for what the child can accomplish. The solution is the same, namely, start at the known functional level of the child in the group, assist as necessary but be quick to extinguish or drop the prompting as soon as possible since, of course, the ultimate objective is for behavior to be spontaneous rather than staged. Remember that the objective the therapist sets for the child in the activity is based on awareness of what the child can do. When the child surpasses the initial objective, the objectives need to be adapted. In this sense, then, the therapist is viewing developmental challenges, objectives, as embedded in varying musical experiences. As discussed in Chapter 6, "Methods," materials will be adapted to suit the completion of objectives. If, for example, the therapist is working on motor planning with children in the group through the realization of a simple dance experience, the beginning rendition of the song could conceivably involve over 20 steps (see below). Rather than expecting all children to complete this sequence, it will make more sense to adapt the dance to a few movement directives. As the children improve their motor planning, auditory processing and ability to follow directions, the dance can be adapted to accommodate greater challenge. Children motor plan at their appropriate developmental level within the group activity.

Appropriate Embedding of Clinical Short-Term Objective in Musical Task

This issue leads to the proverbial question, "What comes first, the chicken or the egg?" The direction of the child's musical interest should pave the way for the therapist to embed the short-term objectives into the musical task. This can be accomplished on two levels: 1) Preplanned experiences or repertoire of materials that the children are fond of in order to embed short-term objectives; 2) Spontaneous musical experience based on what happens in the session that also embeds short-term objectives. *Ideally, the session should contain both preplanned and improvisational and/or spontaneous musical material . . . as the session unfolds.* What this ultimately means is that the *therapist must have a very comfortable grasp of what the goals and objectives are for the children and how these embed themselves into musical materials.*

Clinical Understanding of why the Musical Task Easily Embodies the Clinical Short-Term Objective

The joy of doing music therapy for the children in the group frequently involves what is called a *naturalistic* approach. That is to say that the music therapy takes advantage of child-initiated interactions and uses naturally occurring consequences. While the therapist may premeditate a certain level of developmental learning through music activities, *it is the momentum of the musical moments themselves that leads to more and more naturally occurring developmental interactions through singing, playing instruments, moving to and listening to music.*

REVIEW OF GOAL INFORMATION, ORGANIZATION OF IDEAS FOR WRITING OBJECTIVES

Following are the *suggested steps the therapist can take when formulating objectives.* These steps will be demonstrated through the following of the four case studies originally presented in Chapter 4.

Suggested Steps for Writing Music Therapy Objectives

1. Review group goals.
2. Anticipate which musical interests/activities the group is working on in the session.
3. Establish which goals are logically embedded in music interests/activities the group is working on in the session (i.e., communication linked to songs; motor linked to movement; cognition linked to problem-solving musical solutions and levels of play; social goals linked to behavior throughout session) in order to link goals and music interests/activities.
4. Break down goals into gradations of expectation (clinical objectives) frequently based on quantitative criteria.
5. Modify the clinical objectives to suit the context of the musical activities.

6. As necessary, vary the expectations for each child involved in the objective.
7. A logical format for writing the goals and objectives is the following:

Goal 1:
1a. Objective
1b. Objective
1c. Objective

CASE EXAMPLES

As the reader will remember, four sample groups are presented in Chapter 4 and set forth goals for these groups. These groups are presented here again in order to demonstrate the process of setting up sample short-term objectives.

Case Example One: Developmentally Delayed Preschoolers (Goodman, K., 1992–1998)

Step One: Review Goals Previously Established for Group (see Chapter 4)

Cognitive Goals

1. Increase ability to classify (Paula, Samantha, Lawrence)
2. Increase ability for pattern imitation (Samantha, Lawrence)
3. Increase ability for one-to-one correspondence (Paula, Lawrence)
4. Establish appropriate level of learning
   • Functional (Amanda)
   • Decentered (Joseph)
   • Sequential (Tommy)

Communication Goals

1. Increase comprehension of "Wh" questions (Samantha, Lawrence)
2. Increase ability to sequence and retell stories (Paula, Lawrence, Samantha)
3. Increase grammatical complexity (Samantha, Lawrence), comments on actions (Joseph) and 3-word combination sentences (Tommy)

Social Goals

1. Increase attending skills (Paula, Samantha, Amanda, Joseph)
2. Decrease impulsivity in reference to extraneous talk (Paula), tantrumming (Samantha), shoving and impulsive behavior (Tommy)
3. Increase ability to take turns (Joseph) and share (Lawrence)

Motor Goals—to be clarified by occupational and physical therapists in classroom, working in tandem with sending district professionals.

Step Two: Anticipate which Musical Interests/Activities the Group is Working on in the Session

This group is enthusiastic about taking turns for drum/piano improvisation, imitating short melodies on the xylophone, helping the therapist set up and put away the instrument families in the music room, getting ready for their Halloween party in the classroom, and learning short movement activities.

Step Three: Establish which Goals are Logically Embedded in Music Interests/ Activities the Group is Working on in the Session in Order to Link Goals and Music Interests/Activities

Classification is logically linked to setting up and putting away the instruments. Pattern imitation is logically linked to playing melodic and rhythmic sequences.

Communication (comprehension, grammatical complexity, retelling stories) is linked to ongoing communication about materials being using in the group as well as the use of song material, both precomposed and spontaneous. Socializing skills and impulse control are linked to the temporal nature of all music activities and the interaction inherent in sharing time and materials in the session.

Step Four: Breakdown Goals into Gradations of Expectation, Frequently Based on Quantitative Criteria

These objectives demonstrate beginning and intermediate (see *classify half, imitate at least two of the pitches, match one of five photographs, etc., duration of two minutes*) levels of progress toward the goal.

Step Five: Modify the Clinical Objectives to Suit the Context of the Musical Activities

The objectives are staged within music activities involving the set-up of the instruments, instrument selection, and sharing instruments as well as playing of pentatonic patterns on the xylophone, and vocal selections that allow the children to expand vocabulary and interact appropriately with each other.

Step Six: As Necessary, Vary the Expectations for Each Child Involved in the Objective

This is a more homogeneous group since there are more overlapping objectives. Attending skills for Paula, Samantha, Amanda and Joseph vary in the objective under Social goals (1a).

Sample Objectives Related to Goals Arrived at for this Group

Cognitive Goals/Objectives

1. Increase ability to classify (Paula, Samantha, Lawrence)
   1a. Given a variety of four percussion and four melodic instruments, children (Paula, Samantha, Lawrence) will *classify half* of the instruments appropriately into two groups and *receive verbal cues* as necessary in order to complete this task.
2. Increase ability for pattern imitation (Samantha, Lawrence)
   2a. Given a model of a simple pentatonic pattern, 1–2–3–2–1, on the xylophone, the children (Samantha, Lawrence) will *imitate at least two of the pitches* in the pattern correctly and *receive visual prompting* as necessary in order to complete this task.

3. Increase ability for one-to-one correspondence (Paula, Lawrence)
   3a. In this session, given photographs of instruments in the music room, the children (Paula, Lawrence) will *match one of five photographs to the appropriate instrument on the table.*
4. Establish appropriate level of learning: functional (Amanda), decentered (Joseph) or sequential (Tommy)
   4a. Given a drum to beat, child (Amanda) will play in rhythm with the piano for a *duration of two minutes,* thereby establishing functional use of the instrument
   4b. Given a drum to beat, child (Tommy) *will follow at least two of five sequences of sound rhythms modeled* by the therapist.

Communication Goals/Objectives

1. Increase comprehension of "Wh" questions (Samantha, Lawrence)
   1a. Given the activity song, (name), based on comprehension of "what," "which," "when," "where," child (Samantha, Lawrence) will respond appropriately to at least one directive.
2. Increase ability to sequence and retell stories (Paula, Lawrence, Samantha)
   2a. After hearing a familiar Halloween song, child (Paula, Lawrence, Samantha) will sing with the group, repeating two of three sequential details in the song.
3. Increase grammatical complexity (Samantha, Lawrence), comments on actions (Joseph) and three-word combination sentences (Tommy)
   3a. Given the song, "Windy Wind" (Levin & Levin, 1997), child will sing about what the wind can do in a subject-verb combination (Tommy, Samantha) or subject-verb-direct object combination (Lawrence, Joseph) (2 out of 3 times).

Social Goals/Objectives

1. Increase attending skills (Paula, Samantha, Amanda, Joseph)
   1a. Given the song, "Hokey Pokey," Joseph will follow one of three directives in a given

sequence and Paula, Samantha and Amanda will follow two of three directives in a given sequence.

2. Decrease impulsivity in reference to extraneous talk (Paula), tantrumming (Samantha), shoving and impulsive behavior (Tommy)

   2a. During a 40-minute session, children will be able to avoid tantrumming (Samantha), as well as shoving or impulsive behavior (Tommy) during the first 20 minutes, with slow firm guidance as necessary.

3. Increase ability to take turns (Joseph) and share (Lawrence)

   3a. Given a variety of musical activities that require taking turns and sharing, children (Joseph, Lawrence) will be able to spontaneously take turns one of three times and share one of three times with verbal prompting.

Case Example Two: Preschool Autistic (Goodman, K., 1992–1998)

Step One: Review Goals Previously Established for Group (see Chapter 4)

Social goals:

1. Participate in peer interaction:
   • In routine (Jonathan, Theo, Jacob)
   • Sharing and taking turns (Jonathan, Theo, Jacob)
   • Increasing length of interaction (Jonathan, Theo, Jacob)
   • Responding (Andrew, Mark)
   • Initiating (Mark)
   • With words (Theo)
   • By conforming to game rules (Jonathan)
   • With joint regard (Andrew, Mark)
   • Decentered play (Andrew, Mark))
2. Complete activity (Mark)

Communication goals:

1. Extend expressive language in the following manner:
   • Plan and describe (Jonathan, Theo)

   • Respond contingently (Jonathan, Theo, Mark)
   • "Ing" (Jonathan)
   • Past tense (Jonathan)
   • Respond to directions (Andrew)
   • Commenting (Andrew)
   • Recurrence (Andrew)
   • Causality (Andrew)
   • 'And' and 'because' (Theo)
   • Informing (Jacob)
   • Narrate events (Jacob)
   • Stay on topic and complete sentences (Jacob)
   • Practice connecting (Mark)
   • Ask "what" and "where" questions (Jacob)
   • Respond to "what" and "where" questions (Mark)

Cognitive goals:

1. Extend ideas:
   • Nonroutine directions (Jonathan)
   • Problem solving (Jonathan, Andrew, Theo)
   • Acting out stories (Jonathan, Theo)
   • Add new components in play (Theo, Jacob)
   • Changes in scripts (Mark)
2. Increase ability to discriminate and classify information:
   • Discriminate labels and shapes (Jacob)
   • Grouping by attributes (Jacob)
   • Generalizing size concepts (Jonathan)
   • Categorizing (Andrew)
3. Increase memory and sequential ability:
   • Recall (Theo, Jonathan) and sequence past events (Jonathan)
   • Complete sequences (Jacob)

Motor goals:

1. Respond to directions in games, (Jonathan, Andrew, Theo, Jacob, Mark)
2. Increase motor skills by:
   • Galloping (Jacob)
   • Balancing on one foot (Theo)
   • Skipping (Jonathan)
   • Catching a ball (Jonathan)
   • Alternating feet (Mark)

Step Two: Anticipate which Musical Interests/Activities the Group is Working on in the Session

This group is enjoying here and now language songs from Raffi, Nordoff-Robbins Playsongs Collections: the beginnings of representational play in the play, "The Three Bears" and choreographed movement directives in standard songs such as "Old Brass Wagon."

Step Three: Establish which Goals are Logically Embedded in Music Interests/Activities the Group is Working on in the Session in Order to Link Goals and Music Interests/Activities

Communication is linked to the song materials of Raffi and Nordoff and Robbins, motor is linked to the movement songs such as "Old Brass Wagon," cognition is linked to acting out dramatic roles in the play "The Three Bears" and social goals are linked to interactive behaviors throughout all activity. The higher functioning children can act as role models for the lower functioning children.

Step Four: Break Down Goals into Gradations of Expectations, Frequently Based on Quantitative Criteria

An example of a quantitative term included in some of the following case objectives is "one" or "two of three."

Step Five: Modify the Clinical Objectives to Suit the Context of the Musical Activities

Whenever possible, incorporate varying expectations for different children involved in the music activity. It is easiest to put the first initial or name of the child in parentheses following their goal(s).

Step Six: As Necessary, Vary the Expectations for Each Child Involved in the Objective

There are multiple levels of peer interaction and communication in this group so the therapist must keep these in mind while working with the group (see below). This case example presents so many levels of peer interaction, expressive language and types of cognitive tasks that it is probably easiest to stage the objective after the main goal heading and delimit the nature of the task below by name.

Sample Objectives Related to Goals Arrived at for this Group

Social Goals/Objectives

1. Participate in peer interaction:
   1a. Given the song, "The Sharing Song" (Raffi) and a tambourine to shake and pass, the children will *participate at their appropriate level* 1 out of 2 times with *prompting* as necessary.
      * In routine (Jonathan, Theo, Jacob)
      * Sharing and taking turns (Jonathan, Theo, Jacob)
      * Increasing length of interaction (Jonathan, Theo, Jacob)
      * Responding (Andrew, Mark)
      * Initiating (Mark)
      * With words (Theo)
      * By conforming to game rules (Jonathan)
      * With joint regard (Andrew, Mark)
      * Decentered play (Andrew, Mark))
2. Complete activity (Mark)
   2a. Given the song, "We'll Make Music Together" (Nordoff-Robbins, 1968), Mark will follow his cue to play the drum twice, 1 out of 2 times, thereby completing the activity.

Communication Goals/Objectives

1. Extend expressive language in the following manner:
   1a. Given the song, "What did you see" (on your way to school)? (Nordoff-Robbins, book 5, 1980c), children will respond at appropriate expressive language level, *with musical prompting* as necessary, 1 out of 2 times.
      * Respond contingently (Jonathan, Theo,

Mark)
- "ing" (Jonathan)
- Plan and describe (Jonathan, Theo)
- past tense (Jonathan)
- Respond to directions (Andrew)
- Commenting (Andrew)
- Recurrence (Andrew)
- Causality
- "And" and "because" (Theo)
- Informing (Jacob)
- Narrate events (Jacob)
- Stay on topic and complete sentences (Jacob)
- Practice connecting (Mark)
- Ask what and where questions (Jacob)
- Respond to what and where questions (Mark)

Cognitive Goals/Objectives

1. Extend ideas by:
   1a. Given the third scene in "The Three Bears" (Nordoff-Robbins, 1964), the children will follow *one* nonroutine direction (Jonathan), act out *one* role in the story (Jonathan, Theo) and be musically and verbally assisted as necessary to add *one* new component to the play (Theo, Jacob), solve *one* problem encountered during the play rehearsal (Jonathan, Andrew, Theo) and change *one* part of the script (Mark).
2. Increase ability to discriminate and classify information:
   2a. Given the song "What's That?" (Nordoff and Robbins, Playsongs, Book 2), children will classify *one* group of instruments by label and shape (Jacob), size (Jonathan), instrumental family (Andrew) and sound attributes (Jacob).
3. Increase memory and sequential ability:
   3a. At the end of the music therapy session, children will recall (Theo, Jonathan) *two of three* details of what was done in the session and in what sequence (Jonathan, Jacob).

Motor Goals/Objectives

1. Respond to directions in games, (Jonathan,

Andrew, Theo, Jacob, Mark).
   1a. Given the song, "The Old Brass Wagon," the children will correctly follow at least half the directions in the dance (Jonathan, Andrew, Theo, Jacob, Mark).
2. Increase motor skills.
   2a. Given a modified/adapted version of "The Old Brass Wagon," the children will *approximate* galloping (Jacob), balancing on one foot (Theo), skipping (Jonathan), catching a ball (Jonathan) and alternating feet (Mark), 50% of the time.

Case Example Three: Latency-age Multiply Handicapped (Goodman, K., 1996–2002)

Step One: Review Goals Previously Established for Group (see Chapter 4)

Social Goals

1. Increase participation in activity with:
   - a maximum of two verbal redirections (Richard)
   - ten-minute period with minimal verbal prompting, 4 out of 5 trials (Jared)
   - in gross motor/balance activity with verbal prompts only (Patrick)
   - with minimal verbal prompting and decreased behavioral response at least once during session (Jared)
   - with interest (Evan)
   - for up to 1/2 hour during each school day with prompting and redirection (Evan)
   - Participate in group gross motor activities with minimal verbal redirection on 3/5 occasions (Evan)
2. Increase awareness:
   - of the need for help by appropriately accessing pictures or gesturing on 3/5 (session) days (Evan)
   - of emotional states by spontaneously verbalizing feelings (Jared)
   - of increased frustration tolerance by maintaining appropriate behaviors when challenged (Jared)
   - of attention from peers and adults (Dora)

3. Practice behavior that indicate
   - appropriate volume of verbalizations, reduction of inappropriate behaviors and attention-seeking noises (Jared)
   - appropriateness in challenging circumstances (Jared)
4. Initiate parallel play with a classmate once during each school day (Evan).

Communication Goals

1. Expand use of low-tech augmentative device with voice output for communication and interaction (Evan, Dora).
2. Increase receptive vocabulary according to appropriate developmental level:
   - Improve response to yes/no questions (Dora)
   - responding appropriately through pictures or action during one activity per day (Evan)
   - Demonstrate comprehension of verbal information through appropriate verbal responses on 4/5 opportunities (Richard)
3. Increase expressive communication according to appropriate developmental level:
   - Spontaneously verbalize wants, needs, and feelings to appropriate staff (Richard)
   - Verbalize wants and needs clearly and intelligibly by repeating a 4-word phrase (Patrick)
   - Demonstrate comprehension and retention of auditory input during group activity by responding appropriately, given adequate processing time (Patrick)
   - Intelligibly verbalize wants, needs, and feelings given only one chance for self-correction (Richard)
   - Correct use of temporal terms in response to simple questions, with verbal prompts, 3 out of 5 trials (Jared)
   - Develop gestures to communicate needs and wants (Dora)

Cognitive goals

1. Preacademic:
   - Identify all 26 manuscript letters and their sounds (Dora)
   - Identify 11 color words (Dora)

- Identify 12 words frequently seen on signs and 13 others sight words (Dora)
- Identify numerals to five (Dora)
- Use whole numbers to count groups of objects within the context of everyday tasks (Richard)
- Find correct monetary amounts from coins presented in order to "purchase" snack daily (Richard)
- Verbally communicate home address including street, town, state, and country when asked (Richard, Patrick)

Motor goals

Motor goals are, relatively speaking, the most underdeveloped part of the grid.
1. Modify movement to participate in variations of gross motor activities (Jared).

Step Two: Anticipate which Musical Interests/Activities the Group is Working on in the Session

This group uses a greeting song to open group and a good-bye song each session. These openings and closings incorporate a variety of clinical goals. The content of each session is based on choices: instrumental activity, movement activity, discriminatory listening activity and vocal activity. Group members select the order in which they want to proceed, often through picture exchange with the music therapist

Step Three: Establish which Goals are Logically Embedded in Music Interests/Activities the Group is Working on in the Session in Order to Link Goals and Music Interests/Activities

Instrumental activities are both improvisational and precomposed (simple orchestrations based on motor and language goals); vocal activities are based on here and now subjects, sometimes "filling in the blank" with an augmentative switch which has been prepared for vocal response.

Movement activities are adapted to two or three-step directions, often given one directive at a time for children who have auditory processing problems (see Chapter 7, "Methods").

Step Four: Breakdown Goals into Gradations of Expectation Based on Quantitative Criteria

In many of these examples the number of successful trials expected is stated. The types of and degrees of prompting are indicated.

Step Five: Modify the Clinical Objectives to Suit the Context of the Musical Activities

Step Six: As Necessary, Vary the Expectations for Each Child Involved in the Objective

Here again, there are multiple levels of peer interaction and communication in this group that the therapist must keep these in mind while working with the group. This case example presents so many levels of peer interaction, expressive language and types of cognitive tasks that it is probably easiest to stage the objective after the main goal heading and delimit the nature of the task below by name.

Sample Objectives Related to Goals Arrived at for this Group

Social Goals /Objectives

1. Increase participation in activity:
   1a. Given a movement song, children will follow directions with:
      • A maximum of two verbal redirections (Richard)
      • Ten-minute period with minimal verbal prompting, 4 out of 5 trials (Jared)
      • In gross motor/balance activity with verbal prompts only (Patrick)
      • With minimal verbal prompting and decreased behavioral response at least once during session (Jared)
      • With interest (Dora)
      • For up to 1/2 hour during each school day with prompting and redirection (Evan)
      • Participate in group gross motor activi-

ties with minimal verbal redirection on 3/5 occasions (Evan)
2. Increase awareness:
   2a. Given an instrumental orchestration and appropriate prompting, children will participate by following directions and communicating need for help:
      • By appropriately accessing pictures or gesturing on 3/5 (session) days (Evan)
      • By spontaneously verbalizing feelings (Jared)
      • In conjunction with maintaining appropriate behaviors when challenged (Jared)
      • from peers and adults (Dora)
3. Practice behavior that indicates the following:
   3a. Given the opportunity to select a picture (one of two) in order to elect a particular song, child will participate with:
      • appropriate volume of verbalizations, reduction of inappropriate behaviors and attention-seeking noises (Jared)
      • appropriateness in challenging circumstances (Jared)
4. Initiate parallel play with a classmate once during each school day (Evan).
   4a. Given a choice of rhythm instruments, Evan, will tolerate playing a dyad improvisation with another classmate (note: step one toward initiation).

Communication Goals/Objectives

1. Expand use of low-tech augmentative device with voice output for communication and interaction (Evan, Dora)
   1a. Given a "Big Mac," children (Evan, Dora) will respond by pressing the vocal output device when asked to sing in the "hello" song.
2. Increase receptive vocabulary according to appropriate developmental level:
   2a. During activity songs, children will attempt participation at their developmental level at least once during the session:
      • Improve response to yes/no questions (Dora)
      • Responding appropriately through pic-

tures or action during one activity per day (Evan)
- Demonstrate comprehension of verbal information through appropriate verbal responses on 4/5 opportunities (Richard)

3. Increase expressive communication according to appropriate developmental level:
   3a. In the course of the music therapy session, children will use words or picture exchange to express music activity choices, problem solve during music activity and express communicative reactions:
   - Spontaneously verbalize wants, needs, and feelings half of the time to appropriate staff (Richard)
   - Verbalize wants and needs clearly and intelligibly by repeating a 4-word phrase at least once (Patrick)
   - Demonstrate comprehension and retention of auditory input during group activity by responding appropriately half of the time, given adequate processing time (Patrick)
   - Intelligibly verbalize wants, needs, and feelings given one chance for self-correction (Richard)
   - Correct use of temporal terms in response to simple questions, with verbal prompts, 3 out of 5 trials (Jared)
   - Develop gestures to communicate needs and wants half of the time (Dora)

Cognitive goals/Objectives

1. Preacademic:
   - Identify all 26 manuscript letters and their sounds (Dora)
   - Identify 11 color words (Dora)
   - Identify numerals to five (Dora)
   - Use whole numbers to count groups of objects within the context of everyday tasks (Richard)
   - Find correct monetary amounts from coins presented (Richard) in order to purchase snack
   1a. During the song, "C" is for Cookie (Sesame Street), child (Dora) will select manipulative

letters and spontaneously approximate the sound while the therapist supplies a related object (*note:* signs can be incorporated into the song).
1b. During the song, "C" is for Cookie, child (Dora) will point to the appropriate object by color 5 out of 7 times.
1c. During the song, "Penny-Nickel-Dime-Quarter-Dollar Song" (Nordoff and Robbins, Playsongs, book five), children will select appropriate manipulative to count out five pennies in the nickel (Dora, Richard), two nickels in the dime (Richard), four quarters in the dollar (Richard).
1d. After the song, "Penny-Nickel-Dime-Quarter-Dollar Song," child (Richard) will think of what he wants for snack that day and select the correct coins to purchase his snack (another appropriate song for this purpose can be spontaneously composed).

Motor goals/Objectives

Motor goals are, relatively speaking, the most underdeveloped part of the grid.
1. Modify movement to participate in variations of gross motor activities (Jared).
   1a. During the song, "Oh, What a Miracle am I" (traditional), Jared will attempt to modify his gross motor movement half the time in order to appropriately monitor his impulsivity.

Case Example Four: Latency-age Child Psychiatric (Goodman, K., 1981–1984)

Step One: Goals Previously Established for Group (see Chapter 4)

Social Goals

1. Increase peer interaction (Edgar, Debbie, Betsy, Alan)
2. Reduce suicidal ideation (Edgar, Debbie, Betsy, Alan)
3. Increase awareness of mood (Edgar, Debbie, Betsy, Alan)
4. Decrease impulsivity (Edgar, Alan)

5. Reduce rigidity in play patterns (Debbie)
6. Increase positive affect (Betsy)

Communication Goals

1. Use of first person pronouns (Alan)
2. Thought completion (Betsy)
3. Decrease irrelevant communication (Debbie)
4. Decrease ideas of flight (Edgar)

Cognitive Goals

1. Increase ability to problem solve (Edgar, Debbie, Betsy Alan)

Motor Goals

1. Reduce self-stimulating habits (Alan)
2. Increase participation in movement (Betsy)
3. Increase flexibility in movement (Debbie)
4. Decrease impulsivity in movement (Edgar)

Step Two: Anticipate which Musical Interests/Activities the Group is Working on in the Session

This is an intellectually high functioning group interested in improvisation, sharing reactions to song materials they choose, and using the percussion instruments.

Step Three: Establish which Goals are Logically Embedded in Music Interests/Activities the Group is Working on in the Session in Order to Link Goals and Music Interests/Activities

Peer interaction is logically linked to antiphonal playing and shared thoughts after music listening. Reduction of suicidal ideation and increase in positive self-esteem are possibly related to expression and redirection of negative feelings as well as the mastery of musical skills.

Step Four: Breakdown Goals into Gradations of Expectation Frequently Based on Quantitative Criteria

Most indications in these objectives are quanti-

tative. Note that in child psychiatric settings, there will be a greater emphasis in reducing pathological symptoms that led to the hospitalization (note: vs. IEP goals in the school setting). The average psychiatric stay is about 3 weeks.

Step Five: Rewrite the Clinical Objectives to Suit the Context of the Musical Activities

Step Six: As Necessary, Vary the Expectations for each Child Involved in the Objective

There is more overlap in goals and objectives in this type of group, however, the goal of reducing rigidity and increasing positive affect are directed at specific children in the group. There is also further individuation when communication and motors goals/objectives are addressed. Since the group is higher functioning, there is greater likelihood that the children will spontaneously initiate material for the therapist to musically facilitate.

Sample Objectives Related to Goals Arrived at for this Group

Social Goals

1. Increase peer interaction (Edgar, Debbie, Betsy, Alan)
   1a. Given a modal improvisation and visual cues, children will engage in antiphonal percussive musical exchange with a minimum of two exchanges.
2. Reduce suicidal ideation (Edgar, Debbie, Betsy, Alan)
   2a. Children will reduce the number of suicidal thoughts expressed in music group (note: baseline needs to be taken here) from baseline behavior.
3. Increase awareness of mood (Edgar, Debbie, Betsy, Alan)
   3a. After choosing and singing a song with the group, each child will identify how they feel with a minimum of one thought.
4. Decrease impulsivity (Edgar, Alan)
   4a. Children will follow a copycat pattern on the drum and cymbal with the therapist, with correct imitation at least half the time.
5. Reduce rigidity in play patterns (Debbie)

5a. Debbie will extend a given drum pattern on her instrument at least once given musical support from the therapist.
6. Increase positive affect (Betsy)
   6a. Betsy will spontaneously express positive affect at least once during the music therapy session.

Communication Goals

1. Use of first person pronouns (Alan)
   1a. In the normal course of the music therapy session, Alan will use the personal pronoun 'I' at least twice.
2. Thought completion (Betsy)
   2a. given the song, "Down by the Bay," Betsy will contribute an original song lyric as a completed thought at least two out of four times
3. Decrease irrelevant communication (Debbie), ideas of flight (Edgar)
   3a. During the music therapy session, Debbie and Edgar will respond to questions about music making without tangentially going off topic.

Cognitive Goals

1. Increase ability to problem solve (Edgar, Debbie, Betsy Alan)
   1a. While choosing instruments for an orchestration to "Tomorrow" (Annie), the children will problem solve in a minimum of one situation, aided by the therapist.

Motor Goals

1. Reduce self-stimulating habits (Alan)
   1a. During the music therapy session, Alan will avoid self-stimulating habits during the first 20 minutes.
2. Increase participation in movement (Betsy)
   2a. During 'Rock and Roll Song (Greg and Steve, Sclesa, 1986 CD), Betsy will participate at least half the time.
3. Increase flexibility in movement (Debbie)
   3a. During "Rock and Roll Song" (Greg and Steve, Sclesa, 1986 CD), Debbie will imitate flexible movements modeled by the therapist at least two out of four times.
4. Decrease impulsivity (Edgar, Alan)
   4a. During "The Freeze Dance" (Greg and Steve, Sclesa, 1986 CD), Edgar and Alan will stop and start on cue with the music.

SUMMARY

In this chapter, the therapist continues the thought process following long-term goal setting, namely that of formulating short-term objectives embedded in musical experiences. The four music therapy groups presented in Chapter 4 are again presented in this fifth chapter as the therapist relates the music therapy objectives to the clinical goals. Although there is a natural resistance to tracking the progress or lack of progress of student objectives, the outcome of the accountability will be impressive to any logical administrator, school district, parent, peer therapist/teacher and, in a larger sense, to the credibility of the work itself. The beauty of music therapy is seeing the inherent developmental baby steps each student takes while making music.

In the next chapter, Chapter 6, the therapist begins to plan the musical materials that will lay the groundwork for developmental expression and progress.

STUDY GUIDE QUESTIONS

1. What is a short-term objective?
2. How is a short-term objective written in the music therapy session?
3. Give examples of three types of music therapy objectives: a) nonmusic behavior in the music therapy session; b) nonmusic behavior supported by the musical experience in the music therapy session; and c) musical behavior indicative developmental gain.
4. What are the suggested steps for arriving at music therapy objectives?
5. What are some of the practical ways a therapist can evaluate objectives in the session?
6. Given the group that you defined goals for in the Chapter 4 study guide questions, provide a series of short-term objectives other than those presented in this chapter for those goals now.

Chapter 6

Where Is the Music? Materials in Group Music Therapy

INTRODUCTION

The use of *music* in therapy is the single most therapeutic tool the music therapist has. In the presentation of any musical experience, planned or spontaneous, it is the elements of the music that provide curative value for the children in the group.

Music therapists say that it is the *selective use of music* that is one of the defining features of a music therapist's work. In recognition of this principle of music therapy, *this chapter discusses considerations in selecting music for vocal, instrumental, movement and listening purposes* as well as *considerations in selecting instruments and ancillary materials. Since the use of music will frequently invite adaptation in response to the children in the group, this chapter also suggests how the material itself may be modified.* This part of the writing is a bridge to the next chapter, "Methods."

In presenting musical experience for any child or group of children, two essential principles emerge: 1) *The therapist must present music that is physiologically processed by the children;* and 2) *The therapist must present music that is adaptable for in the moment experiences (see Chapter 7, "Methods") to accommodate the developmental needs of the child or children in the group.*

In order to allow for the selection of materials that are adaptable enough to provide for varying levels of functional responses within a group, the concept of *Continuum of Music Response, CMT* (Goodman, 1996–2002) is presented and demonstrated with case examples in this chapter.

Finally, a listing of different materials used over a five-year period with multiply handicapped children is presented as a sample of a repertoire that a music therapist can develop with simultaneous presentation on different functioning levels.

CONSIDERATIONS IN SELECTING AND CREATING MUSIC VOCAL

VOCAL

The use of vocal materials in music therapy is multi-faceted and therefore the therapist needs to evaluate the potential use of songs in terms of their *musical structure, lyrical content,* and *adaptability.* These aspects of the song will be critical for satisfying the developmental goals of not just one child, but the needs of several children in the group simultaneously.

Musical Structure and Lyrical Content

The musical structure of the song can be considered as follows: 1) vocal range of melody and key signature; 2) form; 3) intervals, phrasing and melodic rhythm of song lyrics; 4) harmonics; 5) dynamics; 6) tempo; 7) mood; 8) amount of musical information; 9) repetition; and 10) mood that the song creates.

The lyrical content of the song can be considered as follows: 1) level of developmental awareness required to sing as well as understand the song lyrics; and 2) thematic relevance of the song lyrics for the child.

Some children will, of course, be familiar with commonplace children's songs, such as 'Old MacDonald', "Twinkle, Twinkle Little Star," "Bingo," "Wheels on the Bus," "Happy and You Know It," and so forth. These songs can be a beginning "comfort zone" for children to sing. However, they are not necessarily useful as therapeutic vehicles to build speech and language. There is so much wonderful song material for the therapist to introduce to children and songs must be considered in terms of their overall developmental value. Types of songs with inherent therapeutic value are indicated in this chapter.

Musical Structure of the Song

Key of Song and Intervals Related to Vocal Range

The key of the song as well as the intervals contained within the song must be suited to the vocal range of the children. Obviously, every child in the group will vary in their *vocal range.* Hopefully, the variation from child to child will not be so dramatic as to become problematic. With a simple vocal warm-up, the therapist can usually ascertain what vocal ranges suit the group. The C an octave above middle C is generally a reasonable guideline for the upper limit of a song since many special learners have lower vocal ranges. If the ranges are dramatically different, the therapist may consider dividing the vocal parts of a song (see form) and transposing while modulating to another key as necessary. Flexibility in considering the range of a song is also important for a child in a psychiatric setting since anxiety or depression can affect the range, pitch-matching ability and the quality of the singing voice (Goodman, 1989). Singing in one's appropriate vocal range is important for every child but particularly critical for a child with a narrow range. Children with a particularly narrow vocal range may need one-on-one vocal experience within the context of the group in order for the therapist to imitate the pitch of the child, supporting these pitches with chords containing them and trying to introduce a tone higher and/or lower (Nordoff and Robbins, 1971). Furthermore, it is important for the therapist to remember that his or her singing is a vocal model for the children and, ideally, should be in or as close to the children's range as possible and expressive without being overwhelming.

Form of the Song Related to Developmental Purpose

The form of the song must have developmental pur-

pose and therefore different kinds of forms for different purposes can be considered.* For example, the song may consist of simple repetition, verse(s) and chorus, question and answer or model and imitate (antiphonal) dialogue, requests for action or, at its most complex, a round harmony. Form relates to developmental purpose. For example,

- If the therapist is trying to engage a nonverbal or beginning verbal child in song, the antiphonal structure of a song with limited information to imitate is best. *The initial response of a nonverbal or beginning verbal child is most likely on the closing pitches of a phrase.*
- If the therapist is attempting to help the child exercise receptive language, there should be a request for action built into the song and a musical "space" for the child to demonstrate understanding.
- If the therapist is working with beginning speakers, the selection of a song with verses and a simple chorus allow the children to sing on the chorus.
- If the therapist is working with moderately advanced speakers, their singing of both verse and chorus is appropriate.
- If the therapist is working with children who have no problems in speech/language but may have problems in listening to each other or working together, the round may be appropriate.

Intervals, Phrasing, and Melodic Rhythm

The intervals, phrasing and melodic rhythm of the song are particularly important for children trying to develop speech and language. The first composer to realize this in music therapy compositions was Paul Nordoff who, along with Clive Robbins, writes about these ideas in their wonderful book on special education and music (Nordoff and Robbins, 1971).

Nordoff and Robbins suggest the following guidelines regarding rhythmic stressing of syllables, tonal settings that follow inflections of speech, verbal emphasis and melodic rhythm, and speech phrase and melodic phrase:

1. The syllable that is normally stressed in speech

should fall on an accented beat of the music (Nordoff and Robbins, 1971, p. 28).

2. Syllables on which the speaking voice naturally rises should, when sung, be on higher tones than those syllables on which the voice falls (Nordoff and Robbins, 1971.

3. Accented syllables and important one-syllable words may be further stressed by being given a relatively longer time value (Nordoff and Robbins, 1971, p. 29): When a speech phrase or a line of a poem is set to music, only those words and accented syllables which are expressively important should be stressed by pitch and/or prolongation.

4. "Words of secondary importance and unaccented syllables are given shorter time values and are generally lower in pitch" (Nordoff and Robbins, 1971, p. 29).

Ideally, then, therapists working with the beginning speaker should use music therapy compositions that replicate speech intervals (the most common of which is the perfect fourth), speech phrasing and accurate melodic rhythms (melodic rhythm is defined as the rhythm of the sung syllables in the song lyrics).

Harmonics Working to Serve Emotional Needs of Children

In conjuntion with the melody and rhythm, the *harmonics in a song must work to serve different emotional needs for the children.* Harmonics, horizontally implied in intervals, are more commonly thought of as vertical and related to chord progressions even though the harmonic interval should also be of consideration to the therapist as it affects pitch matching and vocal range. Even though it is tempting for the beginning student to use a I–IV–V children's tune, this sequence can easily prove boring in its rote predictability. In order to "spice" up the harmonics and further affect the mood of the child, it is easily possible to add intermediate chords and seventh chords.

Nordoff and Robbins, for example, suggest the addition of secondary seventh chords, those chords on the first, second, third, fourth, sixth and seventh scale tones, used in both root position as well as inversions. Harmonics are a vital element of stimulation and must be used as such in thera-

py. An examination of the Nordoff and Robbins songs (Playsongs, Books 1, 1962) shows a conscious use of what we may hear as dissonant intervals in order to stimulate the listener. Students, in the course of learning songs with more complex harmonics, may be tempted to simplify and therefore alter the harmonics (i.e., by taking out minor or major seconds added to chords, by taking out intermediate chords or modulations into other keys). This attempt to simplify should be avoided. It will not only change the mood of the song but also limit the capacity of the song for stimulating or sedating the child.

Changes in Dynamics

As in speaking, the song should employ demonstrative changes in *dynamics.* This seems obvious but, all too often, songs are sung at the same dynamic, without modeling gradual or sudden changes as appropriate to the content of the song. Without changes in dynamics, the "life" of the song loses meaning and the therapist needs to keep this in mind.

Working Tempo

The working *tempo* of the song must be in accordance with a true sense of pulse in order for the song to be alive. If it needs to be slower in order to meet the auditory processing of group members, it should be musically slower, or, in other words, appropriate to the musical feeling of the song. Likewise, if it needs to be faster in order to accommodate the impulses of hyperactive children, it should also be appropriate to the musical feeling of the song. Songs that allow for modulation of tempi can be useful in working with children of varying sensory needs in order to meet their physiological regulatory needs.

Mood Setting through a Song

It is the composite of the melody, harmonics and rhythm that, of course, create the *mood of the song.* This is essential for motivating the children in the group to respond. Many traditional children's songs, described as happy, delimit the range of emotionality. Nordoff and Robbins add the possibility of happy songs provoking a sense of joyousness or triumph, purposeful songs posing a question or setting actions to song, and lyric songs and thoughtful songs having the potential to help the child express sadness, tenderness or longing (Nordoff and Robbins, 1971, pp. 32–35). Moods can be stimulating, sedating, happy, sad, thoughtful, reflective, and will impact different children in varying ways.

Amount of Musical Information

The amount of *musical information* in a song relates to the child's ability to process, recall and then sing. This idea springs from principles of information processing theory. Therefore, amounts of musical information can become progressively larger as the child demonstrates the ability to process, recall and sing it. This process will be easier with information that is *repeated* in the song. Obviously, with children of varying abilities in the group, each child will perform differently. This is why the use of a musical form that allows for variable participation (i.e., one excellent example is verse and chorus) is realistic for a group.

In summary, the therapist must seek and *create* songs with appropriate vocal range, form, intervals, phrasing and melodic rhythm, harmonics, dynamics, mood-setting, amount of musical information and repetition. Not all music therapy materials or improvisations satisfy these requirements and therefore will require modification on the part of the therapist.

Lyrical Content

The level of developmental awareness required to *sing as well as understand the song lyrics* is critically important in selecting song materials.

Levels of Expressive/Receptive Language Related to Lyrics

In terms of singing, the previous discussion of various *forms* in songs suggests *different kinds of musical song structure for promoting and extending different levels of expressive speech-language development,* beginning with vocalization of vowels and conso-

nants, and proceeding with the use of the holophrase (one word standing for multiple meaning), one-two words, simple sentence (noun-verb-direct object), use of adjectives, pronouns, prepositions, and so forth. It is possible for the therapist to seek out this kind of material, however, more often than not, the therapist may need to adapt selected songs for these purposes. In so doing, it is important to maintain accurate articulation of words with respect to melodic intervals and rhythms.

Children who are just beginning to sing will need material that lends itself to vocalization of vowels and consonants, beginning in their given vocal range. There is a lovely improvisational example of this provided in an individual case study for a child named Nunnu (Nordoff and Robbins, 1977, 2007) where the therapists gently expand the child's limited vocal range. Further, there is a better known case study for "Edward" (Nordoff and Robbins, 1977, 2007) who starts with different kinds of cries related to the key signature of the therapist improvisation and, after a period of increasingly sophisticated vocalization, begins singing on single words. These case examples employ improvisation. Suggestions for learning how to improvise present themselves in recent publications, the earliest of which is a published series of Paul Nordoff's original lectures (Robbins, 1998) and the most recent of which is authored by Wigram (2004). *Improvisation can be simple or complex and it should be a skill that every therapist employs in either adapting material, extending material or creating new material.*

Other songs that employ antiphonal imitative beginning vocalization in the context of simple song lyrics in order to "invite" the child to sing exist throughout music therapy literature. One excellent example of this type of song is composed by Alan Turry (Ritholz, 1999, p. 44), simply entitled, "Let's Sing a Song." In this song, the child is encouraged to imitate the therapist's simple "la la la" vocalization in the rests following the modeling. The harmonic sequence of the song is engaging and provides multiple opportunities for the child to sing as the music proceeds. Other conventional materials can be adapted for vocalization, for example, songs like "Zip a dee doo dah,"

"Chim chimeree" from Disney; "Kumbayah" (vocalize on last syllable of word, changing syllable as necessary and waiting for child to complete musical phrase), and "Sing" from Sesame Street (Moss and Raposo, 1992). For older children, "riffs" from popular music, rock and Broadway can be incorporated for the purpose of free vocalization or scat. Riffs can also be followed by instrumental music or clapping, i.e., Da da da da, da, (clap) da da da da (clap).

Some children who may be uncomfortable vocalizing will "break the ice" with animal sounds. There are a great number of these songs; perhaps one of the best known is a traditional tune, "Bought me a Cat" (see Copland arrangment). This song is a wonderful example of a song that can be used on multiple levels. The accompaniment as well as arrangement can be simple or sophisticated. The therapist can use a visual songboard to help children who require more structure.

Just as important in selecting materials for an appropriate level of expressive language is understanding the *level of developmental awareness required to understand the song lyrics.* There are stories of autistic children, for example, who could sing entire Broadway scores but who could not begin to say "Hello" to another person. Rote kind of singing is to be avoided in music therapy. Probably the best way to evaluate language comprehension is to use an activity song, a song that asks the child to respond to directives. Examples of these follow in this chapter.

Thematic Relevance of Song Lyrics

The *thematic relevance of the song lyrics for the child* is essential. Any song the child sings needs to have *meaning:* "The most effective kinds of songs for handicapped children are those about activities that happen within the songs themselves, or about things or events the children know, or can imagine, or can grow to understand. These songs have a personal reality for them and arouse greater involvement" (Nordoff and Robbins, 1971, p. 22). These types of songs can be found in music therapy collections (Nordoff and Robbins, 1962, 1968, 1980a; Ritholz and Robbins, 1999, 2003; Levin &

Levin, 1997, 1998; Farnan, 1998b; Palmer, 1981) as well as nonmusic therapy collections (Glazer, 1983; Moss and Raposo, 1992; Raffi, 1983, 1984, 1986; Rogers, 1970; Wojcio, 1983). Examples of songs in various categories of content below are taken from the Nordoff-Robbins literature.

Adaptability

As the therapist proceeds with the song, it is necessary to be adaptive in some of the following ways:

- Personalize songs
- Simplify or extend lyrical material depending upon spontaneous information offered by the child.
- Adapt music if adapting song lyrics in order to maintain accurate melodic rhythms.
- Be prepared to provide musical bridges from one section of the song to another should the child need a "break" or if the therapist is incorporating instrumental improvisation or movement into the song.

Types of Songs

Nordoff and Robbins (1971) introduce the therapist to different types of songs possible for therapeutic purposes.

Opening and Closing Songs

Opening and closing songs can be useful vehicles for the structure of a music therapy group. The opening can acknowledge who is in the group. It can also, if appropriate, be used to announce the weather, the day of the week, the month of the year, a special occasion, counting who is present, and spelling the names of the children in the group. The closing is particularly useful for musically incorporating thoughts and feelings about what has happened in the session.

Example of excellent *opening and closing songs* composed by Nordoff and Robbins, 1962, 1968, 1980, are the following:

- "Let's Sing Good Morning" (Book 5, p. 6)

- "So Long" (Book 5, p. 24)
- "Have a Good Day" (Book 4, p. 3)
- "A Song for Julie" (Book 4, p. 10)
- "Good Morning" (Book 3, p. 3)
- "Hello, Girls ! Hello, Boys!" (Book 3, p. 4)
- "Thank You" (Book 3, p. 23)
- "Good Morning Song" (Book 2, p. 2)
- "Greeting Song" (Book 2, p. 3)
- "Goodbye Song" (Book 2, p. 19)
- "Hello" (Book 1, p. 3)

Activity Songs

The concept of the *activity song* is simple. The child is asked, in the context of the song, to *do something*. The beauty of the activity song is its value in developing receptive language and dramatic play which, in the group, easily becomes interactive. Examples of activity songs composed by Nordoff and Robbins, 1962, 1968, 1980, inviting physical or conceptual verbal participation, are the following:

- "I've Got a Hat" (Book 1, p. 7)
- "What Did You See?" (Book 4, p. 6)
- "Shoe-making Song" (Book 1, p. 10)
- "Shoe-tying Song" (Book 1, p. 11)
- "The Counting Song" (Book 2, p. 8)
- "Safety Song" (Book 3, p. 6)
- "Penny-Nickel-Dime-Quarter-Dollar Song" (Book 3, p. 9)
- "What Did You See?" (Book 4, p. 6)
- "The Way I Like To Sit" (Book 4, p. 12)
- "A New Baby" (Book 4, p. 14), using a doll for a prop
- "Water, Air, Sunshine, Fire, Earth" (Book 5, p. 3)
- "Safety Song" (Book 3, p. 6)

Songs that Explore Emotions

Songs that *explore emotions* are important for the life of any child but for special needs children who may otherwise have difficulty communicating and expressing their feelings, these songs are critical. It is important not to introduce songs with emotional content in a haphazard way. The therapist

should make every effort to be sensitive to the mood of the group as well as particular moods of children in the group who may need to express certain feelings. Example of songs composed by Nordoff and Robbins, 1968, 1980, that explore emotions, inviting feelings that are either self-identified or projective are the following:

- "I'm Mad Today" (Book 5, p. 14)
- "The Sunny Side" (Book 4, p. 18)
- "You Never Can Tell" (Book 3, p. 12)
- "Crying Song" (Book 2, p. 11)

Songs that Tell a Story and Introduce Cognitive Concepts

Songs that *tell a story and introduce cognitive concepts* are also key sources of therapeutic value, particularly for child psychiatric patients who may need to use songs of this nature for projective play. In cases where the songs introduce preacademic or academic content, the concepts should be functional for the children, concepts that the children can apply in their everyday setting (i.e., counting out lunch money; knowing colors in order to express the desire for a particular color of rhythm sticks). Examples of songs composed by Nordoff and Robbins, 1980a, b, and c, that tell a story and introduce cognitive concepts are the following:

- "Dream Song" (Book 5, p. 8)
- "They Each Walked Along" (Book 5, p. 12)
- "Audrey's Hair" (Book 5, p. 16)
- "Green Grass, Little Wind, Big Sky, Blue Sky" (Book 5, p. 16)
- "The Old King" (Book 5, p. 20)
- "I Have a Friend" (Book 4, p. 20)
- "Color Song" (Book 4, p. 22)

Songs that Invite Dramatic Play

Similar in scope to songs that tell a story, songs that invite *dramatic play* will help children who are capable of representational play act out their feelings and thoughts. One simple example of a song that invite dramatic play is "Bill's Train" (Nordoff and Robbins, 1962, Book 1, p. 16).

Songs Introducing Instrumental Play

Finally songs that introduce the *different playing of instruments* incorporate vocal and instrumental impulses in the children. These songs provide the opportunity for musical flexibility on the part of the therapist if the song material is used as an opportunity for the children to improvise on their instruments and be supported musically by the accompanying therapist.

Examples of songs composed by Nordoff and Robbins, 1962, 1968, 1980a, b, and c, that *introduce the different playing of instruments* include:

- "We'll Make Music Together" (Book 5, p. 10)
- "Who Would Like To?" (Book 3, p. 13)
- "Hocus Pocus" (Book 3, p. 16)
- "Drum Talk" (Book 2, p. 12)
- "Listen to the Birds" (Book 1, p. 6)
- "Charlie Knows How to Beat That Drum" (Book 1, p. 15)

INSTRUMENTAL

In what might be termed *clinical orchestration,* the therapist needs to evaluate the potential use of instrumental materials in terms of their *musical structure, strategic developmental purpose, and adaptability*. These aspects of the orchestration or improvisation will be critical for satisfying the developmental goals of not just one child, but the needs of several children in the group simultaneously.

Clinical Orchestration

The music composed or arranged for instrumental experiences in music therapy must be progressively structured to invite challenging listening experiences and strategic use of instruments.

The Importance of a Role in the Music-making

One of the most important principles for the therapist to remember when using precomposed or improvised instrumental selections is to make sure each child has a specific role to play in the composition. This principle eliminates what is commonly known as "rhythm band" where all the children play on the basic beat whenever they are comfortable so doing. *In music therapy, it is too easy for children to become uninvolved or unmotivated unless they have the responsibility of playing a specific part.* The goal of each child playing a specific role in the musical composition is to keep them listening to each other, watching the conductor, and strategically employing the physical and cognitive responsibility of playing their instrument. Music that accomplishes this is generally music composed and arranged for music therapy either by the therapist or another professional in the field (Levin & Levin, 1977a, 1997b, 1998; Nordoff, 1972, 1979, 1981).

Levels of Functioning in Clinical Orchestration

Clinical orchestrations can employ various levels of challenge to help children respond. This point is beautifully illustrated in the music of Gail and Herbert Levin (1977a, 1997b, 1998) who provides preprimary, primary, intermediate and advanced orchestrated pieces. What sets these levels apart from each other in terms of their musical structure?

In a piece at the preprimary level, a music "lead-in" precedes the child's rhythmic entrance: *It's Billy's turn to beat the drum. It's Billy's turn to beat the drum. Listen to the drum. Oh, listen to the drum* (Levin & Levin, 1998, p. 17). This type of piece would be considered a *preprimary* level of response since it uses only one instrument and implies a straightforward musical directive.

Similarly, Levin's "Play Your Bell One Time" employs one directive at a time, one instrument and one pitch: *Play your bell one time (bell). Play your bell one time (bell). Play your bell one (bell) time (bell). Play it again (bell)* (Levin & Levin, 1998, p. 37). However, in this piece, the quarter notes and eighth notes are supplemented with a triplet and the use of additional rests to employ a slightly more challenging listening experience which is now *primary* level.

In a further example, "The Drum Caught Cold" (Levin & Levin, 1998. p. 44), considered an *intermediate* level challenge, Levin *employs two instruments,* the drum and the cymbal. The cymbal only plays one time, at the end, requiring a long waiting time for the musician. The challenge of playing the drum in this case is the musical requirement of the child playing a tremolo which follows a series of straightforward quarter notes and then again, immediately before the cymbal crash.

Finally, at the *advanced level* of clinical orchestration, "Spooky Bells" (Levin & Levin, 1998, p. 84), *four types of instruments are used* (cymbal, drum, triangle, resonator bells). *This song has an ABA structure.* In both A and B sections, the low G resonator bell and the drum always play three times in unison immediately after the cymbal. In section A, the triangle always plays after each set of three bell and drum beats, and is followed by the A, high g, and the E bells played in sequence. In section B, the triangle and A, high g and e bells are omitted; the pattern of cymbal, then low G bell and drum in unison is repeated four times. The cymbal plays the last response (Levin, 1998, p. 83).

To summarize, *the greater the number of instrumental roles and the greater the amount and complexity of the information in the music, the greater the challenge to the children.*

How can these pieces be modified for a group where the number of children in the group is greater than the number of players called for in the orchestration? In situations where the orchestration appears to be composed for one child, the therapist can vary the piece by passing the instrument, i.e., the drum, around to the children in the group, one beat per child. In situations where the orchestration is composed for three children and there are six, the parts can be doubled. There is always a solution on the part of the clever therapist to accommodate the needs of the group.

Suggestions for Clinical Orchestration

Although there are many fine music therapy pieces to use for instrumental work, it is important for the therapist to flexibly employ classical music as well as various genres of folk music, childrens' tunes, and so forth when orchestrating for the group. When the therapist is orchestrating a piece

of music, the easiest way to do this is to xerox the score and paste it onto another piece of paper with sufficient space on the page to incorporate graphics (based on a key illustrating a graphic for each instrument used) above each musical line. Levin (1998) employs simple graphics in his orchestrations for bell, drum, slide whistle, cymbal, and so on.

Here are some suggestions regarding your own clinical orchestration.

Resonator Bell Arrangement

The role of resonator bells in music therapy is an important one and therefore receives detailed treatment in the writing of Nordoff and Robbins (1971). Resonator bells play a varied role in providing melodic and harmonic accents. They can be used by more than one child at a time in the group setting and they promote both fine and gross motor development. In addition to using the fine pieces available in music composed for music therapy (Levin, 1977b, 1998; Ritholz, 1999; Nordoff and Robbins, 1977, 1979, 1981) bells can be orchestrated for popular, folk and classical material by the music therapist.

In an arrangement of Bach's "Jesu, Joy of Man's Desiring" (Goodman, 1996–2002), resonator bells were used on the downbeat of each musical line for rhythmic and harmonic emphasis. This is a simple way to orchestrate. The bells were arranged this way in order to provide straightforward rhythmic anticipation for a moderately functioning group of multiply handicapped children. Other possibilities for the use of resonator bells are celebrated by Nordoff and Robbins (1971, pp. 56–72):

1. Play each tone of a melody with the resonator bells.
2. Accent the the rise and fall of a melody with the bells.
3. Emphasize the phrase form of a melody with the bells.
4. Create arrangements calling for alertness and quick striking of the bells, pitches can provide dissonance and also require one player to play two pitches, the second pitch

...ediately played after the first.

. ...mphasize a particular interval, i.e., outline the melody of the song by using ascending octaves followed by a dissonance in the fourth measure.

6. Play the bells entirely on the rests.
7. Have the bells echo, answer, or imitate a melodic phrase; this sounds like a canon.
8. Bells answer melodic phrases by playing contrasting phrases.

Percussion

As the therapist creates various orchestrations, percussion instruments can be used for basic beat, melodic rhythm, accents and in dialogue with each other. It is also valuable to remember that percussion instruments can be played in traditional or nontraditional manners and the use of ethnic percussion will prove stimulating in any orchestration.

Xylophone

Less frequently employed in group orchestrations for children, xylophones of varying sizes and materials provide important melodic elements in improvisational or planned orchestrations. The therapist should make sure that the pitches on the xylophones conform to the key of the piano or guitar accompaniment; using the pentatonic scale assures the most freedom in harmony.

Adaptability During Instrumental Experience

As the therapist proceeds with instrumental material, it is necessary to be flexible in accompaniment for the following situations:

- Child creatively extends their instrumental part.
- Melodic or percussion portions have to be added or deleted without previous intention.
- Child needs repetition or variation in

accompaniment in order to provide additional practice or additional processing time.

Strategic Developmental Purpose in Instrumental Assignment

In terms of deciding on a piece of music and assigning the instrumental parts, it is essential that the therapist think in terms of developmental appropriateness. What can the child physically handle? How many directives can the child follow? (*Note:* not to mention how many directives can the therapist conduct.) What kind of auditory processing and/or visual motor planning will be necessary to follow the instrumental cue? What kinds of orchestral instruments might be useful in terms of physical ability and disability? (*Note:* see Elliott, 1982.) The answers to these kinds of questions can help the therapist decide on what will be possible in the group and what kinds of methods (see Chapter 7) will be necessary for the therapist to effectively introduce instrumental work.

Case Example (Goodman, K., 1996–2002)

Paul, 13 years old and diagnosed with a mild/moderate degree of retardation, appeared awkward in the music therapy group (Goodman, 1996–2002). He had difficulty paying attention much of the time and was resistive to participation. However, when the student therapist brought in her cello and played 'Swan' from the *Carnival of the Animals* (Camiille Saint-Saens), Paul sat up straight, was captivated and asked to try using the cello himself. Everyone in the group was amazed to see Paul's posture adapt to holding the cello and purposefully and musically use the bow to play his first pitch. The student therapist brought in another cello for the next session and was able to provide Paul with a simple repetitive harmonic accompaniment that worked well with her playing of the melody. Paul's attention span and self-esteem became noticeably different in the group as other peers admired his musicianship and supported him emotionally.

MOVEMENT

Structure of the Movement Piece

Live vs. Recorded Music: The Dilemma

One of the very realistic problems in presenting movement experiences for the group is the issue of live vs. recorded materials. Live music is always best in any therapy situation since it provides maximum flexibility for the therapist to adapt tempo and minimize or maximize the choreography as needed in the session. However, recorded music can be useful for the therapist to have hands free to demonstrate and assist as the children are moving. A compromise between the live and recorded accompaniment to a movement experience is for the therapist to learn the recorded song either by ear or finding the sheet music and then, using the record function on a casio, record an accompaniment appropriate for the pace of the learning situation. This can be done prior to or during the music therapy session. Assuming this effort is successful, the therapist will sing "voice over" to remind the children of the steps in the movement experience.

Amount of Information in Choreography

As with orchestrations, *the greater the amount and complexity of the information in the music, the greater the challenge to the children.* Therefore, it behooves the therapist to think in terms of simplifying the movement experience and consciously think about the number of directives a child can follow. Materials that cannot be modified are less desirable to use in therapy. Examples of materials that can be modified for therapy include the music of Hap Palmer (1981, 1982, 1994a, 1994b) Greg and Steve (1983), Georgianna Stewart (1977, 1984, 1987, 1991, 1992) and compact discs for Dalcroze exercises (Abramson, 1997). Hap Palmer as well as Greg and Steve materials are available in songbook form; many of the dances from the Georgianna Stewart tapes can be learned by ear. Other music, including "Children of the World" (Stewart, 1991), cannot.

Included in materials for movement are activi-

ties that involve catching or passing manipulatives such as a ball or a beanbag and raising or lowering a parachute. These provide additional sensory input and can be valuable for children requiring multisensory experience. The parachute experience to music can be further supplemented by manipulating a soft ball or balloons in the center and, as these items roll around to each child, the child must push them back into the center of the parachute.

Suggestions for Choreography and Voice Over

When creating simple choreography to fit a piece of world or classical music, keep in mind the following:

- Xerox the lyrics (from the inside of the CD insert) to the dance in order to write out the steps you wish to emphasize as you choreograph the piece.
- Use simple steps to emphasize the basic beat of the music.
- Use one direction at a time if the children cannot handle multiple directions.
- Select music that has a simple ABA structure. This will allow you to return to the familiar "A" portion of the dance.
- Always use a simple repetitive sequence that matches changes in the structure of the music.
- As the children become more comfortable with motor planning, ability to follow more than one or two steps at a time and the ability to recall previous sequence, the choreography can become more complex. Not until then!
- Simple beginning formations for movement experiences might include: 1) Asking the children to stand on a masking tape in line formation while you stand in front of them to model or, even better, while each child is paired with an adult or higher functioning child to act as a model; and 2) Circle formation
- Simple steps can include: 1) Clapping to the beat while standing; 2) Clapping and walking in place to the beat; 3) Clapping and/or walk-

ing into the circle on the beat; 4) Clapping and /or walking back out; 5) Turning to the side and walking around in a circle formation (this is easy for us but deceptively difficult for children who are special learners); and 6) Turning to the other side and walking around in a circle formation.

- When directing the children for movement, make certain that the rhythm of your voice entrains with the basic beat and/or the melodic rhythm of the music. This will help the children neurologically as they take in auditory information and convert it into movement.

LISTENING

Structure of the Listening Experience

Amount of Information in Listening

It is worthwhile to repeat this concept again: *the greater the amount and complexity of the information in the music, the greater the challenge to the children.* Children can enjoy listening to many types of music but their levels of auditory processing and their attention span must be respected. The purpose of the listening can be varied. Children enjoy listening to music for relaxation and this experience can be particularly useful when aides, teachers and therapists move the limbs of physically involved children in rhythmic fashion to the music. Children with abstract imaginations enjoy listen to music that tells a story, for example, "Peter and the Wolf" (Prokofiev), "Mother Goose Suite" (Ravel). This music can suggest a projective reaction on their parts, a point realized early in the music therapy literature (Crocker, 1968).

MUSICAL DRAMA

Structure of the Dramatic Experience

There are many fine plays adapted and orchestrated for music therapy experience. They include the following:

- *The Three Bears* (Nordoff and Robbins, 1964)
- *The Christmas Play* (Nordoff and Robbins, 1970)
- *Pif-Paf Poultrie* (Nordoff and Robbins, 1969)
- *A Message for the King* (Nordoff and Robbins, 1976)
- *Fairy Tales: Musical Drama for Children* (Ginger Clarkson, 1986)
- *Snow White: A Guide to Child-Centered Musical Theater* (Rickard-Lauri, Groeschel, Robbins, Robbins, Ritholz, Turry, 1997)
- *The Story of Artaban, The Other Wise Man* (Nordoff and Robbins, 1964)

These plays involve characters that allow the children a variety of emotions and character development. The music itself is suited to therapy in terms of moderate degrees of information, melodic rhythm and phrasing imitative of speech/language and themes that live for the children. Multiple scenes are included in each play, scenes that will require *introduction and repeated rehearsal over a period of many sessions.* This is a fine idea for a high functioning group since it teaches the group perseverance and the play can be performed for the school. "The Three Bears" (Nordoff and Robbins, 1964) is an example of a familiar story that, for music therapy purposes, employs clinical orchestration as well as chanted speech. The songs composed by Paul Nordoff to accompany the story are composed in line with speech (see selection of song material) and the speech fugues compliment the efforts of any speech-handicapped child to rhythmically order their speech.

Likewise, the therapist can adapt and orchestrate any play really for music therapy or the music therapist can compose one. However, the introduction of musical drama need not be restricted to a large scale production. As soon as a child is capable of representational play, there is opportunity for small-scale drama and the therapist needs to be alert for these possibilities in precomposed or improvisational music.

Case Example: Neals (Goodman, K., 1996–2002)

While the group was singing "Sammy" (Palmer,

1981) relaying a story about a child who experimented his ego by flying like a bird, crawling like a worm, etc, one of the children in the group, Neals, a blind multiply-handicapped child, spontaneously began to reenact the entire sequence of events in the song. This allowed him to explore an added sense of orientation and mobility as well as enjoy his imagination. The other children in the group became captivated in watching Neals, encouraged him to repeat his "acting" and then started imitating him.

CONSIDERATIONS IN SELECTING MATERIALS: INSTRUMENTS AND ANCILLARY MATERIALS

COMMONLY USED INSTRUMENTS IN MUSIC THERAPY

Instruments used in therapy need to be considered for their sensory quality primary in terms of auditory and tactile properties. A variety of instruments will create a pleasing rhythm, melody and harmony rather than just one of these elements. In addition to commonly used instruments detailed below, it is important for the therapist to search for alternative world music instruments of good quality. Here are the instrument families commonly used in therapy.

Percussion

There are so many kinds of drums available and they may serve different purposes depending on the way in which a child needs to physically approach them and the sound one is trying to produce. Orff drums are usually played standing; the djembe drum of all sizes can be played while sitting but tipping it will produce greater sound. The gathering drum is useful if small children wish to sit around it and play together; band size snare, bass and timpani are not commonly found in therapy settings but can be used, especially to create large sounds or to invite particular sensory stimulation. The ocean drum (i.e., manufactured by Remo) is celebrated as a source of multisensory

stimulation since it invites unusual visual, tactile input. Smaller percussion would include claves, rhythm sticks, maracas, triangle, uli-uli shakers (Hawaiian feather gourds), guiro, afuche cabasa (of varying sizes with beads surrounding its head), and tambourines. These must be of professional quality to be useful.

Likewise, cymbals and gongs must be of professional quality. Two cymbals can be available, one 14–16 inches in diameter and another about 10 inches in diameter, both mounted on a stand with a soft mallet beater. If a heavy gong with a mysterious tone is available to add to the music therapy collection, this is useful.

Melodic

The first melodic instrument is the voice. Other melodic instruments commonly used in therapy include the resonator bells, reed horns, bird calls, slide whistle, xylophones of various sizes and materials, and, of course, the piano. Resonator bells that produce the clearest sound are made by Suzuki and require a full arm motion to play most effectively. Reed horns, the most commonly used blowing instrument in therapy, help children form a proper embouchure and practice regulated breathing. The simple kazoo and bird calls can also be used for these purposes. The loveliest xylophones are made as Orff instruments, soprano, alto and bass, played with appropriate beaters to suit the materials they are made of. These xylophones are most easily adapted for visual motor ease by removing the bars that are not being used in the musical composition.

Harmonic

The autoharp, generally used to accompany songs, can be thought of as a harmonic instrument since it plays strummed chords; likewise the guitar and the omnichord. Autoharps come in various sizes and with a varied number of chord possibilities. When "shared" across the laps of a child and a therapist, the autoharp promotes eye contact and has been used in primary assessment by paraverbal therapists (Heimlich, 1975). It can be strummed, percussed with a small beater or plucked. The physical situating of the omnichord shares an attention-getting purpose similar to the autoharp. If one child in the group is higher functioning, that child can be given the job of strumming accompaniment chords to a song the group is singing.

Adaptive Means to Use Instruments

In situations where children are physically challenged, it is important to consider not only positioning and handling but also the selection and use of adaptive means to use instruments. The best source for understanding and adapting instruments is the work of Clark and Chadwick (1980). Adapting instruments and adaptive means for positioning and handling instruments can be done by the therapist often working with the occupational therapist or physical therapist. Other designs for purchase are available through West Music.

The adapted designs allow the child to experience the sensory input of the instruments and/or play them. Simple adaptations include adapted picks, adapted beaters, pocket palm straps, frames and stands. Possibilities such as suspending instruments from the ceiling, the use of foam wedges to provide an alternative angle for the child to play a positioned instrument, and a rubberized bath mat on top of a child's lap to keep the drum in place are example of everyday solutions the creative music therapist can use to help the physically challenged child (Chadwick, 08/20/06, personal communication).

USE OF ANCILLARY MATERIALS

Augumentative Communication Devices

Communication impaired children have the option to use either switch activated or touch activated means to activate messages previously programmed by the therapist or teacher. The beauty of this is: 1) The child is self-selecting the communication message (see touch activated Boardmaker) or 2) The child is self-selecting a sung portion of a song or a recorded instrumental portion of an orchestration which will be activated at the appropriate musical time during the musical experience (see switch activated devices, SAD, such as touch talk devices, known as Big Mack). The Step by Step Big Mack can record several verses in sequence in order to allow a nonverbal child to respond to musical cues while using the device as a surrogate singer. Guided composition, using a yes/no elimination system for selection of topics, allows the therapist to record selected sung information as part of a song; following this, the therapist can provide a musical accompaniment (Chadwick, 08/25/06, personal communication). Out of the session, the child can use a switch to activate music toys or a tape recorder. These devices need to be used judiciously. Boardmaker, a touch activated communication system, contains over 3,000 picture communication symbols which the music therapist can select in order to help the child communicate in music. The system resembles a board and has room for one primary communication symbol as well as adjunctive symbols. For example, the music therapist can use the "I want" as a primary symbol on the board and use "tambourine, drum, horn, and so on" as adjunctive symbols on the board. Another idea in connection with the device, however, is for the music therapist to create a one-to-one correspondence system so the child could first physically touch the instrument they want and then activate the corresponding picture, thereby encouraging preliminary reading.

A device similar to Boardmaker but more elaborate is a 32-message communicator which has 6 levels with 192 three-second messages. Each picture reminds the child what the communication is about. This communication board resembles a breakfast tray and can be placed atop the tray on a wheelchair.

Manipulative Visuals with Songs

Additional materials to present songs can include stuffed animals, puppets, small mirrors, manipulatives such as alphabet forms (in single or three-dimensional form), number forms (single or three-dimensional form) and songboards. Meyer-Johnson pictures for picture exchange and Big Mack speech talkers (also see Augmentative communication) should be used in conjunction with the speech therapy plan. The therapist can photograph instruments and laminate these in order to use them for picture exchange in the music session. Additional therapist-made visuals can serve as picture exchange for types of activities. All can be maintained with a Velcro board and kept in the music room.

Creating Songboards

Songboards can be generated by using music therapy prepared songs (Coleman and Brunk, 2001) or by making your own. In order to make your own, the therapist needs the following materials:

- 8.5 x 11 file folder
- Drawings, photographs or pictures that reference to the content of the song story
- Music for the song
- Two-sided Velcro
- Access to a laminating machine

On the front cover, draw a picture that represents the content of the song. Add the title of the song on the front cover. Paste the music to the back cover. Laminate the front and back at one time, inside the folder next. After selecting the song the therapist wants to illustrate, the therapist cuts out the drawings, photographs or pictures that reference the content of the song story and laminates these. These are added to the inside cover with velcro.

Puppets

Puppets are very useful in helping the therapist act out a story song with the children. In other cases, all the children are given a stuffed animal or doll to help act out a story song, i.e., "Teddy Beat" (Palmer, So Big, 1994 CD), "A new baby" (Nordoff and Robbins, Book 3, 1980a). In a song, where the child is singing about their face, it is appropriate to give them small mirrors.

Materials to Supplement Movement Experience

Materials used to supplement the movement

experience can include the parachute, streamers, a soft middle-sized ball, beanbags and a buddy band. The parachute, as aforedescribed, is used for children to collectively raise and lower and may have a soft ball or balloons thrown in the middle in order to balance these as the parachute motion proceeds. Streamers can be as simple as colored scarves which each child has while moving to music. Beanbags, used as manipulatives, accompany music as they are passed or tossed. The buddy band is an item that all children will hold onto during a movement experience and can be useful for helping the children maintain physical boundaries. Another way to set physical boundaries is to use a hula hoop on the floor for a small group or masking tape on the floor for a larger group.

CONTINUUM OF MUSIC RESPONSE (CMR)

Continuum of Music Response (CMR) (Goodman, 1996–2002) is a system for anticipating different levels of musical response in a group, from lowest to highest functioning levels, adapting materials as necessary with varying methods as necessary for children in the group. The concept of graduated expectations in music therapy was originally presented by Edith Boxill (1985) in her work with the adult developmentally delayed. However, it is helpful in the group setting for the therapist *to further consider the concept of Continuum of Music Response as it applies to the specific members of the group.* The inclusion of CMR in this chapter on materials makes sense if the therapist considers that the *material used must be selected for its possible versatility* in order to be presented (see "Methods," Chapter 7) in different ways to various members of the group. Hence, the adaptation of the material overlaps methodology (see Chapter 7). For this reason, *the CMR concept overlaps planning of objectives, methods and the adaptive nature of using materials.* The therapist creates the continuum in each musical experience dependent upon the functioning levels of children within the group. One example of a continnum for groups of multiply handicapped children is outlined here with general suggestions for vocal, instrumental and movement experiences. Further, examples of specific continuum of musical responses are presented through case examples.

VOCAL EXPERIENCE

General, Continuum Musical Response

1. Listening and watching, some affective reaction, vocal may be combined with movement/instrumental
2. Vocalization (may be delayed)
3. Pitch approximations, phrase singing
4. One word
5. More than one word song lyric(s)
6. Song lyrics to convey feelings, thoughts

Specific, Continuum Musical Response

Case Example One

Song: Bought me a Cat.
Group Members: Multiply handicapped children
Specific, Continuum Musical Response:

- imitate animal sound
- respond with single word response when therapist points to animal being sung about
- approximate parts of sung sentences with therapist
- sing complete sentences with therapist
- recall sequence of sung animals at the end of the song

Discussion: The children in this group are functioning on multiple levels. The highest functioning children are able to sing with the therapist, recall the sequence of sung animals at the end of the song and encourage their peers to approximate parts of sung sentences with the therapist. The therapist is able to prompt lower-functioning children to activate a switch at the appropriate musical moment to imitate the animal sound being sung about or, alternatively, point to it on the songboard.

Case Example Two

Song: "C" is for Cookie (Henson, Muppets, 1986, p. 10)
Group Members: Multiply Handicapped Children, pre-reading skills
Specific, Continuum Musical Response:

- choice of alphabet letter to physically manipulate
- choice of alphabet letter while imitating initial sound of letter with aide
- choice of alphabet letter to physically manipulate while selecting appropriate picture to go with starting letter
- approximation of word while selecting appropriate picture to go with starting letter
- physical manipulation of letter, correct choice of picture and sung lyrics, prompted
- physical manipulation of letter, correct choice of picture and sung lyrics, without prompting

Note: Therapist modifies lyrics of song and choice of visuals to suit alphabet choice, i.e., "" is for banana; "D" is for donuts; "E" is for an egg; "F" is for French fries; "G" is for grapes; "H" is for hot dogs; "I" is for ice cream; "J" is for jello; "K" is for ketchup; "L" is for lemons; "M" is for marshmallows; "N" is for noodles; "O" is for oranges; "P" is for peanuts; "R" is for raisins; "S" is for strawberries; "T" is for tuna; and so on.

Discussion: The children in this group function on multiple levels but many are at the level of pre-reading even though their verbal skills are mixed. The highest functioning children are able to reach the highest point of the continuum while the other children are assisted or prompted to reach their appropriate step of the continuum musical response. The modification of the song lyrics and choice of visuals fit a food theme which also paves the way for another functional academic task, that of classification.

INSTRUMENTAL EXPERIENCE

General, Continuum Musical Response

1. Listening while instruments are being played (sensory intake can include visual, auditory, tactile, kinesthetic)
2. Exploring instrument at beginning level (assisted or unassisted)
3. One step directive (can include stop/start and can include "body percussion")
4. Two-step or multiple directive
5. Instruments as representational
6. Instruments for preacademic directives

Specific, Continuum Musical Response

Case Example One

Instrumental: "Drum caught cold" (Levin & Levin, 1998) (note: children take turns with this piece or, alternatively, the therapist doubles the parts with two drum parts and two cymbal parts)
Group members: Autistic spectrum disorder, mentally retarded
Specific, Continuum Musical Response:

- Physical exploration of drum and cymbal without music
- Physical exploration of drum and cymbal accompanied by music
- Watching therapist model activity while therapist is singing a cappella
- Watching therapist model activity with aide while therapist is singing a cappella and playing the piano accompaniment to the song
- Playing the drum part with visual cues
- Playing the drum and cymbal parts with visual cues
- Playing the drum and cymbal parts without cuing
- Playing the drum and cymbal parts without cuing and with rhythmic stability
- Creative extension of drum and cymbal parts while therapist improvises

Discussion: The children in this group all have very different sensory approaches. The Retts child with the most physical resistance is able to physically explore at successively higher levels until he was up to the fifth step of the continuum, playing the drum part with visual cues. The Downs child with significant motor planning problems is able to start at the third level of the continuum and go to the final level, rather quickly! The emotionally disturbed child in the group was eager to play and, starting at the fourth level of the continuum, was able to play without cuing. However, she had a problem remaining rhythmic, possibly due to her distracting thoughts. It later turned out that she had been a victim of child abuse.

MOVEMENT EXPERIENCE

General, Continuum Musical Response

1. Listening while being physically manipulated to music (sensory intake)
2. Watching while a visual is physically manipulated
3. Gross motor start and stop
4. Finger plays
5. One-step directions
6. Multiple directions
7. Representational play
8. Preacademic directives in the context of movement

Specific, Continuum Musical Response

Case Example One

Movement activity: Hokey pokey
Group members: Mentally retarded, multiply handicapped
Specific Continuum of Response:

- Child is provided hand-over-hand assistance to go through three-step directive
- Child follows three-step directive (step in, step out, clap)
- Child follows five-step directive (step in, step out, step in, shake, clap)
- Child follows six-step direction (step in, step

out, step in, shake it, turn around, clap)

Discussion: The children in this group have difficulty with physical boundaries so the therapist provides masking tape on the floor to help the children stand on the line and use this visual as a way to step in and step out. Only one member of the five-person group has a sense of left vs. right and imitation of the therapist standing in front of the children would contradict these terms anyway, therefore, the words "left" and "right" are changed to "this" and "that." Those children who have language sing along with the therapist, initially following a sequence of three directives and gradually adding more directives up to the six in the first stanza. This gradual introduction to the song allows the children to begin to effectively motor plan, and each week more stanzas can be added. The music itself is adapted accordingly and can be presented in terms of theme and variation as the children progress motorically.

Case Example Two

Movement activity: "Pita Pata" (Stewart, 1991)
Group members: The group of multiply handicapped children is following a four-step sequence to African American music, Pita Pata (Stewart, Music from around the World). The sequence is: Clap, Stamp, Pat, Kick
Specific, Continuum Musical Response:

- Child is physically assisted through motions, using arms instead of legs if nonambulatory
- Child is physically assisted through motions
- Child follows one directive successfully
- Child follows two directives successfully
- Child follows three directives successfully
- Child follows four directives successfully
- Child recalls sequence
- Child is able to extend choreography with prompting
- Child is able to extend choreography independently.

Discussion: In order to adapt the music, the therapist has recorded the melody over a beat replicating the music. She sings a voice over with repeti-

tion of each directive two or more times, as necessary for each child to master the step at least once. Then she moves on. The song is simple enough to accommodate spontaneous repetition and still remain musical.

LISTENING EXPERIENCE

General, Continuum Musical Response

1. Listening to live music without song lyrics in order to receive sensory stimulation
2. Listening to live or recorded music without song lyrics in order to receive sensory stimulation
3. Listening to music for relaxation
4. Listening to music as a means of emotional awareness and projective thinking

General, Continuum Musical Response

Case Example One (Goodman, K., 1996–2002)

Listening Selection: Peter and the Wolf
Group: Emotionally Disturbed
Specific, Continuum Musical Response:

- Child attends to music
- Child watches puppet characters manipulated to music as thematic roles in music are presented (Peter, Grandfather, cat, bird, wolf, duck, hunters)
- Child independently manipulates puppet characters as they appear in the music
- Following the music, child recalls story sequence
- Following the music, child provides projective free association

Discussion: Mason, a disturbed child who has, unfortunately, been refused reentry into four special education schools because of assaultive behavior, loves music. Nurtured by the other children in the group, he becomes a helper and leader. He is able to work through challenging tasks in music and requested the music experience of, "Hand

Jive," Sclesa, 1983), as a reward. As I realize that Mason has an able musical ear, I introduce a tape of musical instruments, part of a musical lotto game, into the music therapy session. Mason is able to win frequently and his self-esteem grows. He starts to ask for classical music. While listening to "Peter and the Wolf," he grows animated and starts to identify with the character of Peter, who sneaks up to the top of the tree, lassos the wolf by the tail, and is helped by the hunters to take it to the zoo. Mason is proud and tells the therapist he is powerful, he is in control. She confirms that he is able to take control of situations without getting out of control. This is music therapy at its finest moment!

MUSICAL DRAMA

General, Continuum Musical Response

1. Child watches other children engage in drama
2. Child holds object of representational play (i.e., teddy bear, doll, mirror) and is given assistance, cues and modeling to replicate what other children are doing
3. Child independently manipulates object of representational play
4. Child extends representational play independently or in conjunction with other children
5. Child's attention span allows participation in larger scale musical drama

Specific, Continuum Musical Response

Case Example (Goodman, K., 1996–2002)

Dramatic Selection: Does anyone have a new baby? (Nordoff and Robbins, 1980, Book 5)
Group: Multiply disabled preadolescents
Specific Continuum of Musical Response:

- Child observes other children or therapist engage in drama
- Child holds doll and is given verbal directives to follow directions in song

- Child independently projects his feelings onto doll, initiating his own actions
- With verbal support, child is able to reflect on his actions and their possible meaning
- Independently, child is able to reflect on his actions and their possible meaning

Discussion: Luis is 13, largely nonverbal, retarded and emotionally disturbed. He has a history of assault with peers and teachers in the building. One day he is particularly volatile and the therapist learns that his mother has given birth to his new sibling. In music therapy, he is given a baby doll to handle while the therapist introduces a song entitled, "A New Baby." The first version of the song proceeds as composed; "Does anyone know a new baby? Does anyone see a new baby? Take a look at the baby's eyes. Take a look, take a look at the baby's eyes. Take a look at the baby's nose. Take a look, take a look at the baby's nose. Oh! Oh! Don't forget to sing to the baby! Don't forget to sing to the baby." (Nordoff and Robbins, 1980, Book 4, p. 14). Following this rendition, Luis throws the doll down on the floor. The children in the group are not sure how to react. They appear uncomfortable. The therapist adapts the words, "Sometimes you feel mad at the baby. Sometimes you feel mad at the baby Sometimes you don't like the baby. Sometimes you don't like the baby." Following this musical acknowledgment of his feelings, Luis laughs and then picks up the doll, holding it tenderly. The therapist continued singing, "And then sometimes you love the baby. Sometimes you love the baby."

The experience of small scale drama helps Jose externalize his feelings. His escalating behavior is eased and other children who are capable of understanding his feelings appear to have their own discomfort eased when Jose becomes more comfortable in the group.

SAMPLE MATERIALS WITH CHILDREN OF DIFFERENT FUNCTIONAL LEVELS

Music therapists collecting lists of materials used in daily clinical work can organize it in various ways. These listings are organized by modality (vocal, instrumental, movement) and by composer or the name of the collection. Other possible ways to organize the material would include classification according to developmental purposes, or according to diagnostic populations as well as developmental purposes.

In the age before computers, students were encouraged to save 3x5 or 5x7 cards with the following information: Name of song, composer, reference, developmental purposes, suggested presentation (methods), adaptations or variations. This type of information is useful for the therapist building a repertoire of materials that have been successfully used and adapted with children.

The following sample listing of materials was arranged over a five-year period while conducting therapy with multiply handicapped children (Goodman, 1996–2002). It is based on Continuum of Musical Response (CMR) (Goodman, 2002).

VOCAL EXPERIENCES

Materials listed below are used on the following levels: 1) Listening and watching (some affective reaction); vocal may be combined with movement/instrumental; 2) vocalization (may be delayed); 3) pitch approximations; phrase singing; 4) one word; 5) more than one word song lyric(s); and 6) song lyrics to convey feelings, thought.

Sample uses or themes follow the listing of various songs here.

1. Disney Collection, abstract thoughts, feelings (Disney Collection, 1993)
   - Candle on water (p. 19): friendship
   - I've got no strings (p. 56): independence
   - It's a small world (p. 61): friendship
   - Zip a dee doo dah (p. 156): happiness
   - Let's go fly a kite (p. 74): seasonal, spring
   - When you wish upon a star (p. 129): motivation
   - Love is a song (p. 80): attachment; Valentine's Day
   - Little April shower (p. 78): seasonal, spring
   - Baby mine (p. 4): separation/individuation
   - Supercalifragalistic (p. 118): articulation

   - Chim chim cherri (p. 24): vocalization
   - Whistle while you work (p. 144): embouchure
   - Give a little whistle (p. 48): embouchure
2. Music Connection (Silver-Burdett, 1995)
   - Sound Poem (grade 5, p. 31): dramatic play
   - Read me a story (K, p. 178): preacademic
   - Falling Rain (grade 2, p. 106): dramatic play with rainsticks
   - I shall sing (grade 4, p. 138): free vocalization
   - Zuni Song (p. 192): vowel sounds
   - Think positive (book 5, p. 4): self-esteem
   - One moment in time (grade 5, p. 140): self-esteem
   - Somewhere out there (grade 5, p. 128): representational play; mood song
   - Under the sea (p. 160): representational play
   - I can do it (K, p. 182): affirmation
   - I feel tall inside (K, p. 172): sense of self
   - You're not everybody (K, p. 170): sense of self
   - Magical me (K, p. 168): sense of self
   - There's just something about a song (grade 5, p. 21): mood song
   - A round of good-byes (grade 5, p. 28): closure
   - Bounce and catch (ball play)
   - One, two, three alary (grade 2, p. 30): rhythmic play
   - Come sailing with me (grade 2, p. 124): antiphonal movement
   - Talking on the telephone (grade K, p. 152): representational play
3. Traditional
   - Down on Grandpa's farm; sequential sounds, vocalization, use of puppet; cock a doddle do, moo, oink, wuff, neigh, gobble, he haw, how do you do; verse chorus structure, sequential actions
   - Bingo: adapt to spell child's name, projective use
   - Kimbayah: vocalize on last syllable, "yah"; substitute syllables for vocalization following the developmental order of acquisition
   - You gotta sing: multi-directional
   - Twinkle twinkle little star: use of small lights

for auditory tracking
- Wheels on the bus: series of imitative movements
- Whole world in his hands: series of imitative movements
- Pat a cake: beginning intimacy
- Row, row, row, your boat: antiphonal rhythmic movement
- Michael row your boat ashore: antiphonal movement
- Down by the riverside: multiple directives

4. Grace Nash (1988)
- Fifty States United (Nash, Holidays and Special Days, p. 120)

5. Raffi (1983, 1984, 1986, 1989)
- Bathtime (Everything grows CD): ADL
- Brush your teeth (*Raffi Singable Songbook*, p. 16): ADL
- Over in the meadow (*Baby beluga*, p. 28): animal sounds
- Six little ducks (*Raffi Singable Songbook*, p. 78): animal sounds
- Listen to the horses (*Raffi Singable Songbook*, p. 50): animal sounds, vocalization
- Good-night Irene (*Raffi Singable Songbook*, p. 34): representational play
- Going to the zoo (*Raffi Singable Songbook*, p. 32): animal sounds, representational play
- Five little frogs (*Raffi Singable Songbook*, p. 28): animal sounds, representational play, object permanence, counting, dramatic play.
- Cluck, cluck red hen (*Raffi Singable Songbook*, p. 18): animal sounds, representational play
- Finger play (*Everything grows songbook*, p. 40)
- You'll sing a song (*Raffi Singable Songbook*, p. 101): antiphonal play, extend to instruments, movement
- Mary wore her red dress (*Raffi Singable Songbook*, p. 22): colors, clothing
- Aikendrum (*Raffi Singable Songbook*, p. 7): sense of humor, parts of body; food (songboard adaptation)
- Willoughby, wallowby: rhyming, sound substitution, humor (*Raffi Singable Songbook*)
- Who built the ark? (*Raffi Singable Songbook*, p. 90): antiphonal, rhyming

- Peanut butter sandwich (*Raffi Singable Songbook*): ADL, sharing
- Going on a picnic (*Raffi Singable Songbook*, p. 31): classification, possible visuals and use of songboard
- This old man (*Baby beluga*, p. 32): counting, movement sequence
- If I had a dinosaur (*Raffi Singable Songbook*, p. 44): representational play
- Down by the bay (*Raffi Singable Songbook*, p. 26): rhyming
- My way home (*Raffi Singable Songbook*, pp. 60–61): transition, short-term memory
- It's mine but you can have some (*Raffi Singable Songbook*, p. 18): sharing
- I wonder if I'm growing: transition (*Raffi Singable Songbook*)
- Swing low (*Raffi Singable Songbook*, p. 86)
- Pick a bale (*Raffi Singable Songbook*, p. 70): one step to multistep directions
- Mr. Sun (*Raffi Singable Songbook*): visuals
- To everyone in all the world (*Baby beluga*): shake hands
- Slow day (Bananaphone CD): vocals
- The world we love (Bananaphone CD): conceptual

6. Tom Glazer (1973, 1983)
- The little white duck (*Eyewinker*, p. 46)
- Old Macdonald (*Eyewinker*, p. 56): fingerplay
- Baa, baa, black sheep, traditional
- Barnyard Song (*Eyewinker*, p. 10)
- Bought me a cat, traditional: sequence, representational play, animal sounds
- The bear went over the mountain (*Eyewinker*, p. 11)
- Bingo (*Eyewinker*, p. 13)
- Baby's going bye-bye (*Music for ones and twos*): representational
- Pull my wagon (*Music for ones and twos*): representational
- Blocks (*Music for ones and twos*): representational
- Rock my doll (*Music for ones and twos*): representational
- Bang hammer (*Music for ones and twos*): representational
- Roll my ball (*Music for ones and twos*): repre-

sentational
7. Songboards
   • Six little ducks
   • Eensy weensy spider
   • Old McDonald
8. Greg and Steve (1983, 1986)
   • Little Sir Echo (*We all live together,* p. 17): auditory tracking
   • Rainbow of colors (Greg and Steve Live Together, Vol. 5): red, yellow, green, blue, white, orange, brown, black: touch, identify, match
   • Piggy bank (Greg and Steve Live Together, Vol. 3): counting
   • Days of the week (Greg and Steve Live Together, Vol. 4)
   • Months of the year (Greg and Steve Live Together, Vol. 2)
   • Sing a happy song (*We all live together*): free vocal
   • Let's go to the market (Greg and Steve Live Together, Vol. 5)
   • We're all together again (Greg and Steve Live Together, Vol. 5)
   • The number game (Greg and Steve Live Together, Vol. 5)
9. Levin, Herbert and Gail (1997a, 1998)
   • The hungry song (*Learning Through Songs,* p. 31): question/answer
   • Happy things (*Learning Through Music,* p. 115): free vocalization in chorus
   • When it rains (*Learning Through Songs,* p. 38): cause and effect
   • Rhyme time (*Learning Through Songs,* p. 5): rhyming
   • Friends (*Learning Through Songs,* p. 47): friendship
   • Everybody makes mistakes (*Learning Through Songs,* p. 19): process of learning
   • Sad things (*Learning Through Songs,* p. 44): mood
   • Friends (*Learning Through Songs,* p. 47): interpersonal concept
   • Yes, I can (*Learning Through Songs,* p. 24): affirmation
   • Some people (*Learning Through Songs,* p. 36): reflection
   • Windy wind (*Learning Through Songs,* p. 28): reflection

   • What's in your house? (*Learning Through Songs,* p. 9): sentence building, pronouns, verbs, plurals, classification, short-term memory
   • How old are you? (*Learning Through Songs,* p. 12): preacademic
   • Now and before (*Learning Through Songs,* p. 15): cause and effect
   • What do you say? (*Learning Through Songs,* p. 21): contractions
   • Learn about things (*Learning Through Songs,* p. 33): senses
   • Today, yesterday and tomorrow (*Learning Through Songs,* p. 40): time sequences
   • Silly song (*Learning Through Songs,* p. 42): logic
10. Nordoff and Robbins: Playsongs (1962, 1968, 1980a, 1980b, 1980c)
   • Penny-nickel-dime-quarter-dollar song (Book 3, p. 9): counting; articulation
   • Color song (Book 4, p. 22): colors
   • Green grass, little wind, big sun, blue sky (Book 5, p. 18): moods, colors, visualization, extend to instrumental drama
   • Safety song (Book 3, p. 6): boundaries
   • What did you see? (Book 4, p. 6): chatty
   • The way I like to sit (Book 4, p. 12): autonomy
   • Let me tell you (Book 4, p. 16): story
   • I have a friend (Book 4, p. 20): interpersonal
   • I'm mad today (Book 5, p. 14): negative emotion, coping
   • A new baby (Book 4, p. 14): transition, representational play
   • Good-bye (Book 2, p. 19): closure
   • A brand new day (Book 4, p. 8): mood
   • A song for Julie (Book 4, p. 10): personalize, reinforce date
   • Thank you (Book 3, p. 23): closure
   • Roll Call (Book 2, p. 4): opening
   • Hello (Book 1, p. 3): opening
   • Good morning (Book 3, p. 3): opening
   • You have a name (Book 1, p. 19): ego
   • Let's sit and talk (Book 1, p. 20): matching/identification
   • What's that? (Book 2, p. 10): matching,

identification
- It's a rainy day (Book 2, p. 9): mood
- You never can tell (Book 3, p. 12): mood, reflective
- Green grass, little wind, big sun, blue sky (Book 5, p. 18): mood
- Who would like to take a little walk with me (Book 3, p. 13): movement
- I've got a hat (Book 1, p. 7): representational play, directives, weather

11. Greetings and Goodbyes (Ritholz and Robbins, 1995)
- Goodbye and tootleloo (p. 18): closing
- Dismissal song (p. 18): closing
- Thank you for the music (p. 20): closing
- Now it's time to say good-bye: closing
- Clap hands (Novickes): multiple directives
- Good morning, everyone (p. 3): opening
- Good morning to you (p. 4): opening
- It's your turn to sing (p. 6): free vocalization
- What shall we do (p. 8): simple language
- Calypso greeting (p. 10): movement

12. Sesame Street (Prebenna, D., Moss, J., Conney, J., 1992; Henson, 1986; Moss and Raposo, 1992)
- Picture a world (*Sesame Street, vol. 2*, p. 46): reflective
- Sing (*Sesame Street, vol. 2*, p. 35): free vocalization
- What do I do when I'm alone (*Sesame Street, vol. 2*, p. 26): mood, conceptual, loneliness
- The Grouch song (*Sesame Street, vol. 2*, p. 51): mood
- I'm pretty (*Sesame Street, vol. 2*, p. 59): self-esteem
- Green (*Muppets*, p. 28): individuation
- One of these things is not like the other (*Sesame Street Songbook*, p. 50): classification; matching
- Everybody makes mistakes (*Sesame Street, vol. 2*, p. 10): coping
- Word family song (*Sesame Street, vol. 2*, p. 24): family
- Over, under, around and through (*Sesame Street, vol. 2*, p. 67): prepositions, directionality

13. Hap Palmer (1969b, 1981a, 1981b, 1994)
- Triangle, circle or square (*Favourites*, p. 68):

preacademic
- So Big (So Big, #6): comparison
- So happy you're here (So Big, #1): one-step direction, imitative vocal
- Letter sounds (*Favourites*, p. 73): preacademic
- Pocket full of B's (*Favourites*, p. 74): preacademic
- Making letters (*Favourites*, p. 76): preacademic
- Marching around the alphabet (*Favourites*, p. 78): movement, preacademic, dramatic play
- Let's hide the tambourine (Learning Basic skills, #7, vol. 2): object permanence
- Big things come from little things you do (So Big): representational play
- Rub a Dub (More Baby Songs, #1): representational play
- My baby (More baby songs): representational play
- The hammer song (Tickey Toddle): representational play
- Big things come from little things you do (So Big): representational play
- My baby (More Baby Songs, #2): reresentational play
- The hammer song (More Baby Songs, #4): representational play

14. Tom Pease (Pease and Stotts, 2003)
- Read a book with me: preacademic
- Love grows: gestural

INSTRUMENTAL EXPERIENCES

Materials listed below are used on the following levels: 1) Listening while instruments are being played (sensory intake can include visual, auditory, tactile, kinesthetic); 2) Exploring instrument at beginning level (assisted or unassisted); 3) One-step directive (can include stop/start and can include "body percussion"); 4) two-step or multiple directive; 5) instruments as representational; 6) instruments for preacademic directives.

1. Music Connection
- Environmental Sounds Bank (K, CD 7): autoharp, hand cymbals, jingle bar, rhythm

sticks, sandblocks, stepbells, tambourine, tom-tom, triangle, woodblock

2. Greg and Steve: backdrop for instrumental music as well as vocal and movement (Sclesa and Millang, 1983)
   - It's a beautiful day (vol. 4)
   - Everyone has music inside
   - Siesta
   - Sing a happy song (vol. 3)
   - Friends forever (vol. 5)
   - Lullaby tape (K, CD 2, ostinato with D, G, B)
   - Big ol storm a coming
   - Something about a song

3. Levin & Levin, (1997) Learning Through Song
   - Quietly: beginning tone chimes
   - Play your bell one time (p. 62): beginning tone chimes
   - Bell dance (p. 80): beginning tone chimes
   - Take turns (p. 40): drums
   - One (p. 52): drums
   - One (p. 58): drums
   - Copycat (p. 55): drums
   - Two (p. 59): drums
   - Three (p. 60): drums
   - Alternate hands (p. 64): drums
   - Four and five (p. 76): drums
   - With cymbal (p. 44)
   - Two and three (p. 72): horns
   - Slow horns (p. 78): horns

4. Raffi (1982, 1983, 1984, 1989)
   - Let's make some noise (Everything Grows, p. 26): sing, clap, shake
   - Working on the railroad (p. 94): whistle, horn
   - Morningtown (Baby beluga): train whistle, ring bell
   - Old MacDonald had a band (p. 66)
   - Twinkle (use with bell tree)
   - Rise and shine: visuals

5. Nordoff and Robbins (1962, 1968, 1980a, 1980c)
   - Fun for four drums
   - Charlie knows how to beat that drum (Book 1)
   - Drum talk (Book 2)
   - Who would like to? (Book 3, p. 13): group instrumental possibility

   - We'll make music together (Book 5, p. 10)
   - What shall we do on a sunny sunny morning?: use picture exchange

6. Ritholz and Robbins (1999, 2003): Themes for Therapy

7. Sesame Street (Prebenna et al., 1992)
   - Play along (p. 5)
   - I've got a new way to walk (adapt to shake, ring, sing, etc.)

8. Tom Glazer (1983)
   - What does baby hear?: auditory discrimination, object permanence

9. Hap Palmer (1981, 1987 CD)
   - Family Harmony (Tickley Toddle)
   - Harmonica happiness: clap/march
   - I'm a little wood block (p. 104, Favourites): basic beat
   - Tap your sticks (p. 110)
   - Clap and rest (p. 120)
   - Play your sticks (p. 122)

10. Greg and Steve (Scelsa and Millang, 1983)
    - Rock and roll rhythm band (vol. 5): cumulative playing includes tambourine, sticks, shaker, bells, triangle, block, soft and loud, stop

11. Ella Jenkins (1994)
    - Play your instruments and make a pretty sound (shake your head, listen to cowbell, rhythm sticks, maracas, softly, triangle, castanets)
    - Traditional: Come on and join into the game.

MOVEMENT EXPERIENCES

Materials listed below are used on the following levels: 1) listening while being physically manipulated to music (sensory intake); 2) watching while a visual is physically manipulated; 3) gross motor start and stop; 4) finger plays; 5) one step directions; 6) multiple directions; 7) representational play; 8) preacademic directives in the context of movement.

1. Hap Palmer
   - Rock and Roll Freeze Dance (So Big, #5, 1994 CD): impulse control

- Five little monkeys (So Big, 1994 CD): dramatic play involves monkeys (fingers), jumping on bed, fall down, bump head, call doctor, no, repeat sequence with hopping on bed, turning on bed, jumping on bed
- Let's Dance (Learning basic skills, vol. 2, 1969b CD): children in line, circle or scattered, also see "Partners," multiple direction with partner
- Marching around the alphabet (Learning Basic Skills, vol. 1, 1969a CD): use with alphabet beanbags: bend/grasp at beginning level
- Put your hands up in the air (Learning Basic Skills, vol. 1, 1969a CD): multiple directives
- Ten Wiggle Worms (So Big, 1994 CD): finger isolation
- Toes (Tickley Toddle): with shoes and socks off, piggy toes, sensory stimulation (Palmer, 1981b, CD)
- Parade of colors (Learning basic skills, vol. 2 recording): march around the circle with color card (blue, red, black, green, yellow, pink, purple, brown, white, orange). Stand and sit as directed in song lyric, adapt as necessary, also see below:
  a. Move around the color
  b. Colors
  c. Parade of colors
  d. What are you wearing?
- Bluegrass jambouree (So Big, #12, 1994 CD): clap, stamp, jump and spin, hop and grin, step and swing, run in place, all fall down. Fast paced sequence, can simplify if recording is not used.
- Growing (So Big, #11): imitative gesture
- Teddy bear playtime (So Big, 1994 CD): visual modeling for representational play with teddy bear; multiple directions

2. Raffi (1989)
- Ha ha this away (Everything Grows, p. 33, songbook and tape): visual localization
- Shake my sillies out (Singable songbook, p. 74): repetition, body parts
- Walking (rise and shine): march

3. Ella Jenkins (1994)
- Follow the leader: clap hands, beat chest, slap thighs, tap knees, stamp feet, slide feet

- Let's listen to the band:conducting and marching
- This is the way to lead the band: march, waltz, jazz beat: add tape on floor as necessary for visual cues

4. Greg and Steve (Scelsa and Millang, 1983)
- Simon Sez, vol. 3: can also use with free accompaniment and do voice over. First rendition includes the following directives: touch head, eyes, nose, mouth, eyebrows, ears, teeth, hair, cheeks, chin, neck, shoulder, arms, fingers, hands, elbows
- Rainbow of colors
- Bingo (vol. 4): sound effects
- Happy and you know it (vol. 3): directions, call/response, cumulative response, creative directives to make up
- A walking we will go (CD 5): walk, stomp, skip, slide, bounce, tiptoe, march, hold hands, sit down (slow paced)
- Old brass wagon (CD 5) circle to left, to right, in, out, run around, shoulder/ knees, clap three times, toes and jump, shout hurrah
- Hand Jive (vol. 4): antiphonal, simple to complex
- Dancing machine (vol. 3): imaginative play
- Just like me (vol. 4): fast paced imitative
- Shapes (vol. 3): use beanbag shapes or laminates for children to respond to movement cues
- When I'm down I get up and dance (CD 5): representational play
- Disco limbo (vol. 3)

5. Tom Pease (1983)
- Apple Pickin Time: two lines opposite each other, choreograph for higher functioning as follows: stamp feet, march in time, hands on hips, kick legs up, swing partner to right, to left, return to line and renew with next pair of students. Do see doe twice and go on to next pair of students. Form bridge and all go under–go on to next pair. End or return to stamp/march until music ends
- Walk a mile in your shoes
- Love grows: gestural, sign
- Rain comes down: gestural, sign

6. Music Connection (Silver-Burdett, 1995)

- Jig along home (K, CD 7, #5): voice over: clap, stamp, dosey-do, down under bridge, also see Bluegrass jambouree
- Zion's children (K, CD 7, #7): fast paced marching, can slow down and do on casio related function
- Will you follow me (K, p. 260): imitative movement
- Hokey Pokey (p. 274, K, CD 7, #2 and #4): Sequence One: right foot in, right foot out, right foot in, shake it all about (do the hokey pokey and you) turn yourself around (that's what its all about) clap: Sequence Two: left foot in, left foot out, left foot in, shake it all about, turn yourself around, clap. Sequence Three: right hand, etc.; Sequence Four: left hand, etc. Sequence Five: head in, out, in, shake, turn around. Clap; Sequence Six, whole self in, out, shake, turn, clap. Add or eliminate sequences as necessary. Keep in mind that one sequence is six progressive steps.
- Lullabye tape
7. Tom Glazer (1964, 1983)
  - Where are your eyes?: multiple directives to use with hand mirrors (eyes, nose, ears, mouth, hands can clap, shut eyes, wiggle nose, open mouth, clap hands and kick). Option to use puppet for visual modeling.
  - Ten fingers (p. 72, Eye Winker)
  - Ten Little Indians (p. 74, Eye Winker)
  - Peters hammers (p. 61, Eye Winker): personalize
  - Where is thumbkin?
  - One finger, one thumb: finger isolation
  - Hickory dickory dock
  - Ten fingers (p. 60, Eye Winker)
  - Eeentsy weentsy spider (p. 59, Eye Winker)
  - Here is the church (p. 52, Eye Winker)
  - I'm a little teapot (p. 53, Eye Winker)
  - What will we do with the baby? (p. 51, Eye Winker)
  - Pat a cake (p. 50, Eye Winker)
  - Roll the Ball: simple passing
8. Abramson (1997) Dalcroze Exercises: can lead to awareness of beginning notation

- Bounce and Catch, #5
- Catch, #6
- Clap beat, #7
- Swing to beat, #8
- Walk to beat, #10
- Clap vs. walk, #11
- Skip/gallop, #12
- Count to 8, #13
9. Disney (1993)
  - Following the leader (Peter Pan, p. 42): march
  - Heigh-ho (p. 52): march
  - Mickey Mouse march, p. 82
10. Georgianna Stewart (1977, 1984, 1987, 1991, 1992): beanbag, parachute play
  - Beanbag Parade (#7): march
  - Pass (1): beanbags
  - Catch (5): beanbags
  - Bumping/jumping (#1, parachute play): lift/shake up/down/shake around: multiple directives
  - Mountain high (#2, parachute play): abstract play
11. Classical
  - Turkish March, Beethoven: march
  - Dreams: stretch
  - Swan: slow stretch (Carnival of the Animals, Camille Saint-Saens)
  - Mother Goose Suite (Ravel)
  - Brahms lullaby: rocking, slow stretch
  - Girl with flaxen hair (Childrens Corner, Debussy): slow stretch
  - Parade of wooden soldiers: march
  - March of the toys (Nutcracker, Tchaikovsky): march
  - March of Siamese children: march
  - Bizet: march
  - Gallop: running (Schumann, Kinderscenen)
  - Hoedown (Copland): square dance choreography
  - Pachabel Canon: stretching, breathing exercises.
12. Moss and Raposo (1992): Sesame Street
  - Circles, p. 63
  - Follow the leader: movement imitation (also vocal and instrumental)

SUMMARY

This chapter has outlined considerations in selecting and adapting materials for music therapy: vocal, instrumental, movement, listening and musical drama. Further, the concept of Continuum of Musical Response (CMR) allows the therapist to conduct group music therapy experiences while anticipating different responses from different children in the group. Creativity and flexibility must be the hallmarks of the therapy approach in using music. A detailed list of resources for music therapy materials is included in the Appendix of this book.

STUDY GUIDE QUESTIONS

1. What are the considerations in selecting vocal materials?
2. What are the considerations in selecting instrumental materials?
3. What are the considerations in selecting movement materials?
4. What are the considerations in selecting materials for listening?
5. What are the considerations in selecting materials for musical drama?
6. What is the Continuum of Musical Response?
7. Practice making a songboard for your music therapy group.
8. Practice choreographing a piece of recorded music.
9. Practice orchestrating a piece of classical music from the Schumann Kinderscenen.

Chapter 7

How Do I Do It? Methods in Group Music Therapy

INTRODUCTION

After the music therapist arrives at goals, objectives and materials for the group session, it is of paramount importance to consider the methodology or specific steps taken to present music for the children.

As previously discussed, initial long-term goals, established both through IEP review and music therapy assessment, lead to the formulation of short-term objectives based on the therapist's awareness of how steps toward the goal present in context of the music-making experience. The materials, which need to be adaptable, are based on the various developmental needs, musical interests and cultural backgrounds of the children and may suggest a type of activity. *The way in which the therapist presents the music activity or experience, premeditated or spontaneous, constitutes methodology, also known as procedures, strategies or interventions.*

Music Therapy as a Unique Discipline

Selected methodology from allied fields such as special education, music education, occupational therapy, physical therapy, speech language therapy and various theories of psychology music therapy can be "translated" into the context of the music therapy session. This is interesting from a historical perspective since, as the fields of special education, music education and psychology have changed, music therapy has been influenced by these changes. However, as a profession, it is important not only to be influenced by new information from related fields but also to craft the music therapy field as one of unique identity and value. One important way in which music therapy

professionals accomplish this is to *understand how to modify the use of musical elements*–rhythm, melody, harmony, timbre, dynamics, form–when selecting music, adapting music and improvising music (see Chapter 6, "Materials"). The music therapy profession has done and continues to do this.

In the course of crafting the profession and being influenced by related disciplines, music therapists selectively develop and use music therapy approaches. These approaches dictate and subsume methodology. For example, Orff, Kodaly, and Dalcroze are examples of music education approaches adapted for music therapy while "Nordoff-Robbins," "Behavioral," "Neurologic," and "Psychodynamic" are examples of music therapy approaches.

In a straightforward world, one approach would simplify the use of methods. However, *quite often the therapist finds that the needs of the children in the group necessitate a mix of approaches or possibly adaptation of approaches.* There is validity to the use of many approaches in music therapy, depending, of course, on the needs of the client. This is an eclectic rather than a purist way of thinking. First and foremost, the therapist needs to evaluate any method for its appropriateness in meeting the developmental levels and needs of the group. That thinking process is demonstrated in this chapter.

Planning Methods vs. Internalizing the Understanding of Methods

The fact that the word "method" is defined as a planned orderly way to do something implies *forethought and consistency,* two hallmarks of successful outcomes, assuming the methodology is a good "fit" for the children in the group.

Forethought and consistency are overlapping concerns in methodology whether the music is planned or spontaneous.

As a beginning means toward forethought and consistency, it is valuable to detail the methods in a written session plan so that they can be carried out in a deliberate therapeutic manner and later evaluated for efficacy. As the student therapist gains clinical expertise and begins to internalize the methods needed to carry out therapeutic musical experiences, the need for writing out methodology decreases

Flexibility in the Session

Even as methods for various kinds of musical experiences are premeditated and eventually become internalized thinking, these plans must only be considered a *beginning* game plan. In fact, *what happens with a seasoned therapist is the understanding of methodology to respond to any spontaneous events in the music therapy session. It is critical for the therapist to be flexible and adaptive in formulating goals, objectives, methods and materials as the session or sessions evolve. This process is created by interpersonal and musical exchange between the therapist and the children.*

The Why and the How of Methodology

There is, potentially, an enormous amount of information to consider in terms of methods. Deciding on methods depends upon the perspective of the therapist and the degree of specificity the therapist has in understanding the clinical populations represented in the group. Further, the music therapy profession has thankfully reached the point where the "why" as well as the "how" behind methodology should always be considered. This chapter invites a critical process and is a start for the therapist to be mindful of the reasons why particular methods are a beginning but by no means an end.

Considerations in Methodology

Methodology in the music therapy group involves multiple considerations, all of which are described in this chapter and can serve as review

points for the therapist to reflect upon when deciding how to run a music therapy session:

1. The *space* being used for music therapy.
2. Physical arrangement of the group.
3. Music therapy activity levels that are consistent with the various functioning levels of the children in the group.
4. Music therapy strategies related to the diagnoses and primary strengths and weaknesses of the children in the group.
5. Music therapy strategies linked to goals and objectives for all group members, often resulting in adaptation of music materials.
6. Incorporation of support and professional staff for interdisciplinary, multidisciplinary and transdisciplinary work.
7. Music therapy strategies designed to invite and promote group process.
8. Music therapy session *format* that makes sense given the purpose, preferences and functioning level of the group.
9. *Adaptive* nature of the methodology.
10. Therapist knowledge base and philosophy of helping that are suited to the methodology being used.

Again, regardless of the type of approach used in music therapy, the strategies must be consistent with the current functional level and needs of the children, be adaptive in response to changing functional levels and needs, and, finally, be an approach or a combination of approaches the music therapist is personally comfortable working with.

These points, a critical review of various music therapy approaches possible in groupwork with children, as well as a working case example, are presented in this chapter.

CONSIDERATIONS IN METHODOLOGY

THE SPACE BEING USED FOR MUSIC THERAPY

Ideally, the music therapist should have a music

room equipped with appropriate instruments and instrumental storage, a piano, sheet music, compact discs, good quality audio equipment, songboards, chairs appropriate for the children, and mats for relaxation to music. The room should be large enough to accommodate musical experiences for vocal, instrumental, movement and listening enjoyment. The room should have windows and proper lighting. Florescent lighting that emits high frequency sounds, for example, can be disturbing to sensitive children with hyperacusis. The issue of storage is also important since an overstimulating or disorganized room can be very distracting to children and, for some children, serve as an open invitation to grab whatever seizes their fancy at the moment. For children who are understimulated, it can be helpful to take out an assortment of instruments that are visible and invite spontaneous choice-making.

Unfortunately, the music therapist does not always have an ideal space. In these cases, it is important to realize the impact of the space on the children in the session and try to explain this to an administrator.

PHYSICAL ARRANGEMENT OF THE GROUP

In order to promote eye contact with the therapist and with each other, it is helpful to arrange the children in a semicircle. When the therapist is using the piano, it is possible to arrange this semicircle around the piano. In cases where this is not possible, it may be necessary for the therapist to work with a keyboard in order to maintain eye contact with the children. This is, however, an unhappy compromise and should be avoided if at all possible. Children should be seated adjacent to peers who have the least possibility of disrupting them in the session.

In situations where the music therapist is asked to go room to room, sessions lose some element of flexibility since the space cannot be in any kind of controlled environment conducive to the music therapy session. However, using a horseshoe type of table where the therapist can be seated in the center and have physical and visual access to all

the children in the group is making the best of a difficult situation.

MUSIC THERAPY ACTIVITY LEVELS THAT ARE CONSISTENT WITH THE VARIOUS FUNCTIONING LEVELS OF THE CHILDREN IN THE GROUP

Developmental Perspective

Music therapy activity levels consistent with the various functioning levels of the children in the group must be considered in order to use age-appropriate methodology. The developmental frameworks presented in Chapter 3 (Briggs, 1991; Greenspan and Wieder, 1998) provide unique perspectives in terms of the child's capacity to move from individual to group therapy. In addition to those perspectives, elementary concepts from the work of Piaget are presented in this chapter in order for the music therapist to further develop a working picture of how the child will react in musical experiences during the session.

Developmental Expectations During Music

According to the developmental psychologist, Jean Piaget (Ginsburg and Opper, 1969), the developmental levels may be sensorimotor (birth to 2 years), preoperational (2–7 years), concrete operational (7–11) or formal operational (11 years and above). Frequently, the therapist is involved with a group of children working on different levels. No matter what the developmental frame of reference is, the material used must be adaptable enough so that it can be presented on various developmental levels not only to meet the needs of a homogeneous group but, more likely, to meet the needs of a heterogeneous group.

For example, children functioning at an infant/toddler or sensorimotor level of development, regardless of chronological age, cannot be expected to participate in music activities requiring abstracting or projective skills. Likewise, children functioning at a latency or concrete operational level need to move beyond a simple drum/cymbal antiphonal duet and should not be presented with nursery rhymes requiring simple imitation.

Sensorimotor

This developmental level, which Piaget writes about as the first 24 months of life (Ginsburg and Opper, 1969) and Greenspan umbrellas under realms of self-regulation, intimacy, two-way communication and the beginnings of complex communication (Greenspan, 1998), begins with the child experiencing the music through all the senses. It is not a developmental level conducive to group process (see Chapter 2) but, realistically speaking, developmentally delayed children at this level are frequently placed in music therapy groups and they can progress on a one-to-one level within the group (Coleman, 2002; Oldfield, 2006). There is much change in terms of different developmental (cognitive, communication, social, motor) milestones through the first two years of development and this is spelled out in developmental profiles used with children (Furuno et al., 2005).

In terms of music activity, the emphasis in the first developmental year of the child is on self-regulation through listening to and watching musical experiences as well as egocentric exploration of musical materials. In the second year of development, the music therapy emphasis is on active response to simple directions for concrete music tasks, tasks that address the here and now rather than the abstract.

In terms of vocal activity, the child may be listening to and watching the therapist sing. While this may look like passive activity to the therapist, it is very much active activity on the part of the child. The therapist needs to be responsive to the changing physical postures, facial or breathing changes on the part of the child. If the child appears disturbed by the singing, the therapist needs to consider the dynamic, rhythm, and amount of information being conveyed. In conjunction with the listening and watching, the child will frequently vocalize as a shared beginning with the therapist and/or peers. The therapist should use materials that allow for free vocalization.

Further, the therapist should be cognizant of the order of vowels and consonants in language acquisition and the amount of information presented to the child for imitation or antiphonal exchange.

Dr. Daniel Stern (1977, 1985) beautifully describes the level of vocal attunement suggested in this period. At the highest level within this period, the child will sing selected words of a song (see Briggs, Chapter 3) and follow one- or two-step directions within the context of an "activity" song. In order to truly evaluate the receptive language, the therapist should sing the direction without prompts or cues.

In terms of instrumental activity, the sensorimotor level child will listen and watch while instruments are being played and also enjoy firsthand exploration of the textures and resultant sounds of various instruments. Sensory intake here can include visual, auditory, tactile and kinesthetic awareness. The exploration of the instrument at this beginning level can be assisted or unassisted. Not infrequently a child with a unique sensory profile may be higher functioning developmentally but choose to explore an instrument in a developmentally regressive manner. Presumably this serves some kind of need for the child and, if not disruptive to the group, should be allowed. The following of musical cues for orchestrated instrumental pieces or simple improvisation comes next.

In terms of movement activity, the sensorimotor level child will listen while being physically manipulated to music and begin to react, albeit dysrhythmically to music (see Briggs, Chapter 3). After that stage, the same child can begin to follow simple choreographed movement pieces.

One example of a realistic music therapy continuum (Goodman, 1996–2002) for a child in the sensorimotor period might be the following hierarchy in terms of expectations:

In terms of vocal activities: 1) listening and watching (sensory intake), some effective reaction, vocal may be combined with movement and/or instrumental; 2) vocalization (may be delayed); 3) pitch approximation, phrase singing; 4) one-word response; and 5) more than one word song lyrics

In terms of movement activities: 1) listening while being physically manipulated to music (sensory intake); 2) watching while a visual is physically manipulated; 3) gross motor start and stop; 4) finger plays; 5) one-step directions; and 6) multiple directions.

In terms of instrumental activities: 1) Listening while instruments are being played (sensory intake can include visual, auditory, tactile, kinesthetic); 2) exploring instrument at beginning level (can be assisted or unassisted); 3) one step directive (can include stop/start and can include 'body percussion') in music; and 4) two-step or multiple directive in music.

Symbolic

The symbolic function of the early (age 2–4) preoperational period that Piaget writes about overlaps with Greenspan's milestones of emotional ideas and emotional thinking (see Chapter 3, Greenspan) that allow the child to engage in representational play through the use of singing, instrumental work and movement.

At the preoperational period progresses (through age 7), the music can serve as an increasingly sophisticated projective and lead to some necessary verbal process (Grinnel, 1975) associated with what Wolberg referred to as a second level of psychotherapy called insight therapy at the reeducative level (Wolberg, 1977). At this level, song lyrics can convey feelings and thoughts whether they are selected unconsciously for that purpose or spontaneously composed with the therapist. Also at this level, feelings are unconsciously channeled into instrumental playing experience, some of which can be verbally processed. Instruments may take on attributes of personalities, thoughts and feelings. Likewise, instruments can convey the elements of a story. Finally, movement activity can serve as a communication of thoughts, feelings and ideas. The symbolic period is ideal for beginning simple musical theater with the group, theater that can be precomposed or composed with the group based on selected themes the group elects.

An example of a hierarchy of expectations for children at this level (Goodman, 1996–2002) might be:

In terms of vocal activities: 1) child selects familiar song he/she can relate to emotionally; 2) child expresses emotion appropriate to song choice; 3) child unconsciously chooses song that reflects emotional disposition or preoccupation; 4) child is able to verbally reflect on the song; and 5) child is able to spontaneously compose simple lyrics reflecting his/her feelings, thoughts, emotions. These feelings, thoughts and emotions can be in the past, present or projected future.

In terms of instrumental activity: 1) child selects instrument he/she can relate to emotionally; 2) child expresses emotion appropriate to instrumental choice; 3) child unconsciously uses the instrument to reflect emotional disposition or preoccupation; 4) child is able to verbally reflect on the instrumental experience; and 5) child is able to improvise reflecting his/her feelings, thoughts, emotions. These feelings, thoughts and emotions can be in the past, present or projected future.

In terms of movement activity: 1) child is able to follow a sequence of movement; 2) child channels emotional energy that is appropriate to movement choreography; 3) child is able to verbally reflect on the dance; and 4) child is able to spontaneously compose simple dance reflecting feelings, thoughts, emotions. These feelings, thoughts and emotions can be in the past, present or projected future.

Concrete Operational

This developmental period conforms to latency age (7–11) and the age range of a typically developing grammar school child. Children at this age are comfortable with rule-based structure but have sufficient skills of their own to help create the musical activities and goals they pursue. More sophisticated orchestrations can be used; music can be "taught" within the context of therapy (Ostwald, 1968); movement can be self-choreographed and songs can be composed by the children themselves. In other words, the therapist can provide musical instruction (how to read, write and play music) in order to enable children at this level to express themselves more thoroughly and relate to each other through the elements of music. Projective content continues at a more emotionally invested level. If it makes sense for the therapist to introduce alternative ways of teaching academics, these can be introduced at this level.

Psychotherapeutic Perspective

The ambitiousness of goals, linked to the current level of functioning, also impacts on methodology. As smaller increments of progress will be expected for lower functioning children and greater increments of progress will be expected for higher functioning children, the level of the group "ambition" will be variable. In using music therapy as an activity therapy, Wheeler (1983) has defined this level as one in which "goals are generally achieved through the used of therapeutic activities rather than through insight" (Wheeler, 1983, p. 9). This is also a reference to the use of a product-oriented group.

Although some therapists find the term "activity therapy" pejorative, the reality is that this level is one used with children who are not yet ready to abstract in order to reach a level of insight, associated with another level of therapy, that of insight therapy with reeducative goals. "The major focus of this kind of music therapy (insight therapy with reeducative goals) is on feelings, the exposition of and discussion of which lead to insight" (Wheeler, 1983, p. 9). Insight therapy with reeducative goals frequently leads to the therapist awareness of transference (Turry, 1998), an active component of how the therapist will lead the session. Although transference has been mentioned in the literature only in connection with the second level of psychotherapy, it is entirely probable that the therapist can be aware of transference on any level of therapy.

The likelihood of a third level of psychotherapy, that of insight therapy at a reconstructive level is unlikely in music therapy group work with children since most groups are conducted on an annual basis and the possibility of insight therapy at a reconstructive level would be delimited to children who require personality redefinition. Insight music therapy with reconstructive goals occurs when music therapy techniques are utilized to elicit unconscious material, which is then worked with in an effort to promote reorganization of the personality (i.e., see personality disorders in DSM IV–TR).

MUSIC THERAPY STRATEGIES RELATED TO THE DIAGNOSES AND PRIMARY STRENGTHS AND WEAKNESSES OF THE CHILDREN IN THE GROUP

Overview

Diagnoses

Within special needs population areas, there are many *diagnoses.* The definitions of most categories of educational classification by IDEA are provided in the *Diagnostic and Statistical Manual of Mental Disorders,* currently in its fourth edition, DSM–IV–TR (1994): mental retardation, learning disorders, communication disorders, pervasive developmental disorders, attention-deficit and disruptive behavior disorders (i.e., includes conduct disorder). Mood disorders, anxiety disorders, personality disorders and schizophrenias are also included but generally do not surface until the teen or young adult years.

"Individuals with Disability Education Act" (IDEA) which mandates services for special needs learners, ages 3–21 includes definitions detailed in this chapter for the following: mental retardation, learning disabilities, emotionally disturbed, autistic, communication disorders, hearing impairment, visual impairment, and severe disabilities.

While diagnosis and classification are necessary in order to provide services for the child, this book chooses to look at children in terms of personality, sensory profile, and developmental functioning. *Where various diagnoses lead to different emphases in terms of methodology, that information is introduced.* Therefore, the *music therapy strategies suggested in this chapter for different populations are not meant to be population specific but, rather, to suggest strengths and weaknesses in various populations.*

Music Therapy Literature on Methods in Group

With the advent of P.L. 94–142 in 1974, federal education for the special needs learner became a *mandate* and, as the field of special education developed, so did the literature in music therapy.

However, much of the music therapy literature

is written as methodology with different kinds of children involved in *individual* therapy, rather than *group*. Further, there is next to no literature describing methodology for mixed diagnoses in music therapy groups. Therefore, two important issues remain largely unaddressed in the literature: 1) *the issue of methods in group;* and 2) *the issue of groupwork with different kinds of diagnoses in the group.*

While there is excellent material regarding general strategies for special needs children in schools available to the reader (Hughes, et al., 2002, pp. 364–368), the music therapist can expect to have *different* clinical considerations for different diagnoses of children: mental retardation, physically handicapped, speech handicapped, serious emotional disturbance, autistic, learning disabled, and so forth. The wealth of information in the music therapy literature on special needs learners, both early in the life of the music therapy profession (Gaston, 1968; Schneider, 1964) and recently (Lathom-Radocy, 2002; Adamak & Darrow, 2005; Jellison, 2006), tends to focus on the *uses* (i.e., generic goals) of music therapy in individual and group settings. Those writings that include methods are included in this chapter.

The detailing of *which methods are best for different types of children and how methods need to be mixed to meet the needs of different children in the group* will profit from ongoing inquiry and this chapter is an ongoing effort toward that end.

As presented in Chapters 4 and 5, the therapist must work toward varying goals and objectives. Likewise, each music experience must be presented with varying clinical consideration or methods. As a student, these considerations can be spelled out in the methods section of the session plan. As a professional, these considerations will become ingrained knowledge in presenting music to the children.

Overlapping Considerations in Working with Special Needs Children

It is helpful to consider what one might term *principles of music therapy group work* with special needs children as overall issues in running the group. These principles include concepts related to the following:

- *Degree of structure* in the group
- The *format* of the group
- The *repetition of material*
- *Accommodations for various disabilities*
- *Modeling*
- *Prompting*
- *Verbal process*
- *Sensory profiling*
- *Intentionality to make music requires emotional engagement*
- Presentation of material at *graduated levels of expectation and emphases* given the needs of different children in the group
- *Evaluation*

Degree of Structure in the Group

The *degree of structure, for example, that is required by the therapist in setting up the group activity is greater for lower functioning groups. Conversely, the degree of structure required by the therapist in setting up the group activity is lesser for higher functioning groups.* Structural considerations will vary depending upon the type of group and the stage of the group as a cohesive unit (Hibben, 1991a). In general, as the lower functioning groups begin to gain a sense of group cohesion, familiarity with possible materials and methods in the session and a sense of confidence amongst each other, they will rely less on the therapist to structure the group.

Format

One way of setting up structure is to provide a format for the session. There are many options for a session format (see *music therapy session format that makes sense given the purpose, preferences and functioning level of the group*). One common example of a session format includes an opening and closing as well as varied options for instrumental, vocal and movement activities that the therapist initially introduces. As the children gain familiarity with these materials and activities, they will begin to choose what it is they would like to do in a particular session. Another option for format is to create a group for a specific musical purpose: guitar group, rock ensemble, choir, composition, musical drama. Further, the therapist can create a group for a specific clinical purpose: relaxation, vocal dialogue, physical therapy, music therapy, and so forth.

Repetition of Material

Repetition of material should be tempered with the needs of the children to avoid rote learning. Children in some groups, particularly lower functioning groups, rely upon the comfort of repetition. It allows some children the elements of comfort and predictability which are particularly important when the children need to develop a sense of mastery or have difficulty adapting to new material. However, it is of limited value to the children to set up rote-like imitation of material. The therapist can think creatively when repeating material either by repeating the material in a different way (i.e., theme and variations) or the way in which it is presented. One simple example of this is the use of the well-worn song, "Head, Shoulders, Knees and Toes." Rather than presenting this in the predictable order of the song, the therapist can "mix it up," thereby presenting a more valid manner of seeing whether or not the children really know where their knees are! Another suggested way to vary the use of material is to extend its use. Where the children are used to singing a particular song, the therapist can extend its use by orchestrating it or choreographing it or acting it out. In short, do not present a carbon copy of each session each week.

Accommodations for Various Disabilities

Accommodations need to be made for various disabilities and will be spelled out in this chapter. Suffice it to say that, depending upon the disability of the child, there may be more emphasis on one area of development than another. For example, the physically disabled child requires physical positioning and handling as well as adaptive equipment; the emotionally disturbed child requires multiple opportunities for channeling of the emotions; the autistic child requires initial emotional bonding and redirection of echolalia and perseveration in the course of the music therapy process; the learning disabled child needs multisensory supports in

order to accommodate to music learning requiring reading, writing and mathematical operation during music; the cerebral palsied child requires positioning and handling for mobility during music activity and the retarded child benefits from a step-by-step breakdown of material presented during each music activity.

Modeling

The role of *modeling,* on the part of the therapist, *is an important way to help the children feel comfortable with what is expected of them and gain a contagious sense of excitement for what they are about to do through the music.* Modeling can be as simple as demonstrating an instrument, singing a part of a song, or performing part of a musical drama or movement routine. Children generally enjoy watching the therapist and modeling also creates a valuable opportunity for the special education teacher, assistant teacher or aide to get emotionally involved in the session. As the children gain competence and familiarity with session materials and spontaneous possibilities, the need for modeling from the therapist will decrease and possibly fall to one of the student "leaders" in the group.

Prompting

The need for prompting (physical, visual, verbal) is variable. One lovely moment in the documentary film, "The Music Child," reminds the music therapist of this: Paul Nordoff says, "I play bum, bum, bum; the child plays bum, bum, bum. I haven't said 'Imitate me on the drum.' I don't need to! It's the music child!" While many children will need cuing in the group, particularly during a group orchestration, these cues should be used as needed and invariably *faded* as children gain mastery.

Verbal Process

The level of verbal process in the music therapy group is variable and depends upon the expressive/receptive language abilities of group members as well as the abstracting abilities of the children. Certainly, children who have beginning language skills need clear, concrete, simple directions and feedback.

Generally, at this level, more action rather than talk is called for in order to draw the children into activity. Going straight into the music is much more effective than any verbal description of what the group is about to do. After the music is over, simple feedback is appropriate. Even better, the idea of introducing self-assessment helps the child begin to feel a sense of empowerment in controlling what it is he or she wants to accomplish in the session.

With children who are verbal, particularly emotionally disturbed children, it is helpful to encourage verbal reflection following music experience. This need not be sophisticated. A simple, "How do you think the music sounded?" or "What did you think of our music?" is a good introduction for talking about the musical experience. In these situations, the child may use the music experience as a projective, i.e., "The music sounded scary, like someone was going to come out of the woods and attack another person." Rather than encouraging the child to immediately personalize this thought, e.g., "did you feel scared? What are you scared about?" it is best to keep the projective thoughts safely contained to the music, extend the musical "story" if possible and allow the child or children, as a group, to personalize their thoughts and feelings when necessary. For a therapist who has limited to no training in verbal psychotherapy, this approach would require clinical supervision.

Sensory Profiling

The therapist learns from the child's reactions how the rhythm, melody, harmony, timbre, dynamics and form used impact on potential learning and contribute to the overall sensory profile and therefore the methodology necessary to acclimate to that profile (see Chapter 6, "Materials"; see Berger, 2002). In recent work on sensory reactivity, presented at the Tenth International World Congress, Oxford, U.K. (Goodman, 2002), sensory reactivity and integration with the multiply handicapped child were detailed. Sensory systems include the use of sight, sound, smell, touch, taste, and motion as well as the body senses such as the vestibular system (sensitive to gravity and movement, therefore influencing musical tone, balance and arousal) and the

proprioceptive system (provides awareness of movement and the position of the body in space, thereby influencing body schema and motor control). *Sensory systems in the special learner are generally uneven and it is the job of the therapist to return a child to an optimal level of arousal, known as sensory modulation.* It is not uncommon to work with children who are either sensory defensive, hyperreactive or hyporeactive. The child who is sensory defensive has a tendency to react negatively or with alarm to sensory input that is usually considered harmless or nonirritating. Berger (2002) refers to these reactions as "fight or flight." The hyperreactive child is the one who experiences overload or sensory shutdown, has difficulty sorting out stimuli, difficulty in focus, is easily overwhelmed and responds to many stimuli in the environment. The hyporeactive child is underresponsive, requires multisensory inputs, can benefit from proprioceptive input (information from muscles, joints and ligaments, or has sensory regulation problems). In order for the therapist to modulate the child to optimum arousal, it is necessary to use music to either stimulate the system or relax the system. In conjunction with the musical experience, it may be useful to simultaneously use other sensory inputs (i.e., visual, kinesthetic), or conversely, limit sensory input.

Sensory integration, a method first introduced to occupational therapy by Jean Ayers (Ayers, 1979) and later adopted by many different professions working with the special learner (Kranowitz, 1999), helps the child integrate information and relies on the child either needing more multisensory information or less multisensory information depending upon their reactivity to the different senses.

Music therapists have also cited the use of music as a listening backdrop to help structure the sound environment and these experiences will benefit from greater study in groupwork. A rock music backdrop, for example, was successfully used with ADHD children (Cripe, 1986) to help them focus. Classical as well as popular folk music was selected for its rhythmic and dynamic regularity as a background for a child with borderline personality and phobias who was involved in play therapy and art. In this latter study, the therapist reports that the music not only reduced anxiety but also led into an active music-making experience of singing, and free associating to the music that helped her structure her thinking (Cooke, 1969). These experiences may be related to sensory profiling since these children were all responsive to certain kinds of music which helped them return to an optimal sense of arousal referred to earlier.

Sensory profiles of the children in the group will also necessitate flexibility and sensitivity on the part of the therapist in determining the *order* of the musical experiences as they provide stimulative or sedative effects.

Intentionality to Make Music Requires Emotional Engagement

Intentionality to make music requires emotional engagement. The motivation of the child to take in information (also see Chapters 2 and 3) is beautifully explained in the writing of Dr. Stanley Greenspan & Wieder (1998). According to Greenspan, it is helpful to keep in mind the number of components at work while the child is emoting, thinking and doing. These components include, for example, motor planning and sequencing, auditory processing and verbal comprehension, speech, visual-spacial (decoding and comprehending what we see), sensory regulation (modulating sensation to avoid being underaroused or overwhelmed) and affective regulation (Greenspan and Wieder, 1998, p. 339). Without the child being engaged emotionally to use these components, they become underutilized or even nonoperative.

For the autistic child, for example, the difficulty in feeling intent or emotion in order to provide purpose and meaning to the component functions we just outlined, is the primary problem to overcome. The best way to overcome this is to pull the autistic child into a musical interaction. In so doing, emotions become connected, for example, to the therapist through music and there is a motivation to do and act and think.

With other special education diagnoses, such as cerebral palsy, retardation, language disorders, and so forth, the ability to connect emotionally is operative and functioning but the deficits in com-

ponent skills make it difficult for the child to function. The music therapist can help the cerebral palsy child by encouraging the easier movements first, such as tongue movement, trunk movement, head-turning movement, through structured musical experience in order for the child to gain confidence in trying to work with more difficult movements of the arms, legs and hands. Similarly, the music therapist can help the language disordered child begin with simple speech and language skills, progressively becoming more motivated with exponential successes.

Children with Down syndrome, generally low tone with severe motor-planning difficulties, tend to be slower to register sound and challenged by auditory and visual spacial processing problems. However, many therapists enjoy working with the Downs child due to a invariably engaging and warm temperament. This emotional strength can therefore be used as a means of motivating and interesting the child in using music for developing weaker developmental areas.

Presentation of Material at Graduated Levels of Expectation

Thus far in the book, the importance of setting functionally appropriate goals and objectives that can be staged in the music therapy group at different levels of expectation has been presented. *Music therapy materials must be presented at graduated levels of expectation and emphases given the needs of different children in the group.* This point cannot be emphasized enough.

Many music therapists tend to conduct the therapy session based on one level of expectation, using generic simplistic goals and objectives. This chapter continues to emphasize the ways in which this simplistic approach is to be avoided. It takes a skilled therapist to present material in as adaptive a manner as possible in order to structure different levels of response and, at the same time, encourage group awareness.

Evaluation

Evaluation of the session is important to determine whether or not the group is progressing, regressing or maintaining different levels of behavior. In the course of therapy, it is normal for clients to maintain, progress or regress in terms of their behavior. It is critical for the therapist to keep track of these changes in order to periodically reevaluate how the therapy is or is not working, and what changes were made in the session to acclimate to the changing needs of the children (see Chapter 8, Evaluation).

Considerations in Working with the Mentally Retarded Child

IDEA, Definition

In IDEA, mental retardation is defined as "significantly subaverage general intellectual functioning existing concurrently with deficits in adaptive behavior and manifested during the developmental period that adversely affects a child's educational performance" (34 C.F.R., Sec.3000.7(b)(5). Levels of retardation include mild, moderate, severe and profound.

Special Education Strategies

Instructional methods detailed in the special education literature with the mentally retarded child often include many techniques associated with behaviorism. This methodology has a history dating from the fifties and sixties when behaviorism was a popular force in this country. There are many educators today, as well, who believe that, in general, children who are mentally retarded reportedly learn best with explicit, systematic methods of presentation, briefly summarized as "demonstration-prompt-practice" (Stevens and Rosenshine, 1981, p. 37).

One need not be a behaviorist to practice these methods; they are not necessarily inconsistent with other philosophies of helping. They can be considered part of the method. Probably the best-known instructional technique in working with the retarded child is *task analysis.* Here the therapist breaks down complex or multistep skills into smaller, easier-to-learn subtasks. One of the best music therapy resources (e.g., Levin and Levin, 1998) suggests this breakdown in the presentation

of a song, or instrumental orchestration. Helping the children learn one step at a time is not a practice alien to working musicians or to many other disciplines, for that matter. Suffice it to say, that the breakdown in presenting a piece of music must be *musical,* e.g., one musical phrase or idea at a time, not one note! Children may need to take the time to learn only a portion of a song, an instrumental piece, a movement song and/or the music may have to be simplified in terms of the amount, not the potential musical enjoyment, of the content.

While the student is in the process of learning, an *active student response* should be expected. Simply put, *active student response* is an observable response made to an instructional antecedent. This seems obvious but the regularity of feedback from the children helps the therapist determine what the children are decoding and able to respond to. Following the children's response, the therapist can provide systematic specific feedback: e.g., "Tommy, great job playing the drum today!" An important suggestion here is not to praise the children inappropriately when they are unsuccessful; a more realistic approach involves true feedback: "that is tough, isn't it? Let's try it again and remember to keep your eye on the drum while you are playing it." This process of true feedback is, in behavioral terms, referred to as *contingent reinforcement, instructional feedback and error correction.*

The stage of active learning can be considered the *acquisition stage of learning,* a realistic period for mastery of most tasks. In order to help in this stage, the therapist frequently employs different levels of *cuing or prompting* which can include physical guidance, verbal directions, picture cues, prerecorded auditory prompts. This is sometimes referred to as *mediated scaffolding* since the therapist provides and then fades prompts and cues so student can respond to naturally occurring stimuli. The "naturally occurring stimulus," in the context of music therapy, is, of course, the music itself. *The ultimate prompting for musical response lays in the structure of the music itself* and it is for this reason that the selection of music must be appropriate to encouraging active musical response.

The hope that the children will be able to *gener-*

alize and maintain what they have learned in music requires a *functional use of skills,* mastery level and internalization of skills. In these situations, this may be problematic for the child coming from music therapy. For example, prompting and inviting appropriate speech and language through music, e.g., singing hello, can be replicated in another environment where it may be deemed inappropriate, e.g., is *singing* hello expected when someone walks into your living room? Therefore, the generalization of this particular skill would require that the child understand how to *say* hello.

Music Therapy Strategies

Least Restrictive Environment and General Suggestions:

The least restrictive educational continuum generally mainstreams mildly retarded children and, at times, the moderately handicapped in self-contained classrooms, to music education rather than music therapy.

General considerations cited by Adamak and Darrow (2005) in working with these children include varying levels of participation expected of children, adapting the manner is which instruction is provided, adapting how children respond to instruction, adapting the difficulty of skill levels, allowing sufficient time for learning and responding, adapting expectations of children within a group, adapting instruments as necessary, increasing amounts of support from ancillary staff and adapting the classroom space as necessary. These guidelines can be applied differently and specifically to every special education population. In the case of the moderately retarded child, for example, it is important to model the expected musical behavior so that it becomes concrete information. An imitative level can then follow with time for auditory processing and decision-making. As the children become more proficient in their music skills, the amounts of information that need to be mastered become greater with more directives, more sequential responses and greater challenges. In a sense, this is comparable to a format of "theme and variations." Infrequently, severely handicapped children may be mainstreamed, a sit-

uation that has been investigated by Jellison and her colleagues (Jellison, Brooks, and Huck, 1984). In most of these situations, the music educator is not trained to work with mainstreamed students (Darrow, Colwell, and Kim, 2002) and, ideally, the school system will hire a music therapist as a consultant to the music education program. More frequently, self-contained moderately retarded children in a public school or private special education school will have music therapy.

Severely/profoundly handicapped children, thankfully the lowest incidence of mental retardation, in out-of-district special education schools (i.e., Coleman, 2002) or residential developmental centers (i.e., Farnan, 2002), are the most likely group to have music therapy and, historically, profit in the areas of sensorimotor, auditory-visual perceptual, communication and social skills (Grant, 1989). Obviously the considerations in working with the mentally retarded child are dramatically variable depending upon the functioning level of the child.

Children who are classified, as severely/profoundly retarded will be at a development level years below their chronological age. For example, Farnan (2002) describes a group chronologically 9–17 years old, with developmental ages of 2.7 to 5.7 months. As previously suggested in developmental considerations ingroup work, the sensorimotor period of development, appropriate for children functioning at an infant level, invites multisensory stimulation, response to which can be frequently delayed. In terms of instrumentation, children can achieve auditory, tactile and visual stimulation by touching the vibrating sound surface of an ocean drum, shaking the Hawaiian feather gourd called an uli-uli, playing the omnichord or autoharp,and putting their hand inside the reed horn as the therapist blows it, These tasks can be achieved within the context of a song (i.e., "Let's make Music," Nordoff and Robbins, Book 5, 1980) thereby providing a musical structure to invite group awareness. In terms of vocal activity, children can be stimulated to vocalize sounds, sign, move to the rhythm and use a programmed "Big Mack" (made by Ablenet) for appropriate response. Finally, in the course of practicing music therapy, it is important for the therapist to employ *direct and frequent measurement* (see Chapter 2, assessment and Chapter 8, evaluation) as one aspect of *objective* assessment and evaluation. Objective evaluation is an important aspect of working with any special needs group in order to derive an accurate sense of how the group members are *progressing, regressing or maintaining* the skills presented. This measurement need not be limited to nonmusical behaviors. Indeed, the tracking of musical responses in the Nordoff-Robbins method is a perfect example of direct and frequent measurement even though it is part of a humanistic philosophy of helping.

Summary

In summary, music therapy suggestions for the mentally retarded child include the following:

1. Provide a clear structure for the session while allowing the children to choose options.
2. Model each musical task as necessary.
3. Task-analyze the musical task in order to present one step at a time to the children.
4. Model - practice - praise or correct.
5. Repeat musical materials as requested by the children but add variety in order to provide more developmental challenge.
6. Infuse language in a naturalistic manner as the session proceeds.
7. Evaluate responses on a regular basis.

Considerations in Working with the Learning Disabled Child

IDEA, Definition

In IDEA, learning disabilities is referred to as "specific learning disability," meaning a "disorder in one or more of the basic psychological processes involved in understanding or in using language, spoken or written, which disorder may manifest itself in an imperfect ability to listen, think, speak, read, write, spell, or to do mathematical calculations" (IDEA, 2004, H.R. 1350, Sec. 602(301).

Music Therapy Strategies

Least Restrictive Environment and General Suggestions:

Many learning disabled (LD) children, all with varying degrees of deficit, are mainstreamed for music education and do not have music therapy available to them in the school setting. Those who attend a school for learning disabilities children have a greater prospect of music therapy services. Those who attend a music therapy clinic may be grouped with other LD children or with children of different diagnosis. Since the learning disability is specific it is set apart from the general intellectual aptitude of the child; there is a severe discrepancy between the student's intellectual ability and academic achievement. Since many of the deficits for the LD child show up in reading, mathematics and writing, LD children may be referred to music therapy for alternative means of instruction, with the referring professional possibly overlooking the area of self-esteem and social skills. Whether or not skills of reading, writing, and mathematically decoding musical rhythms generalize to other learning environments of reading, writing and mathematics is a topic that needs further exploration in the music therapy literature.

Gfeller (1984) presents the possible music therapy methodology for LD students within the context of three instructional philosophies: underlying skills theory, behavioral theory and cognitive theory.

Underlying skills theory, emphasizing the development of prerequisite skills in perception, motor and linguistic processing (i.e., auditory memory or discrimination) in preparation for academic skills such as reading and mathematics, suggests that improvement in perceptual-motor skills will automatically result in improved academic skills or, at least, serve as skills acquired before pursuing academic tasks. perceptual or psycholinguistic skills (Reid and Hresko, 1981). This is highly controversial. Nevertheless, the appeal of sensory-motor integration through music is a natural process and shows up in such activities as sequencing of musical tones or timbres, or crossing the midline during instrumental activity (Gfeller, 1984).

BEHAVIORAL: Behavioral theory for LD children, suggests a behavioral approach both for teaching academics and managing behaviors such as impulsivity or distractibility, thought to interfere in learning. In addition to task analysis of music tasks, this approach can include the use of music as a reward for successful academic work (Yarbrough, Charboneau and Wapnick, 1977). These approaches are also used with the mentally retarded child.

COGNITIVE: A cognitive approach for LD children suggests that new information, rather than being accumulated in a step-by-step process, is assimilated or accommodated through an understanding of what the student already knows and then relating new information to material that is already mastered. Active learning may require the development of strategies. For example, the use of music to aid recall of information is termed a mnemonic strategy (Gfeller, 1984) proven effective in the Gfeller research (1982, 1983).

BEHAVIORAL/COGNITIVE: Gfeller (1984) suggests a combination of approaches depending upon the nature of the goal for the learning disabled child.

- A behavioral approach can be employed to manage distractibility and/or hyperactivity as well as reinforcement for academic success.
- Academic concepts and processes can be presented through music activity.
- Music therapy can allow children with social or emotional issues to channel their activity and express themselves.
- Write stories or songs in which the initial vocabulary is based on the child's experiences and ideas. This allows the child to improve reading comprehension and written language.
- Use instruments in a way that can present academic concepts. For example, Orff instruments can act as mathematical manipulatives for exploring concepts of number, amount, greater or less than, even and odd, bigger and smaller, and so on.

- Use the lyrics of a song in order to carry information and act as a mnemonic for recalling being remembered information such as a rule of grammar or the order of computational steps.

In addition to the previous mention of guidelines for the music therapy room and the physical arrangement of the children, Gladfelter (2002), a music therapist working with the LD child, offers additional input regarding this population. He reminds the therapist to be cognizant of varying learning styles of problems, allow the children to move around the room one at a time, keep verbal directions simple, and specific, use the music as the attention-getting device rather than talking, present material in multisensory fashion, and one piece of new information at a time, add variety to repetition, use visuals such as letters, numbers, music notation and words as well as an overhead projector for song lyrics or visual symbols, use adapted music and laminated charts for visual tracking, use fill-in-the blank songwriting to simplify the songwriting process, simple poetry forms (i.e., haiku) for a possible base of song lyrics and, finally, use headphones for children who need to filter out extraneous sound.

SUMMARY: Many of these suggestions relate to skills needed for reading (e.g., visual tracking; awareness of rhythmic structure) and writing (creating and decoding symbols) while other suggestions relate to a need for structure, a sensitivity to different sensory profiles, a need for different activity levels, defining the sense of space and systematic learning. While the therapist may wish to avoid presenting music with the use of visuals since this seems more "academic," it is important to realize that, for the learning disabled child, the visuals may help the child integrate the skills necessary for other academic processes.

Considerations in Working with the Emotionally Disturbed Child

IDEA, Definition

The IDEA definition of emotional disturbance reads as follows:

(I) The term means a condition exhibiting one or more of the following characteristics over a long period of time and to a marked degree that adversely affects educational performance,

    a) An inability to learn which intellectual, sensory and health factors; cannot explain;

    b) An inability to build or maintain satisfactory interpersonal relationships with peers and teachers;

    c) Inappropriate types of behavior or feelings under normal circumstances;

    d) A general pervasive mood of unhappiness or depression; or

    e) A tendency to develop physical symptoms or fears associated with personal or school problems.

(II) The term includes schizophrenia. The term does not apply to children who are socially maladjusted, unless it is determined that they have an emotional disturbance. (U.S. Department of Education, 1999, p. 12422)

Music Therapy Strategies

Least Restrictive Environment and Diagnosis:

As mentioned before, there is a wide variation of diagnoses and nomenclature within the category of emotionally disturbed children. For example, recent music therapy literature has focused on the needs of children and adolescents in *bereavement* (Hilliard, 2001; Dalton and Krout, 2005) as well as the SED (Hussey, Laing, and Layman, 2002), seriously emotionally disturbed, and EBD (Sausser and Waller, 2006), *emotional behavioral disturbance.* The therapist needs to become quite schooled in the use of the *Diagnostic and Statistical Manual of Mental Disorders IV–TR* (1994) in order to consider different kinds of methods for conduct disorders, and possibly emerging mood disorders, psychotic disorders, personality disorders, phobias, and so forth. It is also necessary to understand multiaxial diagnosis, particularly for children who have a dual diagnosis, for example, mental retardation along with conduct disorders. Further, it is important to understand disturbed children in terms of their behavior rather than a given nomenclaure such as seriously emotionally disturbed (SED) and emotional behavioral disturbance (EBD).

For children who may have difficulty holding a conversation, expressing their feelings, participating ingroup activities and responding to failure or criticism in positive and constructive ways, music therapy is a blessing.

BEHAVIORAL: The traditional emphasis on discipline, well represented in the music therapy literature of the sixties and seventies (e.g., Steele et al., 1976) and largely introduced through the work of Clifford Madsen (Madsen, 1998, 1981) relates to what educators call "behavior management." Music therapists using these techniques incorporate the following into their planning: 1) Behavior expectations are stated; 2) Behavioral expectations are defined and taught; 3) Appropriate behaviors are acknowledged; and 4) Behavioral errors are corrected proactively.

A behavioral system would encourage tools such as shaping, contingency contracting, extinction (ignoring disruptive behavior), differential reinforcement of other behavior (reinforcement of any behavior except the undesirable behavior), response cost, time-out, and overcorrection (restitution beyond the damaging effects of the antisocial behavior, as when a child who takes another child's instrument must return it plus one of her own).

One recent example of a behavioral approach with disturbed children is described at the Rutland Psychoeducational Center, Athens, Georgia (Sausser and Waller, 2005). The article presents group goals, "group cohesion and cooperation using a check-in methods incorporating drumming and chanting, on-task and appropriate behavior using immediate positive reinforcement, second chances, and music as a contingency for appropriate behavior" (Sausser and Waller, 2005, p. 2). "Session activities include a variety of established techniques such as lyric analysis, song writing, instrumental improvisation, instrumental ensembles, group singing, group drumming, movement to music, and musical games. To provide closure for each session, the therapist plays a drum and chants each student's name as a prompt to line up" (Sausser and Waller, 2005, p. 9). Note that the word *techniques* rather than experiences is used to describe the kind of *session activities* presented rather than the way (*method*) in which these experiences are presented.

Another example of a behavioral approach with disturbed children, the work of Presti (Presti, 1984). sets up music therapy groups encompassing four levels of expectations based on varying degrees of behavioral control in motor behavior, verbal behavior and social behavior exhibited in the completion of music tasks. The behaviors of the children in the music therapy groups are recorded and involve reinforcement and consequences. "Adapting the levels system to music therapy capitalizes on the reinforcing value and motivational potential of the music medium" (Presti, 1984, p. 123).

Then, the question arises, "Why not rely upon those values of the music experience rather than employing external reinforcements?"

The issue with behavioral strategies may be that, for the music therapist, *they imply that the channeling of emotions into music and the pleasure (positive reinforcement) derived from the music-making experience is not enough to correct inappropriate behavior,* when many music therapists have experienced the cessation of inappropriate behavior on the part of the disturbed child soon after the child begins music therapy.

RELATIONSHIP-BASED APPROACH: In contrast to strictly behavioral strategies, a relationship-based approach, suggested early in the music therapy literature by Gewirtz (1964), emphasizes the growth in musical relatedness and therapist-children interrelatedness. This type of approach has further precedent in the approach of play therapy (Linder, 1990), introduced into music therapy by Grinnel (1975) where the therapist follows the child's lead in play in order to use the vehicle of projective play as a channel to play out thoughts, feelings and emotions. Relationship-based music therapy is supported by success in published accounts of individual case study material (e.g., Nordoff-Robbins, 1971, 1977; Goodman, 1989) with the emotionally disturbed child and is gaining further legitimacy by published accounts of relationship-based group music therapy case study material with emotionally disturbed children (Friedlander, 1994; Oldfield, 2006) and adolescents (Aigen, 1997; Brooks, 1989; Haines, 1989; Henderson, 1983; Mark, 1988; McFerran-Skewes, 2000; Wells, 1984).

A specific manual which relates symptoms of emotionally disturbed children with tried and true methods used by music therapists throughout the United States is that of Cassity and Cassity (2006). The usefulness of this approach is that the symptoms, rather than the diagnosis lead the therapist to treatment choices. The majority of the methods in this manual tend to be activity based, product oriented vs. process-oriented, but do not detail the methods or steps used to present the music experiences.

Summary

If the therapist would like to run the session as both product and process oriented and the disturbed child has the potential for abstracting and problem-solving ability and can learn to express the self and respond to the expression of others in a group, the therapist can structure the session in the following ways:

1. Help the children define their own expectations of their behavior and post these on a large piece of oak tag, if they like.
2. Encourage the children to bring in music they relate to and identify with.
3. Help the children channel their feelings, positive and negative, into instrumental, vocal and movement experience.
4. Respect the need of each child to act out their feelings through music without necessarily talking about their experience if they are not ready to do this.
5. Help the children begin to identify how they are feeling.
6. Simple verbal techniques with disturbed children include acknowledging emotional issues, being supportive without solving the problem for the child or denying the existence of the issue, helping the child extend his/her thoughts, posing the issues to the rest of the group members; discussing various solutions to the problems, including use of the music.
7. Help the children work with each other toward completion of musical projects.
8. Help the children recognize how they are problem-solving in music and generalize these solutions to other aspects of daily life.

9. Help the children self-assess how they followed their own behavioral guidelines in the
session.

Considerations in Working With
the Autistic Spectrum Child

IDEA, Definition

The term "autistic spectrum child," also
referred to as *pervasive developmental disorder*
includes *autistic disorder, Asperger syndrome, Rett's
syndrome, childhood disintegrative disorder and pervasive developmental disorder not otherwise specified.*

Autism was added to the IDEA definition as
late as 1990 (P.L. 101–476) as follows:

> (i) Autism means a developmental disability
> affecting verbal and nonverbal communication
> and social interaction, generally evident before
> age 3 that adversely affects a child's performance.
> Other characteristics often associated with autism
> are engagement in repetitive activities and stereo-
> typed movements, resistance to environmental
> change or change in daily routines, and unusual
> responses to sensory experiences. The term does
> not apply if a child's educational performance is
> adversely affected primarily because the child has
> a serious emotional disturbance as defined in
> paragraph (c) (4) of this section.
> (ii) A child who manifests the characteristics of
> 'autism' after age 3 could be diagnosed as having
> "autism" if the criteria in paragraph (c) (1) (i) of
> this section are satisfied. (34 C.F.F., Sec. 300.7 (c)
> (1) (1999)

Special Education Methods

The special education literature distinguishes
between research-based methods of positive
behavior support and relationship-based
approaches that do not necessarily provide systematic environmental arrangements and differential consequences for behavior. This is a controversial topic in working with the autistic child
(Bailey, 1992; Heflin and Simpson, 2002; Cullen
and Mudford, 2005; Romanczyk, Weiner,
Lockshin, and Ekdahl, 1999).

BEHAVIORAL: There are different special educa-

tion methods for working for the autistic child and
perhaps one of the most celebrated is that of
applied behavior analysis. ABA, as it is commonly
known, is a systematic approach for designing,
conducting and evaluating instruction based upon
scientifically verified principles describing how
the environment affects learning (Alberto and
Troutman, 2006; Cooper, Heron, and Heward,
2006). Stated in simpler terms, the ABA method
determines individual specific goals based on
assessment of behavior and functional usefulness
and it records achievement of "target behavior" as
it occurs in the natural environment for that skill.
Surprisingly, it is not a method restricted to special
education nor is it restricted to behavioral philosophy since there can be systematic learning
through music that is evaluated regularly and need
not be presented through a behavioral methodology. The strategies used in an ABA system are varied and include the following:

1. Strategies for shifting control over a student's
responses from contrived stimuli to naturally
occurring stimuli and events he encounters
in his environment (Green, 2001).
2. Alternative forms of communication such as
the Picture Exchange Communication
System (Bondy and Frost, 2002; Schwartz,
Garfinkle, and Bauer, 1998; Sundberg and
Partington, 1998).
3. Peer-mediated interventions for social relationships (McConnell, 2002; Strain and
Schwartz, 2001).
4. Methods of errorless discrimination learning
(Sidman, 1994).
5. Development of stimulus equivalence classes
in which students learn relationships that are
not taught directly, thereby expanding the
power of instruction (Sidman, 1994).
6. Functional assessment of challenging behavior (Horner, Carr, Strain, Todd, and Reed,
2002).
7. Pivotal response intervention (Koegel,
Koegel, Harrower, and Carter, 1999).
8. Naturalistic language strategies (Goldstein,
2002; McGee, Morrier, and Daly, 1999).
9. Discrete trial method (DTT) is a method
wherein the therapist has a set of problems

and presents these to a student one at a time, presumably in an optimum order for teaching and learning, responds to each of the child's responses or nonresponses, rewarding or acknowledging correct responses, ignoring, correcting, or reproving incorrect responses; and either ignoring or prompting responses after nonresponse (Baer, 2005).

Probably some of the commonly employed approaches mentioned above that are included in music therapy include the use of the Picture Exchange Communication System (PECS) as well as that of naturalistic language strategies (Goldstein, 2002; McGee, Morrier, and Daly, 1999). The question of whether or not a relationship-based approach could be overlapped with a behavioral support design has not been pursued in music therapy with the autistic child.

RELATIONSHIP-BASED APPROACHES: Relationship-based approaches in psychiatry and special education include the work of Stanley Greenspan's "Floortime" approach (Greenspan and Wieder, 1998) and a philosophical attitude that McGee refers to as "Gentle Teaching" (McGee, 1991, 1992). Further, the "play therapy" approach, first presented by Virginia Axline (1969) years ago continues to receive validation (Linder, 1990). These approaches are initially employed in *individual therapy* in an effort to bond with the autistic child. The Greenspan "floortime" approach, while immensely helpful in understanding developmental milestones (see Chapter 3), sensory reactivity and initial methods for bonding and interaction through music (Goodman, 1996), has not proven valid in group work (Goodman, 1998) due to the intensive nature of the child interacting with the therapist. Nevertheless, the developmental progression suggested in the Greenspan model, the emphasis on emotional engagement as a prerequisite for cognitive involvement and the awareness of sensory profiling are all essential aspects of working with special needs children.

Music Therapy Approaches

SENSORY CONSIDERATIONS: The unique sensory profiles of children with autism (Greenspan and Wieder, 1998) suggest that auditory and visual physiological processing for each group member requires assessment to "ensure that treatment in a group can comfortably address the various functioning levels and physical problems that could arise as a result of group encounters" (Berger, 2002, pp. 172–173). As mentioned in Chapter 3 of this book, sensory profile is an important consideration in determining individual or group placement. Not only is it critical in terms of determining how a child learns best but, in terms of the specific presentation and use of music, *the therapist essentially learns from the child's reactions how the rhythm, melody, harmony, timbre, dynamics and form used impact on potential learning* (Berger, 2002) (see Chapter 6, "Materials"). This is particularly true in work with autistic children since they have unusual sensory profiles. Because of these challenged systems, it is not unusual for a music therapist to watch the autistic child wander the room while the therapist wonders why the child is not initiating play. In working with the autistic child, it is important to remember the limitations of the child and their need for prompting. Dr. Stanley Greenspan suggests structuring "playful obstruction" in order to foster reaction from the child (Greenspan and Wieder, 1998). The music therapy alternative might be the Nordoff-Robbins approach which fosters interaction through musical improvisation. The alternative, allowing a child to wander about the room aimlessly, is not productive.

RELATIONSHIP-BASED: The primary relationship-based approach used with autistic children in music therapy is that of Nordoff-Robbins, based on the humanistic concepts presented by Dr. Abraham Maslow. Introduced by the pianist and composer, Paul Nordoff, and his colleague, a special educator, Clive Robbins, the Nordoff-Robbins approach encourages an improvisational entre into the world of the autistic child. It seems to make total sense that music, a language of the emotions, should be the basis of a relationship-based therapy because it has the capacity to bring the therapist and childback to the primary relationship of nonverbal attunement, a relationship written about in the psychiatric literature (Stern, 1977). However, the bulk of this work is done in *individual* therapy.

In the Nordoff-Robbins approach, as the child progresses in musical and interpersonal relatedness, he/she is able to become part of a group. Once the group is formed, however, it appears that the therapist becomes more reliant upon precomposed materials for music therapy (see "Materials," Chapter 6) while still keeping the possibility of improvisation alive. Within the context of a relationship-based approach with the autistic child, whether it be individual or group, the therapist, however, needs to recognize that the autistic child may not have the internal capacity to self-structure. Therefore, *the musical experiences that are improvisational must deliver the sense of structure that the autistic child has difficulty initiating.* A beautiful example of this is viewed in the video, "Here We Are in Music–One Year with an Adolescent Creative Music Therapy Group" described in print by Ken Aigen (1997). In the vignette where one autistic teen provides us with a fragment of speech, "chocolate," the therapist, Alan Turry, seizes on the moment to structure a question, "What kind of candy do you like?" This question is posed three times, beginning with a melody, a musical question so to speak, that rests at the end, as a question would, and then repeats itself twice, each time starting on another pitch. This musical sequence musically begs for the answer, e.g., "I like chocolate?" Thereafter, other children are asked the same question, give their individual answers and, as a result, the group has a unifying moment. What is the consequence to their wonderful communication? The consequence is the pleasure of shared communication.

GENERAL GUIDELINES/ACTIVITY CHOICES: Adamek and Darrow (2005, pp. 198–199) suggest examples of music therapy activity choices to address various goal areas of development for the autistic child. Although these suggested activities do not include methodology or how to *present* the activities, they are extremely helpful general guidelines for the therapist in arriving at initial choices to address goal areas. This information is summarized as follows:

- Address communication skills as follows: 1) options for choices through instrumental and vocal activities; 2) vocal imitation in songs; and 3) following directions (i.e., stop/go).
- Address social skills as follows: 1) turn-taking and sharing; 2) cooperative music-making as part of an ensemble; 3) self-expression through song, instruments and movement; and 4) self-esteem achieved through mastery of new skills.
- Address changes in behavior as follows: 1) follow directions in music; 2) leadership as well as following roles; and 3) reinforcement of appropriate behavior through the music.
- Promote academic skills as follows: 1) counting songs as well as rhythm activities; 2) movement activity that reinforces directional concepts; and 3) categorizing instruments through the use of colors, size, shapes and sounds.
- Developing physical skills as follows: 1) fine motor skills addressed through the playing of specific instruments; and 2) gait training through patterned music.
- Developing interest in leisure skills: 1) training on instruments such as guitar or piano; and 2) vocal ensemble rehearsal for performance options.

Summary

In summary, some key music therapy suggestions for working with the autistic child include:

1. Consider a relationship-based approach where the emphasis is on musical relatedness and interpersonal relatedness and structured within the musical experience.
2. Provide a clear format for the music therapy session, encouraging the children to choose the materials they would like to work with.
3. Encourage variety rather than rote repetition of music activity.
4. Be sure to use song transitions or simple words to transition from one activity to another.
5. Be responsive to echolalic or perseverative speech/language by extending it further in order to discourage the echolalic or perseverative speech/language.
6. Break down the presentation of music activities, presenting one step at a time, simplify-

ing as necessary and providing modeling and prompting.

7. Encourage shared communication and natural eye contact amongst the children by turn-taking types of instrumental, movement and vocal activities.

8. Take advantage of spontaneous nonverbal or verbal communication of the children in order to form further musical and interpersonal connections.

Considerations in Working with the Communication Disorders Child

IDEA, Definition

The definition of speech or language impairments in IDEA follows: "a communication disorder, such as stuttering, impaired articulation, a language impairment, or a voice impairment that adversely affects a child's educational performance" (20 U.N.C. 1401 (3), Section 300.7 (c) (11).

Music Therapy Methods

Music therapy is a natural way of working with the communication disorders and has a history of a large literature base (Galloway, 1975). As a part of the developmental sequence, children *"sing" before they talk and all the components of speaking are virtually musical elements: dynamic, phrase, rhythm, inflection, and timbre.* While children go through "normal stages" of such "errors" as articulation difficulty, substitutions and omissions in sounding words (12–18 months) and being echolalic (up to about 4 years), these errors become deviant when they are still happening in later developmental periods.

MOVEMENT AND SPEECH/LANGUAGE: Condon, a psychologist at Boston University, was among the first to study the matching of movement with speech as the individual talks (1974, 1975), considered a form of entrainment, and relate a possible dysfunction in this ability to the diagnosis of autism (1986). The music therapist who encourages the *pairing of movement and singing* will see that this essentially *sensory integrative effort stimulates speech,* a concept that was first utilized in the development of *melodic-intonation therapy* (Sparks, Helm, and Marin, 1974), a music therapy technique initially employed with the aphasic patient.

Further, *music therapy songs encourage the here and now development of receptive and expressive language* assuming they are precomposed or spontaneously composed materials that utilize natural speech elements, here and now language, antiphonal response, and requested actions through song (see Chapter 6, "Materials").

GENERAL GUIDESLINES/"ACTIVITY CHOICES": Adamek and Darrow (2005, p. 207) suggest music therapy "strategies" which, in effect, constitute suggested music therapy activities for the communication disordered child within the context of broad goal areas. Their suggestions are summarized as follows:

- Address expressive language skills as follows: 1) the writing of songs to help children express ideas; 2) choice-making in terms of song, instruments and movement; and 3) acquiring and practicing words in the context of simple repetitive songs.
- Address receptive language skills as follows: 1) active response to directives in songs; and 2) active response to nonverbal cues such as stopping when a drum stops and moving when a drum plays.
- Address social skills as follows: 1) group music-making in the course of a tone chime or percussion ensemble; 2) playing and then passing instruments; 3) decision-making during music-making; taking on leadership roles; and 4) listening, responding, and decision-making.
- Address memory and attention difficulties as follows: 1) therapist motivates with simple activities, gradually increasing the length and complexity of these in order to increase attending skill; and 2) rhythmic imitation; call and response.

PROTOCOL FOR APRAXIA, DYSARTHRIA, DYSPHAGIA: Adamek, Gervin and Shiraiski (2000) suggest specific protocols for brain-injured patients with apraxia of speech, dysarthria and dysphagia. Although the case examples are all individual adults, it may be possible to use these protocols with children as well and this would constitute valuable research. For apraxia the interventions include inhalation/exhalation breathing exercises, the use of wind instruments, vowel imitation and consonant vowel blends (first used in isolation, then in song lyrics and then again in isolation), melodic intonation therapy and instrumental exercises. For dyarthria, the interventions include inhalation/exhalation breathing exercises, the use of wind instruments, the strengthening of oral-motor mechanisms through exercises with rhythmic pacing and, finally, instrumental exercises. For dysphagia, breathing exercises with inhalation and exhalation as well as the use of wind instruments are followed by vowel and consonant/vowel blends, phrase completion and singing, then oral-motor strengthening similar to that used with dysarthria, followed by falsetto exercises and, again, instrumental exercises.

PROTOCOLS, ARTICULATION, PHONOLOGY, FLUENCY, LANGUAGE DISORDERS: The breakdown of speech and language difficulties can be addressed with the following suggestions from the author (Goodman, 2006).

The *correction of articulation errors through singing* can be achieved with the therapist introducing *discrimination activities.* Within the context of a song, the child learns to match his speech to that of a standard model by using auditory, visual, and tactual feedback. The *production* of sounds, within the context of a song, can be practiced first in isolation, then in syllables, words, phrases, sentences, and musical conversation until it can generalize to unstructured conversation.

Phonological errors, where the child is inconsistent about articulating the sound correctly, can be corrected by asking the child, within the context of an activity song; to distinguish between closely-related words (i.e., sea vs. seat).

Fluency disorders may be more difficult to generalize beyond the music therapy setting since it is well known that stutterers do not stutter when they are singing! It is this increased awareness of "slow start" and rhythmic patterning in speech that helps the dysrhythmic speaker become rhythmic.

Language disorders, frequently showing up as

delayed language development in children that are autistic, retarded, communication disordered, and multiply handicapped, benefit from the rich possibility of vocal material in music therapy. Further, language can be infused into the music session by asking for language before giving the child what it is he or she wants. This is an example of *naturalistic intervention* also known as *milieu teaching strategy.* Rather than inviting artificial situations for language intervention, naturalistic intervention teaches when the child is interested, teaches what is functional for the student at the moment and stops while both the student and the teacher/therapist are still enjoying the interaction. A simple situation such as choice-making, "What do you want, the tambourine or the reed horn?" compels the child who is capable of approximating or articulating words to speak. Further, the decoding of the child's nonverbal communication is considered a naturalistic intervention. For example, if the child points to the horn, the therapist decodes, "Oh, you want the horn. Can you use your words?" Of course, these are all preliminary efforts to infusing language into activity songs composed for music therapy (see Chapter 6, "Materials").

It is critical for the music therapist to encourage language response within the context of a song. Here, it is important to consider the level of language used in the song (also see Chapter 6, "Materials") as well as the way in which the song is presented to the child.

For example, the structure of the song, particularly for a child beginning language must be simple, repetitive, and predictable and allow for auditory processing time (i.e., several seconds more than usual), possibly within the context of a musical rest, while still maintaining the musical tempo of the song. Common examples of this kind of presentation follow:

1. A song with one verse at a time followed by a simple chorus, often on one word or syllable. The therapist can sing the verse; the children can sing the chorus. As the language potential of the children increases, the words of the chorus can be amended accord-

ingly.

2. A song that is antiphonal, thereby creating a musical dialogue, particularly one that is imitative at the language level of the child.

3. A song that incorporates singing about one object at a time (i.e., an instrument), which is physically used after it is sung about.

4. A song that allows the child to "fill in the blank" at the end of a musical phrase with one or two words, depending upon their language level.

5. An activity song that musically asks the child to respond physically with one or two directions, depending upon the receptive language level of the child, at a time.

THE USE OF AUGMENTATIVE AND ALTERNATIVE COMMUNICATION: *Augmentative and alternative communication (AAC) methods* are frequently used in music therapy, particularly with children who are not able to physically produce speech and language. AAC has three components (Kangas and Lloyd, 2002): 1) a representational symbol set or vocabulary; 2) a means for selecting the symbols; and 3) a means for transmitting the symbols.

The most common AAC communication methods in music therapy would be considered unaided techniques such as oral speech, gestures, facial expressions, general body posture and manual signs.

Aided techniques involve a series of picture symbols, an external device or a piece of equipment. After the therapist, in conjunction with the speech-language pathologist (SLP), has selected the vocabulary for an AAC system, symbols can be selected or developed to represent the vocabulary. In the case of music symbols, for example, they are frequently developed with simple drawings or actual photographs in order to look like the object or concept they represent. Commercial symbol set frequently used in music therapy include the Oakland Picture Dictionary (Kirsten, 1981), Picture Communication Symbols (Mayer-Johnson, 1986) and the Pictogram Ideogram Communication symbols (Johnson, 1985). Contrary to symbol sets, symbol systems constitute, in effect, their own graphic language, the most well known of these being Bllisssymbolics, frequently used with cerebral palsied children. Most commonly, the child in the music therapy group can point to, touch, eye gaze or select and hand a picture symbol or photograph to the therapist in order to communicate choice or response to a question. These symbol cards can be shown directly to the child by the therapist (i.e., select one of three), be a part of a communication board on the tray of a wheelchair, or be arranged in a photo album.

There are several systems of computerized speech selection or transmission such as the Prentke Romich Intro Talker, the Prentke Romich Liberator, DECtalk (Digital Equipment Company), and Sentinent System's Dynavok generally seen with the most physically compromised children.

In terms of the music therapy session, a device commonly known as a "Big Mack" which records a spoken voice or musical sound can be prerecorded in the music therapy session as a means of inviting the nonverbal child to touch the device at the correct musical moment in a song. Further suggestions are discussed in Chapter 6, "Materials."

Considerations in Working with the Blind Child

IDEA, Definition

"An impairment in vision that, even with correction, adversely affects a child's educational performance."

Music Therapy Methods

In a review of music therapy literature and clinical applications for the blind and severely visually impaired that scans a 60-year period, 1940–2000 (Codding, 2000), the research on the blind and visually impaired child is surprisingly scant. Codding finds 44 studies, 17 of which are case studies and 27 of which are data-based research studies. Between the years of 1975–1999, Jellison (2000) finds only two research studies on the blind/visually impaired child, suggesting that there was more interest in this population in earlier years. None of the studies suggest methods specific to the visually impaired child although the focus of therapy with visually impaired involves music as an auditory cue for special awareness and travel, provision of directional cues, as an contingency to establish, maintain or eliminate inappropriate nonmusic behavior (i.e., motoric stereotypic movement).

Music therapists have often been under the impression that visually impaired children compensate for their visual deficiency with a heightening auditory sense and therefore are excellent candidates for music therapy. In many cases, this is true. In other cases, however, the heightening response to sound may sound overwhelming to the visually impaired child and a sense of precaution in dynamics must be considered for these children.

SUMMARY SUGGESTIONS: Some simple suggestions for working with the blind child involve their needs for auditory awareness of other children in the group, orientation to the musical instruments being used in the session and one's sense of physical space and movement in the music room. Because of these concerns, the following simple methods are suggested:

1. Allow the visually impaired child to physically explore a musical instrument before attempting to play it in a conventional fashion.
2. If the child does not play at an appropriate musical moment, verbally or physically prompt her.
3. Encourage the visually impaired child to have a physical sense of the space in the music room, to the extent that she can move from one instrument to another within an orchestration.
4. Consider hand-over-hand physical assistance with movement activities, gradually fading this assistance out.
5. Encourage the child to look in the direction of the peer or therapist who is speaking.
6. Intellectually advanced children can use Braille printed music.

Considerations in Working with the Deaf/Hard-of-Hearing Child

IDEA, Definition

IDEA uses the category label hearing impairment to indicate a hearing loss that adversely affects educational performance and thereby makes the child eligible for special education.

Special Education Methods

ORAL/AURAL METHODS: Oral/aural methods help the child develop residual hearing and possible verbal intelligibility (Stone, 1997). Auditory, visual and tactile methods for doing this include amplification, auditory training, speech-reading, cued speech, the use of technological aids and, certainly, talking. Total communication, using speech, and options for sign language (manually coded English, fingerspelling, American Sign Language) simultaneously has been the most widely used method of instruction in schools for the deaf since the 1960s but has been a subject of debate recently since some educators believe that "teachers typically emphasize speech and audition at the expense of sign language, or vice versa. And students attend more to one mode than to the other . . . it is not possible to speak and use ASL at the same time" (Schirmer, 2004, 441–442).

The beauty of American Sign Language (ASL) is its bilingual-bicultural approach. As a visual-spacial language, ASL utilizes the shape, location, and movement pattern of the hands, intensity of motions and the signer's facial expressions to communicate meaning and context. ASL has its own unique phonology, morphology, syntax, semantics and pragmatics and therefore does not correspond to spoken or written English. Proponents of a bilingual-bicultural (bi-bi) approach suggest that ASL be considered a deaf child's first or native language with the mastery of a second language as an additional goal.

Music Therapy Methods

LEAST RESTRICTIVE ENVINRONMENT: Descriptive terms in referring to the deaf or hard-of-hearing child include Deaf, deaf (individuals who are oral largely because they have lost their hearing adventitiously rather than at birth) and hard-of-hearing (residual hearing functional for processing speech). Approaches to teaching deaf and hard-of-hearing children (D/HH) today include the oral/aural approach, total communication, and bilingual-bicultural approaches. All these play a part in music therapy and have been most prominently presented in the work of Robbins and Robbins (1980), Darrow and Grohe (2002), Darrow (1995), and Darrow and Gfeller (1991), to name a portion of the literature. The deaf and hard-of-hearing population may be mainstreamed for music (Darrow and Gfeller, 1991) or attend a private or public school where music therapy is offered. A good deal of the placement decision will depend, of course, on the developmental level of the child and other possible handicapped conditions (see *Considerations in Working with the Severe/Multiply Disabled Child, Deaf-Blind and Traumatic Brain Injury,* p. 203).

PRIORITIES: Darrow and Grohe (2002) present an overview of the Deaf/Hard of Hearing (D/HH), a comprehensive literature review, and the multiple uses of music therapy to address the needs of this population. In their writing, there are many practical suggestions as well. According to Darrow and Grohe (2002), priorities in adapting to the D/HH client in the music therapy setting concern the physical environment and interpersonal communication.

In addition to the previous mention in the chapter of appropriate lighting and circle formation for group work, Darrow and Grohe (2002) add the following suggestions regarding the physical environment:

1. Absorbing unnecessary sound with draperies, carpeting and upholstery
2. Children with hearing aids should be positioned with their hearing aids toward the group
3. Speaker's face must clearly be seen
4. Speech-reading distance is optimal at 6 feet
5. Additional communication devices such as microphones, visual aides, tactile aids, sign language interpreters and technological aides can be added in the music therapy room.

Darrow and Grohe (2002) suggestions for interpersonal communication, based on information for the National Technical Institute for the Deaf at the Rochester Institute of Technology, are summarized as follows:

1. Before speaking, use a physical (i.e., tap on the shoulder) or visual (i.e., wave) prompt to get the child's attention.
2. Speak clearly and slowly, allowing time for auditory processing (not necessarily for the purpose of speech-reading),
3. Face and look directly at the child you are talking to without obscuring, in any way, your communication; try to maintain eye contact; do not pace and speak at the same time.
4. An alternative means of communication may be paper and pencil as necessary.
5. Rephrasing of a thought or restating a sentence with alternative words may be necessary at times for successful communication.
6. Demonstrative communication such as pantomime, body language and facial expression is encouraged.
7. Seat the deaf person near you.
8. Avoid standing in front of a window or other light source since this will make speechreading more difficult for the deaf child.
9. Use visual aids.

STRATEGIES RELATED TO GOALS FOR HEARING IMPAIRED: Music therapy strategies for the deaf and hard-of-hearing child focus toward the goals of *auditory training, language acquisition and speech production.* While the first two levels of auditory discrimination, those of *detection* (listener can determine the presence, absence, initiation or termination of music source) and *discrimination* (listener can perceive difference in the music source) are normally developed by the D/HH child in the context of the environment, the second two levels, namely *identification* (applying musical labels to musical sources) and *comprehension* (making critical judgments about music related to form, harmony or texture) need to be presented in music therapy. Other auditory processing skills that precede auditory comprehension include *awareness of acoustic stimuli, localization, attention, discrimination between speech and nonspeech, auditory discrimination* of different instruments within a total music context, discrimination about expressive qualities of music such as dynamics, tempo and phrasing (this is referred to as *suprasegmental discrimination*), *auditory memory, auditory sequential memory,* and *auditory synthesis* (in order to make critical judgments regarding form, texture and harmony).

Language acquisition and development for the D/HH child will focus on vocabulary knowledge and word-class usage. Songwriting, song signing, small group ensembles requiring communication, and the study of song texts are some of the methods used for these purposes and specifically described in further writings by Gfeller (1987, 1990).

Speech production and reception for the deaf/hard-of-hearing child includes the possibility of hearing one's own voice through the use of residual hearing. As with other special needs children needing to develop speech and language, rhythmic chanting and singing of syllables, syllable combinations, words, word combinations, phrases and the simple sentence are the order of acquisition provided through song material. Issues in articulation can be addressed though songs which focus on specific speech sounds or words.

MUSIC FOR AUDITORY TRAINING: In using music instruction as a means of auditory training, Darrow and Grohe (2002) remind the therapist of several basic attributes of the deaf/hard-of-hearing child:

1. Rhythmic abilities are generally stronger than pitch-related abilities and therefore deaf and hard-of-hearing children will be more response to rhythmic vs. tonal aspects of music.
2. Beat reproduction is easier than discrimination of or production of rhythmic patterns.
3. Amplification must be appropriate for the child to hear the music.
4. Tactile perception is helpful for partial compensation of auditory deficits.
5. Visual cues (i.e., tapping the beat) aid the learner.
6. Music skills, rather than being considered deviant, are delayed.
7. Lower frequency ranges are easier for the discrimination of pitch.
8. Training can develop pitch discrimination.

9. Language problems will frequently interfere with the child's ability to describe what is heard.
10. Vocal range is limited and lower; this should be taken into account when selecting the vocal range of song literature.
11. Deaf and hard-of-hearing children may require greater amounts of experience in music in order to achieve.
12. Sustaining instruments may provide more useful aural feedback than do percussive instruments.
13. Greater rhythm performance accuracy may be achieved with the use of moderate tempi,
14. Standard music notation may lead to more accurate performance than a reliance on the ear to imitate. This reading ability, of course, will benefit from instruction in the use of musical vocabulary.
15. Deaf and hard-of-hearing children can improve vocal intonation and ear training with practice.
16. Vibrotactile stimuli can be used in a supplementary manner for music instruction.
17. The deaf and hard-of-hearing child, like other children, can exhibit certain musical preferences in terms of sound, source, intensity and listening conditions.
18. Appropriate sound amplification and sound quality are vital.

SIGNING IN MUSIC THERAPY: Darrow and Grohe (2002) encourage the use of interpreting songs into sign, a method, by the way, that is also used with nonverbal children, such as the young autistic child. Guidelines for this activity basically encourage the signing to be compatible with the features of the music, which might be referred to as musical signing. These guidelines are summarized as follows:

1. Signs can reflect elements of music such as volume, pitch, rhythm and mood as well as the emotional interpretation of lexical content though body language, facial expression, space and manner of execution.
2. Signing should be rhythmically paced to match the rhythm of the words; this would include the duration of the sign matching the

duration of the word.

3. Instrumental sections, humming, figurative language or symbolism will require creative use of mime.

4. A single sign can often signify an entire phrase of a song (note: not dissimilar to the use of the holophrase when a child is beginning to talk).

5. The option of the signs moving upward as the melody moves upward and the signs moving downward as the melody moves downward can be employed but is not necessarily helpful to the D/HH audience.

6. Signs for *forte* can be larger and executed with more force vs. signs for *piano*.

7. Likewise, signs for *crescendo* can be demonstrated by gradually making signs larger and more intense while signs for *decrescendo* can be expressed by making signs smaller and more gentle.

8. The phrasing of the sign should reflect the phrasing of the song.

9. Song style (i.e., classical, folk, rock, country or pop) can be interpreted through the rhythm of the sign, facial expression, body language and even the dress of the child.

10. Just like voices, signers need to blend so no one person stands out in the group.

11. One child can serve to lead the musical ensemble as a "sign master."

SUMMARY STATEMENT: Therapists working with the deaf/hard-of-hearing child are encouraged to make full use of the child's residual hearing and innate musicality, leading the child into musical co-activity and making full use of total communication systems.

Considerations in Working with the Physically Disabled Child

IDEA, Definition

Children with physical disabilities and health conditions requiring special education are described under two separate IDEA disability categories, orthopedic impairment and other health impairments. Orthopedic impairment is described as follows: "adversely affects a child's educational performance. The term includes impairments caused by congenital anomaly, impairments caused by disease, and impairments from other causes" (e.g., cerebral palsy, amputations, and fractures or burns that cause contractures) (C.F.R. Sec. 300.7 (b)(7)).

Special Education Strategies

POSITIONING AND HANDLING: Probably the most prevalent physical disability music therapists encounter is cerebral palsy, classified in terms of the affected parts of the body (i.e., monoplegia, hemiplegia, triplegia, quadriplegia, paraplegia, diplegia, double heiplegia) and by its effects on movement (hpertonia, athetosis, and hypotonia). A cerebral palsy diagnosis does not necessarily impact on intellectual aptitude and this is an important consideration in music therapy methods. The importance of positioning, seating and movement are critical elements for children who are physically disabled. These elements impact on success in singing, playing instruments and movement. Therefore, the music therapist should work in tandem with the physical therapist regarding these considerations, for the following reasons:

1. Good positioning results in alignment and proximal support of the body.

2. Stability positively affects use of the upper body.

3. Stability promotes feelings of physical security and safety.

4. Good positioning distributes pressure evenly and provides comfort for seating tolerance and long-term use.

5. Good positioning can reduce deformity.

6. Positions must be changed frequently.

7. Proper seating helps combat poor circulation, muscle tightness and pressure sores and contributes to proper digestion, respiration and physical development.

Heller, Alberto, Forney, and Schwartzman (1996) suggest the following techniques for positioning and handling:

1. Face should be forward, in midline position.

2. Shoulders should be in midline position, not hunched over.
3. Trunk should be in midline position, maintaining the normal curvature of the spine.
4. Seatbelt, pommel or leg separator, and/or shoulder and chest straps may be necessary for shoulder/upper trunk support and upright positions.
5. Pelvic position is defined as having the hips as far back in the chair as possible in order to allow for even weight distribution on both sides of the buttocks.
6. Foot support is achieved with both feet level and support on the floor or wheelchair pedals.

Music Therapy Strategies

MOVEMENT AND MUSIC: When positioned and handled properly, the physically handicapped child is most likely to benefit from movement activity as well as movement activity resulting from the playing of instruments. According to Thaut (1999), particular techniques in movement training are associated with the following attributes of music: 1) the ability of music to organize rhythmic patterns and therefore use the rhythmic accents and phrases as timing cues; 2) when sound is below the intensity level of the startle reflex and when sound is organized in rhythmic pattern, the motor system in the central nervous system is activated, allowing the muscles to synchronize with the rhythm in order to anticipate and time the movement properly; 3) rhythmic entrainment, defined as a synchronization of "frequency and pattern of movement locked to the frequency and pattern of an auditory rhythmic stimulus" (i.e., rhythmic patterns in music) resulting in scaling the duration of the movement to the duration of the beat interval (Thaut, 1999, p. 238).

These three attributes of music are a solid rationale for techniques used in music therapy. Rhythmic Auditory Stimulation and Patterned Sensory Enhancement is used with the physically handicapped as well as the neurologically handicapped client. Although these techniques are detailed for the physically handicapped as well as the neurologically handicapped client, there seems to be no reason why they could not help,

for example, the autistic child or the retarded child in need of neurological movement cues through music. "Rhythmic Auditory Stimulation (RAS) uses rhythmic movement to facilitate gait. Patterned Sensory Enhancement (PSE) uses temporal, visual-spacial and dynamic patterns in music to creative structures for cuing discrete movement or longer movement sequences during functional tasks or exercises, especially during hand and arm training" (Thaut, 1999, p. 158).

Therapeutic instrumental music playing, a third technique, employs the use of musical instruments for exercise and simulation of functional movement patterns. Range of motion, endurance, strength, functional hand movement and finger dexterity, limb coordination, and so forth. are facilitated by adaptive instrumental designs (Clark and Chadwick, 1980) as well as the prescriptive use of commonly used instruments (Elliot, 1982).

ADAPTED INSTRUMENTS: The use of adapted instruments, coupled with appropriate positioning and handling, helps make the playing of instruments accessible to the physically handicapped child, thereby relieving the need for hand-over-hand assistance. Adamek and Darrow (2005, p. 283) remind the therapist of practical considerations regarding the use of instruments: 1) in order to encourage range of motion, the instrument must be strategically placed so the child will reach for it; 2) in order to increase hand grasp strength, the weight of the instrument the child will hold can be gradually increased; 3) in order to increase hand dexterity, the therapist can increase the complexity of manual manipulation necessary to play an instrument; and 4) in order to encourage digital flexibility, the therapist should encourage the use of instruments that use individual fingers, such as a keyboard. Other instrumental considerations are mentioned in Chapter 6 of this book.

ASSISTIVE TECHNOLOGY: Finally, assistive technology is often critical for a child who is otherwise nonverbal. Low-tech assistive devices, picture communication books, and high-tech assistive devices include computerized synthetic speech devices, and electronic switches that can be activated by eye movement (Parette, 1998). Further, there is an electronic device called a "soundbeam" (Tomaino, ed., 1998) which is activated by the child's movement.

Considerations in Working with the Severe/Multiply Disabled Child, Deaf-Blind and Traumatic Brain Injury

IDEA, Definitions

The term 'children with severe disabilities' refers to children with disabilities who, because of the intensity of their physical, mental, or emotional problems, need highly specialized education, social, psychological, and medical services in order to maximize their full potential for useful and meaningful participation in society and for self-fulfillment. The term includes those children with disabilities with severe emotional disturbance (including schizophrenia), autism, severe and profound mental retardation, and those who have two or more serious disabilities such as deaf-blindness, mental retardation and blindness, and cerebral palsy and deafness. Children with severe disabilities may experience severe speech, language, and/or perceptual-cognitive deprivations, and evidence abnormal behavior such as failure to respond to pronounced social stimuli, self-mutilation, self-stimulation, manifestation of intense and prolonged temper tantrums, and the absence of rudimentary forms of verbal control; and may also have extremely fragile physiological conditions. (34 C.F.R., Sec. 315.4(d))

Special Education Methods

Children in this category tend to have a slow acquisition rate for learning new skills and difficulty in generalizing and maintaining these skills once learned. Communication skills can be extremely limited, along with impaired physical and motor development, a paucity of social interaction and stereotypic and challenging behavior. For these reasons the following special education strategies, emphasized with other populations introduced in this chapter already, are germane: 1) assess current level of performance; 2) clearly define skill(s) to be taught; 3) break down skill into component parts; 4) provide clear prompting and/or cuing; 5) supply feedback and reinforcement; 6) repeat learned skills in different environments in order to help child generalize skills; and

7) ongoing assessment.

Music Therapy Strategies

DEVELOPMENTAL FUNCTIONING LEVEL: Children in this category generally operate at a sensorimotor level (see beginning of this chapter) and do not necessarily fit into the structure of a group (see Chapter 3). Nevertheless, they are frequently sent to music therapy when the therapist is servicing the entire population of the school. In order to provide appropriately for them, the therapist needs to help adjunctive staff in the room essentially provide one-on-one support for each child while the session in ongoing. Vocal songs can provide opportunities for practicing beginning speech sounds and holophrases as well as the use of sign and programmed "Big Mack." Songs can also direct children to follow simple one-step directive, allowing auditory processing time. Movement songs must be accepting of dysrhythmic movement common at a low functioning developmental level (see Briggs, Chapter 3) and instrumental materials can be introduced on an exploratory level. Increments of progress will be small and the therapist working with this population must be patient with these small levels of change.

MUSIC THERAPY STRATEGIES LINKED TO GOALS AND OBJECTIVES FOR ALL GROUP MEMBERS, OFTEN RESULTING IN ADAPTATION OF MUSIC MATERIALS

Thought Process

After the music therapist goes through the process of initially prioritizing goals (see Chapter 4) following assessment and review of the Individual Education Plan, it is helpful to reflect on these goals and speculate about how they will affect the planning of the methods and materials. Three primary questions include: *What kind of musical experiences will provide opportunity for the child(ren) to demonstrate progress* toward their developmental goals? *How must the material used be adapted in order for the therapist to help structure the varying response(s) of the child(ren) in the group? How* must the material be presented(methods) in order for the therapist to help structure the varying response(s) of the child(ren) in the group?

In situations where the therapist is familiar with a wide repertoire of songs, movement experiences and instrumental orchestrations composed for therapy, and feels confident in improvising material, orchestrating music and composing songs (see Chapter 6, "Materials"), the initial choice of musical experience and materials, even though they will need adaptation, is easy. It is the adaptation that may get tricky. It may be an easier process for the therapist to procedurally write out the steps in presenting the basic musical experience and then, considering all the goals of the children, go back and detail the methods further (see case examples below).

Adapting Methods where there is Little Overlapping of Goals

In a group where there is little overlapping of goals (see Case Example One below), it may be helpful to think first in terms of a musical experience for one child and then the necessary adaptations to include the other children in the group as well, bearing in mind that not all musical experiences in the session will promote developmental growth equally for the children. Different musical experiences will emphasize different developmental purposes which will be of varying concern for different children.

Case Example One: Preschool Developmentally Delayed Group (Goodman, K., 1992–1998)

One of the communication goals for Samantha, a four-year-old developmentally delayed child (note: included in example one group, Chapters 4 and 5), is to comprehend "Wh" questions appropriately. What kind of song will provide that experience and how will the therapist *musically structure* the response for the child? Further, how will the therapist *include the other children in the group* in this musical experience?

What kind of song will provide that experience and how will the therapist musically structure the response

for the child? The song, "Questions" (Levin & Levin, 1981, p. 10) explains the purpose of "Wh" questions: "*what, where, why, who . . . these are words that start a question. What, where, why, who . . . Pick one word and ask a question. What is it? (Solo) That's a question (Class). Where are you? (Solo) That's a question. (Class). Why me? (Solo) That's a question (Class). Who are you? (Solo) That's a question (Class). What, where, why, who. . . . These are words that start a question. What, where, why, who?*"

At first glance, this song is fine to use for Samantha. However, there are some issues with using the song that relate to Samantha's learning style. She is a concrete learner. Therefore, it is not enough to sing "That's a question." It makes more sense to ask a question within the context of the song and then answer it! This technique would require adaptation of the song (see Chapter 6, "Materials"), changing the method as seen in the written plan below:

Goal 1: Increase comprehension of "Wh" questions.

Objective 1a: Samantha will demonstrate understanding of a "Wh" question by appropriately responding within the context of an activity song.

Material: "Questions" (Learning Songs, Levin & Levin, 1997, p. 10).

Method:

1. Therapist will model the use of the song with an aide, adapting the question/answer portion of the song by pointing to a musical instrument (i.e., maraca, tambourine, ocean drum) after musically posing the question, "What is it?" then placing it on a chair and musically posing the question, "Where is it?" and finally musically asking "Who will play it?"
2. Therapist will hand the selected instrument to the aide who is being questioned, assuming she has sung, "I will play it."
3. Therapist will adapt musical intervals, tempo and melodic rhythm appropriately in order to conform to natural speech.
4. Therapist will adapt tempo in order to allow time for sufficient auditory processing.

5. Therapist then improvises on original melody for several bars while aide plays.
6. Therapist then sings, "Who will play next?" Aide supplies name of a child.
7. Therapist continues use of song with each child.
8. Therapist can use ocean drum for any child in the group, however, for a more advanced child who can think abstractly (Tommy), ask, following the playing of these instruments, "What does it sound like?"

But, *how will the therapist include the other children in the group in this musical experience?* With the exception of Lawrence, who also has "comprehension of 'Wh' questions" as an expressive language goal, the other children in the group have different expressive language goals which can be included in the methodological presentation of this song. In order to accommodate Joseph, who is to "increase comments upon actions," Joseph will be asked the same questions as Samantha. In order to accommodate Amanda who is to "use single word approximations to request and to comment on existence, nonexistence and recurrence," the therapist will ask only one question of her, the "Where" question. Further, the instrument can be hidden under a blanket in order for Amanda to comment on nonexistence; the instrument can be placed back again on the chair to comment on recurrence. Tommy, the child with the most expressive language can use a "three-word combination" in his sung response (object + attribution + object). Therefore, in response to the question, "What is it?" the therapist can use both a small tambourine and big tambourine and, in picking up the big tambourine, sing, "It's a big tambourine." Paula, who is expected to "sequence and retell stories" as well as "have memory of information" can be asked, following the activity, what the group did. Now it is necessary to amend the original methods section of this musical experience by amending step 7 of the methods:

Method:

7. Therapist continues use of song with each child, adapting the method as necessary:

- Following response to "where" question in respect to tambourine placed on chair, hide tambourine under a cloth and repose question (Amanda). Then repeat question with tambourine placed on chair. Model and/or prompt one word response to these questions, as necessary.
- Model, as necessary, a three-word combination response, object + attribution + object, for higher functioning child (Tommy).
- Following song, ask for retelling of what the group just did (Paula).

Adapting Methods where there is a Greater Degree of Overlapping Goals

In a group where there is a greater degree of overlapping goals, the materials and methods may be easier to premeditate (see Case Example Two below).

Case Example Two: Clinical Example, Latency-Age Psychiatric (Goodman, K., 1981–1984)

As presented in Chapters 4 and 5, a group of four latency-age children, ages 9–12, are all admitted to a private psychiatric hospital because of attempted suicide or consistent suicidal ideation. They are diagnosed with various psychiatric disturbances such as conduct disorder (Alan), clinical depression (Betsy), schizophrenic (Debbie) and bipolar disorder, manic phase (Edgar) and yet their social/interpersonal goals, provided by the team of mental health professionals at the hospital, overlap. All the children need to "increase peer interaction," "reduce suicidal ideation," and "increase awareness of mood." Edgar and Alan need to "decrease impulsivity," Debbie needs to "reduce rigidity in play patterns" and Betsy needs to "increase positive affect." The task of the inpatient psychiatric unit staff, therapists, doctors and teachers, is to emotionally stabilize the child over their average three-week stay so that they may leave the hospital in due time and return to their homes or residential settings, as necessary.

Methods for Psychiatric Stabilization: Product to Process

What kind of musical experience will provide that experience and how will the therapist musically structure the response for the child? Children of latency and preadolescent age, in this case, often prefer contemporary music. With the exception of Debbie, who is prone to difficulties in reality testing, all the children in the group are cognitively capable of abstract thinking. A product-oriented experience such as an ongoing simple rock group, can be used to bring the group together and introduce reflection, a process-oriented experience, on interpersonal relatedness. This would be the written plan for such a musical experience.

Goal:

1. Increase peer interaction (Edgar, Alan, Debbie, Betsy).
1a. Children will participate in singing and playing with each other, watching the therapist and each other for starting, unison playing, solo playing, musical entrances, exits and stopping (Edgar, Alan, Debbie, Betsy).
2. Reduce suicidal ideation (Edgar, Alan, Debbie, Betsy).
2a. Children will participate in musical experience, focusing solely on that experience, with a maximum of two distracting suicidal thoughts (Edgar, Alan, Debbie, Betsy).
3. Increase awareness of mood (Edgar, Alan, Debbie, Betsy).
3a. Children will verbally reflect on their mood following the musical experience (Edgar, Alan, Debbie, Betsy).
4. Decrease impulsivity (Edgar, Alan).
4a. Children will follow musical boundaries set by the therapist (Edgar, Alan).
5. Reduce rigidity in play pattern (Debbie).
5a. Child will follow musical cues of therapist to extend percussive accompaniment patterns to song (Debbie).
6. Increase positive affect (Betsy).
6a. Child will spontaneously express one positive feeling regarding the musical experience in the reflective discussion following the singing and playing.

Materials:

Song #1. "I can see clearly now" (J. Rivers)
Song #2. "Feelin the Same Way" (Norah Jones)
Song# 3. "Digging a Ditch" (working through issues–Dave Andrews)

Method:

1. After listening to a selection of three contemporary songs, the group members will cooperatively decide which song they want to sing and rhythmically improvise on.
2. The therapist will "rehearse" the singing of the song, using chaining method as necessary to review the song lyrics.
3. After the children are comfortable singing the song, the therapist, playing the accompaniment, will help the group members select and experiment with various rhythmic patterns, using the snare drum, timpani, maracas, cymbal and claves. Each child will play with the therapist alone while the others listen. As necessary, therapist will help the child musically follow boundaries (Edgar, Alan) or expand possible rigidity in their playing (Debbie).
4. Then all will play together.
5. Following the song, the children will reflect on the ways in which their sounds fit together, and how this made them feel.
6. The therapist will acknowledge, clarify and help extend verbal processing.
7. Assuming the group is still able to attend, the therapist will offer the children an option to select another song to learn and accompany.

How will the therapist include the other children in the group in this musical experience? Since this example includes children who share common social goals, the developmental emphasis in any plan involving emotionally disturbed children in an activity group, methods are easier to plan. However, there are still varying considerations which need to be addressed. For example, one child, Debbie is rigid in her playing, while others, Edgar and Alan, are impulsive and have difficulty setting boundaries. These tendencies, no doubt, relate to their diagnoses. Debbie is depressed and may be "stuck" in a low level responsiveness in terms of the musical experience; Edgar is in the manic phase of bipolar disorder and Alan is a conduct disorder: both of these diagnoses imply a difficulty with boundaries. Debbie, who is schizophrenic, has boundary issues in terms of her thinking and therefore may need further definition through music as well.

INCORPORATION OF SUPPORT AND PROFESSIONAL STAFF: INTERDISCIPLINARY, MULTIDISCIPLINARY AND TRANSDISCIPLINARY METHODS

In the Session

Roles for Support Personnel

Frequently, teachers, teacher assistants, personal aides and nurses, depending upon the number of children in the group and the functioning level of the children, accompany the children in the music therapy group. The goal of involving these personnel in the music therapy session so that there is mutual benefit and enjoyment for all is important. Personnel can take on a number of roles in the music therapy session: 1) serving as models for music tasks; 2) providing hand-over-hand assistance as necessary for children; 3) physical prompting and cuing for lower functioning children; 4) tracking and noting behavioral responses on the part of children; and 5) careful observation in order to provide carryover of relevant techniques in classroom music.

Directing Additional Staff

Generally speaking, additional staff in the music therapy session is helpful and adds to the success of the session. However, invariably, there are cases where this does not happen and the therapist must attempt to introduce a more positive involvement. In situations where staff help the child too much and do not allow the child to initially try things independently, the music therapist may simply say, "Let's let Jimmy try that on his own first and see what happens." Somehow the use of the word "Let's" dilutes the possibility of the

staff member being offended. Likewise, if there is resistence from a staff member to being involved at all, the therapist can specifically suggest what is to be done next, "Let's try positioning Johnny with upright trunk so he can breathe more easily while he is singing." As staff begin to get more physically and emotionally involved in the music session, they spontaneously look forward to music therapy and can be an enormous benefit to the therapist.

Multidisciplinary, Interdisciplinary, and Transdisciplinary Work

Planning and the delivery of such related therapies as occupational therapy, physical therapy, speech-language therapy and music therapy proceeds on three possible levels: multidisciplinary, interdisciplinary and transdisciplinary. The word "multi," meaning "having many" refers to the existence of multiple disciplines, not necessarily linked to each other in terms of goal setting or strategy planning. The word, "inter," meaning "between" refers to the cooperative planning between disciplines. Finally, the word, "trans," meaning "across," refers to cross-disciplinary planning and delivery of services. These terms are also applied to levels of planning for the individual education plan (Johnson, 2002).

The abundance of interdisciplinary teamwork in school settings creates opportunity for the music therapist to educate other professionals about the purposes and strategies associated with music therapy during the course of cooperative goal planning. If the therapist is operating in an outpatient clinic, it is important to communicate those efforts with the rest of the team.

The growth of transdisciplinary methods in music therapy has been a boon to music therapists. As the fields of speech-language pathology, physical therapy and occupational therapy developed, the tendency to compartmentalize these services for "pull-out" sessions has diminished. Today, it is commonplace to infuse learning in all environments of the school, including motor learning, communication learning, positioning and handling, and so on. This tendency extends to the music therapy room where many therapists in allied fields find the children more emotionally and physically available for therapy as a result of the music. Transdisciplinary work not only results in double goals between music therapist and allied therapists but also, further, a sense of doing co-therapy that crosses disciplinary lines. A recent example of this is detailed by Oldfield (2006) who describes a session with a physical therapist and a speech therapist. A session with an occupational therapist and a music therapy (Goodman, 1996–2002) is detailed below.

Case Example: Cathy in Occupational Therapy and Music Therapy

Marleen, the occupational therapist, and I have detailed goals and objectives for Cathy, hoping to integrate our work in the coming weeks. Cathy is a multiply handicapped eleven-year-old, nonambulatory with sensory weaknesses in vision and hearing as well as very low motor tone. She has difficulty lifting her head and trunk, is nonverbal and operates at an infant-toddler level. She is in a group of six with half the children functioning marginally above her level and the other half functioning at a preschool level. All are multiply handicapped. Marleen reports, "Cathy has been working on functional hand skills, both at lunchtime and during music. While she has generally been very alert and more conscious about events in her environment, an increase in independent, self-initiated hand use has not been forthcoming. On some days, Cathy performs tasks with only minimal assistance and/or physical prompting. At other times, everything is done hand-over-hand. She does respond well to both music and food so motivation does not appear to be a compromising factor during therapy sessions. Visual attention, or interest, however, is not always present throughout an activity, which does affect her level of function."

Our goals and objectives are as follows: 1) enhance sensory processing; 1a) consistently localize to sound source in music with carryover to the classroom; 2) Improve functional hand use; 2a) will reach for and grasp an object other than food without prompting.

We start out with Marleen sitting behind Cathy who is positioned in her wheelchair with maximal efforts for her to keep her head and trunk up. I begin with a greeting song and Marleen is able to provide hand-over-hand assistance for Cathy to pat her chest in response to the question, "Where is my friend Cathy?" As we move to a song entitled, "Oh, what a miracle am I (traditional)," I play the piano, sing and turn to model, "I got hands," while higher functioning children in the group repeat after me, "Watch me move them," while higher functioning children in the group repeat after me and move their hands, "Oh what a miracle am I." In order for Cathy to attend and localize sound while keeping her trunk and head upright, Marleen strokes her spine periodically for proprioceptive input. Seated behind Cathy, Marleen is able to provide hand-over-hand assistance in rotating the hands or, as the second directive in the song dictates, moving the head from side-to-side and the third directive in the song involves moving the shoulders up and down. As processing time for Cathy becomes more of a challenge, I slow down the music and anticipate reaction time. In order to evaluate how far away I can sing and still have Cathy localize sound, I leave the piano and being to move at limited distances singing a cappella. She is still tracking my efforts. Finally, I add the tambourine to the song, "I've got a tambourine (imitative response from higher functioning children and staff). 'Watch me play it' (shake, shake, shake, shake). Oh, what a miracle am I." Following this, I have the children pass the tambourine to each other, in order to provide opportunity for each one of them to participate. When it reaches Cathy, I offer it to her from the front. Maureen and I are very pleased to see her spontaneously reach out for it and attempt to shake it! The next time we meet we are going to use "The Echo Song" with Marleen echoing my vocalizations from another part of the room to see if Cathy will turn around to localize those sounds.

Out of the Session

It is helpful for the music therapist to provide taped recordings as well as access to instruments and music (i.e., if the special education teacher or assistant teacher is a musician) that may be used during the week as supplementary material for the children. While this is not music therapy, per se, it helps the teacher reinforce many efforts of the music therapy sessions and builds positive rapport. An initial memorandum to teachers as an open-ended invitation for the creation of supplementary music materials can provide the following check-off possibilities:

- Developmentally appropriate song materials linked to classroom themes
- Developmentally appropriate instrumental activities
- Developmentally appropriate movement activities
- Developmentally appropriate listening materials
- How to integrate music into preacademic or academic goal areas
- Other

Further, the music therapist can plan in-service workshops to educate staff about the purposes and techniques of music therapy. These workshops should include experiential work as well as handout materials and brainstorming question and answer sessions.

MUSIC THERAPY STRATEGIES DESIGNED TO INVITE AND PROMOTE GROUP PROCESS

Overview

The music therapy literature detailing strategies to invite and promote group process in the children's group is scant. Greater degrees of responsibility in group activity have been suggested by Hibben (1991a) and Presti (1984) as children advance to more demanding levels of group work but this writing is related more to the advancing stages of the group. The actual *methods for creating group cohesion* will benefit from further writing, possibly influenced by the abundance of writing on groupwork music therapy interventions for the adolescent (Joseph and Freed, 1989) and adult psychiatric population.

Review of Literature, Child Music Therapy Group

Although possible techniques for promoting group cohesion in music therapy groupwork with children seem implicit, there is a paucity of music therapy literature on this subject. One article, which paves the way for subsequent work, may be the one written by Friedlander (1994), previously presented in Chapter 3 of this book.

Friedlander details several curative factors cited by Yalom, including cohesion, universality, identification, enhancement of interpersonal learning and social coping. She proposes to meet these through positive interrelatedness and problem solving. Tracking the group process through what she terms group developmental stages, Friedlander (1994) identifies four stages, previously introduced to the music therapy literature through Hibben (1991) which bear repeating: 1) preaffiliation; 2) power and control; 3) intimacy: 4) differentiation and separation. She describes the first three of these four phases as they manifest themselves in the music therapy group.

Preaffiliation is marked by approach-avoidance behavior where the child explores the use of musical materials and must have enough ego strength to avoid open conflict and hostility. *Power and Control* involve challenging the authority of the therapist and competing for attention, both verbally and nonverbally through the music; *Intimacy,* after several weeks of intensive work, relies on familiarity, structure and music to help members work toward a common musical goal as they listen to and support each other. These stages, along with the fifth stage of separation-individuation (Garland et al., 1976) are also discussed by Hibben (1991a) with the suggestion that demands of the groupwork increase as the children gain the ability to share, become intimate and assume greater responsibility. The challenges of promoting group cohesion are entirely possible in developmentally age-appropriate groups and can and should be written about in greater detail in the music therapy literature.

Review of Literature, Adolescent

What is group cohesion? Joseph and Freed (1989) cite observable aspects of group cohesion. For example, members actively listening and participating in the giving and receiving of feedback, create a supportive group environment, a trusting environment for risk-taking and self-disclosure. Members who see and use their groupwork as a potential environment for the achievement of personal goals begin to achieve self-esteem and self-respect, translating their insight into action.

However, in order to achieve levels of cohesiveness, several methods are necessary. First, the therapist needs to establish a working alliance "by setting clear goals, challenging group members and clarifying for the clients how completion of the goals can meet their needs" (as cited in Joseph and Freed, 1989, p. 29). Further, the therapist can make appropriate interventions by focusing on experience and the shared feelings of clients. An important extension of this method can mean prompting and cuing clients to take risks in order to help them make more progress through the group. Further, challenging clients must be accompanied by acceptance and understanding. Finally, we return to the aforementioned *principle of structure* in the group. Structuring is, in fact, an important consideration in working toward a cohesive group since a higher degree of structure in a beginning group may alleviate unnecessary anxiety in the early stages of groupwork. Interpersonal trust and stable relationships may more easily flourish when there is unnecessary anxiety, sometimes the result of lack of structure in a group.

In order to facilitate group cohesion with a group of adolescents, Joseph and Freed (1989, p. 30) identify five stages with related goals and emphases:

1. *Goal setting:* identify need for music therapy service and reinforce sense of client responsibility in therapy group.
2. *Individual/parallel activity:* in order to develop interpersonal awareness, this stage will also emphasize similar life experiences through music.
3. *Cooperative activity:* in order to advance inter-

personal cooperation, this stage emphasizes the reality that the group can work toward an objective.
4. *Self-disclosure:* in order to develop trust, this stage works to accept self-disclosure in the group.
5. *Problem solving:* the clarification of individual issues in therapy can be clarified in this stage in order to work through what may be individual and/or group ineffectiveness in problem solving. This stage may involve interpersonal confrontations and therefore help the members handle these confrontations, hopefully generalizing these skills to other environments.

Although the Joseph and Freed model was used with adolescents, *it is possible for the therapist to facilitate a sense of group process, beginning with children functioning at a latency age level.* Prior to this age level, group process is difficult and, as pointed out in Chapter 3, children are effectively operating on a one-to-one level within the group.

In her casework with latency-aged children who were suicidal, Goodman (1989) suggested that the abilities to problem-solve and gain insight through musical experience profit from music therapy.

Types of Groups Relevant to Music Therapy Groupwork with Children

Slavson and Schiffer (1975): Play Group Therapy

In their noteworthy work on group therapy with children, Slavson and Schiffer (1975) note two types of groups and approaches with children.

The first type of group is termed the *play group therapy,* "a group treatment method for *prelatency* children where various types of age-appropriate play materials are supplied and where the therapist may speak with individual children and/or the group, at opportune times, explaining and interpreting their feelings and behavior on their level of understanding; includes dyadic triadic and total group interactions and attitudes" (Slavson and Schiffer, 1975, p. 465). The prelatency ages are typically developmental ages 3–5, associated with preschool. Children at this age are prime candidates for play therapy; their work of thinking, feeling, conceptualizing and problem solving is essentially accomplished through play. The transfer of these functions through music play would constitute the music therapy group with developmentally appropriate children.

MUSIC THERAPY GROUP PROCESS FOR PLAY THERAPY GROUP: What can the music therapist do to encourage group process at these developmental ages? Several suggestions are appropriate here: 1) structure turn-taking activities with instruments, vocals and movement; 2) encourage the development of representational play through creative improvisation and associated thoughts through improvisational song, movement, musical theater and instrumental creations; 3) encourage interpretive listening to music; and 4) help the children become aware of what they are all contributing to the sense of group by commenting on what is happening in the group, possibly drawing their attention to various members of the group with respect to perseverance, altruism, success and handling challenges.

Slavson and Schiffer (1975); Activity Therapy

The second type of group is termed the *activity group therapy,* a type of group structure cited by Friedlander (1994) in helping disturbed children make progress in social skills, motor skills and internal organization. Slavson and Schiffer describe the activity group therapy "as a method of group treatment of specially selected latency children where the corrective modality is experiential, flowing from significant activities and interactions in a group (vs. analytic group psychotherapy)" (Slavson and Schiffer, 1975, p. 463). The latency ages are typically ages 5–12, associated with grammar school. Children at this age are beginning to develop notions of morality, decision-making skills, following rules, and working to get along with each other. They accomplish their work of thinking, feeling, conceptualizing and problem solving in a more traditional environment of academics and product-based projects as opposed to play.

MUSIC THERAPY GROUP PROCESS FOR ACTIV-

ITY THERAPY GROUP: What can the music therapist do to encourage group process with children functioning at the ages of latency-aged children? These children can be involved in longer and more sophisticated musical projects that involve cooperative work and decision-making, therefore inviting a greater responsibility for group process. Examples of this could include working on a musical play, developing a series of songs around selected themes, orchestrated pieces that can be performed at school assemblies, ensemble group work such as chorus, modified orchestra and band groups, rock ensemble, relaxation to music listening for stress reduction, and so forth.

Passive vs. Active Music Therapy Approaches Related to Group Cohesion

As the group begins the task of trusting each other enough to profit from working with each other and taking interpersonal and musical risks, the therapist must be mindful of inviting musical experiences that are *progressively* conducive toward these ends. Coons and Montello (1998), in their work with two groups of emotionally disturbed learning disabled preadolescent boys, found that passive-listening approaches, helping children share their music with each other, could teach the children trust and tolerance, thereby paving the way for active music making.

Keeping the principle of successive expectations in mind, the therapist needs to be aware of what the group can comfortable tolerate in terms of new learning, problem solving, getting along with each other and taking risks.

Therapeutic Factors in Groupwork: Irving Yalom

Psychodynamic: Interpersonal Group Therapy

Irving Yalom introduced the original models for groupwork with adults in the seventies. Several therapeutic factors of group therapy all contributing to a sense of group cohesion were identified by Irving Yalom (1985). Although originally written in reference to group therapy with adults, these factors are arguably operative in latency-aged children and can be encouraged in the music therapy group. As a psychodynamic model, the curative factors in Yalom's group therapy model move beyond the activity therapy model toward a process-oriented group. They include the *installation of hope, universality, altruism, development of socializing techniques, imitative behavior, interpersonal learning, group cohesiveness and catharsis.*

Catharsis/Interpersonal Learning in Child Group Music Therapy

It is the very essence of music therapy that allows the children in the group to channel their energies through the musical experience. This *catharsis* will happen. The question is how the therapist uses the cathartic experience as an opportunity for insight. The very simple question of "What was it like beating the drum?" for example, will pave the way for the cognitively higher functioning child to reflect on the emotional release of music-making. Other children in the group can learn from this type of process-oriented experience and know that they, too, can safely express their impulses through music. In sharing these experiences, the children learn from each other, otherwise a process known as *interpersonal learning.*

Instillation of Hope/Sense of Universality/Imitative Behavior in Child Group Music Therapy

The *installation of hope as well as a sense of universality* invariably results from children identifying with other children in the group who have similar or even dissimilar challenges and are rising to meet these challenges. Music presenting challenges to be handled, for example, is commonplace in younger children's song material (see Chapter 6). For example, "What do I do when I'm alone?" (Moss and Raposo, 1992); "I'm Mad Today" (Nordoff and Robbins, 1980); "Everybody makes mistakes" (Moss and Raposo, 1992). This installation of hope and a sense of universality, on the part of a child in the group, may not even happen consciously. The therapist can encourage this identification and admiration from peers by prais-

ing the efforts of a child meeting different types of challenges and simply saying, "Look what Johnny has done! Let's all try that too." This type of comment, by the way, further encourages *imitation* on the part of other children in the group, another corrective element identified by Yalom.

Altrusim in Child Group Music Therapy

As children in the group begin to feel a further sense of attachment to each other, they become *altruistic,* receiving gratification from giving to their peers. These giving acts are usually as simple as spontaneously praising each other, comforting each other or helping each other physically in the group. The therapist can support these actions by recognizing them and praising them with a simple acknowledgment.

Socializing Techniques in Child Group Music Therapy

The development of *socializing techniques,* referred to in the Yalom literature, comes about naturally through the necessary efforts to make music together. Particularly in the latency-age groups, children must learn to work with each other cooperatively. When this becomes difficult, it is the working-through process of getting along with each other and problem-solving conflicts that becomes the work of the therapist and the group members.

Recapitulation of the Primary Family Group in Child Group Music Therapy

Part of the music therapy effort may impact on what Yalom calls *"corrective recapitulation of the primary family group"* particularly if the children unconsciously take on the roles of competing siblings for the attention of the surrogate mother or father therapist. In order to help the group work together cooperatively, the therapist can help the group members set ground rules for the functioning of the group.

Further, the success of the music product itself can serve as a reflection of the group's ability to work together and this should be acknowledged and praised by the therapist, possibly even discussing what kinds of positive interpersonal behaviors led to the success of the outcome. When there are difficulties in music-making as a result of interpersonal conflicts, the therapist can initially try to correct the musical problems. If the children are ready to verbally process the success or lack of success in the musical problems which may stem from interpersonal conflict, the therapist can proceed on that level as well, asking simple questions like "Our music is not 'working' today. What do you think is going on? What can we do to make it sound better?" In these cases, the music may be serving as a projective of how the children are able to work or not work successfully with each other in terms of assuming various roles in the music, listening to each other, controlling their impulses, and so on.

MUSIC THERAPY SESSION FORMAT THAT MAKES SENSE GIVEN PURPOSE, PREFERENCES AND FUNCTIONING LEVEL OF THE GROUP

Although a format of suggested types of activity does not constitute any kind of method, it helps the therapist forecast an organization to the session and this can be helpful, particularly to children in need of structure.

General Session Formats

As aforementioned, one common example of a general session format includes *an opening and closing as well as varied options for instrumental, vocal and movement activities* that the therapist initially introduces. As the children gain familiarity with these materials and activities, they will begin to choose what it is they would like to do in a particular session. Apart from the choice of materials happening in a structured way (i.e., through picture exchange or verbal request), choices often happen spontaneously as children begin to sing a particular song or approach a certain instrument. This is fine as long as the group agrees with the momentum of the moment.

Specific Group Format

A more specific format for a multiply handicapped group (Coleman, 2002), includes the following: hello song, puppet play, use of percussion instruments, vocal imitation using voice-activated device, motor imitation, visual following of tagboard books, use of song file folders, use of large tone bars as ostinato patterns for simple songs, manipulatives such as beanbags or hoops within the context of a song, and, finally, a good-bye song.

In a situation where the therapist has the possibility of setting up many different types of session formats, these can follow a developmental progression, possibly be modified from existing adult models (Unkefer, 2000), and be organized under various main categories:

1. Movement
   • Sensory stimulation
   • Relaxation through music group
   • Movement, based on precomposed choreography
   • Movement, creative/improvisational
2. Instrumental
   • Sensory stimulation group
   • Instrumental work, based on orchestrated arrangements, Preprimary, Primary, Intermediate, Advanced (Levin & Levin, 1998)
   • Instrumental ensemble, precomposed music
   • Instrumental ensemble, creative/improvisational
   • Composition group
3. Vocal
   • Sensory stimulation–beginning vocalization
   • Vocal work, based or music therapy materials, Preprimary, Primary, Intermediate, Advanced (Levin & Levin, 1997a; Ritholz and Robbins, 1999, 2003; Nordoff and Robbins, 1962, 1968, 1980).
   • Vocal ensemble, precomposed music
   • Vocal ensemble, creative/improvised
   • Vocal songwriting group
4. Listening
   • Auditory discrimination activities
   • Guided music listening

- Music appreciation
5. Musical Drama
   - Simple drama, activity songs
   - Intermediate to advanced drama, music therapy dramas
   - Drama, creative/improvised
   - Musical playwriting group

As the children move from one level of participation to another within given formats, the therapist can expect a more reasoned, abstract level of response. While some group members may be expected to work together toward completion of a *product* (i.e., playing the instrumental orchestration, singing the song, listening to a piece of music, carrying out a musical drama), other group members will be expected to work together toward completion of a *product* through *process-oriented work* that further involves their problem solving and psychodynamic awareness of what is happening in the group during the musical work. This would constitute a goal for the increasing sophistication of the group.

ADAPTIVE NATURE OF THE METHODOLOGY

As the sample case study in this chapter will hopefully illustrate, *it is of paramount importance that the methodology in the music therapy session not become stagnant.* What this means in very practical terms is that *the music therapist must be responsive to the evolving needs of group members as they suggest alternative or extended activity levels* in the group or, conversely, object to what is going on in the group and need to problem solve. Examples of this are presented in Chapter 1 as well as Chapter 8 within the context of subjective evaluation.

THERAPIST KNOWLEDGE BASE AND PHILOSOPHY OF HELPING SUITED TO THE METHODOLOGY

As the student therapist becomes involved in hands-on training, it is necessary and natural to develop a philosophy of helping. This is further propelled by what the student may be learning in the training program. Some programs, for example, will emphasize a behavioral approach in conducting group therapy with children; others will emphasize a relationship-based approach; others will make many approaches available to the student, and suggest that an eclectic approach is possible in conducting group music therapy.

Development of Critical Thinking

No matter what the training and education program presents, it is incumbent upon the student therapist to develop a critical approach in reviewing music therapy literature and sharing in the dialogue of students and professionals when discussing the appropriateness of music therapy approaches with different population groups.

How is this accomplished? One suggestion is that the student remain open to different possibilities. In doing so, the student can evaluate the efficacy of a certain approach with a certain population by reviewing the music therapy literature, observing, assisting, and finally trying different kinds of music therapy groupwork with children. Another suggestion is that the student personally ascertains what type of helping philosophy suits their particular needs and temperament.

EXAMPLE OF SESSION PLAN METHODOLOGY FOR MIXED GROUP DIAGNOSES: FLEXIBILITY IN ADAPTING TO RESPONSE OF GROUP

THE GROUP

Thoughts About Group Members

This group of seven latency-age children, five of whom, Jared, Evan, Richard, Dora, and Patrick, were previously grouped together and initially introduced to the reader in Chapters 4 and 5 of this book, range in age from 10 to 13 years old. They attend a regional day school in New Jersey. Since last year, two children have joined this group, Abby and Gabriel. Since the functioning levels of these seven children range from pre-school to early grade school and the children present with a variety of physical and attentional difficulties (diagnoses include different ranges of mental retardation, autistic spectrum disorder, cerebral palsy, emotional behavioral disorder, and communication disorders), methods will be varied.

A group of very different personalities, strengths and weaknesses, this group will not be easy to "juggle." In order to provide a sense of carryover from the classroom, I have italicized student strengths and weaknesses as well as classroom strategies mentioned. This will help me formulate some observations and questions that go beyond the IEP goals and objectives. Let me introduce you to the children:

Dora, a slim tall teenager with brown hair and blue eyes, is 13. Her mother and her nurse, who has been caring for Dora since infancy, report that she absolutely loves music and listens to classical music and opera at home in order to relax. Dora is medically fragile, quadriplegic and nonverbal. Despite all her physical involvement, she perseveres in music therapy activity and is motivated to try challenging physical tasks in movement, playing instruments and vocalizing. She has specific *music choices* which she *indicates through picture exchange, eye gaze to sight words* (25 personally relevant sight words) or adaptive switch and speech output device. The physical therapist reports that she is spontaneously *using her right hand more frequently* and she has the ability to maintain a more upright posture when in a gait trainer or on an adaptive trike. However, the contractures that appear to be developing in her right elbow are becoming a problem since she is *resistive to manual stretching of these joints.* Dora understands a great deal, is able to make definitive choices, and is the strongest reader in the group. The other children relate to her as a friend, reading her nonverbal cues comfortably, despite her restrictions.

Jared, a stocky good looking 10-year-old with curly black hair and green eyes, smiles and laughs frequently in music. According to his mother and his teacher, music is "his thing" and he approaches musical experience with a tremendous amount of excitement. This, tempered with his already impulsive hyperactive temperament, needs to be

channeled and *sometimes he has difficulty working with the rest of the group in making choices about what to do next in music.* He has an excellent *sense of humor* and makes jokes, not all of them appropriate. He is a very demonstrative child and is learning to *identify his emotions and discuss them.* His diagnoses are broad: both mentally retarded and emotional behavioral disorder (EBD). In terms of communication, Jared is now *self-correcting his sentences,* with good recall of previous learning, and also elaborating his thoughts with longer sentences. He is *able to answer simple "Wh" questions, such as who, what and why.* In terms of receptive language, Jared can follow two-step motor commands. In his academics, Jared identifies numerals and counts objects up to ten, is working on identifying numbers 11–20 and counting objects up to 20. His sight word vocabulary is about 7 words and he can classify pictures into categories such as food, clothing and animals. *Frustration tolerance* remains a primary goal for Jared in conjunction with developing leisure skills and continuing to improve academic, language, early math and reading and fine and gross motor skills.

Abby, a petite Afro-American 10-year-old with black braids and brown eyes, comes to music eagerly despite her shy temperament. Given her reticence in terms of being the only girl who is verbal in the group, Abby has had to develop more skills in *standing up for her rights with her peers.* Abby is challenged with *auditory processing* disorder, *cognitive and language delays* and a *left-side motor weakness.* She is able to follow a *one-step routine without prompts* and is *working on two-step routines.* Given her temperament, her voice tends to be soft and she *needs encouragement to project* it when spontaneously using short sentences and phrases. Her *motor planning is dependent upon her organization of sensory functions* which vary daily. When she is functioning well, for example, the physical therapist reports that she can follow directions requiring gross motor skills including riding an adaptive trike around obstacles and attaining and maintaining various positions on a scooter board. Since auditory processing is weak, Abby *has difficulty at this time with more complex directions and responding to why questions.* She continues to rely on *prompts.* Could this be related to her relatively passive temperament as well as her auditory processing disorder? This year, she joins this group, five of whom were together and therefore bonded as a unit previously.

Patrick, a well-built handsome 11-year-old with light brown hair and blue eyes, comes to music with his personal aide. Patrick *seems anxious to please* his aide, Bill, and turns to Bill constantly throughout the session looking for guidance and direction, further indications of Patrick's lack of self-confidence. Patrick *follows activity related one and two-step directions and is possibly a better visual learner* than an auditory learner since his success improves with visual cues. He is nonverbal but communicates using a *combination of gestures, sign approximations, pictures and vocalization.* Patrick's efforts to verbally communicate are compromised by his *poor oral motor skills* which result in lack of saliva control and speech intelligibility. Moreover, he seems to get discouraged easily and *does not seem motivated to tolerate correction of speech sounds.* Further, his *resistence to extending manual sign vocabulary* as well as *his confusion and aggression during classroom transitions* makes one wonder if these behaviors are only secondary to *poor auditory processing skills.* Patrick is not yet toilet-trained, has below-age level academic skills, unrefined fine motor skills and needs monitoring by the physical therapist for coordination and balance activities. He comes to music with positive anticipation.

Evan, a 12-year-old with sandy-colored hair, electric blue eyes and freckles across his nose and cheeks, comes to music with an impish grin. He is a Retts child and wears gloves on his hands to protect them from impulsive biting. Despite the fact that he is nonverbal, he understands a great deal and his *receptive language continues to be a strength.* He communicates by using his communication book and *responding to pictures presented.* He has been introduced to a low-tech augmentative device but needs more vocabulary and additional content in order to really use it. His attention is described as *brief but focused* and, with frequent verbal redirection, he is *responsive to verbal directions in order to complete a task.* Evan has *a strong personality* in terms of ordering his own environment and *will tantrum when imposed upon to perform tasks or activi-*

ties. He is orally self-stimulatory, frequently putting his fingers in his mouth and biting, a behavior associated with the Retts syndrome. *He seems to socially isolate himself although he smiles with pleasure when ongoing actions in the group engage and stimulate him.* I wonder about his will to order his environment and how much of this is sensorily protective.

Gabriel, a 12-year-old Downs child, wears an engaging smile. He is of small stature with a bowl haircut and soft brown eyes. He has always loved music and his transition to this group is a bit difficult because many of the other boys are physically larger and more aggressive than he is. *Gabriel learns well by rote* and has apparently learned the class routine following a picture schedule with prompting. He is *social* and makes it clear that he wants to play with his new friends, *preferably with physically active games.* His *auditory processing skills are inconsistent and he sometimes has difficulty following two-step directions.* In terms of communication, there is a good deal of *self-talk, echolalia and perseveration despite his extensive expressive vocabulary* which needs to be channeled into complete sentences. He has *low tone and can have slow motor planning skills.*

Richard, an 11-year-old moderately retarded child with apraxia, has adorable dimples and a wave in his hair. *He loves being the leader in the group, "conducting" the group and trying to change from one song to another as he sees fit.* In short, he has a fine ego and demonstrates this in music. Despite his apraxia, *his spontaneous speech has markedly increased and shows up through appropriate questioning as well as active response.* He is *eager to please and participate,* especially during music. His *fine and gross motor abilities are becoming more organized, reflect more weight-bearing and are beginning to demonstrate left to right sequencing skills.* In contrast to the growth in physical skills, academic skills are of inconsistent performance, largely due to *auditory processing problems* which make it difficult for him to retain information. He is a child of the moment and *if he sees no internal reason to learn something, he makes limited effort to do so.* His *attention may be fleeting* and he has *difficulty* in organizing his work space or *sequence the process* needed to complete his work. *The teacher recommends that rote skills compensate for the lack of generalization.*

FORMULATION ABOUT GROUP MEMBERS

We will summarize the considerations outlined earlier at the beginning of the chapter in thinking about what methods to use with this group.

The Space being Used for Music Therapy

The space available for these sessions was a former classroom now equipped for both art and music, a shared space. Fortunately, the room was large enough to share although it would have been preferable to have my own space, as I originally did before enrollments in the school climbed.

Sheet music, music books, music games and books were housed in bookshelves to the left of the piano. A few feet from the piano there were shelves that had square cubbies so smaller percussion instruments could be organized. Larger instruments such as glockenspiel, autoharps, omnichord, standing drums and suspended cymbal were arranged in proximity to the cubbies. In back of the piano was a blackboard wall as well as a chalkboard and a Velcro board with pictures of instruments. My primary problem was fluorescent lighting but, fortunately, I also had natural light.

Physical Arrangement of the Group

The children were seated in a semicircle around the piano.

Music Therapy Activity Levels that are Consistent with the Various Functioning Levels of the Children in the Group

Activity levels in this group are primarily in the symbolic period (developmental ages 2–7) but at least half the children still have lower functioning skills, as far as language, in the sensorimotor period. Sensory and concrete presentations would have to occur simultaneously; representational play will remain a challenge for all.

Music Therapy Strategies Related to the Diagnoses and Primary Strengths and Weaknesses of the Children in the Group

Although Dora is severely physically compromised, she has a high degree of motivation and emotional intentionality. I remember what Greenspan writes about when he refers to this component of the child so positively. I do believe that I can take advantage of this trait in Dora as well as her love of music to have her make specific music choices, continue to use her right hand frequently with positioning and handling and adapted instruments and possibly even come to music in a gait trainer for the possibility of free vocalization and breathing and spontaneous movement. I wonder why she is resistive to manual stretching of the joints in her right elbow. Can I give her an instrumental task that will motivate her to follow through on stretching these joints? This could be done in conjunction with the physical therapist as a transdisciplinary.

Like Dora, Jared is blessed with a high degree of motivation for music. Although he is prone to impulsivity and hyperactivity, I do believe that these traits can be channeled through the music and eventually motivate him to get along with the rest of the group. The fact that he can self-correct his sentences makes me think that he can also self-correct his impulsive behavior particularly since he has good recall of previous learning. The ability to follow two-step commands will be valuable in giving him somewhat more sophisticated musical roles in orchestrations.

Abby, also motivated to perform in music, will, I believe, overcome her reticence through vocal projection. I believe that the music, if properly timed, will help her with auditory processing and the motor tasks will challenge her left side motor weakness.

Patrick is also motivated to perform in music but gets easily discouraged due to his anxiety and lack of confidence. He also has auditory processing disorder but seems to perform at a higher level with visual cues. I would like to take advantage of this strength in learning as I offer musical experiences to him.

Evan, armed with stronger receptive language than most, also responds to pictures like Patrick. His sensory style is hyperactive; he is sensitive to sound and touch and can easily get overwhelmed; perhaps his efforts to control his environment are a means to protect his sensory overload. The fact that he is smiling during moments of engagement in the group is very positive; it is an indication of emotional engagement on his part, an opportunity to enter his world.

Gabriel, also strongly motivated through music, is said to learn well by rote. While this may be so, it would be great to encourage his conceptual creativity through music in order to give him emotional freedom he is not accustomed to, at least in the classroom. The fact that he is social and enjoys physically active games may be a precursor to dancing in music as well as using his body while playing the instruments to increase motor planning skills. Further, I believe the inconsistent auditory processing which sometimes gets in the way of following two-step directions can be retrained through music.

Finally, Richard, another lover of music, can show off his leadership skills in the group if he learns to self-organize, increase his attention span, continue his curiosity and develop internal reason to learn. Like Gabriel, Richard has been encouraged to learn by rote. Yet he has a propensity for drama and pantomime, indicating to me that he can go beyond rote learning and perhaps, in this way, develop conceptually in other ways. I also think that movement, in conjunction with singing, will help him overcome his apraxia. Perhaps the drama can also be utilized to teach him academics.

Summary, Strengths, and Weaknesses Related to Methods

As I think about the strengths and weaknesses of the children, I am pleased to realize that *they all seem very motivated to work through music.* According to Greenspan, this *emotional intentionality,* as previously discussed in this chapter, can work wonders in helping the children have a reason to work on

their challenges. Several of the children have *difficult sensory profiles* but, on a positive note, *they have self-awareness and a beginning sense of insight.* Because of that, I can *talk* to them about what is happening: Evan is *hyperreactive but knows his limits;* Dora and Abby are *protective of the limbs they know are weak;* Jared is *impulsive and has a low frustration tolerance but also has the ability to self-correct and learn from past experience;* Gabriel and Richard *have been taught in a rote style but have a flair for dramatic experience, socializing and potential leadership;* Abby, Patrick, Richard, and Gabriel all have varying degrees of *auditory processing disorders* which will necessitate *my careful awareness to tempo.* Richard's difficulty is further compromised by apraxia, the oral motor planning issue which I can address *through paired movement and singing.* Abby and Patrick learn well when *supplemented with visuals.* Further, both of them need to boost their confidence and allay their anxiety by gradually *taking on solo roles* within the group. Fortunately, Richard and Gabriel are socially comfortable and can take their place in the group *as role models for more reticent members.*

Music Therapy Strategies Linked to Goals and Objectives for all Group Members, Often Resulting in Adaptation of Music Materials

In terms of session planning, this group is a challenge. There are few overlapping goals and therefore I am going to have to be very inventive in terms of finding musical experiences I can adapt to all the needs of the children. I do not have to feel overwhelmed by this, even though that may be my first reaction. I remind myself that each musical experience will provide varying degrees of benefit for the children in the group. My purpose is to include them in the group experiences to whatever extent possible, prioritize what I want to accomplish in the sessions and what musical experiences can focus on those priorities. In this group, social issues seem paramount. Some children are reticent (Abby), anxious (Patrick), dependent (Patrick), self-absorbed (Dora, Evan) while others are social but possessive in terms of needing the therapist's attention (Jared, Richard). Following the social aspects of the group dynamics, I am concerned with the communication goals. Abby, Patrick, Richard, Gabriel, and Jared have very different levels of verbal communication while Dora and Evan, even though they have a relatively high level of receptive language, are nonverbal. Finally, I look at the motor goals and prioritize the music experience as one where Abby and Dora can maximally benefit in terms of motor experience. I have to admit that I am not that concerned about the preacademic goals even though I have included them in my developmental grid. To me, they are an ancillary element of the music therapy session.

It is helpful to see the goals within the context of certain kinds of musical experience first. Communication goals are, in my opinion, best addressed through singing. Motor goals are, in my opinion, best addressed through movement and strategic instrumental tasks. Interpersonal goals

remain a constant throughout all musical experiences although experiences requiring attention to a group product rather than a one-on-one product within the group are the most effective for interpersonal awareness in a lower functioning group like this.

With this in mind, I think group instrumental orchestrations, songs which are structured in antiphonal or solo/group fashion and movement experiences that involve partner play, passing a beanbag, passing a ball or moving a parachute to music provide more interpersonal awareness and cooperation. As the group becomes more aware of each other, I can progress to experiences that will necessitate their spontaneously waiting and taking turns in order to participate. If you look at Table 7.1, you will see a summary of the goals for this group. The objectives are organized per session plan.

TABLE 7.1. GOALS FOR GROUP.

Social goals
1. Increase participation in activity with:
   a. a maximum of 2 verbal redirections (Richard)
   b. ten-minute period with minimal verbal prompting, 4 out of 5 trials (Jared)
   c. with minimal verbal prompting and decreased behavioral response at least once during session (Jared)
   d. interest (Dora)
   e. for up to 1/2 hour during each school day with prompting and redirection (Evan)
2. Increase awareness:
   a. of the need for help by appropriately accessing pictures or gesturing on 3/5 session days (Evan)
   b. of emotional states by spontaneously verbalizing feelings (Jared)
   c. of increased frustration tolerance by maintaining appropriate behaviors when challenged (Jared)
   d. attention from peers and adults (Dora)
3. Practice "appropriate" behavior as defined below:
   a. appropriate volume of verbalizations, reduction of inappropriate behaviors and attention-seeking noises (Jared)
   b. appropriateness in challenging circumstances (Jared)
   c. Auditorally and visually attend to peers for 2 turns during group activity (Gabriel)
4. Initiate parallel play with a classmate once during each school day (Evan)

Communication goals include the following:
1. Use of augmentative device in order to expand use of low-tech augmentative device with voice output for communication and interaction (Evan, Dora)
2. Receptive vocabulary
   a. Improve response to yes/no questions (Dora)
   b. responding appropriately through pictures or action during 1 activity per day (Evan)
   c. Demonstrate comprehension of verbal information through appropriate verbal responses on 4/5 opportunities (Richard)
   d. Follow three-step activity-related directions with gestural prompts once (Gabriel)

continued

TABLE 7.1. GOALS FOR GROUP–*Continued.*

3. Expressive communication
    a. Spontaneously verbalize wants, needs, and feelings to appropriate staff (Richard)
    b. Verbalize wants and needs clearly and intelligibly by repeating a 4-word phrase (Patrick)
    c. Demonstrate comprehension and retention of auditory input during group activity by responding appropriately, given adequate processing time (Patrick)
    d. Intelligibly verbalize wants, needs, and feelings given only one chance for self-correction (Richard)
    e. correct use of temporal terms in response to simple questions, with verbal prompts, 3 out of 5 trials (Jared)
    f. Develop gestures to communicate needs and wants (Dora)
    g. Spontaneously use a 4-word phrase to answer a simple activity based "Wh" question for 3 out of 5 trials with a pictorial prompt (Gabriel)
    h. Inhibit vocalizations and quietly attend to speaker on 3 of 5 occasions within 1 activity with a gestural prompt (Gabriel)
    i. Verbally instruct a peer to do a three-step activity with visual, gestural and verbal prompts on 3/5 trials (Abby)
    j. Recognize when it is his turn to participate without gestural or verbal prompting during group activity (Gabriel)

Cognitive goals
1. Preacademic:
    a. Identify all 26 manuscript letters and their sounds (Dora)
    b. Identify 11 color words (Dora)
    c. Identify 12 words frequently seen on signs and 13 others sight words (Dora)
    d. Identify numerals to 5 (Dora)
    e. Use whole numbers to count groups of objects within the context of everyday tasks (Richard)
    f. Find correct monetary amounts from coins presented in order to "purchase" snack daily (Richard)
    g. Verbally communicate home address including street, town, state, and country when asked (Richard, Patrick, Abby)
    h. Demonstrate 1:1 correspondence up to number 5 by responding to the request "give me" (Gabriel)
    i. Indicate which group as "more" when presented with a choice of 2 groups with 1 verbal prompt on 3 of 5 tries (Gabriel)
    j. Sort 10 objects of 3 different materials into appropriately marked bins with no more than 2 verbal and/or gestural prompts (Gabriel)
    k. Read a daily picture/word schedule and follow 3 activities sequentially with 1 verbal prompt (Gabriel)

Motor goals
1. Modify movement to participate in variations of gross motor activities (Jared)
2. Carry out desired motor activity in response to verbal directive, within 30 seconds of the directive (2/3 trials) (Abby)
3. Maintain balance in a challenged position for the duration of the activity (Abby)
4. Spontaneous use of left upper extremity during bilateral activites without verbal prompting (Abby)
5. Reposition herself in her classroom chair with verbal prompting only to attain an appropriate seated posture 2/3 times (Abby)
6a. Follow directions and participate in group gross motor activities without physical prompts on 3 out of 5 trials (Gabriel)
6b. in gross motor/balance activity with verbal prompts only (Patrick)
6c. Participate in group gross motor activities with minimal verbal redirection on 3/5 occasions (Evan)

Incorporation of Support and Professional Staff for Interdisciplinary, Multidisciplinary and Transdisciplinary Work

I am fortunate in this group. The primary teacher is going to skip his preparation period and attend the music therapy session. I also have the assistant teacher, a private aide (for Gabriel) and a nurse (for Dora)–five adults in a group of seven children. At times, I wonder if I even need this many people; the room sometimes feel crowded.

Music Therapy Strategies Designed to Invite and Promote Group Process

Although Patrick, Evan and Dora are largely nonverbal and Richard, Abby, Jared and Gabriel are limited in their verbal communications, I do believe they have the degree of *comprehension* necessary to profit from many of the therapeutic factors in a group.

Music Therapy Session Format that Makes Sense Given the Purpose, Preferences, and Functioning Level of the Group

I decided to keep the opening, vocal, instrumental, movement, closing format for this group, subject to change as the group became cohesive.

Adaptive Nature of the Methodology

All of the music will be adaptive subject to the children's responses and in this manner, I can profit in my evaluation process in planning for the subsequent sessions (see Chapter 8, "Evaluation").

Therapist Knowledge Base and Philosophy of Helping

This is an ongoing challenge to define one's knowledge base and philosophy of helping while emotionally growing through clinical experience. At this point, I am comfortable and confident incorporating elements of Nordoff-Robbins, my starting point in music therapy, with developmental theory and behaviorism into my working model. More simply stated, I work from the per-

spective of developmental psychology, staging the children at their functioning levels, in order to understand what they are currently capable of and what they can aspire to. The verb "aspire" leads me into the Nordoff-Robbins thinking, the humanistic part of me that believes in what Paul Nordoff describes as "The Music Child," the part of the child that is not handicapped, the soul that aspires for self-actualization. Yes, this is poetic. I personally relate to it and it is this thinking that got me emotionally involved in music therapy to begin with. The behavioral elements of my work come with my increased awareness of how breaking down musical experiences relate to task analysis, and how modeling and prompting play an important behavioral role in teaching and leading children into their discovery of self-actualization. With some groups, I will encourage the children to set their own rules and reward themselves with a record (usually a sticker on a chart) of their achievement; this external reward becomes less necessary as the children internalize their productive and creative behaviors. Finally, the evaluation of my aspect is both behavioral, keeping note of responses, and humanistic, subjectively keeping track of transferences and subjective responses that affect my work.

Summary of Initial Methods

Uniform use of specific praise and encouragement of self-assessment for self-correction for all the children. Ask teachers and aides, as appropriate, to help with modeling, hand-over-hand assistance, physical prompting during session experiences. Choose musical experiences that incorporate different objectives simultaneously in the group using varied format of opening, movement, instrumental, vocal, closing with choice making from children for musical preferences.

- *Dora*–positioning and handling as well as adaptive use of instruments to help her with movement.
- *Evan*–respect need for sensory self-protection; move in slowly if providing hand over hand assistance
- *Abby*–model vocal projection inviting her

imitation; utilize instrumental work that involves bilateral beating; invite solo work as she gains confidence; allow time for auditory processing; utilize visuals.

- *Jared*–channel impulsivity through start and stop activity; encourage dialogue and self-correction when he has difficulty with frustration tolerance. Be aware of increased length of time he has to wait for his turn in music sharing activity.
- *Richard*–encourage dramatic experience in singing, instrumental and movement experience; document differences in communication with and without paired movement, singing; allow time for auditory processing and supplement with visuals; serve as role model and "conductor" for group.
- *Gabriel*–allow time for auditory processing; supplement with visuals; move from rote learning to encourage creative experimentation; serve as role model for group; invite participation in transition tunes (i.e., time to go to lunch).
- *Patrick*–allow time for auditory processing; allow him to sing "solo" initially paired with

his aide (as a model), then by himself.

Thoughts about Initial Materials

As I consider which materials to use (see Chapter 6, "Materials"), I think about materials that will accommodate the following considerations: adequate auditory processing, modeling, verse and chorus vocal structure, antiphonal vocal structure, simple song lyrics, repetition, strategic physical movement, dramatic experience, nonverbal choicemaking, use of visuals, antiphonal singing, different social roles within the group, sharing, passing and sharing, rote to creative learning, easily adapted for changes in song lyrics or different uses in instrumentation, simple structure without being musically stagnant or age inappropriate, one- to two-step directives

There is, admittedly, quite a lot to think about! I have come up with initial music choices and created the materials necessary for choice-making in order to allow the children choices as they began to familiarize themselves with the possibilities from week to week. See Table 7.2 for initial music options.

TABLE 7.2. INITIAL MUSIC OPTIONS.

Openings

- Let me Introduce Myself (Turry and Beer, Themes for Therapy, p. 31)
- Roll Call (Nordoff and Robbins, Book 2, p. 4)
- It's Good to See You (Carol Robbins, Alan Turry, More Themes for Therapy, p. 33)

Vocals

- "C" is for Cookie (Muppets, p. 10)
- Penny-Nickel-Dime-Quarter-Dollar Song (Nordoff and Robbins, Book 4)
- Let's sing our song together (Ritholz, Themes for Therapy, p. 50)
- What shall we do (Carol Robbins, Themes for Therapy, p. 80)
- When you see a friend, say "Hi!" (Turry, Themes for Therapy, p. 36)
- Everybody makes mistakes (Levin & Levin, Learning through Songs, p. 19)
- Everyone makes mistakes (Moss, Sesame Street, p. 10)
- The Word Family Song (Moss and Raposo, Sesame Street, p. 24)
- What do I do when I'm alone (Moss, Sesame Street, p. 26)
- Sing (Raposo, Sesame Street, p. 35)

TABLE 7.2. INITIAL MUSIC OPTIONS–*Continued.*

- Mad (Moss, Sesame Street, p. 39)
- Picture a World (Raposo, Sesame Street, p. 46)
- The Grouch Song (Moss, Sesame Street, p. 51)
- Friends (Levin & Levin, Learning through Songs, p. 47)
- Songboards: Going on a Picnic (Raffi), Got Me a Cat (traditional)
- How Many People in the Room? (Turry, Themes for Therapy, p. 42)
- Let's look and see (Ritholz, Themes for Therapy, p. 29)

Instrumentals

- Play Along (Raposo, Sesame Street, p. 24)
- Busy Hands (Levin & Levin, Learning through Music, p. 38)
- Now Beat One (Levin & Levin, Learning through Music, p. 24)
- Taking Turns (Levin & Levin, Learning through Music, p. 16)
- Copycat I; Copycat II (Levin & Levin, Learning through Music, p. 30)
- Play your bell one time (Levin & Levin, Learning through Music, p. 36)
- Slow Horns (Levin & Levin, Learning through Music, p. 52)
- Bell Dance (Levin & Levin, Learning through Music, p. 54)
- Spooky Bells (Levin & Levin, Learning through Music, p. 83)
- Who would like to? (Nordoff and Robbins, Book 3, p. 13)
- We'll make music together (Nordoff and Robbins, Book 5, p. 10)
- Tis a Gift (orchestrated by therapist)
- Pacabel Canon (orchestrated by therapist)
- Shenadoah (orchestrated by therapist)
- Let me hear you beat that drum (Ritholz, Themes for Therapy, p. 76)
- Can you play the bell? (Lee, Themes for Therapy, p. 76)
- Are you ready? (Carol Robbins, Themes for Therapy, p. 69)
- Hand Jive (Greg and Steve): body percussion
- Let's make some music (Ritholz, Themes for Therapy, p. 2)
- You can play the tambourine (Ritholz, Themes for Therapy, p. 2)
- Drum-Talk (Nordoff and Robbins, Book 2, p. 12)
- Rock and Roll rhythm band (Greg and Steve, vol. 5): cumulative playing includes tambourine, sticks, shaker, bells, triangle, block, soft and loud, stop

Movement

- Rock and Roll Freeze Dance (Hap Palmer, So Big, #5): impulse control
- Marching around the alphabet (Learning Basic Skills, Vol. 1): use with alphabet beanbags, bend/grasp at beginning level.
- Simon Sez (Greg and Steve, vol. 3): can also use with free accompaniment and do voice over. First rendition includes the following directives: touch head, eyes, nose, mouth, eyebrows, ears, teeth, hair, cheeks, chin, neck, shoulder, arms, fingers, hands, elbows
- Old brass wagon (Greg and Steve, CD 5) circle to left, to right, in, out, run around, shoulder/knees, clap three times, topes and jump, shout hurrah
- Hand Jive (Greg and Steve, vol.4), antiphonal, simple to complex
- Dancing Machine (Greg and Steve, vol. 3): imaginative play
- Just like me (Greg and Steve) vol. 4: fast-paced imitative
- Disco Limbo (Greg and Steve, vol. 3): use with limbo stick
- Hokey Pokey (Music Connection, p. 274, K-CD 7, #2 and #4). Sequence One: right foot in, right foot out,

continued

TABLE 7.2. INITIAL MUSIC OPTIONS–*Continued.*

right foot in, shake it all about (Do the hokey pokey and you) turn yourself around (That's what its all about) clap; Sequence Two: left foot in, left foot out, left foot in, shake it all about, turn yourself around, clap; Sequence Three: right hand, etc.; Sequence Four: left hand, etc.; Sequence Five: head in, out, in, shake, turn around. Clap; Sequence Six: whole self in, out, shake, turn, clap. Add or eliminate sequences as necessary. Keep in mind that one sequence is six progressive steps.
- Bounce and Catch (Abramson Dalcroze exercises #5)
- Catch (Abramson, Dalcroze exercises, #6)
- Bean Bag Parade (#7, Stewart): march
- Pass (1, Stewart): beanbags
- Catch (5, Stewart): beanbags
- Bumping/jumping (Stewart,#1, parachute play): lift/shake up/down/shake around, multiple directives
- Mountain High (Stewart,#2, parachute play): abstract play.
- Turkish March, Beethoven: march
- March of Siamese Children: march
- Hoedown (Copland): square dance choreography
- Pachabel Canon: stretching, breathing exercises.
- Girl with Flaxen Hair (Childrens Corner, Debussy): slow stretch

Closings
- Adios (Sorel, More Themes for Therapy, p. 48)
- Ready to Say Good-bye (Sorel, More Themes for Therapy, p. 57)
- Yes, I Can (Music Connection)
- Good-bye Song (Nordoff and Robbins, Book 2, p. 19)

Beginning Session Planning

Now I am ready to put the goals, objectives, methods, and materials together. Here is a sample session plan followed by a firsthand description of what happened in the session that required my flexibility and changes in methodology as the session progressed.

TABLE 7.3. SESSION PLAN, SAMPLE.

Opening

Goals/Objectives
1. Expand use of low-tech augmentative device with voice output for communication and interaction (Evan, Dora).
   1a. Given a "Big Mac," children (Evan, Dora) will respond by pressing the vocal output device when asked to sing their name in the "Let Me Introduce Myself" song.
2. Increase receptive language at appropriate developmental level (Evan, Richard, Gabriel).
   2a. Responding appropriately through action at least once during opening song (Evan).
   2b. Demonstrate comprehension of verbal information through appropriate verbal responses on 4/5 opportunities during and after opening song (Richard).
   2c. Follow three-step activity-related direction (face the group, point to himself, sing his name within the context of the opening song) with gestural prompts (Gabriel).
3. Increase expressive communication according to appropriate developmental level (Richard, Patrick, Jared, Abby).

continued

TABLE 7.3. BEGINNING SESSION PLANNING–*Continued.*

3a. Spontaneously verbalize wants, needs, and feelings half of the time during opening song to appropriate staff (Richard).

3b. Demonstrate comprehension and retention of auditory input during opening song by responding appropriately half of the time with repetition of the four word phrase, "Let me introduce myself" given adequate processing time (Patrick).

3c. Abby will use simple language to instruct Gabriel in the three-step activity of facing the group, imitating a gestural motion to point to himself, and sing his name on "My name is _____."

3d. With correct use of temporal terms (Jared) in response to at least one question.

Material

Let me Introduce Myself (Turry and Beer, Themes for Therapy, p.31–32).
Choices with picture exchange, on Velcro board for types of activities and then specific choices of activities.

Method

1. Therapist models song a cappella, standing, in theatrical presentation, pointing to self on word "myself."
   Let me introduce myself.
   My name is ( ).
   Let me introduce myself.
   My name is ( ).
2. Therapist visually invites aides and teachers to sing chorus in order to continue modeling.
   Here we are in music, Here we are in music, Here we are in music, today, today.
3. Therapist continues modeling song a cappella,
   Let me introduce my friend,
   Let me introduce my friend,
   Let me introduce my friend,
   His/her name is ( ).
   (Pointing to an aide or teacher on the word "friend" and then singing their name).
4. Therapist signals selected aide or teacher to model song while therapist accompanies, moderate tempo, pausing after each line and visually reminding other aides/teachers to sing chorus. In closing portion of song, aide points to a child who appears to be eager to sing.
5. Therapist visually and verbally invites first child to piano, and positions the child accordingly to allow the child to visually scan the group as well as see the therapist for visual cues while singing.
6. Therapist accompanies child in entire song, providing verbal and visual prompting and cues as necessary.
   Let me introduce myself.
   My name is ( ).
   Let me introduce myself.
   My name is ( ).
   (or stay seated and "perform" song in modified fashion by pointing to self on the word "myself" and approximating the speaking of their name or generating touchtalker at that point in song, Evan and Dora).
7. Therapist visually reminds group to sing on chorus. All children, aides, and teachers sing on "chorus.
   Here we are in music, Here we are in music, Here we are in music, today, today.
8. Therapist provides prompts as necessary to help child complete song.
   Let me introduce my friend, His/Her name is ( ).
   (child points to next child to sing; next child comes up; first child sits down).
9. Therapist assists Abby as necessary in order to introduce and cue three-step activity for Gabriel.
10. During song, therapist prompts for language expression and comprehension by asking questions prior to singing and after song, such as, Who are we singing to? What are we singing? Where are we? Etc. What time is it, morning, lunchtime, or afternoon?
11. Therapist redirects children as necessary if calling out in disruptive fashion reminding them of the need to wait their turn (Jared).

continued

TABLE 7.3. BEGINNING SESSION PLANNING– *Continued.*

12. Therapist asks children, following the activity, to share how they felt during or after the activity, prompting for appropriate level of language (Richard, Patrick, Abby).

Transition

Goals/Objectives

1. Increase expressive communication according to appropriate developmental level (Richard, Patrick, Jared, Gabriel).
   1a. Spontaneously verbalize wants, needs, and feelings half of the time during transitions to appropriate staff (Richard).
   1b. Verbalize wants and needs clearly and intelligibly during transitions by repeating a 4-word phrase at least once (Patrick).
   1c. Demonstrate comprehension and retention of auditory input during transitions by responding appropriately half of the time, given adequate processing time (Patrick).
   1d. Intelligibly verbalize wants, needs, and feelings during transitions given one chance for self correction (Richard).
   1e. Correct use of temporal terms in response to simple questions during transitions, with verbal prompts, 3/5 trials (Jared).
   1f. Use a 4-word phrase to answer "Who" question at least once with a pictorial prompt (Gabriel).
2. In the course of the music therapy session, children will use words or picture exchange to express music activity choices, problem-solve during music activity, and express communicative reactions (Dora, Evan).
   2a. Develop gestures and use of picture exchange during transitions to communicate needs and wants half of the time (Dora, Evan).

Method

1. Therapist shows child Velcro board which has visuals for movement, instrumental, singing, and listening and, using "Wh" questions, asks child to verbally (Gabriel, Jared, Richard, Patrick) or nonverbally, through eye gaze or picture exchange (Dora, Evan), select the next kind of musical experience he or she would like (the following music experiences with selected goals and objectives will be possible, not necessarily in order of their written presentation in plan).
2. Therapist informs the children of the group choice.
3. If there are objections, Therapist will remind child (i.e., Jared) that if not now, we can do another activity later (temporal).
4. Therapist sings an original transitional tune, "Time to play the instruments (alternatively, time to sing a song; time to dance to music; time to listen to music, etc.), Time to play the instruments, Time to play the instruments, Getting ready now."

Vocal/Instrumental

Goals/Objectives

1. Increase participation in activity at appropriate developmental level (Richard, Jared, Dora, Evan, Gabriel).
   1a. With a maximum of two verbal redirections during vocal/instrumental activity (Richard).
   1b. Over a ten-mionute period with minimal verbal prompting, 4/5 trials, during vocal/instrumental activity (Jared).
   1c. With minimal verbal prompting and decreased behavioral disruption (Jared) during vocal/instrumental activity.
   1d. With interest (Dora) during vocal/instrumental activity.
   1e. With prompting and redirection (Evan) during vocal/instrumental activity.
   1f. Without physical prompts (Gabriel) during vocal/instrumental activity.

continued

TABLE 7.3. BEGINNING SESSION PLANNING–*Continued.*

Materials

"You can play the tambourine'" (Ritholz, Themes for Therapy, p. 90).

Method

1. Therapist introduces song by having the aide come up by the piano and play the tambourine as directed in the song (note: therapist has adapted words of song to turn question into a positive statement):

   You can play the tambourine (visual prompt leads to shake).
   You can play the tambourine (visual prompt leads to shake).
   Yes, you can (visual prompt leads to shake).
   Yes, you can (visual prompt leads to shake).
   You can play the tambourine (visual prompt leads to shake).

2. Therapist shows aide a choice of two instruments, asking him to choose either the tambourine or the drum. He chooses the drum.

3. Therapist continues modeling of song. This time the aide plays the drum to the song; therapist adapts words but maintains melodic rhythm of song:

   You can play the drum, drum, drum (visual prompt leads to quarter-note beat).
   You can play the drum, drum, drum (visual prompt leads to quarter-note beat).
   Yes, you can (visual prompt leads to quarter-note beat).
   Yes, you can (visual prompt leads to quarter-note beat).
   You can play the drum, drum, drum (visual prompt leads to quarter-note beat).

4. Therapist and aides help children take turns, either seated or coming up by the piano, in selecting one of two instruments and singing and playing song.

5. Therapist provides verbal prompting as necessary (Abby, Patrick, Evan, Jared, Richard).

Transition

Goals/Objectives

1. Increase expressive communication according to appropriate developmental level (Richard, Patrick, Jared, Gabriel).

   1a. Spontaneously verbalize wants, needs, and feelings half of the time during transitions to appropriate staff (Richard).

   1b. Verbalize wants and needs clearly and intelligibly during transitions by repeating a 4-word phrase at least once (Patrick).

   1c. Demonstrate comprehension and retention of auditory input during transitions by responding appropriately half of the time, given adequate processing time (Patrick).

   1d. Intelligibly verbalize wants, needs, and feelings during transitions given one chance for self correction (Richard).

   1e. Correct use of temporal terms in response to simple questions during transitions, with verbal prompts, 3/5 trials (Jared).

   1f. Use a 4-word phrase to answer "Wh" question at least once with a pictorial prompt (Gabriel).

2. In the course of the music therapy session, children will use words or picture exchange to express music activity choices, problem-solve during music activity, and express communicative reactions (Dora, Evan).

   a. Develop gestures and use of picture exchange during transitions to communicate needs and wants half of the time (Dora, Evan).

Method

1. Therapist shows child Velcro board which has visuals for movement, instrumental, singing, and listening and using "Wh" questions, asks child to verbally (Gabriel, Jared, Richard, Patrick) or nonverbally, through eye gaze or picture exchange (Dora, Evan), select the next kind of musical experience he or she would like (the following music experiences with selected goals and objectives will be possible, not necessarily in order of their written presentation in plan).

continued

TABLE 7.3. BEGINNING SESSION PLANNING–*Continued.*

2. Therapist informs the children of the group choice.
3. If there are objections, Therapist will remind child (i.e., Jared) that if not now, we can do another activity later (temporal).
4. Therapist sings an original transitional tune, "Time to move to music now (alternatively, time to sing a song; time to dance to music; time to listen to music, etc.), Time to move to music now, Time to move to music now, Getting ready now."

Movement

Goals/Objectives
1. Increase participation in activity at appropriate developmental level (Richard, Jared, Dora, Evan).
   1a. With a maximum of two verbal redirections (Richard) during movement.
   1b. Over a ten-minute period with minimal verbal prompting, 4/5 trials (Jared) during movement.
   1c. With minimal verbal prompting and decreased behavioral disruption (Jared) during movement.
   1d. With interest (Dora) during movement.
   1e. With prompting and redirection (Evan) during movement.
2. Reposition herself in her classroom chair with verbal prompting only 2/3 times (Abby).
   2a. Reposition herself in her classroom chair during movement with verbal prompting only to attain an appropriate seated posture during sone 2/3 times (Abby).
3. Carry out desired motor activity in response to verbal directive, within 30 seconds of the directive (Abby).
   3a. Given the song, Stand Up, Abby will respond to verbal prompting within 30 seconds by the third mention of "up" and the third mention of "down."

Materials
Stand Up (Levin & Levin, Stand Up, p. 22, Learning through Music); Piano

Method
1. Therapist models song with aide. Tempo is moderate in order to allow for adequate motor planning and auditory processing. Words are adapted in last line so children do not finish the song standing. If therapist wishes to personalize song, sing, for example, "Gabriel can stand up," emphasizing original melodic rhythm. Dissonant chords can be added for stimulation.
   Let's all stand up (pause).
   Up, up, up.
   Let's all sit down
   Down, down, down.
   Stand up
   Up, up
   Up, up
   Up, up
   Sit down
   Down, down
   Down, down
   Down, down
   Now clap (one-quarter note clap).
2. Therapist verbally invites children to try the stand up, sit down motion as well as singing.
3. Therapist can modify singing by emphasizing the words, up and down, instead of all the lyrics.
4. Therapist can further modify the singing by pausing before last rendition of the word "up" or "down" and waiting for children's vocal response.
5. Therapist can modify for Dora by separately inviting her to:
   Put your arms up
   Up up up

continued

TABLE 7.3. BEGINNING SESSION PLANNING–*Continued.*

Put your arms down
Down down down
(Etc.)
Nurse or physical therapist can assist Dora in manually stretching her contracted elbow.

Transition

Goals/Objectives

1. Increase expressive communication according to appropriate developmental level (Richard, Patrick, Jared, Gabriel).
   1a. Spontaneously verbalize wants, needs, and feelings half of the time during transition to appropriate staff (Richard).
   1b. Verbalize wants and needs clearly and intelligibly during transitions by repeating a 4-word phrase at least once (Patrick).
   1c. Demonstrate comprehension and retention of auditory input during transitions by responding appropriately half of the time, given adequate processing time (Patrick).
   1d. Intelligibly verbalize wants, needs, and feelings during transitions given one chance for self correction (Richard).
   1e. Correct use of temporal terms in response to simple questions during transitions, with verbal prompts, 3/5 trials (Jared).
   1f. Use a 4-word phrase to answer "Wh" question at least once with a pictorial prompt (Gabriel).
2. In the course of the music therapy session, children will use words or picture exchange to express music activity choices, problem-solve during music activity, and express communicative reactions (Dora, Evan).
   2a. Develop gestures and use of picture exchange during transitions to communicate needs and wants half of the time (Dora, Evan).

Method

1. Therapist shows child Velcro board which has visuals for movement, instrumental, singing, and listening and, using "Wh" questions asks child to verbally (Gabriel, Jared, Richard, Patrick) or nonverbally, through eye gaze or picture exchange (Dora, Evan), select the next kind of musical experience he or she would like (the following music experiences with selected goals and objectives will be possible, not necessarily in order of their written presentation in plan).
2. Therapist informs the children of the group choice.
3. If there are objections, Therapist will remind child (i.e., Jared) that if not now, we can do another activity later (temporal).
4. Therapist sings an original transitional tune, "Time to play the instruments (alternately, time to sing a song; time to dance to music; time to listen to music, etc.), Time to play the instruments, Time to play the instruments, Getting ready now."

Vocal/Instrumental

Goals/Objectives

1. Increase participation in activity at appropriate developmentally level (all).
   1a. With a maximum of two verbal redirections during vocal/instrumental activity (Richard).
   1b. Over a ten-minute period with minimal verbal prompting, 4/5 trials, during vocal/instrumental activity (Jared).
   1c. With minimal verbal prompting and decreased behavioral disruption (Jared) during vocal/instrumental activity.
   1d. With interest (Dora) during vocal/instrumental activity.
   1e. With prompting and redirection (Evan) during vocal/instrumental activity.

continued

TABLE 7.3. BEGINNING SESSION PLANNING–*Continued.*

2. Increase awareness of the need for help (Evan), of emotional states (Jared), of increased frustration tolerance (Jared), getting attention from peers and adults (Dora), and helping others (Abby).
    2a. By appropriately accessing pictures or gesturing on 3/5 (session) days during vocal/instrumental activity (Evan).
    2b. By spontaneously verbalizing feelings (Jared) during vocal/instrumental activity.
    2c. By getting attention from peers and adults (Dora) during vocal/instrumental activity.
    2d. By instructing a peer, Gabriel, to do a three-step activity with visual, gestural, and verbal prompts (Abby) and spontaneous modeling (Abby) during vocal/instrumental activity.
3. Initiate parallel play with a classmate once during each school day (Evan).
    3a. Given a choice of rhythm instruments, Evan, will tolerate playing a dyad improvisation with another classmate (note: step one toward initiation).

Materials
Let's make some music (Nordoff and Robbins, Book 3);

Instruments
ocean drum, claves, standing orff drum, tone bells, reed horn, tambourine, cymbal.

Methods
1. Therapist asks aides and teachers to come up in front of children, select an instrument and model the song while therapist accompanies (Note: The song is structured to provide solo and group playing by allowing the therapist to call on one child at a time to play their selected instrument as the class listens and alternatively invite the group to play together).
2. Therapist asks the child to point to the picture/photograph or name their assigned instrument while they are seated. Patrick, due to his difficulty with oral-motor musculature, is encouraged to play the reed horn. Dora is encouraged to play the cymbal in order to use her left arm; likewise Abby is encourged to use the drum and Jared is encouraged to use the ocean drum because of the amount of physical control it takes. Richard is encouraged to use the tone bell to develop auditory processing; Evan is given the tambourine because he enjoys its multifaceted sensory input and Gabriel is given the claves since he enjoys keeping the beat in the group.
3. Therapist helps the children sing the words of the song by adapting to their tempo and waiting for the last word of each musical phrase.
4. The children are encouraged to signal for help as necessary through verbal and/or gestural communication.
5. Therapist personalizes the verses and melodic rhythms as necessary,
    i.e., verse.
    Gabriel plays the claves. (rest, rest, rest), Gabriel plays the claves (rest, rest rest); Gabriel plays the claves (rest) right now (rest).
    i.e., chorus.
    Everybody. (rest) Let's make some music (rest, rest, rest). Let's make some music (rest, rest, rest). Let's make some music (rest). Music right now (rest).
    i.e., verse 2, etc.
6. Therapist structures dyadic playing with Evan and Abby as follows: "Let's make some music (drum, drum, tambourine), repeated two more times. "Music right now"–cymbal (Dora).
7. Further, during the song, Abby is asked to assist Gabriel by providing multiple song and gestural directions for him (Play claves, rest, rest; Play claves, rest; Play claves, rest).
8. Following the song, one child helps collect the instruments (Richard) and the children are encouraged to verbally reflect on their musical experience, recalling the sequence of solos if possible.
9. If there is a request for a second rendition of the song, the children can be conducted by Richard.
10. Therapist provides transitional tune to movement activity.

continued

TABLE 7.3. BEGINNING SESSION PLANNING—*Continued.*

Movement

Goals/Objectives

1. Increase participation in activity at appropriate developmental level (all).
   1a. With a maximum of two verbal redirections during movement (Richard).
   1b. Over a ten-minute period with minimal verbal prompting, 4 out of 5 trials, during movement (Jared).
   1c. With minimal verbal prompting and decreased behavioral disruption (Jared) during movement.
   1d. With interest (Dora) during movement.
   1e. With prompting and redirection (Evan) during movement.
2. Children will increase physical mobility through spontaneous use of left upper extremity during bilateral activities without verbal prompting 2/3 times (Abby).
   2a. During the Beanbag Song, child will use her left arm to pass the beanbag (Abby) without verbal prompting 1/3 times.
3. Modify movement to participate in variations of gross motor activities (Jared).
   3a. During Beanbag Song, attempt to modify his gross motor movement half the time in order to appropriately monitor his impulsivity (Jared).

Materials

Pass (1, Stewart): beanbags

Methods

1. Therapist asks aides and teachers to come up in front of children in order to model beanbag passing game.
2. Therapist and teacher group model Beanbag Pass, emphasizing rhythmic movement of passing, which conforms to basic beat of recorded music and sung directions, while children watch.
3. Therapist hands beanbag to first child to her left of the semi-circle and signals the children to start passing the beanbag on repeat of "Pass your beanbag." No recorded accompaniment is used at this time so that the working tempo of the group can be established while the therapist sings a cappella.
4. Therapist uses recorded music or, alternatively, plays the accompaniment of the song on a casio at an appropriate working tempo, using the record function, in order to have working physical access to the children.
5. Therapist signals nurse to assist Dora with manual stretching of left elbow as Dora reaches from the left and uses palmer grasp to hold the beanbag.
6. Therapist prompts Abby to use her left arm in receiving and passing the beanbag.
7. Therapist asks children how they did. Were they able to follow the beat of the music and pass the beanbag "in time"? Were they able to wait their turn (Jared)?
8. Therapist uses transitional tune for next vocal.

Vocal

Goals/Objectives

1. Expand use of low-tech augmentative device with voice output for communication and interaction (Evan, Dora).
   1a. Given a "Big Mac," children (Evan, Dora) will respond by pressing the vocal output device when asked to sing "Yes I Can."
2. Increase receptive language at appropriate developmental level as specified below (Evan, Richard).
   2a. During opening and activity songs, children will attempt participation at their developmental level at least once during the session responding appropriately through pictures or action during one activity (Evan).
   2b. Demonstrate comprehension of verbal information through appropriate verbal responses on 4/5 opportunities (Richard).
3. Increase expressive communication according to appropriate developmental level (Richard, Patrick, Dora).
   3a. Spontaneously verbalize wants, needs, and feelings half of the time to appropriate staff during song (Richard).

continued

TABLE 7.3. BEGINNING SESSION PLANNING–*Continued.*

3b. Demonstrate comprehension and retention of auditory input during group activity by responding appropriately half of the time, given adequate processing time (Patrick), during song.

3c. Expressive gestures (Dora) during song.

Materials

"Yes, I Can" (Music Connection, Adapted)

Methods

1. Therapist uses pictures to remind children of what they did in session.
2. Therapist asks children to pick the picture that describes their favorite musical experience (Evan, Patrick) or respond nonverbally with gesture to the same question (Dora), with therapist modeling as necessary.
3. Therapist asks children to recall verbally what they did in music today and how they liked it (Richard).
4. Therapist incorporates the information about what was accomplished in music today, using the song, "Yes, I Can" which requires a sung response of "Yes, I Can" after each sung detail of what happened.
5. Therapist adapts tempo and melodic rhythm as necessary to improvise on song and personalize as appropriate.

Closing

Goals/Objectives

1. Expand use of low-tech augmentative device with voice output for communication and interaction (Evan, Dora).

   1a. Given a "Big Mac," children (Evan, Dora) will respond by pressing the vocal output device when asked to sing "Goodbye."

2. Increase receptive language at appropriate developmental level (Evan, Richard).

   2a. Responding appropriately through pictures or action during closing song (Evan).

   2b. Demonstrate comprehension of verbal information through appropriate verbal responses on 4/5 opportunities during closing song (Richard).

3. Increase expressive communication according to appropriate developmental level (Richard, Patrick).

   3a. Spontaneously verbalize wants, needs, and feelings half of the time during closing song to appropriate staff (Richard).

   3b. Demonstrate comprehension and retention of auditory input during closing song by responding appropriately half of the time, given adequate processing time (Patrick).

Materials

"It's time to sing good-bye" (Nordoff and Robbins, Book 2, p. 19).

Methods

1. Therapist initiates Good-bye song, pausing at end of musical phrase for lower-functioning children to approximate the sung word "good- bye," wave, or use "Big Mac" (Evan, Dora).
   - It's time to say good-bye.
   - Good-bye, good-bye, *good-bye.*
   - Boys and Girls and everyone say *good-bye.*
   - Oh.
   - Boys and Girls and everyone say *good-bye.*

2. Therapist provides final opportunity for children to reflect on session and suggest what they might want to work on next time, either verbally (i.e., Richard, Jared, Abby, Patrick) or through picture choice or gesture (Dora, Evan).

What actually happened in the session and how did I adapt methodology as well as materials?

Note: ongoing changes in methodology are italicized below.

The children entered the room in an upbeat mood. This was a morning session and this was fortuitous since they were full of boundless energy. Jared practically threw himself into the seat and Abby started to laugh at that fierce opening! Then Jared started to laugh and Dora, although she has difficulty with any kind of demonstrative facial expression, tried to smile. I have to admit that I starting laughing too, at Jared's energy.

After the children sat down, I opened with "Let me introduce myself." I sang with great enthusiasm and it was apparently contagious for the children since they laughed with pleasure while watching me. I then picked as my "friend" Patrick's aide, Bill. Bill was a pretty quiet guy and this song seemed to bring out his alter ego. He opened up his arms as he sang the song and his voice opened up as well. Patrick, usually quiet and anxious, was really enthralled with this. He could not stop staring at his aide! He was ready to perform like his aide now! As soon as his aide called on him, he panicked a bit and decided to sing from his seat. He was given very positive attention from his aide and this seemed to spur him on. He finished his part of the song by calling on Richard. Richard, a natural "clown," as he is jokingly referred to by his teacher, became quite theatrical in front of his peers. After he finished, he begged to repeat his performance. *I said fine.* He did it again and begged again to repeat the performance. He just could not get enough of this! I noticed that the second rendition had resulted in a stronger mastery of articulation and told him about this. He seemed pleased. I must admit that I had to be a bit stern in *setting limits for him to finally choose another child to sing!* By this time, Jared was jumping up and down in his seat, waiting for his turn, and *I told him I was very proud of him being able to wait.* He would be next after Dora. *Dora did not choose to use the Big Mack; rather she preferred to gesture to herself on the word "myself" and point to Abby on the word "friend."* This was fine, especially since I

noticed that *she spontaneously stretched the contractured left arm to perform these gestures.* Abby, verbally encouraged by Jared and Richard to "come on," stood up haltingly and came by the side of the piano to sing her solo. She was hesitant. I started her off and continued to *help her approximate the words she was having trouble with as she tried to open up her arms to the group,* smiling all the while. After she was finished, the group clapped for her, a wonderful display of support! By this time, Evan had his hands over his ears; the excitement might have been both overwhelming and intimidating for him. I wasn't sure which. At any rate, *he passed on participating* even though *he was watching every step of the action and I commented on how great that was.* Gabriel, the last group member to sing, had profited from all the modeling thusfar and sang many of the words in the song, to the surprise of the teacher.

We transitioned smoothly to the group choice of "Stand Up, Sit Down" song particularly because the children had already been getting up to do the greeting song and were now "warmed up." The excitement escalated as I modeled the song first and then invited the children to participate. Evan was laughing as he got up and down in his seat, sharing in the contagion being created by Jared and Richard. Abby, Richard, Patrick were a bit slower physically and, *in my efforts to accommodate their delayed auditory processed and motor planning, I created a challenge for Jared to manage his hyperactivity.* I had not really forecast this but it worked out well in terms of group dynamics.

I asked the children to cast their "votes" for the next choice of music activity. They all chose the picture of the instruments. I introduced the tambourine song with the option of choosing the drum as well. The aide modeled with me. While I briefly demonstrated for him how to model the tambourine as well as the drum, I realized that playing the tambourine and the drum can actually be done in many ways, each way inviting a different kind of sensory stimulation. I wasn't sure if I should model the easiest way (merely shaking the tambourine; striking the drum three times) or a more complex sequential technique (shake the tambourine up on first beat, in the middle on second beat, down on third beat; strike the drum with a different rhythmic combination on each quarter note beat) or a yet more complex manner (shake the tambourine on first beat, strike with elbow, strike on knee; strike the drum with three different dynamics). *I became aware that, in my own excitement about presenting the song, I had the potential to go off on musical tangents and this could be confusing for the children. I decided to keep it simple the first time around, shaking the tambourine each time on a beat.* Even this was more of a challenge than shaking it constantly through the three beats. The playing and passing went smoothly although more physical efforts to help the children pass were required than I had anticipated. *In order to help the children with an extra musical prompt for stopping, I changed the music slightly by adding an extra phrase after the last rendition of "you can play the tambourine."* At that point I added two quarter notes and dissonant chords while singing, *"Now Stop!"* That helped. My only problem was Jared. He did not want to let go of the tambourine and he was shaking it vigorously, up and down in the air. *I got up from the piano, took another tambourine and started shaking with him, singing a cappella at the end, "Stop (rest) and rest." He enjoyed the stopping point so much, the moment of musical connection, that he burst out laughing, and gave the tambourine up.*

After the next transition, the vote was cast for "Beanbag." We did it a cappella at first so I could gage the working tempo of the group before using a recording to have my hands free.

When Jared got the beanbag, he tossed it up in the air and it actually came close to striking Abby. She was scared, not expecting the sudden intrusion. *We stopped the music and I asked him to self-assess what he had done.* He muttered, "Sorry, sorry, sorry Abby." I believe he really was sorry. *I told him, "You can control your behavior, Jared. Let's try this again. You need to listen to the music."* He was then okay. *During this episode, I had to keep the attention of the other group members, so I simply said, "Jared is having a little trouble passing the beanbag, but now he can do it."* Richard nodded, Dora looked attentive, and Evan looked interested as though he wanted to toss it too! Well. . . . That's exactly what happened. *Evan ended up throwing the beanbag on the floor and laughing.*

I acknowledged his feeling, "Yes, it can be fun to throw. Now let's try another way." I like to think

this was a redirection rather than a reprimand. For Evan, it is important to have him participate on any level so the seemingly negative behavior was acknowledged even though it felt like a developmental behavior of a two-year-old. Maybe that's where Evan is. At any rate, he complied with changing his throwing and we continued.

By now, we were 35 minutes into the 45-minute session and I had to use my time-management skills, not always the best, to anticipate how long we would have for the affirmation/recall (Yes, I Can) *and Closing.* Richard was asking me if we could "act" again, remembering the opening song. *I decided to skip the option of the additional song/instrumental activity and convert the "Yes, I Can" into a more theatrical presentation.* In order to do this, *I asked Richard to model for the class a recollection of what we had done in music.* I helped him remember the sequence by *showing him the picture exchange cards* for "Movement" (Beanbag; Stand Up-Sit Down), "Instruments" (tambourine song) and Opening (Let me Introduce Myself). *With those visual prompts,* he was able to sing and act out, "Oh, I can sing hello (Ohhhhhhh) Oh I can sit down and stand up (demonstrates), Oh, I can play a drum (demonstrates), Oh I can pass the beanbag" (hands it to me) to my accompaniment.

All the children were encouraged to join in on the "Yes, I Can" chorus and seemed to enjoy Richard's antics. *The more concrete visual recall of what we had done in the session was actually a wonderful way to reinforce their memories.*

We closed comfortably and Patrick was able to transition from the classroom without any tantrumming.

Changing Methodology in Subsequent Sessions

As the year progressed, the group became more cohesive in terms of watching each other, emotionally responding to each other, progressing toward their developmental goals and developing a sense of rapport. At Halloween, not long after the group started, they were able to use several subsequent sessions to prepare "Spooky Bells" (Levin & Levin, 1998), a piece involving several different instruments played contrapuntally. My methodology as a therapist did not radically change.

What did change that November, shortly after Thanksgiving, was my realization that the capacity of some of the group members to accept greater emotional and cognitive challenge had progressed.

There was one very sad day after Thanksgiving when the teachers and therapists found out that one of the students, Paul, a student in an adolescent class, had been killed in a car crash. In music therapy, I helped the children in Paul's class write a song about their classmate, Paul. It was based on a familiar melody, the melody of "Let me Introduce Myself." They all supplied information about what their classmate liked to do, favorite things which I incorporated into the song, Paul likes to (_____), etc. Paul likes to (_____), Yes, Paul likes to (_____). Let me introduce my friend, his name was Paul.

The adolescent group was leaving the music room as the younger group entered. They asked if they could sing their song for the younger group. There was noted empathy from everyone in the younger group in terms of their facial expressions, tears in their eyes and thoughtful simple comments like "I'm sad."

EVALUATION OF MUSIC THERAPY APPROACHES FOR GROUPWORK

INSTRUCTIVE QUESTIONS

Moving on from the experience of a sample case study, the therapist can now reflect on how to evaluate different music therapy approachs for groupwork. As aforementioned, an approach is a series of methods. In music therapy, there are multiple approaches. Therapists trained in these approaches can use them on their own or possible in tandem with each other while developing a unique therapy style that fits the needs of the group and the practical reality of the clinical setting.

Darrow's recent contribution (Darrow, 2004) to the music therapy literature is an anthology detail-

ing approaches in music therapy. It is important for the therapist to selectively review various approaches and consider them for inclusion in group work. Questions presented here summarize the descriptions of the following approaches: Orff (Colwell, C.M., Achey, C., Gillmeister, G., Woolrich, J., 2004), Dalcroze (Frego, R.J.D., Liston, R.E., Jama, M., Gillmeister, G., 2004), OK, Kodaly (Brownell, M.D., Frego, R.J.D., Kwak, E., Rayburn, A.M., 2004), Kindermusik (Pasiali, V., De L'Etoile, S., Tandy, K., 2004), Nordoff-Robbins (Aigen, K., Miller, C.K., Kim, Y., Pasiali, V., Kwak, E., Tague, D.B., 2004), Psychodynamic (Isenberg-Grzeda, C., Goldberg, F.S., Dvorkin, J.M., 2004), Behavioral (Standley, J., Johnson, C.M., Robb, S.L., Brownell, M.D., Kim, S., 2004), and Neurologic Music Therapy (Clair, A.A., Pasiali, V., 2004).

1. What is the description of this method?
2. Is this method appropriate for groupwork?
3. Do I have the necessary background, skills and knowledge to practice this method?
4. How does this method further the developmental goals of the children in the group? Specifically how?
5. Is this methods contraindicated in any way?

ORFF-SCHULWERK

What is the description of this method?

- Initial exploration and imitation of music and words
- Music and words used to improvise
- Music and words used in composing
- Gradual introduction to written music
- Rhythm is the foundation for all work and provides unifying force in speech, dance and movement; moves into metered and unmetered speech.
- Melody is developed through call and response, chanting, pentatonic modes and diatonic modes.
- Unpitched instruments followed by pitched instruments to accompany speech, singing and movement.

Is this method appropriate for groupwork?

Yes, Orff, conceptualized for music education, is a group approach. It is generally introduced to school-age children.

Do I have the necessary background, skills and knowledge to practice this method?

Orff is a music education method and is taught in classes and workshops for music educators. You can probably find music therapists who have adapted this work and offer workshops.

How does this method further the developmental goals of the children in the group? Specifically how?

Orff is a multisensory approach. The pairing of music and movement is a sensory integrative method popular in music therapy for promoting language and motor planning. Further, the fact that Orff gradually moves to music transcription may make it a valuable tool for teaching music reading and writing to learning disabled children who have been exposed to music initially from a multisensory perspective. The Orff instruments themselves have excellent tone quality and therefore are valuable to use with any special needs population.

Orff has been used in group work with adults (Bitcon, 2000) and, according to Colwell, Achey, Gillmeister and Woolrich (2004, p. 10), has application for music therapy as follows:

- Encourage taking turns and following directions through imitation, solo/ensemble playing, ostinatos and rhythmic dancing.
- Encourage the use of speech and question-answer skills through chants, speech ostinatos, call and response activities.
- Encourage motor imitation and the development of palmer grasp through body percussion (imitation/ostinatos) and mallet use.
- Encourage listening skills and name recognition through rote teaching of ensemble parts as well as a variety of name games and chants.

- Encourage stress release and self-control through improvisation, free movement, compositional choices and levels of participation.
- Encourage verbal self-expression and awareness of body language through chants describing the self and mirroring movement.
- Encourage self-expression and discrimination of emotions through improvisation, composition, singing and creative work based on emotion.
- Encourage visual tracking and symbol/letter discrimination though reading charts for rhythms/text and rondo activities using visuals.
- Encourage auditory discrimination and peer interaction through the use of environmental sounds in a composition and, in general, ensemble performance.

Is this method contraindicated in any way?

Children who are very low functioning in terms of ambulation and language will have difficulty with this method.

DALCROZE

What is the description of this method?

- Solfege is taught using a fixed *do* system wherein children develop sensitivity to pitches and tonal relationships. Solfege is always combined with rhythm and movement.
- Improvisation skills develop sequentially.
- Eurhythmics provide symmetry, balance and rhythmic accuracy through movement.
- Solfege, improvisation and eurhythmics are an interdependent system and therefore are taught together.
- A typical beginning Dalcroze lesson will include "walking to improvised music and then responding to changes in tempo, dynamics and phrase in quick reaction games" (Frego, Liston, Hama, Gillmeister, 2004, p. 19) in order to introduce elements such as pulse, beat, subdivision, meter,

rhythm, phrase and form.
- Intermediate lessons can include experiences in polymeters, polyrhythms, canon, tension and relaxation, breathing, conducting, counterpoint, and interactions of anacrusis, crusis and metacrusis.
- All classes are in groups where participants develop nonverbal communications.
- Plastique Animee, based on previous rhythmic learning, is a loose choreography.

Is this method appropriate for groupwork?

Yes, Dalcroze is held in groups.

Do I have the necessary background, skills and knowledge to practice this method?

Dalcroze is a music education method taught in classes and workshops. Music therapists have adapted this approach and may train other therapists in workshops.

How does this method further the developmental goals of the children in the group? Specifically how?

Dalcroze is a multisensory approach, pairing music, vocal exercises of solfege and movement. Beginning Dalcroze experience can help children with reaction time, impulsivity and auditory processing, assuming the therapist can be adaptive in the approach. Intermediate and advanced Dalcroze experiences will be more challenging in terms of integrating sensory input (i.e., polymeter, polyrhythms). Dalcroze has been used in groupwork with learning disabled, emotionally disturbed and mentally retarded children (Hibben, 1984, 1991) in order to help children attend and listen, increase self-awareness of the body in space, control movement, increase peer socialization and self-expression. This method is not to be confused with Steiner eurhythmy (1977, 1983), often referred to a curative eurhythmy.

Is this method contraindicated in any way?

Low-functioning children who are nonambulatory and/or nonverbal will have difficulty with Dalcroze.

KODALY

What is the description of this method?

- Based on *singing a cappela, folk music, solfege and movable do.*
- *Hand signs,* as visual representations of pitches and pitch relationships, correspond to pitches.
- Pentatonic music used extensively in beginning musical work in order for the child to acclimate to major and minor modes later.
- *Solmization* consists of syllables that represent note durations (i.e., Quarter note is Ta, two 8th notes are ti-ti, four 16th notes are ti-ti-ti-ri, half note is ta-a, whole notes is ta-a-a-a).
- *Rhythm first presented though iconic picture cards* that represent the notes with size of note(s) related to duration.
- Learning sequence of songs includes *preparation through new songs that contain material to be learned and experienced on several levels* including rote singing, singing loudly or softly, clapping the rhythm, stepping to the beat; singing faster or slower, playing singing games.
- Learning sequence after preparation includes musical opportunities *for conscious awareness of new concept though one particular song.*
- Reinforcement of new concept is achieved with the children now *reading from notation, using rhythm syllables and solfege.*
- Last stage of learning concept asks the child to read *new* songs with the melodic or rhythmic elements in order to internalize these concepts.

Is this method appropriate for groupwork?

Yes, Kodaly is conducted in groups.

Do I have the necessary background, skills and knowledge to practice this method?

Kodaly is a music education method achieved through workshops and classes. There are minimal instances of this work being adapted for music therapy.

How does this method further the developmental goals of the children in the group? Specifically how?

Kodaly is a multisensory approach since pitches are represented visually, note durations are represented aurally and visually, and learning songs is achieved in a repetitive manner using different sensory inputs. Therefore, it could be useful for sensory integration efforts on the parts of special learners. The visual representations may be particularly useful for deaf/hard of hearing learners.

Is this method contraindicated in any way?

Kodaly is multifaceted and abstract and therefore is probably contraindicated for the concrete learner as well as the nonambulatory and nonverbal learner.

KINDERMUSIK

What is the description of this method?

- Enrichment program for children birth to seven
- Involves parents
- Based on Piagetian stages of cognitive development
- Music skills incorporate nonmusic goals such as socialization (turn-taking), language and auditory skills (exposure to sounds and syllables and changes in the volume, rate and pitch in various songs), increasing physical development (swaying and rocking, repositioning), and socio-emotional development (start and stop to music for regulation).
- Kindermusik Village is for infants up to the age of 1.5 years and incorporates singing, chanting, object play, intentional touch, movement to music and parent education.
- Kindermusik Our Time is for toddlers ages 1.5 to 3 years and incorporates singing, playing rhythmic instruments, creative movement, music listening and participatory

action songs.
- Kindermusik Imagine That, designed for children ages 3–5, ask parents to participate in the last 15 minutes of the 45-minute class. It incorporates music making, performing and ensemble playing. Classes include music games that introduce concepts.
- Kindermusik for the Young Child, for children ages 4.5 to 7 years, increases classtime from 45 minutes of previous programs to 60–75 minutes. It incorporates dancing, listening, reading, playing percussion instruments, and an introduction to writing and reading music. Parents and siblings are involved. There are take-home materials for replication of music experiences.

Is this method appropriate for groupwork?

Yes, Kindermusik is held in groups.

Do I have the necessary background, skills and knowledge to practice this method?

Kindermusik requires a specialized training as a licensed Kindermusik educator.

How does this method further the developmental goals of the children in the group? Specifically how?

Kindermusik is developmentally based and therefore appropriate to the functional development of any child from infancy to age seven. However it was created for typically developing children and special learners in the program would need accommodations depending on their particular disabilities.

Pasiali, DeL'Etoile, and Tandy (2004) suggest that the music therapist as Kindermusik Specialist can provide an adapted experience for the special learner, essentially a mainstreamed experience. For example, the visually impaired learner will need instruments and materials that provide tactile stimulation (i.e., with different textures) and the hearing impaired child will require greater degrees of volume and feeling via vibrations (i.e., near the speakers). The autistic child may profit from a visual reminder of the structure of the session which can remain a constant even though the materials used within the activity areas will change. The physically impaired child may need to partially participate or be carried by the parent during ambulatory activity. The encouragement of the parent-child relationship is positive since it encourages replication of music at home. Likewise, the ability to separate from the parent at an appropriate developmental age is recognized in programming.

Is this method contraindicated in any way?

Kindermusik appears appropriate for a child who is appropriate for music mainstreaming.

BEHAVIORAL

What is the description of this method?

• First principle: "The object of behaviorism to identify, modify, count or otherwise observe a behavior or behavioral indicator of a cognitive or affective process" (Standley, Johnson, Robb, Brownell, Kim, 2004, p. 107).
• Second principle: Use observation to document the occurrence and magnitude of events.
• Third principle: Introduce contingencies into the client's environment in order to positively modify behavior. Specific operant techniques include task analysis, prompting, errorless learning, chaining, successive approximation, modeling, premack principle, generalized reinforcer, group contingencies, negative reinforcement, differentiated reinforcement, extinction, time out, all described by Standley, Johnson, Robb, Brownell, Kim (2004).
• Fourth principle: Evaluate results through continued or post observation of targeted behavior.

Is this method appropriate for groupwork?

Yes. Behavioral methods, initially introduced

into the music therapy literature in cases of individual therapy (Madsen, 1979) have been used in groupwork with profoundly handicapped children (Ghetti, 2002; Jellison, Brooks, and Huck, 1984), deaf and hard-of-hearing (Darrow, Gfleller, Gorsuch,Thomas, 2000), emotionally disturbed (Hanser, 1974; Presti, 1984; Wilson, 1976), and preschool children (Steele, 1971; Wolfe, 1993; Harding, et al., 1982).

Do I have the necessary background, skills and knowledge to practice this method?

Behavioral training is a component of many music therapy training programs. Florida State is notable for teaching this approach.

How does this method further the developmental goals of the children in the group? Specifically how?

Through the use of various operant techniques, contingencies using music are a reinforcement for both education and therapy objectives (Standley, 1996) that is superior to traditional contingencies (Standley, 1996).

Is this method contraindicated in any way?

For the therapist who wishes to achieve insight-oriented work, behaviorism is contraindicated.

NORDOFF-ROBBINS

What is the description of this method?

• No prescribed format.
• Music is primary vehicle of change.
• During improvisation, elements of music are used with conscious intent (i.e., direction and construction of melody, degree and type of dissonance, use of cadence, use of specific style and scale patterns, use of timbre).
• Prewritten pieces are used in conjunction with improvisation.
• Match, accompany and enhance client emotions from moment-to-moment.
• Long-term therapeutic growth (vs. short-term

behavioral goals) "characterized by expressive freedom and creativity. Communicativeness, self-confidence and independence" (Aigen, Miller, Kim, Pasiali, Kwak, Tague, 2004, p. 72).

· Clinical goals attained within musical goals'(Aigen et al., 2004, p. 72).

· Original model is two therapists, one at piano (or guitar) and the other interacting with the child(ren); as a matter of practicality, this model is now more flexible.

Is this method appropriate for groupwork?

Yes. Although most of the breakthroughs in Nordoff-Robbins are written about individual children, Nordoff and Robbins spent many years conducting groupwork, especially in the Philadelphia school systems. Their book on music in special education has many fine suggestions for group work (Nordoff and Robbins, 1971, first edition). According to the assessment scales used in the Nordoff-Robbins approach, the child who progresses along the continuums of musical responsiveness and interpersonal relatedness is ready to join a group. This makes developmental sense.

Do I have the necessary background, skills and knowledge to practice this method?

The Nordoff-Robbins methods are taught in their clinics throughout the world and, in this country, in New York City, the completion of which grants the designation, NRMT. However, classes encouraging beginning stages of clinical improvisation are taught at select university programs (i.e., Montclair State University) and pre-composed materials are available for use by any music therapist.

How does this method further the developmental goals of the children in the group? Specifically how?

Musical gains lead to developmental gains in areas of cognition, socialization, language and motor planning.

Is this method contraindicated in any way?

No. However, schools requiring documentation of short-term behavioral goals in music therapy, may not accept this approach. Therefore, the therapist will have to modify the assessment measures. In addition to tracking the musical gains of the child, developmental gains will have to be stated and tracked.

PSYCHODYNAMIC

What is the description of this method?

· "Based on the concept that events in the past have an impact on the present and that unconscious material drives current behavior. The goal of therapy is to uncover and work through the past and unconscious elements that interfere with current functioning" (Isenberg-Grzeda, Goldberg, Dvorkin, 2004, p. 100).

· Associated with music as a form of free association (Freud-based).

· Associated with music as a projective mechanism with parts of the self "split" from each other (Klein-based).

· Associated with music as a transitional object (Winnicott-based).

· Associated with music as a container or holding environment (Bion-based).

· Associated with music as a mirror (Kohut-based).

· Associated with the musical experience as one inviting transference, countertransference and intersubjective responses (Freud and Stern-based).

· Descriptive case material is generally individual and used in the context of long-term therapy with an adult.

· One example of this approach is a related approach called Analytic Music Therapy (Priestley, 1975).

Is this method appropriate for groupwork?

Largely described in accounts of individual work, including individual accounts with disturbed but cognitively high functioning children (Goodman, 1989), this method could conceivably be used in groupwork with children but they would have to be a cognitively high-functioning, ego-intact, long-term group.

Do I have the necessary background, skills and knowledge to practice this method?

This approach, since it involves verbal process, would require additional training in psychotherapy, or, minimally, supervision from a psychiatrist or social worker. Background training in analytic methods as an adjunctive knowledge base is recommended, particularly the theorists stated before (Freud, Klein, Winnicott, Bion, Kohut, Stern).

How does this method further the developmental goals of the children in the group? Specifically how?

The emphasis in this approach is on resolution of unconscious conflict affecting personality.

Is this method contraindicated in any way?

Contraindicated for short-term work, lower-functioning cognitively impaired children.

NEUROLOGIC

What is the description of this method?

- Used for sensorimotor training, speech and language training and cognitive training.
- Sensorimotor training includes Rhythmic Auditory Stimulation (RAS), a technique to facilitate rhythmic gait.
- Sensorimotor training includes Patterned Sensory Enhancement (PSE), a technique using elements of music in order to promote temporal, spatial and force patterns to struc-

ture and cue functional movement.
- Sensorimotor training includes Therapeutic Instrumental Music Playing (TIMP), a technique using strategically selected instruments, in the context of musical accompaniment, to engage the client in physical exercise and simulate functional movement patterns.
- Speech and language training includes Melodic Intonation Therapy (MIT), based on a protocol developed by Sparks and Holland (1976) wherein functional phrases, initially sung in prosody and intonation similar to spoken words, are then incorporated into speech singing and finally normal speech pattern.
- Speech and language training includes Speech Stimulation (MSS) where the client completes or initiates spoken words or functional phrases within the context of a song, chant, rhyme or musical phrase.
- Speech and language training includes Rhythmic Speech Cuing (RSC), especially recommended for clients with apraxia, dyarthria and fluency disorders, where the client listens to a hand tapping or drum playing consistent with a compatible tempo for speech prosody; then the client is asked to speak along with the rhythm.
- Speech and language training includes Vocal Intonation Therapy (VIT), used to train inflection, pitch, breath control, timbre and loudness for clients affected with voice disorders. Sung phrases simulating the prosody, inflection, and pace of typical speech are initially learned and then faded to spoken phrases.
- Speech and language training includes Therapeutic Singing (TS) for the initiation and development of speech, the improvement of articulation and an increase in respiratory function.
- Speech and language training includes Oral Motor and Respiratory Exercises (OMREX), a method which uses musical wind instrumental playing and oral exercises for the purposes of improved sound vocalization, better articulation, better respiratory

strength and better speech mechanism function.

- Speech and language training includes Developmental Speech and Language Training Through Music in order to provide musical experiences (singing, chanting, playing musical instruments and combinations of music, speech and movement) consistent with the development of speech and language. Commonly used with children who are developmentally delayed or autistic with little functional communication.
- Speech and language training includes Symbolic Communication Training Through Music (SYCOM) wherein both structured and/or improvisational musical performances are used to help clients communicate verbally and nonverbally (i.e., listening, question/answer, statement, waiting for input, etc.).
- Auditory Attention and Perception Training includes Auditory Perception Training (APT), a technique to encourage sound discrimination and identification of sounds including time, tempo, duration, pitch, timbre, rhythmic patterns and speech sounds. APT requires the integration of sensory stimuli such as reading symbols or notes that direct instrumental playing, moving or dancing with music or feeling sound while beating a drum.
- Auditory Attention and Perception Training includes Musical Attention Control Training (MACT), a technique where composed or improvised music acts as a cue for varying types of attention (selective, sustained, divided and alternating).
- Memory Training includes Musical Mnemonics Training (MMT), a series of mnemonic exercises that include immediate recall of sensory information (echo mnemonic), remembering rules and previously learned skills (procedural mnemonics) and, finally, teaching semantic and episodic memory skills (declarative mnemonics). All mnemonics are taught with songs, rhymes, or chants.
- Memory Training includes Associative

Mood and Memory Training (AMMT), a technique designed to establish various moods, for example, a mood to facilitate recall, a mood associated with memory and mood conducive to learning and recall.
- Executive Function Training includes Musical Executive Functioning Training (MEFT), a technique where improvisations and compositions help the client in organization, problem solving, decision-making, reasoning and comprehension.
- Psychosocial Behavior Training includes Music Psychotherapy and Counseling (MPC) as a range of music uses for mood induction, cognitive reorientation, training affective behavior response, training social skills and the provision of musical incentive training for behavior modification.

Is this method appropriate for groupwork?

Many of the afore described approaches may be appropriate for group work and some are specifically described for or imply a group option (MEFT, MPC). In his work on physically handicapped children, Thaut (1999) includes techniques for children although he does not specify if these can be used with them as part of a group.

Do I have the necessary background, skills and knowledge to practice this method?

Although many of the mentioned approaches will appear familiar to music therapists, they are described in the Thaut training with a specific protocol that is measurable and therefore useful for research validity. According to Clair and Pasiali (2004), neurologic music therapists are trained in neuroanatomy, neurophysiology, brain pathology, medical terminology and rehabilitation of cognitive and motor functions with the training taking place at Colorado State University.

How does this method further the developmental goals of the children in the group? Specifically how?

Children possibly involved in these protocols could benefit in areas of sensorimotor training, speech and language and higher level organizational, decision making and memory skills.

Is this method contraindicated in any way?

Nonambulatory children are contraindicated in gait control methods. Lower functioning children are contraindicated in executive level training skills.

SUMMARY

This chapter has included a tremendous amount of information simply because the methods section represents a coming together of ideas for the music therapist working with the group. A definition of what constitutes methods, a comprehensive review of considerations in deciding on methodology, a series of detailed suggestions that suggest methods for various populations, a sample case study illustrating the thinking process in deciding on methods for a group and, finally, a suggested process for critically understanding the appropriateness of a music therapy approach complete the chapter.

STUDY GUIDE QUESTIONS

1. What are the considerations Goodman outlines in considering methodology for a group?
2. Why is the history of changes in special education, music education and psychology germane to changes in music therapy?
3. What are some of the many principles Goodman outlines in planning music therapy groups for special learners?
4. Name at least four different population groups and outline specific methodological considerations for each of these groups.
5. Give one example of how a behavioral approach would be used in music therapy.
6. Give one example of how a relationship-based approach would be used in music therapy.
7. What is the difference between multidisciplinary, interdisciplinary and transdisciplinary work in the special education setting?
8. Describe a group you are working with. How do you set up the methods based on their goal? Objectives? Diagnoses?
9. How do you allow yourself flexibility in your methods?
10. Name at least two music education methods and indicate why these would or would not be useful in your work with a given group.

Chapter 8

Reflecting: Evaluation of the Music Therapy Session

INTRODUCTION

THE END AND THE BEGINNING

The evaluation process can be a deceptive one. It feels like it should be an end point but, in fact, it can also be viewed as a new beginning. It comes at the end of the cycle of assessment, goals, objectives, intervention, and data collection (Asmus and Gilbert, 1981), and yet it can ultimately bring the therapist back to another point in this loop. If the therapist realizes that the children in the group have not progressed satisfactorily, it is a realization that requires going back to the "drawing board" and possibly rewriting objectives or modifying interventions. If, on the other hand, the children have progressed satisfactorily, it is time to design higher-functioning objectives and more challenging interventions. This is part of what makes evaluation another step in the ongoing process of music therapy.

AMTA COMPETENCIES FOR EVALUATION OF MUSIC THERAPY

According to AMTA Competencies (AMTA, 2006, date), the evaluation process requires that the therapist "design and implement methods for evaluation and measuring client progress and the effectiveness of therapeutic strategies" (18.7) in order to "recognize significant changes and patterns in the client's response to therapy" (18.3), presumably to "modify treatment approaches based on the client's response to therapy" (18.2) and "revise treatment plan as needed" (18.4).

Further, the therapist needs to be cognizant of the relationship of the treatment plan to the agency guidelines (18.6) and time frames (18.5). The resulting documentation should be supported by clinical data (19.2) with reports that describe the client "throughout all phases of the music therapy process in an accurate, concise and objective manner" (19.3). These competencies may prove challenging in much of the workplace.

RELATIONSHIP BETWEEN MUSIC THERAPY OBJECTIVES AND EVALUATION OF THE SESSION

The music therapy objectives designed for evaluation vary according to the working philosophy of the therapist and the facility in which the therapist works. These objectives may be all data-driven (objective) or a combination of objective and subjective recording. Objectives strive toward understanding the child's progress or lack of progress in music therapy, modification of music therapy as necessary and short-term and long-term reporting on the progress or lack of progress despite logistical issues in observing, remembering and recording information from the session. Examples of this are described in this chapter.

INDIVIDUAL VS. GROUP EVALUATION

The issue of individual vs. group evaluation needs further inquiry and is explored in this chapter as well. Finally, the overall need for music therapists to document behavior for longer periods of time and seek to document the generalization of skills learned in music therapy to natural and inclusive settings (Jellison, 2000) is discussed.

PURPOSES OF EVALUATION

Purposes of evaluation are discussed further here and include the following:

- Measure client progress
- Determine effectiveness of therapeutic strategies
- Recognize changes in client response to therapy
- Recognize patterns in client response to therapy
- Modify treatment approach as necessary
- Revise treatment plan as necessary

Measurement of Progress?

The word "measurement" in measure client progress is a quantitative term and clearly implies that *progress needs to be based on objective measurement of observed behavior.* This observed behavior is based on the objectives, also quantifiable, that the therapist has set up. Setting up objectives, discussed in Chapter 5 of this book, reminds the therapist of the need to observe behavior related to goals. Suggestions for setting up objective evaluation grids are indicated in the next segment of this chapter. The behavior observed may be developmental or it may be musical depending upon the working philosophy of the therapist. Taking a measurement of progress is not contrary to a relationship-based theory of practice. Greenspan, for example, takes note of the number of circles (a term he uses in reference to interaction and closure in a communication) a child closes. Nordoff and Robbins tape music therapy sessions and return to the tapes for analysis of musical response (see Chapter 2, Nordoff-Robbins scales). That is the primary data base and it, in their judgment, is the basis for developmental change. Therapists responsible for working toward IEP goals measure objectives related to those goals.

Rethinking Methods after Evaluation

Effective therapeutic strategies, based on the goals and objectives of the children in the music therapy group, are often premeditated. The basis for these strategies, discussed in Chapter 7 of this book, however sound it may be, may not necessarily work. If a child or more than one child is not progressing in the group, it is a multidimensional issue. It could be related to the inappropriateness of the goal, the objective, or some aspect of the method, in which case these all need reconsideration. Conversely, lack of progress could be related to medical issues, attendance issues, or dysfunctional family issues. It can appear to be a puzzle which the therapist needs to sort out, often with the assistance of the rest of the therapeutic team in the school or psychiatric setting.

What is Significant Change?

The measurement of client progress recognizes *changes in client response* and relates to the measurement of client progress. Although AMTA uses the word "significant" in guidelines regarding the observation of changes, that word is relative to the functioning level of the children in the group. If, for example, a child in the group is only capable of very small increments of change, then those small increments are "significant." If, on the other hand, a child in the group is capable of a major increment of change, then those major increments are "significant." If a child capable of very small increments of change makes a major leap in the therapy session, then the situation seems almost miraculous and the therapist may wonder about the credibility of the stated goals and objectives. Perhaps the ultimate ability of the child was underestimated. Conversely, if a child capable of large increments of change makes only tiny increments of progress, or significantly regresses, the therapist needs to not only consider the accuracy of the stated goals and objectives but also the possibility of a dysfunctional event in the child's life.

Changing Pattern in Client Response to Therapy

The *recognition of patterns* in client response to therapy is different from recognizing changes since *patterns can include positive or negative response within a context* (i.e., reaction to a modality of music therapy, reaction to types of music or instruments, reaction to specific techniques). It is not likely that a therapist will notice patterns of response in a simple checklist; rather these patterns would be noted in a subjective evaluation or a behavioral tool that focuses on specific behaviors and their context for a child. Detecting response patterns is extremely helpful for the therapist to begin to calculate what is an advantageous or disadvantageous context for the child. If, for example, the child consistently generates more language following a movement activity, then movement activity should precede expressive language experiences unless contraindicated for some other reasons in the group. Further, these observations lead the therapist back to a possible link between *theory and practice* (Goodman, 2006), paving the way for a related literature review and experimental research on the issue of the relationship between movement and expressive language, an area that has already received inquiry.

Modification of the Treatment Approach

The therapist frequently reacts to evaluation by *modifying the treatment approach.* The need for modification is often realized through both the objective and subjective reporting on the session as explained further in this chapter. This modification can happen spontaneously in the session as the therapist realizes that the approach is not working appropriately or the modification can be premeditated for subsequent sessions. The modification need not be major. Sometimes, changing something as simple as a prompt or modeling intervention can impact on a child's progress. Remember that the modification can result in more or less challenge for the child. Examples of spontaneous modification in the session are demonstrated in the case examples following in this chapter.

Revision of the Treatment Plan

Revision of the treatment plan is a more radical step in reacting to evaluation. It presupposes that the goals and/or objectives as well as related methods are "off." As stated in Chapter 4, the IEP goals are initially set up by clinicians in the school district and are not always accurate. At the very least, they are variable. Therefore, it is not unreasonable to suggest the possibility that they may require adaptation. Further, since the objectives are linked to the goals, if the goals are changed, so would the objectives.

If, however, the goals are a reasonable estimate of what the child can accomplish in the period of therapy and the objectives are problematic, the therapist should reconsider whether they are too challenging or not challenging enough. Either one of these situations can be changed by altering the quantitative and/or qualitative expectation. For example, instead of "Jared will follow three-step directions independently in movement songs in two out of three sequences," the objective could be less challenging with "Jared will follow three-step directions with verbal and physical prompts in movement songs in two out of three-step sequences." Alternatively, the challenge could increase "Jared will follow three-step directions independently in movement songs in four out of four sequences."

Both objectives and subjective evaluation are necessary in evaluation. They are explained here.

TYPES OF EVALUATION

WEEKLY OBJECTIVE

Objective evaluation must be a part of evaluation. This type of evaluation observes and notes changes in behavior without bias, inference or interpretation. As such, it is almost always based on the initial goals and objectives that were set up for the session. The advantage of objective evaluation is in its supposed lack of bias, inference or interpretation. Oddly enough, that can also be its disadvantage since the therapist can lose sight of additional anecdotal information that can be valuable in why the session went well or did not go well. This is the reason for adding an anecdotal objective observation or, additionally (see below case examples) a subjective evaluation.

Format for Objective Evaluation

Individual evaluation within the context of the group can be documented in various ways. Objective evaluation can follow the log of each planned activity using a coded or uncoded system. Objective evaluation can follow the session in an evaluation form.

The simplest way to accomplish this would be a listing of objectives underneath each child's name adjacent to a column for a check mark (accomplished) or N (not accomplished). This may be too simplistic for the child who has partially responded or responded given various kinds of prompts. Therefore, another sample of a therapist-made (Goodman, 2002) evaluation form below shows the various developmental objectives listed to the left of the form and the evaluation code indicated as follows:

√+ Consistently Observed,

√ Observed When Cued (Physical, Verbal, Visual),

√- Inconsistently Observed,

NO Not Observed,

NA Not Applicable.

This coding can be delimited further by specifying numbers (Charoonsathvathana, 2000) or letters for hand-over-hand assist (1), partial hand-over-hand assist (2), physical prompt (3), verbal prompt (4), visual prompt (5), approximated (6), spontaneously, inconsistent (7), spontaneously-consistent (8).

Case Examples

The two case examples of objective evaluation and subsequent analysis of the objective information represent groups that the reader has met before in this book. Case example one, a group of latency-age multiply handicapped children (Terrence, Simon, Keisha, Maria, Alexander and Linda) are presented in Chapter 1: The Story of a Group. Case example two, another group of latency-age multiply handicapped children (Jared, Evan, Richard, Abby, Patrick, Gabriel, and Dora) are initially presented in Chapters 4 and 5, then in Chapter 7.

TABLE 8.1. CASE EXAMPLE ONE: SAMPLE OBJECTIVE EVALUATION FORMAT.

Objective Evaluation

Regional Day School

Class Number 6

Student Evaluations

Date of this evaluation

CODE

√+ Consistently Observed

√ Observed When Cued (Physical, Verbal, Visual)

√- Inconsistently Observed

NO Not Observed

NA Not applicable

---

continued

TABLE 8.1. CASE EXAMPLE ONE: SAMPLE OBJECTIVE EVALUATION FORMAT–*Continued.*

Objectives	Keisha	Terrence	Maria	Simon	Alexander	Linda
Communicate using programmed touch talker with voice output on 1 of 3 trials when given verbal and gestural prompt (Linda; Simon): Hello, Good-bye.				√		√
Produce 3-word combinations (Here I am; Sing Good-bye) with manual signs when given verbal prompts (Maria).			√			
Use spontaneous and consistent short and appropriate verbal sentences (Keisha) and response to activity-related "Wh" questions (Keisha) with a short phrase or sentence without prompting on 1 out of 3 trials (Terrence).	√√	√				
Attend to musical tasks without biting to hands, given a verbal prompt "hands down" 4 out of 5 trials (Maria).			√+			
Attend to musical tasks by sitting appropriately during 2 other peer turns and not exhibiting aggressive behaviors toward herself or others, when given no more than 2 verbal prompts, on 3 out of 4 occasions (Maria).			√+			
Attend to musical tasks without grabbing/touching objects or people when 1 verbal prompt is provided on 3 out of 5 trials (Keisha).	√+					
Attend to musical tasks without exhibiting inappropriate behavior on 4 out of 5 occasions (Terrence) when following verbal directive.		√+				

continued

TABLE 8.1. CASE EXAMPLE ONE: SAMPLE OBJECTIVE EVALUATION FORMAT–*Continued.*

Objectives	Keisha	Terrence	Maria	Simon	Alexander	Linda
Attend to musical tasks without scratching, pinching or slapping of others when given physical and verbal prompts on 3 out of 5 occasions (Simon).				√-		
Attend to musical tasks by participating in a presented activity, given physical and verbal prompting, without exhibiting inappropriate behavior for a period of 10 minutes (Simon).				√-		
Complete a task without complaint with 1 verbal reminder 4 out of 5 trials (Alexander).					√	
Attend to musical task when transitioning from favored activity, 5 minimal physical assistances, after only 1 verbal prompt (Linda).						√
Follow 2-step directive (Clap your hands, Stamp your feet) without resistance, 3 out of 5 trials (Keisha, Maria).	√		√			
Follow 3-step directive (Clap your hands, Stamp your feet, Pat your knees independently) (Alexander) or given 2 prompts, 2 out of 3 trials (Terrence).		√			√	
Select 1 picture from field of 2 (clap hands or stamp feet) in order to start song (Simon).				√		
During instrumental and movement activity, demonstrate bilateral hand use spontaneously (Alexander) by striking sticks in midline given modified tempo.					√	
Initiate striking sticks together without physical prompts on 3 out of 5 trials (Simon).				√		

continued

TABLE 8.1. CASE EXAMPLE ONE: SAMPLE OBJECTIVE EVALUATION FORMAT–*Continued.*

Objectives	Keisha	Terrence	Maria	Simon	Alexander	Linda
Clap hands in midline, given modified tempo as necessary, in context of song (Alexander).					√	
Initiate clapping hands on 1 out of 3 trials (Simon) in context of song.				√-		
Give 2 rhythm sticks to other children in the group on 3 out of 4 trials (Maria).			√			
Count up to 4 objects (Terrence).		√				
Sit appropriately during 2 other peer turns and avoid exhibiting aggressive behaviors toward herself or others, when given no more than 2 verbal prompts, on 3 out of 4 occasions (Maria).			√			
Initiate turn at the proper time, with 1 verbal prompt, during group activities for 2 reciprocal sequences (Linda).						√
Communicate wants, needs and preferences (i.e., choice of instrument), given up to 5 picture choices and/or using an augmentative device with voice output on 3 to 5 trials when given verbal and gestural prompt (Linda).						√-
Produce 3-word combinations through the use of pictures and/or manual signs when given verbal prompts, but without phrase modeling (Maria).			√			

Anecdotal notes:

Analysis of Objective Information, Case Example One

There is a total of 29 behaviors being tracked in this session. It is going to be next to impossible for even an experienced therapist to track this much behavior. The therapist would need to be assisted by aides, assistant teachers, student therapists, primary teacher or therapists in the session in order to successfully accomplish this task. If that is not possible, the number of objective behaviors tracked over the session should be modified. Four behaviors are rated √+; twenty-one behaviors are rated √; four behaviors are rated √-. Overall, the group is doing very well.

Children who demonstrate consistent behavior (√+ Consistently Observed) over a period of sessions, say 2–3, probably need more challenging objectives. Therefore, the therapist should make note of this possibility for positive attending be-haviors for Maria. If this happens in the next few sessions, then it stands to reason that these objectives may no longer be necessary.

Children who demonstrate appropriate response when cued (√ Observed When Cued–Physical, Verbal, Visual), which includes most children in the group, will benefit from a more accurate breakdown of what kind of cuing and how many times a child was cued before responding in order to modify the expectation up or down. Children who demonstrate inconsistent response (√- Inconsistently Observed) over a period of sessions will benefit from further observation of the context in which there is positive or negative response.

Finally, the therapist working with a child who shows no response to a task (NO) over a period of 2–3 sessions should reconsider the appropriateness of the task and the method.

TABLE 8.2. CASE EXAMPLE TWO: OBJECTIVE EVALUATION FORMAT.

Objective Evaluation

Regional Day School

Class Number 7

Student Evaluations

Date of this evaluation

CODE
√+   Consistently Observed
√   Observed When Cued (Physical, Verbal, Visual)
√-   Inconsistently Observed
NO   Not Observed
NA   Not applicable

Objectives	Jared	Evan	Richard	Abby	Patrick	Gabriel	Dora
Use of augmentative device in context of song (Evan, Dora)		√-					√-
Appropriate response through pictures or action (Evan)		√					

continued

TABLE 8.2. CASE EXAMPLE TWO: OBJECTIVE EVALUATION FORMAT–*Continued.*

Objectives	Jared	Evan	Richard	Abby	Patrick	Gabriel	Dora
Comprehension of verbal information through appropriate verbal response (Richard)			√				
Answer content specific questions about content of song (Abby)				√			
Spontaneously verbalize wants, needs and feelings half of the time (Richard)		na	√+				
Demonstrate comprehension and retention of auditory input during group activity by responding appropriately half of the time, given adequate processing time (Patrick)					√		
Participate in transition without objection (Patrick)		na			√+		
Verbalize wants and needs clearly and intelligible by repeating 4-word phrase at least once (Patrick)					√		
Correct use of temporal terms in response to single questions, with verbal prompts, 3/5 (Jared)	√						
Develop gestures to communicate needs and wants half of the time (Dora)							√+
Participate with a maximum of two verbal redirections (Richard)			√				
Respond over a 10-minute period with minimal verbal prompting, 4/5 (Jared)		√					
Respond with minimal verbal prompting and decreased behavioral disruption (Jared)							
Participate with interest (Dora)							√+

continued

TABLE 8.2. CASE EXAMPLE TWO: OBJECTIVE EVALUATION FORMAT–*Continued.*

Objectives	Jared	Evan	Richard	Abby	Patrick	Gabriel	Dora
Particiapte with prompting and redirection (Evan)		√					
Participate with minimal verbal redirection on 3/5 occasions (Evan)		√					
Particiapte by completing a simple one-step task independently with only two verbal re-directives (Abby)				√			
Particiapte with verbal prompts only (Patrick)					√		
Participate without physical prompts (Gabriel)						√+	
Respond within 30 sec of the directive (Abby)				√+			
Intelligibly verbalize wants, needs and feelings given one chance for self-correction (Richard)			√+				
Maintain balance in challenged position for duration of activity (Abby)				√+			
Reposition herself in her class-room chair with verbal prompting only to attain an appropriate seated posture 2/3 times (Abby)				√			
Attempt to modify gross motor movement half the time in order to appropriately monitor his impulsivity (Jared)	√						
Access pictures or gesturing on 3/5 days (Evan)		√					
Spontaneously verbalize feelings (Jared)	√+						

continued

TABLE 8.2. CASE EXAMPLE TWO: OBJECTIVE EVALUATION FORMAT–*Continued.*

Objectives	Jared	Evan	Richard	Abby	Patrick	Gabriel	Dora
Participate with appropriate behavior when challenged (Jared)	√						
Participate by following directions, helping and communicating need for help from peers and adults (Dora)							√+
Help by instructing a peer to do a three-step activity with visual, gestural, and verbal prompts (Abby)				√			
Help in group by spontaneous modeling of task (Abby)				√			
Initiate parallel play though rhythmic playing with classmate (Evan)		√-					

Anecdotal notes:

Analysis of Objective Evaluation, Case Example Two

There is a total of 31 behaviors being tracked in this session. At first glance, it appears that more behaviors are being tracked in this session than case example one. This is because there is practically no overlap; that makes the task of the observing therapist that much more difficult. As in the first case example, the therapist would need to be assisted by aides, assistant teachers, student therapists, primary teacher or therapists in the session in order to successfully accomplish this task. If that is not possible, the number of objective behaviors tracked over the session should be modified.

Ten behaviors are rated √+; eighteen behaviors are rated √; three behaviors are rated √-. ; zero behavior is rated NO. Note that the √ rating is a bit confusing given the objectives of this group since this rating involves prompts in order to accomplish the task. Does that mean that if the child consistently responds with prompts they will still never receive the √+ rating even though they have consistently met the objective? The therapist needs to consider more specific remarks in the key.

As in the first case example, children who demonstrate consistent behavior (√+ Consistently Observed) over a period of sessions, say 2–3, probably need more challenging objectives.

Children who demonstrate appropriate response when cued (√ Observed When Cued - Physical, Verbal, Visual), which includes most children in the group, will benefit from a more accurate breakdown of what kind of cuing and how many times a child was cued before responding in order to modify the expectation up or down.

Children who demonstrate inconsistent response (√- Inconsistently Observed) over a period of sessions will benefit from further observation of the context in which there is positive or negative response.

Finally, the therapist working with a child who shows no response to a task (NO) over a period of 2–3 sessions, should reconsider the appropriateness of the task and the method. Another item, NOO, could be added to indicate "no opportunity to observe."

WEEKLY SUBJECTIVE

Purposes of Subjective Evaluation

In contrast to the objective reporting, the subjective reporting (see samples below from Chapter 1 and Chapter 7 case study) is less discussed in the literature. While it is true that objective evaluation is the true source of actually measuring what the child does in terms of changes in behavior, the subjective evaluation serves many purposes. It documents the following: 1) reaction of the therapist to the various group members; 2) the therapist interpretation of behavior; 3) the issues that the therapist perceives in connection to the progress or lack of progress on the part of a child in the group; 4) necessary modification made in the session that may be considered in subsequent session planning; 5) issues related to group dynamics and; 6) the realization of a link from theory to practice. These factors provide a basis for reflective understanding of the client and recognition of what the therapist had to change in the session and the possible reasons for those changes following each subjective report below; there is an analysis of these factors.

Case Studies

As in objective reporting, the two case examples of subjective evaluation and subsequent analysis of the subjective information represent groups that the reader has met before in this book. Case example one, a group of latency age multiply handicapped children (Terrence, Simon, Keisha, Maria, Alexander and Linda) are presented in Chapter 1: The Story of a Group. Case example two, another group of latency age multiply handicapped children (Jared, Evan, Richard, Abby, Patrick, Gabriel and Dora) are initially presented in Chapters 4 and 5. Those words in italics represent the content that will be analyzed.

Case Example One: Subjective Evaluation (From Chapter 1) (Goodman, K., 1996–2002)

Opening the group today is comfortable. Even though it is just the second session, *the children seem* very *"up"* as they enter the room. Terrence, Maria, Keisha and Alexander are smiling. *Simon has so much physical limitation in his facial muscles because of his low tone that it is hard for me to figure out how he is feeling.* Linda, in her wheelchair, is drooling and moving arhythmically in the chair. She seems restless and discomforted. Everyone is able to respond to the "Hello" song, either through augmentative device, sign or singing. *They seem to have an instinctive sense of when to enter the song* and *I don't think I will have to prompt* as the sessions progress.

As I move into the clapping song, I notice that Keisha and Terrence lose eye contact with me and *start clapping impulsively. I do not want to interrupt their enthusiasm for the music and so I choose not to "correct" them.* I think there is a grey area between judging impulsivity and enthusiasm here. During the last rendition of the song, where I combine three different steps, I notice that the uninterrupted clapping has turned into intentional rhythmic clapping. *I wonder about the processing time that these children need to decode the pattern I have been introducing.* Clearly, *they process "correctly" after the repetitions in the song.* Likewise, Alexander is having some difficulty bringing his flailing hands to midline in order to physically grasp the beat. Again, *I do not "correct" him.* By the end of the song, he "catches up." Maria is only clapping once each time on her own even though her aide keeps assisting her with the second two beats. Here again, *I wonder about processing time. If I had Maria on an individual basis, I could have her clapping only one beat.*

The transition from opening and clapping to the use of the rhythm sticks works well due to my singing a little tune I spontaneously compose while walking over toward the instruments in the room, "Watch me, watch me, I am looking for the rhythm sticks." *This seems to keep Linda from getting upset* and helps her visually track me moving toward another corner of the room. I return quickly, even walking to the pulse of my singing voice, as the children watch me with the can of sticks. Some of my students in training at the university express a need to "keep the activities going" so the children do not "act out" but *I think transitions are always a welcome comfort to children rather than back-to-back activities which seems robot-like.*

There is a brief moment of *anxious anticipation*

as the children wait for their turn to select rhythm sticks. Again, *I try to keep the momentum stable* while talking through what is happening in the room. It works. As we move into the song, I notice the aides *automatically* trying to do hand-over-hand assistance with the children. *The only gentle way I can encourage autonomy* is to say, "Let's let the children try it on their own first," rather than singling out one particular offender. It works. Granted, the children are all physically limited in one way or another *but it is helpful for me to see how they naturally approach using these materials.* At one point, Terrence playfully tries to play one of his sticks with Keisha. *The visual-motor match is not quite right at first and then it improves. Again, I don't feel a need to change this.* It is a great effort at befriending and sharing each other's musical energy. After a while, laughing, they return to playing their own sticks.

After we put the rhythm sticks away, I again transition with my little song but by this time, *the stimulation has been too much for Linda and she starts crying.* We are about a half hour into a *45-minute session, a session time that easily leads to sensory overload for some of these children.* I suggest that one of the aides take Linda out for a brief reprieve and she ends up going to the nurse for a nap. *I wonder about the balancing act for children who are overly reactive to stimuli,* other children who need to channel their hyperactivity, and finally children who are underreactive. *This remains one of the great challenges in doing groupwork.*

Bringing out the drums and the standing cymbal is an exciting moment for the children and Maria begins to spontaneously clap her hands in anticipation. *I wonder how she can clap her hands several times here but only clapped once before.*

Again, the children are able to wait their turns while I demonstrate with the aide and then offer instrumental preference cards to the first child, Maria. In her excitement, she is spontaneously pointing to herself and *I take advantage of this moment* by acknowledging her communication, "Oh, look everyone, Maria wants music (sign)!" I am trying to involve the other children even though they are waiting. "Maria, do you want (this), or (this)?" and I show her the cards. She chooses the cymbal. After the preliminary modeling, she plays. *Her playing is so loud that Simon begins* to shake. *How do I monitor this level of excitement?* Again, the issue of balancing the sensory input in the session is apparent. Fortunately, Simon is able to contain his reaction to the cymbal "crash" and self-regulate. I can see that *this issue of "self-regulation," the first milestone Stanley Greenspan writes about is such a fundamental issue.* If Maria was truly able to follow the dynamics in the song I was playing, she would be self-regulating . . . but she is not there yet. The same thing happens after Terrence and Keisha play. *I think about the stated goals in the IEP that I have set up for this activity. They don't seem to reflect much humanistic feeling for the developmental goals.* Why didn't the clinicians who set up this plan think about self-regulation as preparatory for any of the behavioral regulating? The music is a perfect way to help with regulation.

By the time I get to Alexander, he is hyperventilating in his excitement. He chooses both the drum and the cymbal so I change the orchestration in "Mary is sleeping" in order for him to basic-beat the melody and play the cymbal at the end of the piece. He tries to acclimate his flailing arms to the dynamics of the piece and is partially successful. *I can tell that, in his mind, he knows what he has to do physically but he is not successful in keeping his body under control. I admire his fortitude* and the other teachers and aides in the classroom are amazed at this. It is hard to believe that this is a child who the teacher says "complains" in the classroom when he is so highly motivated in music.

As we arrive at the end of the music time, *I can tell that the group is still largely attentive and I am truly impressed.* In terms of assessment, when I compare the functioning levels stated in the Individual Education Plans with the functioning levels I see in the music activities, the levels are similar. However, *the emotional relatedness is overwhelmingly positive, something that I did not expect based on my reading of the behavioral goals for the children.* I do think the drive to engage in music channels the energy of the children in such a positive way that they simply do not need to be distracted in negative ways. Even though the children are limited in their functioning, *their enthusiasm is going to override their functioning level and allow them to start facilitating the session* on their own level. Relatively speak-

ing, this is going to be a workable group.

Analysis of Subjective Evaluation: Case Example One

EXAMPLES OF REACTION OF THE THERAPIST TO THE VARIOUS GROUP MEMBERS: This is a low-functioning group and I sense from the subjective evaluation that I have mixed reactions to the children.

Part of the feeling is empathy, particularly for the children who are very physically compromised, for example, *Simon has so much physical limitation in his facial muscles because of his low tone that it is hard for me to figure out how he is feeling* and Alexander, *I can tell that, in his mind, he knows what he has to do physically but he is not successful in keeping his body under control.* With Alexander, I seem to have made a subjective decision that he is higher functioning than his body allows him to communicate and he becomes a figure of admiration: *I admire his fortitude* particularly since *It is hard to believe that this is a child who the teacher says "complains" in the classroom when he is so highly motivated in music.*

Another part of the feeling is my own discomfort and anticipation that I will not be able to meet the needs of the children, given the limitations of the school structure. This is apparent in my comments regarding Linda, *Linda, in her wheelchair, is drooling and moving arhythmically in the chair. She seems restless and discomforted* and Maria, *If I had Maria on an individual basis, I could have her clapping only one beat* and even extends to the entire group at one point, *Why didn't the clinicians who set up this plan think about self-regulation as preparatory for any of the behavioral regulating?*

Yet, despite elements of frustration, I am ultimately positive toward the group as a whole, for some reason making a causal connection between their efforts and their prognosis in music therapy: *Even though the children are limited in their functioning, their enthusiasm is going to override their functioning level and allow them to start facilitating the session, on their own level.*

EXAMPLES OF THE THERAPIST INTERPRETATION OF BEHAVIOR: With nonverbal children, there may be a tendency on the part of the therapist to interpret behavior more frequently. In this group, Terrence is really the only verbal child and therefore I see myself trying to interpret many nonverbal behaviors. The question here for the therapist is, "How does this therapist interpretation of behavior affect the intervention?"

We see my interpretation early in the session as I try to perceive how the children are feeling upon their entry into the session: *Opening the group today is comfortable. Even though it is just the second session, the children seem very "up" as they enter the room. . . . Simon has so much physical limitation in his facial muscles because of his low tone that it is hard for me to figure out how he is feeling.*

As the session proceeds, I make further interpretations about cause and effect; these interpretations lead me into methodology as well. First, I anticipate what will happen in the session: *They seem to have an instinctive sense of when to enter the song* and *I don't think I will have to prompt* as the sessions progress and then I proceed to adjust my methods as necessary. As the sessions move on, I make another causal connection between the sound level in the music therapy session and Linda's reaction: *the stimulation has been too much for Linda and she starts crying,* confirming my initial suspicion that I might not be able to meet her needs given the constraints of the session and her problems.

It is interesting that, at the close of the session, I make an interpretive connection between attentiveness and emotional relatedness, a point that reflects my Greenspan reading (see link from theory to practice): *As we arrive at the end of the music time, I can tell that the group is still largely attentive and I am truly impressed. In terms of assessment, when I compare the functioning levels stated in the Individual Education Plans with the functioning levels I see in the music activities, the levels are similar. However, the emotional relatedness is overwhelmingly positive, something that I did not expect based on my reading of the behavioral goals for the children.*

EXAMPLES OF NECESSARY MODIFICATION MADE IN THE SESSION THAT MAY BE CONSIDERED IN SUBSEQUENT SESSION PLANNING: As aforementioned, therapist interpretation of behavior can lead to modifications in the session. I spontaneously sense the need for a transitional tune

based on my perception of anxiety level, particularly for Linda (see interpretation and therapist reaction to children): *I create a transitional tune, assuming it will hold a corrective opportunity for Linda: This seems to keep Linda from getting upset and helps her visually track me moving toward another corner of the room.* Further, I become aware of how one musical experience following another makes sense: *The transition from opening and clapping to the use of the rhythm sticks works well due to my singing a little tune I spontaneously compose while walking over toward the instruments in the room,* even adjusting my gait pattern to the rhythm of the transitional tune I am singing in order to provide rhythmic stability.

Even when I appear to "lose" the children I interpret the behavior (see the connection here again between interpretation and methodology) favorably and act flexibly. This is particularly noticeable in the interplay between Keisha and Terrence, a dyad within the group: *At one point, Terrence playfully tries to play one of his sticks with Keisha. The visual-motor match is not quite right at first and then it improves. Again, I don't feel a need to change this. It is a great effort at befriending and sharing each other's musical energy. After a while, laughing, they return to playing their own sticks.*

Another example follows: As I move into the clapping song, I notice that Keisha and Terrence lose eye contact with me and *start clapping impulsively. I do not want to interrupt their enthusiasm for the music and so I choose not to "correct" them.* This reaction on my part leads into thoughtful speculation, part theory to practice questions and part reaction to the children: *I think there is a grey area between judging impulsivity and enthusiasm here. During the last rendition of the song, where I combine three different steps, I notice that the uninterrupted clapping has turned into intentional rhythmic clapping. I wonder about the* processing time that *these children need to decode the pattern I have been introducing. Clearly, they process "correctly" after the repetitions in the song.*

I relax my expectation regarding Alexander as well, this time not because of speculation about processing time, but, rather about motor planning: *Likewise, Alexander is having some difficulty bringing his flailing hands to midline in order to physically grasp the beat. Again, I do not "correct" him. By the end of the* song, he "catches up."

Other accommodations in the session include praise in recognition of a spontaneous positive moment: *In her excitement, she (Maria) is sponta-neously pointing to herself and I take advantage of this moment by acknowledging her communication, Oh, look everyone, Maria wants music (sign)!* and musical adaptation for Alexander: *He chooses both the drum and the cymbal so I change the orchestration in "Mary is sleeping" in order for him to basic-beat the melody and play the cymbal at the end of the piece.*

Coupled with my need to be flexible is a grow-ing awareness of the sensory vulnerability of the group given the time constraints: *We are about a half-hour into a 45-minute session, a session time that easily leads to sensory overload for some of these children. I wonder about the balancing act for children who are overly reactive to stimuli, other children who need to channel their hyperactivity, and finally children who are underreactive. This remains one of the great challenges in doing groupwork.*

EXAMPLES OF ISSUES RELATED TO GROUP DYNAMICS: It is interesting that, for this group, the dynamics are limited in comparison to the second case study. This group is lower functioning and therefore limited in their capacity for groupwork (see Chapter 3). Given that scenario, I am still aware of a dyad between Keisha and Terrence and I try to facilitate awareness in the group by com-menting to all the members when I am focusing on Maria's spontaneous positive behavior and Alexander' fortitude in playing the percussion instruments.

EXAMPLES OF LINK FROM THEORY TO PRACTICE: There is a good deal of speculation on my part as I try to connect what is happening in the group with theory. For example, I continue to consider the issues of processing time: *As the sequence of directives in a particular song becomes more demanding I note that, oddly enough, the uninterrupted clapping has turned into intentional rhythmic clapping. I wonder about the processing time that these children need to decode the pattern I have been introducing. Clearly, they process "correctly" after the repetitions in the song.* As well as sensory regulation: *Her playing is so loud that Simon begins to shake. How do I monitor this level of excitement? Again, the issue of balancing the sensory input in the session is apparent. Fortunately,*

Simon is able to contain his reaction to the cymbal "crash" and self-regulate. I can see that this issue of "self-regulation," the first milestone Stanley Greenspan writes about is such a fundamental issue. If Maria was truly able to follow the dynamics in the song I was play-ing, she would be self-regulating . . . but she is not there yet. The same thing happens after Terrence and Keisha play.

Case Example Two

Subjective Evaluation (From Chapter 7)

The children entered the room in an upbeat mood. This was a morning session and this was fortuitous since they were full of boundless energy. Jared practically threw himself into the seat and Abby started to laugh at that fierce opening! Then Jared started to laugh and Dora, although she has difficulty with any kind of demonstrative facial expression, tried to smile. I have to admit that I starting laughing too, at Jared's energy.

After the children sat down, I opened with "Let me introduce myself." I sang with great enthusi-asm and it was apparently contagious for the chil-dren since they laughed with pleasure while watching me. I then picked as my "friend" Patrick's aide, Bill. Bill was a pretty quiet guy and this song seemed to bring out his alter ego. He opened up his arms as he sang the song and his voice opened up as well. Patrick, usually quiet and anxious, was really enthralled with this. He could not stop staring at his aide! He was ready to per-form like his aide now! As soon as his aide called on him, he panicked a bit and decided to sing from his seat. He was given very positive attention from his aide and this seemed to spur him on. He finished his part of the song by calling on Richard. Richard, a natural "clown," as he is jokingly referred to by his teacher, became quite theatrical in front of his peers. After he finished, he begged to repeat his performance. *I said fine.* He did it again and begged again to repeat the perform-ance. He just could not get enough of this! I noticed that the second rendition had resulted in a stronger mastery of articulation and told him about this. He seemed pleased. I must admit that I had to be a bit stern in *setting limits for him to final-*

ly choose another child to sing! By this time, Jared was jumping up and down in his seat, waiting for his turn, and *I told him I was very proud of him being able to wait.* He would be next after Dora. *Dora did not choose to use the Big Mack; rather she preferred to gesture to herself on the word "myself" and point to Abby on the word "friend."* This was fine especially since I noticed that *she spontaneously stretched the contractured left arm to perform these gestures.* Abby, verbally encouraged by Jared and Richard to "come on," stood up haltingly and came by the side of the piano to sing her solo. She was hesitant. I started her off and continued to *help her approximate the words she was having trouble with as she tried to open up her arms to the group,* smiling all the while. After she was finished, the group clapped for her, a wonderful display of support! By this time, Evan had his hands over his ears; the excitement might have been both overwhelming and intimidating for him. I wasn't sure which. At any rate, *he passed on participating* even though *he was watching every step of the action and I commented on how great that was.* Gabriel, the last group member to sing, had profited from all the modeling thus far and sang many of the words in the song, to the surprise of the teacher.

We transitioned smoothly to the group choice of the "Stand Up, Sit Down" song particularly because the children had already been getting up to do the greeting song and were now "warmed up." The excitement escalated as I modeled the song first and then invited the children to participate. Evan was laughing as he got up and down in his seat, sharing in the contagion being created by Jared and Richard. Abby, Richard, and Patrick were a bit slower physically and, *in my efforts to accommodate their delayed auditory processed and motor planning, I created a challenge for Jared to manage his hyperactivity.* I had not really forecast this but it worked out well in terms of group dynamics.

I asked the children to cast their "votes" for the next choice of music activity. They all chose the picture of the instruments. I introduced the tambourine song with the option of choosing the drum as well. The aide modeled with me. While I briefly demonstrated for him how to model the tambourine as well as the drum, I realized that playing the tambourine and the drum can actually be done in many ways, each way inviting a different kind of sensory stimulation. I wasn't sure if I should model the easiest way (merely shaking the tambourine; striking the drum three times) or a more complex sequential technique (shake the tambourine up on first beat, in the middle on second beat, down on third beat; strike the drum with a different rhythmic combination on each quarter note beat) or a yet more complex manner (shake the tambourine on first beat, strike with elbow, strike on knee; strike the drum with three different dynamics). *I became aware that, in my own excitement about presenting the song, I had the potential to go off on musical tangents and this could be confusing for the children. I decided to keep it simple the first time around, shaking the tambourine each time on a beat.* Even this was more of a challenge than shaking it constantly through the three beats. The playing and passing went smoothly although more physical efforts to help the children pass were required than I had anticipated. *In order to help the children with an extra musical prompt for stopping, I changed the music slightly by adding an extra phrase after the last rendition of "you can play the tambourine."* At that point I added two quarter notes and dissonant chords while singing, *"Now Stop!"* That helped. My only problem was Jared. He did not want to let go of the tambourine and he was shaking it vigorously, up and down in the air. *I got up from the piano, took another tambourine and started shaking with him, singing a cappella at the end,* "Stop (rest) and rest." *He enjoyed the stopping point so much, the moment of musical connection, that he burst out laughing, and gave the tambourine up.*

After the next transition, the vote was cast for "Beanbag." We did it a cappella at first so I could gage the working tempo of the group before using a recording to have my hands free.

When Jared got the beanbag, he tossed it up in the air and it actually came close to striking Abby. She was scared, not expecting the sudden intrusion. *We stopped the music and I asked him to self-assess what he had done.* He muttered, "Sorry, sorry, sorry Abby." I believe he really was sorry. *I told him, you can control your behavior, Jared. Let's try this again. You need to listen to the music.* Then he was okay. *During this episode, I had to keep the attention of the other group members, so I simply said, Jared is having a little trou-*

ble passing the beanbag, but now he can do it. Richard nodded, Dora looked attentive, Evan looked interested as though he wanted to toss it too! Well. . . . That's exactly what happened. *Evan ended up throwing the beanbag on the floor and laughing. I acknowledged his feeling,* Yes, it can be fun to throw. Now let's try another way. I like to think this was a redirection rather than a reprimand. For Evan, it is important to have him participate on any level so the seemingly negative behavior was acknowledged even though it felt like a developmental behavior of a two-year-old. Maybe that's where Evan is. At any rate, he complied with changing his throwing and we continued.

By now, we were 35 minutes into the 45-minute session and I had to use my time-management skills, now always the best, to anticipate how long we would have for the affirmation/recall (Yes, I Can) and Closing. Richard was asking me if we could "act" again, remembering the opening song. *I decided to skip the option of the additional song/instrumental activity and convert the "Yes, I Can" into a more theatrical presentation.* In order to do this, *I asked Richard to model for the class a recollection of what we had done in music.* I helped him remember the sequence by showing *him the picture exchange cards* for "Movement" (Beanbag; Stand Up-Sit Down), "Instruments" (tambourine song) and Opening (Let me Introduce Myself). *With those visual prompts,* he was able to sing and act out, "Oh, I can sing hello (Ohhhhhh), Oh, I can sit down and stand up (demonstrates), Oh, I can play a drum (demonstrates), Oh, I can pass the beanbag" (hands it to me) to my accompaniment.

All the children were encouraged to join in on the "Yes, I Can" chorus and seemed to enjoy Richard's antics. *The more concrete visual recall of what we had done in the session was actually a wonderful way to reinforce their memories.*

We closed comfortably and Patrick was able to transition from the classroom without any tantrumming.

Analysis of Subjective Evaluation: Case Study Two

EXAMPLES OF REACTION OF THE THERAPIST TO THE VARIOUS GROUP MEMBERS: The subjective commentary explains the theoretical rationale for much of the reaction to the children, for example, *Yes, it can be fun to throw. Now let's try another way. I like to think this was a redirection rather than a reprimand. For Evan, it is important to have him participate on any level so the seemingly negative behavior was acknowledged even though it felt like a developmental behavior of a two-year-old* and this is helpful. Nevertheless, some reactions proceed without explanation and therefore invite more thought on my part.

For example, *"I have to admit that I starting laughing, too, at Jared's energy"* shows a mixed reaction to Jared's impulsivity. On one hand it is problematic; on the other hand I think it is refreshing and perhaps I relate to it personally. Does this mean, I could be tempted to be inconsistent in the way I handle it in the session? Later on, I push Jared to his limit by asking him to wait for his turn, *By this time, Jared was jumping up and down in his seat, waiting for his turn, and I told him I was very proud of him being able to wait.*

Another example of a particular reaction to a child in the group is my reaction to Richard: *I must admit that I had to be a bit stern in setting limits for him (Richard) to finally choose another child to sing.* The implication here is that I am not really comfortable being "stern" and my spontaneous reaction to Richard would be to encourage his dramatic play, to continue to enjoy it and help him extend it. But . . . as the therapist of a group, I have to be aware of the need for other children to share my time and have their turns in the session.

EXAMPLES OF THE THERAPIST INTERPRETATION OF BEHAVIOR: As indicated in my reaction to Evan in a previous example, I do interpret behavior and react on that basis throughout the session. This is the mark of a seasoned therapist where theory and practice connect.

I seem to create a number of cause and effect interpretations. In this opening description, for example, I make a causal connection between Jared's energy and the behaviors of other children in the group: *Jared practically threw himself into the seat and Abby started to laugh at that fierce opening! Then Jared started to laugh and Dora, although she has difficulty with any kind of demonstrative facial expression, tried to smile.*

Following this, I make a causal connection between Patrick's motivation to sing and his aide's modeling in the session: *I then picked as my "friend" Patrick's aide, Bill. Bill was a pretty quiet guy and this song seemed to bring out his alter ego. He opened up his arms as he sang the song and his voice opened up as well. Patrick, usually quiet and anxious, was really enthralled with this. He could not stop staring at his aide! He was ready to perform like his aide now!*

Finally, in another part of the subjective commentary, I write about Evan and my interpretation of why he has his hands over his ears: *Evan had his hands over his ears; the excitement might have been both overwhelming and intimidating for him. I wasn't sure which.*

EXAMPLES OF THE ISSUES THAT THE THERAPIST PERCEIVES IN CONNECTION TO THE PROGRESS OR LACK OF PROGRESS ON THE PART OF A CHILD IN THE GROUP: It seems that this item is a item under the therapist interpretation of behavior. In this latter section. See the comments regarding Patrick and Evan.

EXAMPLES OF ISSUES RELATED TO GROUP DYNAMICS: Causal connections I make clearly imply group dynamics. For example, my comments under therapist interpretation of behavior suggest a peer reaction that involves two other children in response to Jared. Further comments in the subjective evaluation related to group dynamics follow. We see the advantage of modeling for the more reticent child, first Gabriel. *Gabriel, the last group member to sing, had profited from all the modeling thus far and sang many of the words in the song, to the surprise of the teacher* and then Evan, *Evan was laughing as he got up and down in his seat, sharing in the contagion being created by Jared and Richard.* We also see, that it is possible to accommodate two very different kinds of sensory profiles and therefore try to bring a state of equilibrium to a group: *Abby, Richard, Patrick, were a bit slower physically and, in my efforts to accommodate their delayed auditory processed and motor planning, I created a challenge for Jared to manage his hyperactivity. I had not really forecast this but it worked out well in terms of group dynamics.*

Throughout the session, the "voting" for the next kind of musical experience creates a feeling of democracy although it is difficult to ascertain if the unanimous selection is imitative or possible due to group spirit: *I asked the children to cast their "votes" for the next choice of music activity. They all chose the picture of the instruments.*

The session ends with a positive note and the child who seems to have assumed a leadership role in the group coincidentally, through his visual antics, cements the closing: *All the children were encouraged to join in on the "Yes, I Can" chorus and seemed to enjoy Richard's antics. The more concrete visual recall of what we had done in the session was actually a wonderful way to reinforce their memories.*

EXAMPLES OF NECESSARY MODIFICATION MADE IN THE SESSION THAT MAY BE CONSIDERED IN SUBSEQUENT SESSION PLANNING: There are many modifications in the session that were not previously planned. These point the way to subsequent session planning and would not have shown up in an objective evaluation.

There are many methods that a good therapist spontaneously carries out without articulating in a session plan. One of these is praising a child for spontaneous behaviors. I notice this in my efforts with Richard, *I noticed that the second rendition had resulted in a stronger mastery of articulation and told him (Richard) about this. He seemed pleased,* as well as Jared, *I told him I was very proud of him for being able to wait,* and Evan, *he (Evan) passed on participating* even though *he was watching every step of the action and I commented on how great that was.*

There are also many occasions that surprise the therapist in spontaneously promoting goal behaviors through a choice the child is consciously or unconsciously making: *Dora did not choose to use the Big Mack; rather she preferred to gesture to herself on the word "myself" and point to Abby on the word "friend."* This was fine especially since I noticed that *she spontaneously stretched the contractured left arm to perform these gestures.* These happen, though, due to the therapist's flexibility in opening up alternatives for the child apart from the beginning session plan.

Changes in the way the music is presented is obviously a critical aspect of music therapy: *In order to help the children with an extra musical prompt for stopping, I changed the music slightly by adding an extra phrase after the last rendition of "you can play the tambourine." At that point I added two quarter notes and dissonant chords while singing, "Now Stop!"*

In connection with the music presentation, the ongoing thought process of the therapist creates awareness: *I became aware that, in my own excitement about presenting the song, I had the potential to go off on musical tangents and this could be confusing for the children. I decided to keep it simple the first time around, shaking the tambourine each time on a beat.*

Other examples of changing methodology in the session include the ongoing task of adapting to sensory profiles particularly through musical changes: *in my efforts to accommodate their delayed auditory processed and motor planning, I created a challenge for Jared to manage his hyperactivity. I had not really forecast this but it worked out well in terms of group dynamics,* additional physical positioning and handling, *The playing and passing went smoothly although more physical efforts to help the children pass were required than I had anticipated.*

Further, spontaneous change in the session includes the handling of potentially disruptive situations, situations which can be handled with humor and a sense of emotional connection: *He* (Jared) *did not want to let go of the tambourine and he was shaking it vigorously, up and down in the air. I got up from the piano, took another tambourine and started shaking with him, singing a cappella at the end, Stop (rest) and rest. He enjoyed the stopping point so much, the moment of musical connection, that he burst out laughing, and gave the tambourine up,* followed by verbal redirection, *We stopped the music and I asked him to self-assess what he had done. He muttered, Sorry, sorry, sorry Abby. I believe he really was sorry. I told him, you can control your behavior, Jared. Let's try this again. You need to listen to the music. Then, he was okay.* Another example of a potentially disruptive situation refers to Evan: *Evan ended up throwing the beanbag on the floor and laughing. I acknowledged his feeling.*

Being aware of and facilitating group dynamics, as mentioned earlier, is a constant responsibility: *During this episode, I had to kept the attention of the other group members, so I simply said: Jared is having a little trouble passing the beanbag, but now he can do it,* handled not only through verbal and musical communication but also, in a practical sense, the transition from one musical experience to the next and the need to leave sufficient time for closure:

By now, we were 35 minutes into the 45-minute session and I had to use my time-management skills, now always the best, to anticipate how long we would have for the affirmation/recall ("Yes, I Can") and Closing. Finally, the fluid methodology calls for the therapist to spontaneously follow up on unanticipated but positive forces in the session. A good example of this is my decision to take advantage of Richard's leadership and theatrical skill: *I decided to skip the option of the additional song/instrumental activity and convert the "Yes, I Can" into a more theatrical presentation. In order to do this, I asked Richard to model for the class a recollection of what we had done in music.*

EXAMPLES OF LINK FROM THEORY TO PRACTICE: There are implicit comments throughout the subjective summary that indicate the therapist has studied child development, special education methods, and music therapy. Were it not so, the session could not proceed with positive and changing methods, particularly those that were unanticipated in the session plan. Two specific examples of this include the comments, *The more concrete visual recall of what we had done in the session was actually a wonderful way to reinforce their memories* and *For Evan, it is important to have him participate on any level so the seemingly negative behavior was acknowledged even though it felt like a developmental behavior of a two-year-old.* The first comment shows an understanding of the need for multisensory input, particularly important for the children in this session with poor auditory processing. The second comment shows an understanding of developmental regression.

Case Studies One and Two: Summary, Evaluation Issues

Objective

In both of these case examples, there is room for improvement with the objective grid. The key could be altered as follows:

C, Behavior is consistently observed, without cues
C-P, Behavior is consistently observed, with physical prompting
C-V, Behavior is consistently observed, with ver-

bal prompting

C-Vi, Behavior is consistently observed, with visual prompting

(note: if more than one type of prompting is used, indicate as necessary)

I-P, Behavior is inconsistently observed, with physical prompting

I-V, Behavior is inconsistently observed, with verbal prompting

I-Vi, Behavior is inconsistently observed, with visual prompting

N, Behavior is not observed

NO, There is no opportunity to observe behavior

Na, This objective is not applicable to this child

Alternatively, a numerical equivalent (3 for consistent response; 2 for response with prompt; 1 for inconsistent response; and 0 for no response) could be used to compare degrees of success from one session to the next for each child.

Subjective

Admittedly, the areas outlined under subjective evaluation overlap. Therapist interpretation of behavior, frequently based on a combination of therapist reaction to the children as well as the link from theory to practice, will result in modifications in the session that affect individual children as well as the group. Nevertheless, these are helpful guidelines in the subjective evaluation. Overall, the importance of subjective evaluation is probably underestimated in the music therapy evaluation. Subjective evaluation serve to inform the therapist in terms of self-growth and further investigating why or why not the methods and materials work.

Logistical Issues in Observing: Remembering and Reporting Information from the Session

As previously mentioned, the reality of the music therapist's day may contraindicate the systematic note-taking of what happens in the session. Many therapists do not have breaks between sessions for note-taking and by the time they turn to their notes, they have forgotten some of the observed behaviors. The first and foremost sug-

gestion is for the therapist to only set up the number of behavioral objectives for each child that can reasonably be observed in the session. For the beginning student, for example, it may even make sense to effectively set up one behavioral objective for one child in the group. If the seasoned therapist is able to effectively track a number of objectives for each child, great. If not, quality rather than quantity is the adage.

Other means for handling this issue are the following: have the teacher or aide complete a simple checklist for observed behavior; 2) schedule certain days to record the behavior of specific children in the group; and 3) note only key changes (significant progress or regression) in your notes.

One example of this flexibility in recording changes in behavior is a rotating system of log entries in a model demonstration school for autistic spectrum disordered children where therapists and teachers were asked to log in observed behaviors related to goals for children only when definitively observed (Goodman, 1996–2002). This information became part of mid-year and final year evaluations written by one assigned staff member who reviewed log entries, compiled and summarized them.

A Note on Student Logs As Subjective Evaluation

In many music therapy training programs, it is suggested that students write running logs on their music therapy practicum sessions. In many ways, these session logs contain some of the same elements that have been analyzed in the previous subjective evaluation case material. However, there are differences. There seems to be a greater emphasis on the developing feelings of the student therapist—their doubts about their own levels of competence in making music and making clinical decisions, their anxiety, their great need for positive feedback from the children, their reactions to the supervisor, their emotional attachment to the children, their difficulties with setting limits for the children. The difficulty in realizing the link between theory and practice seems to be exacerbated by anxiety (Goodman, 2005). Some examples of these are indicated below:

Example of Self-Questioning in Reference to Setting Limits: Anxiety Regarding Clinical Decision-Making

I noticed that some of the kids were testing me. I think that they were purposely misbehaving in order to see whether or not I would accept their negative behavior as well as their positive behavior to see if they could trust me. I think they were also testing the boundaries to see what they could get away with when I was there. I had a difficult time setting strict boundaries. I was so afraid that I would upset the kids or make them feel bad. I wanted to increase their sense of self-worth and I was scared that I would hurt them in some way if I was too strict with them.

Example of Link from Theory to Practice in Student Note

Anyway, when I observed this student, who was one of the higher-functioning ones, she was making random verbalizations very much like an infant would make. She seemed to like the "bah buh" sound and looked like she was in the initial stages of learning to talk. I don't think she yet put meaning to the sounds she was making or used them to communicate in any way. Instead, she used gestures much more in order to communicate. As we learned in class, what she was doing verbally was very normal at one time, but because she is now about eight years old, I could see the degree of delay due to her CP and other conditions.

Educator Responsibility Regarding Student Logs

Educators working with students need to help the students sort out their emotional reactions in doing therapy by inviting further objectivity regarding what the student therapist is able to accomplish at a beginning level of training.

PROGRESS REPORTS

Unlike weekly objective and subjective evalu- ation, progress reports are generally written mid- year and end-year or when the child in a group reaches closure in their group therapy (the word termination is also used). The progress reports, then, constitute an overall compilation of informa- tion from previous weeks. The format used can be variable.

Sample Format for Progress Reports, General

Sample formats for progress reports are vari- able, depending upon the facility and can be requested quarterly or biannually. One sample of a format for a 3–4 page progress report would include the following:

Facility Name
Music Therapy Progress Summary

Name of Client:
Date of Report:
Dates of Service:
Music Therapist :

Summary of Services:
Goals and Objectives Addressed:
Interventions:
Summary of Progress:
Recommendation:

Sample Format, Progress Note in the Schools

A typical progress note that is "graded" at a school will include a short one-two paragraph summary of progress, largely based on objective evaluation that leads to recommendations for the following quarter of the academic year. A com- mon example of 'Grading' is "A," Achieved; "P," Progressing Steadily; "I," Inconsistent Growth; "E," Experiencing Difficulty. This evaluation is based on data generated from the achievement or lack of achievement of objectives within the group music therapy session, presumably referring back to the IEP goals.

Another option is to include a note that specifi- cally states objectives to the right with progress "grading" to the left. While this is more specific reporting regarding the achievement or lack of achievement of objectives, what does it tell us about the child?

Anecdotal notes describing the interventions used, the possible patterns of behavior and recommendations would possibly supply that additional information (see author additions following the behavioral reporting).

Sample Format, Objective and Anecdotal Progress Note in the School

Case Example One (Goodman, K., 1992–1998)

Arnold is an autistic ten-year-old participating in a small group with other autistic spectrum disordered children. His clinical objectives are arranged in domains of behavioral deficits, cognitive/attention, social skills, communication, fine/gross motor skills and reading/mathematics. The focus of the music therapy sessions is to address his social skills and communication. "Grading" includes "A," achieved; "P," partially achieved (% achieved), "I," introduced, not achieved; "N," not introduced.

This is the report for the first quarter of the year with objectives related to communication.

Name: Arnold Child
Domain: Communciation
Goal: To demonstrate improved speech and language skills
Progress:
1 2 3 4 Objectives: Student will . . .
P _ _ _ Respond orally by using one-word answers; across a variety of settings and activities, on 3 out of 5 trials.
I _ _ _ Begin combining words into two-word utterances; across a variety of settings and activities; on 3 out of 5 trials
P _ _ _ Respond to yes/no questions through verbalizations and/or appropriate head movement; across a variety of setting and activities; on 3 out of 5 trials.
N _ _ _ Identify 50 objects or pictures of objects by pointing and/or verbalizations (i.e., common household items, objects in a school setting) across

a variety of settings and activities; on 3 out of 5 trials.

Key: A=Achieved; P=Partially achieved; I-Introduced, not achieved; N=Not introduced.
Anecdotal notes:

Arnold is having difficulty functioning in a group, as evidenced by his frequent wandering around the room behavior, difficulty in attending to ongoing musical experiences and lack of eye contact. He resists sitting with the group.

However, the therapist notes that while the group is singing, Arnold is observed humming to himself, frequently in a key related to the song. The recommendation is that Arnold have a trial individual music therapy session. Further, the objectives should be reviewed by the team and reevaluated for their functional value.

INDIVIDUAL VS. GROUP EVALUATION

Reports of group progress in music therapy with children are difficult to find. Hibben (1991) reports the group moving from one stage of group process to another, however. In order for this to include both objective and subjective information, the stages would have to clearly document behavioral changes expected in changing from one group to another as well as reporting inference and interpretation on the part of the therapist. This is a challenge for the music therapist.

A more typical example of a "group music therapy progress report," provided by Gladfelter (Wilson, 2002, p. 287) includes a summary of goals and activities for the group followed by a listing of class attitudes and behavior (follows directions, uses good listening skills, participates in activities, interacts appropriately with peers, works independently, accepts praise and encouragement, respect musical equipment) with the child's participation rated as excellent (E), good (G), Satisfactory (S) or needs improvement (N). Midyear and End-of year comments provide more specific commentary related to the evaluation "grades." This progress report evaluates the child based on group goals. The extent to which these goals are related to the IEP is unclear.

FUTURE RESEARCH/DOCUMENTATION

In her review of research related to clinical work with special needs children, Jellison (1975–1999) documents work completed in the years, 1975–1999. Referred to as music research in special education, the 148 studies included in the Jellison analysis report data and use descriptive or experimental research methodologies. With an average of only six articles per year, the need for more research is pronounced, particularly in inclusive school settings, the types of settings largely referred to in this book. In terms of evaluation of children in music therapy and longitudinal evaluation of the effectiveness of music therapy programs, there is little research. Both the Individual Education Plan (IEP) and the Individualized Family Service Plan (IFSP) need further utilization as tools for research. Jellison also emphasizes the need for studies related to the efficacy of mainstreamed music settings.

SUMMARY

This chapter defines and provides case examples of objective and subjective evaluation. Objectives evaluation measures behavior while subjective evaluation is described as describing therapist bias, inference, interpretation of behav-

ior and modifications in the sessions being described. Typically speaking, both will lead to necessary modification of objectives and interventions.

Resultant progress notes or reports should rely on objective reporting of progress or lack of progress with recommendations for subsequent work.

STUDY GUIDE QUESTIONS

1. Define objective evaluation.
2. What are the possible means of providing objective evaluation in a group?
3. Define subjective evaluation.
4. What are the possible means of providing subjective evaluation in a group?
5. What are the pros and cons of objective evaluation?
6. What are the pros and cons of subjective evaluation?
7. Using one of the groups you are currently working with, devise a system for objective evaluation and use it. Analyze the results.
8. Using of the groups you are currently working with, consider the elements you would like to include in subjective evaluation. After writing subjective evaluation of your group, analyze the results.

Appendix

Appendix
Music Therapy Materials

Music Therapy
Song/Instrumental/Movement Resources

Farnan, L., & Johnson, F. (1998a). *Everyone can move.* New York: Hal Leonard.

Farnan, L., & Johnson, F. (1998b). *Music is for everyone.* New York: Hal Leonard.

Levin, H., & Levin, G. (1977) *A garden of bell flowers.* Bryn Mawr, PA: Theodore Presser.

Levin, H., & Levin, G. (1981). *Learning songs.* Bryn Mawr, PA: Theodore Presser.

Levin, H., & Levin, G. (1997a) *Learning through songs.* Gilsum, NH: Barcelona.

Levin, H., & Levin, G. (1998). *Learning through music.* Gilsum, NH: Barcelona.

Levin, H., & Levin, G. (2004). *Distant bells: 12 delightful melodies from distant lands–Arranged for resonator bells and piano.* Gilsum, NH: Barcelona.

Levin, G., & Levin, H. (2005). *Let's make music.* Gilsum, NH: Barcelona.

Nordoff, P., & Robbins, C. (1962). *The first book of children's play songs.*

Nordoff, P., & Robbins, C. (1964). *The three bears: A musical adventure for an orchestra and chorus of young children, story-teller, and piano.* Bryn Mawr, PA: Theodore Presser.

Nordoff, P., & Robbins, C. (1968a). *The second book of children's play songs.* Bryn Mawr, PA: Theodore Presser.

Nordoff, P., & Robbins, C. (1968b). *Fun for four drums.* Bryn Mawr, PA: Theodore Presser.

Nordoff, P., & Robbins, C. (1969). *Pif-Paf-Poultrie.* Bryn Mawr, PA: Theodore Presser.

Nordoff, P., & Robbins, C. (1970). *The children's Christmas play: For narrator, actors, piano, percussion, instruments, and reed horns.* Bryn Mawr, PA: Theodore Presser.

Nordoff, P., & Robbins, C. (1972). *Spirituals for children to sing and play,* volumes 1 and 2. Bryn Mawr, PA: Theodore Presser.

Nordoff, P., & Robbins, C. (1976). *A message for the King:* *A story with music for percussion, piano, voices, and narrator.* Bryn Mawr, PA: Theodore Presser.

Nordoff, P., & Robbins, C. (1977). *Folk songs for children to sing and play.* Bryn Mawr, PA: Theodore Presser.

Nordoff, P. (1979). *Fanfares and dances.* Bryn Mawr, PA: Theodore Presser.

Nordoff, P., & Robbins, C. (1980a). *The third book of children's play songs.* Bryn Mawr, PA: Theodore Presser.

Nordoff, P., & Robbins, C. (1980b). *The fourth book of children's play songs.* Bryn Mawr, PA: Theodore Presser.

Nordoff, P., & Robbins, C. (1980c). *The fifth book of children's play songs.* Bryn Mawr, PA: Theodore Presser.

Ritholz, M., & Robbins, C. (Eds.) (1999). *Themes for therapy from the Nordoff-Robbins Center for Music Therapy at New York University: New songs and instrumental pieces.* New York, NY: Carl Fischer.

Ritholz, M., & Robbins, C. (Eds.) (2003). *More themes for therapy.* New York, NY: Carl Fischer.

Robbins, C. (1995). *Greetings and goodbyes: A Nordoff-Robbins Collection for classroom use.* Bryn Mawr, PA: Theodore Presser.

Suggested Classical Music
to Use in Therapy

Bach, J.S. Notebook of Anna Magdalena Bach.

Bartok, Bela. *For children,* Piano solo, volumes 1 and 11.

Copland, A. (arranged by) *Old American songs.*

Debussy, C., *Children's corner.*

Gershwin, G., *An American in Paris.*

Pachelbel, J., *Canon in D.*

Prokofieff, Serge, *Peter and the Wolf.*

Prokofieff, Serge, *Music for children, opus 65.*

Ravel, M., *Ma Mere I'oye (Mother Goose).*

Starer, R., *Sketches in color: Seven pieces for piano.* Melville, NY: MCA Music.

Schumann, *Forest scenes for piano solo, opus 82.*

Schumann, *Kinderscenen (Album for the young, op. 68* and *Scenes from childhood, op. 15).*

Miscellaneous Sheet Music Resources to Adapt for Music Therapy

Birkenshaw, L. (1977). *Music for fun, music for learning.* Toronto: Holt, Rinehart & Winston.

Birkenshaw-Fleming, L. (1989). *Come on everybody let's sing.* Toronto, Canada: Gordon V. Thompson Music.

Disney Collection, The (1993). *The Disney Collection: Best loved songs from movies, television shows, and theme parks.* New York: Hal Leonard.

Glazer, J. (1973). *Eyewinker Tom Tinker, Chin Chopper.* New York: Doubleday.

Glazer, J. (1983). *Music for ones and twos: Songs and games for the very young child.* New York, NY: Doubleday.

Henson, J. (1986). *Favorite songs from Jim Henson's Muppets.* New York: Hal Leonard.

Moss, J., & Raposo, J. (1992). *The Sesame Street songbook, Volume 2.* New York: Macmillan.

Nash, G., & Rapley, J. (1988). *Holidays and special days.* Sherman Oaks, CA: Alfred.

Palmer, H. (1981a). *Hap Palmer favorites: Songs for learning through music and movement.* Sherman Oaks, CA: Alfred.

Palmer, H. (1987). *Hap Palmer songs to enhance the movement vocabulary of young children.* Sherman Oaks, CA: Alfred.

Prebenna, D., Moss, J., & Cooney, J. G. (1992). *Sesame Street Songbook: Sixty favorite songs featuring Jim Henson's Sesame Street Muppets.* New York: Scribner.

Raffi (1983). *Baby beluga book.* Toronto, Ontario: McClelland & Stewart.

Raffi (1984). *The Raffi Singable Songbook.* Ontario, Canada, Chappell.

Raffi (1986). *The Second Raffi Songbook.* New York, NY: Crown.

Raffi (1989). *Everything Grows Songbook.* New York, NY: Crown.

Rogers, F. (1970). *Mister Rogers' Songbook.* New York, NY: Random House.

Sclesa, G., & Millang, S. (1986). *We all live together.* Milwaukee, WI: Hal Leonard.

Sharon, Lois, & Bram (1980). *Elephant jam.* San Francisco: McGraw-Hill.

Silver-Burdett (1995). *The music connection.* Morristown, NJ.

Wojcio, M. (1983). *Music in motion: 22 songs in signing exact English for children.* Los Alamitos, CA: Modern Sign Press, Inc.

nition. Miami, FL: Volkwein.

Jenkins, E. (1994). *Play your instrument and make a pretty sound.* Washington, DC: Smithsonian Folkways Recordings.

Morris, S. (1998). *Songs for speech therapy and beyond.* Boulder, CO: Belle Curve.

Orozoco, J. L. (1985). *Canto y Cuento: Latin American childrens' folklore.* Berkeley, CA: Arcoiris.

Orozoco, J. L. (1996). *DeColores.* Berkeley, CA: Arcoiris.

Palmer, H. (1969a). *Learning basic skills through music.* Freeport, NY: Educational Activities.

Palmer, H. (1969b). *Learning basic skills through music, vol. 11.* Freeport, NY: Educational Activities.

Palmer, H. (1972). *Getting to know myself.* Freeport, NY: Educational Activities.

Palmer, H. (1981b). *More baby songs* (formerly Tickley-Toddle). Freeport, NY: Educational Activities.

Palmer, H. (1994). *So big: Activity songs for little ones.* Freeport, NY: Educational Activities.

Palmer, H. (2004). *Two little sounds–Fun with phonics and numbers.* Northridge, CA: Hap-Pal Music.

Pease, T. (1983). *Wobbi-do-wop.* Amberst, WI: Tom Pease.

Pease, T. (1989). *I'm gonna reach.* Amberst, WI: Tom Pease.

Pease, T., & Stotts, S. (2003). Celebrate. Amherst, WI: Tom Pease.

Raffi (1976). *Singable songs for the very young.* Universal City, CA: Troubadour.

Raffi (1977). *More singable songs.* Universal City, CA: Troubadour.

Raffi (1980). *Baby Beluga.* Universal City, CA: Troubadour.

Raffi (1982). *Rise and shine.* Universal City, CA: Troubadour.

Raffi (1985). *One light one sun.* Universal City, CA: Troubadour.

Raffi (1987). *Everything grows. Mary wore her red dress.* Universal City, CA: Troubadour.

Raffi (1994). *Bananaphone.* Universal City, CA: Troubadour.

Sclesa, G., & Millang, S. (1983). *Greg and Steve Live Together, Vol. 1–5.* Los Angeles, CA: Youngheart.

Stewart, G. (1977a). *Beanbag activities and coordination skills.* Long Branch, NJ: Kimbo.

Stewart, G. (1977b). *Playtime parachute fun for early childhood.* Long Branch, NJ: Kimbo.

Stewart, G. (1984). *Folkdance fun and simple folk songs and dances.* Long Branch, NJ: Kimbo.

Stewart, G. (1987). *Good morning exercises for kids.* Long Branch, NJ: Kimbo.

Stewart, G. (1991). *Children of the world.* Long Branch, NJ: Kimbo.

Compact Discs

Abramson, R. (1997). *Rhythm games for perception and cog-*

Stewart, G. (1992). *Multicultural rhythm stick fun.* Long Branch, NJ: Kimbo.

Augumentative Equipment Resource

1) Enabling Devices
385 Warburton Ave
Hastings On Hudson, New York 10706
www.enablingdevices.com

Visual Aids Kit

Coleman, K., & Brunk, B. (2001). *Visual Aids Kit.* Grapevine, TX: Prelude Music Therapy.

Bibliography

Abramson, R. (1997). *Rhythm games for perception and cognition.* Miami, FL: Volkwein.

Adamek, M. S., & Darrow, A. A. (2005). *Music in special education.* Silver Spring, MD: American Music Therapy Association.

Adamany, R. (Ed.). (2006). Amusia. *Medical Dictionary of Terms.* Abstract retrieved May 1, 2006, from www.medterms.com.

Ademek, M. S., Gervin, A. P., & Shiraishi, I. M. (2000). Speech rehabilitation with brain-injured patients. In C. Furman (Ed.), *Effectiveness of music therapy procedures: Documentation of research and clinical practice* (3rd ed.). Silver Spring, MD: American Music Therapy Association.

Aigen, K. (1997). *Here we are in music: One year with an adolescent creative music therapy group.* St. Louis, MO: MMB.

Aigen, K. (1998). *Paths of development in Nordoff-Robbins music therapy.* Gilsum, NH: Barcelona.

Aigen, K., Miller, C. K., Kim, Y., Pasiali, V., Kwak, E., & Tague, D. B. (2004). Nordoff-Robbins music therapy. In A. A. Darrow (Ed.), *Introduction to approaches in music therapy* (pp. 63–77). Silver Spring, MD: American Music Therapy Association.

Alberto, P. A., & Troutman, A. C. (2006). *Applied behavior analysis for teachers* (7th ed.). Upper Saddle River, NJ: Merrill/Prentice Hall.

Alvin, J., & Warwick, A. (1992). *Music therapy for the autistic child.* New York: Oxford.

Amaducci, L., Grassi, E., & Boller, F. (2002). Maurice Ravel and right hemisphere musical creativity. *European Journal of Neurology, 9,* 75–82.

AMTA. (2006). *Effectiveness of music therapy procedures: Documentation of research and clinical practice* (3rd ed.). Silver Spring, MD: American Music Therapy Association.

AMTA. (2006). Standards of clinical practice. In A. Elkins (Ed.), *AMTA member sourcebook 2006.* Silver Spring, MD: American Music Therapy Association.

Amusia. (2006). *Merck Manual.* England: Oxford University Press.

Anshel, A., & Kipper, D. (1988). The influence of group singing on trust and cooperation. *Journal of Music Therapy, 25,* 145–155.

Apprey, Z. R., & Apprey, M. 91975). Applied music therapy: Collected papers on a technique and a point of view. London: Institute of Music Therapy & Humanistic Psychology, International University.

APPI. (1994). *DSM–IV–TR.* Washington, DC: American Psychiatric Publishing.

Arieti, S. (1955). *Creativity: Interpretation of schizophrenia.* New York: R. Brunner.

Arieti, S. (1976). *The magic synthesis.* New York: Basic Books.

Asmus, E. P., & Gilbert, J. P. (1981). A client-centered model of therapeutic intervention. *Journal of Music Therapy, 18*(1).

Axline, V. (1969). *Play therapy.* New York: Ballantine.

Ayotte, J., Peretz, I., & Hyde, K. (2002). Congenital amusia [A group study of adults with a music-specific disorder]. *Brain, 125,* 238–251.

Ayres, A. J. (1979). *Sensory integration and the child.* Los Angeles: Western Psychological Services.

Bach, J. S. *Notebook of Anna Magdalena Bach.*

Baer, D. M. (2005). Letters to a lawyer. In W. L. Heward, T. E. Heron, N. A. Neef, S. M. Peterson, D. M. Sainato, G. Cartledge, R. Hardner III, L. D. Peterson, S. B. Hersh, & J. D. Dardig (Eds.), *Focus on behavior analysis in education: Achievement, challenges, and opportunities* (pp. 3–30). Upper Saddle River, NJ: Merrill/Prentice Hall.

Bailey, J. S. (1992). Gentle teaching: Trying to win friends and influence people with euphenism, metaphor, smoke, and mirrors. *Journal of Applied Behavior Analysis, 25,* 879–883.

Bang, C. (1986). A world of sound and music. In E. Ruud (Ed.), *Music and health* (pp. 19–36). Oslo, Norway: Norsk Musikforlag.

Bartok, Bela, *For children.* Piano solo, volumes 1 and 11.

Bautista, R. E. D., & Ciampetti, M. Z. (2003). Expressive Aprosody and Amusia as a Manifestation of Right Hemisphere Seizures. *Epilepsia, 44*(3), 466–467.

Bean, K. L., & Moore, J. R. (1964). Music therapy from auditory inkblots. *Journal of Music Therapy, 1,* 143–147.

Berger, D. S. (2002). *Music therapy, sensory integration and the autistic child.* London: Jessica Kingsley, Publishers.

Bion, W. R. (1961). *Experiences in groups.* London: Tavistock.

Birkenshaw, L. (1977). *Music for fun, music for learning.* New York: Holt, Rinehart & Winston.

Birkenshaw-Fleming, L. (1989). *Come on everybody let's sing.* Toronto, Canada: Gordon V. Thompson Music.

Bitcon, C. H. (2000). *Alike and different: The clinical and educational uses of Orff-Schulwerk* (2nd ed.). Gilsum, NH: Barcelona.

Bixler, J. (1968). Music therapy practices for the child with cerebral palsy. In Gaston (Ed.), *Music in therapy* (pp. 143–150). New York: Macmillan.

Bondy, A., & Frost, L.. (2002). *A picture's worth: PECS and other visual communication strategies in autism.* Bethesda, MD: Woodbine House.

Boxill, E. (1985). *Music therapy for the developmentally disabled.* Denver, CO: Aspen.

Braswell, C., Brooks, D. M., Decuir, A., Humphrey, T., Jacobs, K. W., & Sutton, K. (1986). Development and implementation of a music/activity therapy intake assessment for psychiatric patients. Part II. Standardization procedures on data from psychiatric patients. *Journal of Music Therapy, 23,* 126–141.

Brazelton, B. (1972). *Infants and mothers.* New York: Dell.

Brazelton, B. (1974). *Toddlers and parents: A declaration of independence.* New York: Dell.

Bricker, D. D., Pretti-Frontczak, K. L., & McComas, N. R. (1998). *An activity-based approach to early intervention* (2nd ed.). Baltimore: Brookes.

Briggs, C. (1991). A model for understanding musical development. *Music Therapy, 10*(1), 1–21.

Brooks, D. (1989). Music therapy enhances treatment with adolescents. *Music Therapy Perspectives, 6,* 37–39.

Brownwell, M. D., Frego, R. J. D., Kwak, E., & Rayburn, A. M. (2004). The Kodaly approach to music therapy. In A. A. Darrow (Ed.), *Introduction to approaches in music therapy* (pp. 25–33). Silver Spring, MD: American Music Therapy Association.

Bruscia, K. (1982). Music in the assessment and treatment of echolalia. *Music Therapy, 2*(1), 25–41.

Bruscia, K. (1987). *Improvisational models for music therapy.* Springfield, IL: Charles C Thomas.

Bruscia, K. (1988). Standard for clinical assessment in the arts. *The Arts in Psychotherapy, 15,* 5.

Bruscia, K. (1989). The practical side of improvisational music therapy. *Music Therapy Perspectives, 6,* 11–16.

Bruscia, K. (1991). *Case studies in music therapy.* Gilsum, NH: Barcelona.

Bruscia, K. (2001). A qualitative approach to analyzing client improvisation. *Music Therapy Perspectives, 1,* 7–21.

Carter, E., & Oldfield, A. (2002). A music therapy group to assist clinical diagnosis. In Davies & Richards (Eds.), *Music therapy and group work: Sound company.* (pp. 149–163).

Cassity, M. C. (1985). Techniques, procedures and practices employed in the assessment of adaptive and music behaviors of trainable mentally retarded children. *Dissertation Abstracts International, 46*(10A), 2955.

Cassity, M. D., & Cassity, J. E. (1994). Psychiatric music therapy assessment and treatment in clinical training facilities with adults, adolescents, and children. *Journal of Music Therapy, 30*(1), 2–30.

Cassity, M. D., & Theobold, K. A. (1990). Domestic violence: Assessments and treatments employed by music therapists. *Journal of Music Therapy, 27*(4), 179–194.

Cassity, M. D., & Cassity, J. E. (2006). *Multi-modal music therapy* (3rd ed.). London: Jessica Kingsley, Publishers.

Cattell, R. B., & Anderson, J. C. (1953). The measurement of personality and behavior disorders by the L.P.A.T. music preference test. *Journal of Applied Psychology, 37,* 446–454.

Cattell, R. B., & Saunders, D. R. (1954). Musical preferences and personality diagnosis: A factorization of 120 themes. *Journal of Social Psychology, 39,* 3–24.

Charoonsathvathana, A. (2000). [Unpublished Evaluation Tool]. Unpublished manuscript.

Chase, K. (2004). Music therapy assessment for children with developmental disabilities. *Journal of Music Therapy.*

Clair, A., & Pasiali, V. (2004). Neurologic music therapy. In A. A. Darrow (Ed.), *Introduction to approaches in music therapy* (pp. 143–157). Silver Spring, MD: American Music Therapy Association.

Clark, C., & Chadwick, D. M. (1980). *Clinically adapted instruments for the multiply handicapped.* St. Louis, MO: West Music.

Clarkson, G. (1986). *Fairy tales: Musical dramas for children.* St. Lawrence, MO: MMB.

Codding, P.A. Music Therapy Literature and Clinical Applications for Blind and Severely Visually Impaired Persons: 1940–2000. AMTA. (2000). *Effectiveness of music therapy procedures: Documentation of research and clinical practice* (3rd ed.). Silver Spring, MD: American Music Therapy Association, pp. 159–198.

Cohen, G., & Gericke, O. (1972). Music therapy assessment: Prime requisite for determining patient objectives. *Journal of Music Therapy, 9*(4), 161–189.

Cohen, N. S. (1986). *Cohen Music Therapy Assessment Tool.* Unpublished document.

Cole, K. (2002). *The music therapy assessment handbook.* Columbus, MS: Southern Pen Publishing.

Coleman, K., & Brunk, B. (1999). *SEMTAP: Special Education Music Therapy Assessment Process.* Grapevine, TX: Prelude Music Therapy.

Coleman, K., & Brunk, B. (2001). *Visual Aids Kit.* Grapevine, TX: Prelude Music Therapy

Coleman, K. (2002). Music therapy for learners with severe disabilities in a public school setting. In B. Wilson (Ed.), *Models of music therapy interventions in school settings.* Silver Spring, MD: American Music Therapy Association.

Coleman, K., McNairn, P., & Shioleno, C. (1996). *Qick Techn Magic: Music-based literacy activities.* Solana Beach, CA: Mayer Johnson.

Colwell, C. M., Achey, C., Gillmeister, G., & Woolrich, J. (2004). The Orff approach to music therapy. In A. A. Darrow (Ed.), *Introduction to approaches in music therapy* (pp. 3–13). Silver Spring, MD: American Music Therapy Association.

Condon, W. S. (1975). Multiple response to sound in dysfunctional children. *Journal of Autism and Childhood Schizophrenia, 5,* 37–56.

Condon, W. S. (1986). Communication: Rhythm and structure. In J. R. Evans & M. Clynes (Eds.), *Rhythm in psychological, linguistic, and musical processes* (pp. 55–78). Springfield, IL: Charles C Thomas.

Condon, W. S., & Sander, L. W. (1974). Synchrony demonstrated between movements of the neonate and adult speech. *Child Development, 45,* 456–462.

Cooke, R. (1969). The use of music in play therapy. *Journal of Music Therapy, 11*(3), 66–75.

Coons, E., & Montello, L. (1998). Effects of active versus passive group music therapy on preadolescents with emotional, learning, and behavioral disorders. *Journal of Music Therapy, 35*(1), 49–56.

Cooper, J. O., Heron, T. E., & Heward, W. L. (2006). *Applied behavior analysis* (2nd ed.). Upper Saddle River, NJ: Merrill/Prentice Hall.

Copland, A. (arranged by) *Old American Songs.*

Cripe, F. (1986). Rock music as therapy for children with attention-deficit disorder. *Journal of Music Therapy, 31*(1), 31–62.

Crocker, D. (1955). Music as a projective technique. *Music Therapy, 7,* 114–119.

Crocker, D. B. (1968). In Gaston (Ed.), *Clinical experiences with emotionally disturbed children* (pp. 202–207). New York: Macmillan.

Cullen, C., & Mudford, O. C. (2005). Gentle teaching. In J. W. Jackson, J. A. Mulic & R. M. Foxx (Eds.), *Controversial therapies in developmental disabilities: Fads, fashion, and science in professional practice* (pp. 423–432). Hillsdale, NJ: Lawrence Erlbaum Associates.

Dalton, T., A., & Krout, R. E. (2005). Development of the grief process scale through music therapy song-writing with bereaved adolescents. *The Arts in Psychotherapy, 32,* 131–143.

Darrow, A. A., & Gfeller, K. (1991). A study of public school music programs mainstreaming hearing impaired students. *Journal of Music Therapy, 28,* 23–39.

Darrow, A. A. (1995). Music therapy for hearing impaired clients. In R. Wigram, R. West, & B. Saperston (Eds.), *The art and science of music therapy: A handbook.* Chur, Switzerland: Harwood Academic.

Darrow, A., Gfeller, K., Gorsuch, A., & Thomas, K. (2000). Music therapy with children who are deaf and hard of hearing. *Effectiveness of music therapy procedures: Documentation of research and clinical practice.* Silver Spring, MD: American Music Therapy Association.

Darrow, A., & Grohe, H. S. (Music Therapy for Learners Who are Deaf/Hard-of-Hearing. Wilson, B. L. (Ed.) (2002), *Models of music therapy interventions in school settings* (pp. 291–317).

Darrow, A., Colwell, C., & Kim, J. (2002). Research on mainstreaming. In B. Wilson (Ed.), *Models of music therapy interventions in school settings* (pp. 41–67).

Darrow, A. A. (Ed.). (2004). *Introduction to approaches in music therapy.* Silver Spring, MD: American Music Therapy Association.

Daugherty, S., Grisham-Brown, J., & Hemmeter, M. L. (2001). The effects of embedded skill instruction on the acquisition of target and nontarget skills in preschoolers with developmental delays. *Topics in Early Childhood Special Education, 21,* 213–221.

Davidson, L., Gardner, H., & McKernon, P. (1981). The acquisition of song: A developmental approach. *Documentary report of the Ann Arbor Symposium:* Applications of psychology to the teaching and learning of music (pp. 301–314). Reston, VA: Music Educators National Conference.

Davis, W., Gfeller, K., & Thaut, M. (1999). *An introduction to music therapy: Theory and practice* (2nd ed.). Boston: McGraw-Hill.

Debussy, C. *Children's corner.*

Disney Collection, The (1993). *The Disney Collection: Best loved songs from movies, television shows, and theme parks.* New York: Hal Leonard.

Doyle, P. K., & Ficken, R. (November, 1981). Application of a stages of therapy model to music therapy activities in adult psychiatric populations. Paper presented at the meeting of the National Association for Music Therapy. Denver, CO.

Edgerton, C. (1990). Creative group song-writing. Music

Therapy Perspectives, 18, 15–19.

Edgerton, C. L. (1994). The effect of improvisational musich therapy on the communicative behaviors of autistic children. *Journal of Music Therapy, 31,* 31–62.

Elliott, B. (1982). *Guide to the selection of musical instruments with respect to physical ability and disability.* St. Lawrence, MO: MMB.

Farnan, L., & Johnson, F. (1998a). *Everyone can move.* New York: Hal Leonard.

Farnan, L., & Johnson, F. (1998b). *Music is for everyone.* New York: Hal Leonard.

Farnan, L. (2002). Music therapy for learners with profound disabilities in a residential setting. In B. Wilson (Ed.), *Models of music therapy interventions in school settings.* Silver Spring, MD: American Music Therapy Association.

Farnsworth, P. R. (1969). *The Social Psychology of Music.* Ames, IA: Iowa State University Press.

Ficken, T. (1976). The use of songwriting in a psychiatric setting. *Journal of Music Therapy, 13*(4), 163–171.

Ford, S. (1984). Music therapy for Cerebral Palsied. *Music Therapy Perspectives, 1*(3), 8–13.

Fox, L., & Hanline, M. F. (1993). A preliminary evaluation of learning within developmentally appropriate early childhood settings. *Topics in Early Childhood Special Education, 13,* 308–327.

Foxton, J. M., Dean, J. L., Gee, R., Peretz, I., & Griffiths, T. D. (2004). Characterization of deficits in pitch perception underlying 'tone deafness.' *Brain, 127,* 801–810.

Freed, B. (1987). Songwriting for the chemically dependent. *Music Therapy Perspectives, 4,* 13–18.

Frego, R. J. D., Liston, R. E., Harna, M., & Gillmeister, G. (2004). The Dalcroze approach to music therapy. In A. A. Darrow (Ed.), *Introduction to approaches in music therapy* (pp. 15–24). Silver Spring, MD: American Music Therapy Association.

Freud, S. (1932). *New introductory lectures on psychoanalysis* (standard ed., Vol. 22, pp. 3–157). London: Hogarth Press.

Fridman, R. (1973). The first cry of the newborn: Basis for the child's future musical development. *Journal of Research in Music Education, 21,* 264–269.

Friedlander, L. H. (1994). Group music psychotherapy in an inpatient psychiatric setting for children: A developmental approach. *Music Therapy Perspectives, 12*(2), 92–97.

Froehlich, M. A. (1996). Orff-Schulwerk music therapy in crisis intervention with hospitalized children. In M. A. Froelich (Ed.), *Music therapy with hospitalized children* (pp. 25–36). NJ: Jeffery Books.

Furuno, S., O'Reilly, K., Hosaka, C., Inatsuka, T., Allman, T., & Zeisloft, B. (2005). *Hawaii Early Learning Profile, HELP–Activity Guide.* Palo Alto, CA: Vort.

Gallagher, L. M., & Steele, A. L. (2002). Music therapy with offenders in a substance abuse/mental illness treatment program. *Music Therapy Perspectives, 20*(2), 117–122.

Galloway, H. (1975). A comprehensive bibliography of musical studies referential to communication development, processing disorders and remediation. Journal of Music Therapy, 12, 164–197.

Gardstrom, S. (2002). Music therapy for juvenille offenders in a residential treatment setting. In B. Wilson (Ed.), *Models of music therapy interventions in school settings.* Silver Spring, MD: American Music Therapy Association.

Garland, J. A., Jones, E., & Kolodney, R. L. (1976). A model for stages of development in social work groups. In S. Bernstein (Ed.), *Explorations in group work: Essays in theory and practice* (pp. 17–71). Boston: Charles River Books.

Gaston, E. T. (Ed.). *Music in therapy.* New York: Macmillan.

Gershwin, G. *An American in Paris.*

Gewirtz, H. (1964). Music therapy as a form of supportive psychotherapy with children. *Journal of Music Therapy, 1*(2), 61–65.

Gfeller, K. E. (1982). The use of melodic-rhythmic mnemonics with learning disabled and normal students as an aid to retention (Doctoral dissertation, Michigan State University, 1982). University Microfilms International, No. 8303786.

Gfeller, K. E. (1983). Musical mnemonics as an aid to retention with normal and learning disabled students. *Journal of Music Therapy, XX* (4) 179–189.

Gfeller, K. E. (1984). Prominent theories in learning disability and implications for music therapy methodology. *Music Therapy Perspectives, 2,* 9–13.

Gfeller, K. E. (1987). Songwriting as a tool for reading and language remediation. *Music Therapy, 6,* 23–38.

Gfeller, K. E. (1990). A cognitive-linguistic approach to language development for preschool children with hearing impairments. *Music Therapy Perspectives, 8,* 47–51.

Ghetti, C. M. (2002). Comparison of the effectiveness of three music therapy conditions to modulate behavior states in students with profound disabilities: A pilot study. *Music Therapy Perspectives, 20,* 20–30.

Gibbons, A. C. (1983). Rhythm responses in emotionally disturbed children with differing needs for external structure. *Music Therapy, 3*(1), 94–102.

Gilbert, J. (1980). An assessment of motoric motor skill development in young children. *Journal of Music Therapy, 29,* 18–39.

Ginsburg, H., & Opper, S. (1969). *Piaget's theory of intellectual development: An introduction.* Englewood Cliffs, NJ: Prentice-Hall.

Gladfelter, N. D. (2002). Music therapy for learners with learning disabilities in a private day school. In B. Wilson (Ed.), *Models of music therapy interventions in school settings.* Silver Spring, MD: American Music Therapy Association.

Glazer, T. (Ed.). (1964). *Tom Glazer's treasury of songs for children.* New York: Doubleday.

Glazer, T. (1973). *Eyewinker Tom Tinker, Chin Chopper.* New York: Doubleday.

Glazer, T. (1983). *Music for ones and twos: Songs and games for the very young child.* New York: Doubleday.

Goldstein, H. (2002). Communication intervention for children with autism: A review of treatment efficacy. *Journal of Autism and Developmental Disabilities, 32,* 373–396.

Goldstein, S. L. (1990). A songwriting assessment for hopelessness in depressed adolescents: A review of the literature and a pilot study. *Arts in Psychotherapy, 17,* 117–124.

Goodman, K. (1977). Unpublished case notes, Brooklyn School for Special Children, Brooklyn, NY.

Goodman, K. (1981). Music Therapy. Arieti, S. (Ed.), *The American Handbook of Psychiatry- New Advances and New Directions,* Vol VII. New York: Basic Books, pp. 564–585.

Goodman, K. (1981–1984). Unpublished case notes, New York Hospital–Cornell Medical Center, White Plains, NY.

Goodman, K. (1982). Unpublished case notes, Creative Arts Rehabilitation Center, New York, NY.

Goodman, K. (1982–1984). Unpublished case notes. Parent-Infant Program. Montclair State University.

Goodman, K. (1983). *Musical development and affective development in infants and toddlers.* Separately Budgeted Research Grant, Montclair State University.

Goodman, K. (1985). *Musical development and affective development in infants and toddlers, phase two.* Separately Budgeted Research Grant, Montclair State University.

Goodman, K. (1986–1992). Unpublished case notes, Private Practice.

Goodman, K. (1989). Music therapy assessment with emotionally disturbed children. *The Arts in Psychotherapy, 16*(3), 179–192.

Goodman, K. (1992–1998). Unpublished case notes, Communication Disorders Demonstration Program, Montclair, NJ.

Goodman, K. (1996). *Greenspan methods applied to individual music therapy for developmentally delayed/emotionally disturbed children.* Separately Budgeted Research Grant, Montclair State University.

Goodman, K. (1996–2002). Unpublished case notes, Regional Day School, Morristown, NJ.

Goodman, K. (1997). *Greenspan methodology applied to individual and group music therapy for autistic spectrum disorder preschoolers, phase two.* Separately Budgeted Research Grant, Montclair State University.

Goodman, K., & Chadwick, D. (1999). *Music Therapy on the I.E.P.* Paper presented at the 9th World Congress, Washington, DC, November, 1999.

Goodman, K. (2002). *Music therapy and sensory integration.* Paper presented at the Tenth World Congress, July, 2002, Oxford, U.K.

Goodman, K. (2002). *Core considerations in forming the music therapy group.* Paper presented at the Annual Meeting of the American Music Therapy Association: November, 2002, Atlanta, GA.

Goodman, K. (2005). *Music Therapy on the Individual Education Plan,* Certification Board for Music Therapy Paper/Workshop, MidAtlantic Regional Conference, Garden City, New York, April 2005.

Goodman, K. (2005). *Theory to practice: The link in undergraduate clinical supervision.* Paper presented at the Eleventh World Congress, July, 2005, Brisbane, AU.

Gordman, E. (1979). *Primary measures of music audiation.* Chicago, IL: GIA Publications.

Gordon, E. (1984). *Instrument preference test.* Chicago, IL: GIA Publications.

Graham, R. (1968). Music therapy for the moderately retarded. In T. Gaston (Ed.), *Music in therapy* (pp. 78–85). New York: MacMillan.

Grant, R. (1989). Music therapy guidelines for developmentally disabled children. *Music Therapy Perspectives, 6,* 18–22.

Green, G. (2001). Behavior analytic instruction for learners with autism. *Advances in stimulus control technology: Focus on Autism and Other Developmentally Disabilities, 16,* 72–85.

Greenspan, S. (1981). *The clinical interview of the child.* New York: McGraw-Hill.

Greenspan, S. (1992). *Infancy and early childhood: The practice of clinical assessment and intervention with emotional and developmental challenges.* Madison, CT: International Universities Press.

Greenspan, S. (1995). *The challenging child: Understanding, raising and enjoying the five 'difficult' types of children.* Reading, MA: Addison-Wesley.

Greenspan, S., & Wieder, S. (1997). Developmental patterns and outcomes in infants and children with autistic spectrum diagnoses. *Journal of Developmental and Learning Disorder, 1,* 87–141.

Greenspan, S., & Wieder, S. (1998). *The child with special needs: Encouraging intellectual and emotional growth.* Reading, MA: Addison-Wesley.

Griggs-Drane, E., & Wheeler, J. (1997). The use of functional assessment procedures and individualized schedules in the treatment of autism: Recommendations for the music therapist. *Music Therapy Perspectives, 2,* 87–93.

Grinnel, B. (1980). The developmental therapeutic process: A new theory of therapeutic intervention (Doctoral Thesis, Bryn Mawr College, PA). Available from University Microfilms.

Gunsberg, A. (1991). A method for conducting improvised musical play with children both with and without developmental delay in preschool classrooms. *Music Therapy Perspectives.*

Haines, J. (1989). The effects of music therapy on self-esteem of emotionally-disturbed adolescents. *Music Therapy, 8*(1), 78–91.

Hanser, S. (1974). Group-contingent music listening with emotionally disturbed boys. *Journal of Music Therapy, 11,* 220–225.

Hanser, S. (1999). *The new music therapist's handbook.* Boston: Berklee.

Harding, C., & Ballard, K. D. (1982). The effectiveness of music as a stimulus and as a contingent reward in promoting the spontaneous speech of three physically handicapped preschoolers. *Journal of Music Therapy, 19,* 86–101.

Heal, & Wigram. (1993). *Music therapy in health and education.* London: Jessica Kingsley, Publishers.

Heflin, L. J., & Simpson, R. (2002). Understanding intervention controversies. In B. Scheuermann & J. Webber (Eds.), *Autism: Teaching does make a difference* (pp. 248–277). Belmont, CA: Wadsworth.

Heimlich, E. P. (1975). An auditory-motor percussion test for differential diagnosis of children with communication difficulties. *Perceptual and Motor Skills, 40,* 839–845.

Heller, K. W., Alberto, P. A., Forney, P. E., & Schwartzman, M. N. (1996). *Understanding physical, sensory and health impairment.* Pacific Grove, CA: Brooks.

Henderson, S. M. (1983). Effects of a music therapy program upon awareness of mood in music, group cohesion, and self-esteem among hospitalized adolescent patients. *Journal of Music Therapy, 20*(1), 14–20.

Henson, J. (1986). *Favorite songs from Jim Henson's Muppets.* New York: Hal Leonard.

Herman, F. (1968). Music therapy for children hospitalized with muscluar dystrophy. In Gaston (Ed.), *Music in therapy* (pp. 152–156). New York: Macmillan.

Herman, F., & Smith, J. (1988). *Accentuate the positive: Expressive arts for children with disabilities.* Toronto,

Canada: Jimani Publications.

Heward, W. L. (2003). *Exceptional children: An introduction to special education* (7th ed.). Upper Saddle River, NJ: Prentice-Hall.

Hibben, J. (1991). Group music therapy with a classroom of 6–8-year-old hyperactive learning disabled children. In K. Bruscia (Ed.), *Case studies in music therapy.* Gilsum, NH: Barcelona.

Hibben, J. K. (1984). Movement as musical expression in a music therapy setting. *Music Therapy, 4,* 91–97.

Hibben, J. K. (1991). Identifying dimensions of music therapy activities appropriate for children at different stages of group development. *The Arts in Psychotherapy, 18,* 301–310.

Hilliard, R. (2001). The effects of music therapy-based bereavement groups on mood and behavior of grieving children: A pilot study. *Journal of Music Therapy, 38*(4), 291–306.

Hollander, F., & Juhrs, P. (1974). Orff-Schulwerk, and effective treatment tool with autistic children. *Journal of Music Therapy, 11,* 1–12.

Horner, R. H., Carr, E. G., Strain, P. S., Todd, A. W., & Reed, H. K. (2002). Problem behavior interventions for young children with autism: A research synthesis. *Journal of Autism and Developmental Disabilities, 32,* 423–441.

Howery, B. I. (1968). Music therapy for the severely retarded. In T. Gaston (Ed.), *Music in therapy* (pp. 56–65). New York: Macmillan.

Hughes, J., Rice, B., DeBedout, J. K., & Hightower, L. (2002). Music therapy for learners in comprehensive public school systems: Three district-wide models. In B. Wilson (Ed.), *Models of music therapy interventions in school settings* (pp. 319–368). Silver Spring, MD: American Music Therapy Association.

Hussey, D., Laing, S., & Layman, D. (2002). Music therapy assessment for severely   disabled children: A pilot study. *Journal of Music Therapy, 39*(3), 167–184.

Hyde, K. L., & Peretz, I. (2004). Brains that are out of tune but in time. *Psychological Science, 15*(5), 356–360.

Isenberg-Grzeda, C. (1988). Music therapy assessment: A reflection of professional   identity. Journal of Music Therapy, 23(3), 166–173.

Jellison, J. (1983). Functional value as criterion for selection and prioritization of nonmusic and music education objectives in music therapy. *Music Therapy Perspectives, 1*(2), 17–22.

Jellison, J. A., Brooks, B. H., & Huck, A. M. (1984). Structuring small groups and music reinforcement to facilitate positive interactions and acceptance of severely handicapped students in regular music classroom. *Journal of Research in Music Education, 32,* 243–263.

Jellison, J. A. A Content Analysis of Music Research with Disabled Children and Youth (1975–1999): Applications in Special Education. AMTA. (2000). *Effectiveness of music therapy procedures: Documentation of research and clinical practice* (3rd ed.). Silver Spring, MD: American Music Therapy Association, pp. 199–264.

Jenkins, E. (1994). *Play your instruments and make a pretty sound.* Washington, DC: Smithsonian Folkways Recordings.

Johnson, F. L. (2002). Models of service delivery and their relation to the IEP. In B. Wilson (Ed.), *Models of music therapy interventions in school settings* (pp. 83–107).

Johnson, R. (1985). *The picture communication symbols: Book II.* Solana Beach, CA: Mayer Johnson.

Jones, R. E. (1986). Assessing developmental levels of mentally retarded students with the musical-perception assessment of cognitive ability. *Journal of Music Therapy, 23*(3), 166–173.

Joseph, M. R. (1984). Sensory integration: A theory for therapy and research. *Journal of Music Therapy, 21*(1), 79–88.

Joseph, M. R., & Freed, B. S. (1989). A sequential model for developing group cohesion in music therapy. *Music Therapy Perspectives, 7,* 28–34.

Josepha, Sister, M. (1968). Music therapy for the physically disabled. In T. Gaston (Ed.), *Music in therapy.* New York: Macmillan.

Jourdain, R. (1998). *Music, the brain, and ecstasy* (pp. 286–293). New York: Bard Press.

Kangas, K. A., & Lloyd, L. I. (2002). Augmentative and alternative communication. In G. H. Shames & N. B. Anderson (Eds.), *Human communication disorders: An introduction* (6th ed., pp. 543–593). Boston: Allyn & Bacon.

Kaplan, P. R. (1977). A criterion-referenced comparison of rhythmic responsiveness in normal and educable mentally retarded children (mental ages 6–8) (Doctoral dissertation, University of Michigan, 1977). *Dissertation Abstracts International, 38*(6A), 3354–3355.

Kegan, R. (1982). *The evolving self.* Cambridge: Harvard University Press.

Kestenberg, J. S. (1965). Role of movement patterns in development. *Psychological Quarterly, 34,* 1–36.

Kirchner-Bockholt, M. (1977). *Fundamental principles of curative eurythmy.* London: Rudolf Steiner Press.

Kirsten, I. (1981). *The Oakland picture dictionary.* Wauconda, IL: Johnson.

Klein, M. (1964). *Love Hate and Reparation.* New York: I.E. Norton & Co.

Knak, D., & Grogan, K. A children's group: An explo-ration of the framework necessary for therapeutic work. Chapter 13. In A. Davies & Richard E. (Eds.) (2002), *Music therapy and groupwork.* London: Jessica Kingsley Press.

Koegel, L. K., Koegel, J. L., Harrower, J. K., & Carter, C. M. (1999). Pivotal response intervention I: Overview of approach. *Journal of the Association of Persons with Severe Handicaps, 24,* 174–185.

Kohler, F. W., Anthony, L. J., Steighner, S. A., & Hoyson, M. (1998). Teaching social interaction skills in the integrated preschool: An examination of naturalistic tactics. *Topics in Early Childhood Special Education, 21,* 93–103.

Kohler, F. W., Strain, P. S., Hoyson, M., & Jamieson, B. (1997). Merging naturalistic teaching and peer-based strategies to address the IEP objectives of preschoolers with autism: An examination of structural and behavior outcomes. *Focus on Autism and Other Developmental Disablities, 12,* 196–206.

Kozak, Y. (1968). Music therapy for orthopedic patients in a rehabilitation setting. In Gaston (Ed.), *Music in therapy* (pp. 166–171). New York: Macmillan.

Kranowitz, C. (1999). *The out-of-sync child.* Los Angeles: Western Psychological Services.

Lathom, W. (1968). The use of music therapy with retarded patients. In Gaston (Ed.), *Music in therapy* (pp. 66–77). New York: Macmillan.

Lathom-Radocy, W. (2002). *Pediatric music therapy.* Springfield, IL: Charles C Thomas.

Layman, D., Hussey, D., & Laing, S. (2002). Music therapy assessment for severely emotionally disturbed children: A pilot study. *Journal of Music Therapy, 39*(3).

Levin, H., & Levin, G. (1977). *A garden of bell flowers.* Bryn Mawr, PA: Theodore Presser.

Levin, H., & Levin, G. (1981). *Learning songs.* Bryn Mawr, PA: Theodore Presser.

Levin, H., & Levin, G. (1997a). *Learning through music.* Gilsum, NH: Barcelona.

Levin, H., & Levin, G. (1997b). *Learning through song.* Gilsum, NH: Barcelona.

Levin, H., & Levin, G. (2004). *Distant bells: 12 delightful melodies from distant lands arranged for resonator bells and piano.* Gilsum, NH: Barcelona.

Levin, H., & Levin, G. (2005). *Let's make music.* Gilsum, NH: Barcelona.

Libertore, A. M., & Layman, D. L. (1999). *The Cleveland music therapy assessment of infants and toddlers: A practical guide to assessment and developing intervention strategies.* Cleveland, OH: The Cleveland Music School Settlement.

Linder, T. (1990). *Transdiciplinary play-based assessment: A functional approach for working with young children.* Baltimore: Paul H. Brankes.

Loewey, J. (2000). Music psychotherapy assessment. *Music Therapy Perspectives, 1,* 47–58.

Loewey, J. (Ed.). (2000). *Music therapy in the NICU.* New York: Satchnote.

Losardo, A., & Bricker, D. D. (1994). Activity-based intervention and direct instruction: A comparison study. *American Journal on Mental Retardation, 98,* 744–765.

Luce, D. W. (2001). Cognitive therapy and music therapy. *Music Therapy Perspectives, 19*(2), 96–104.

Macy, L. (Ed.). (2006). Neuropsychology. *Grove Music Online.* Retrieved April 28, 2006, from www.grove-music.com.

Madsen, C. K. (1979). The effects of music subject matter as reinforcement for correct mathematics. *Bulletin of the Council for Research in Music Education, 59,* 54–58.

Madsen, C. K. (1981). *A behavioral guide for the mentally retarded.* Washington, DC: National Association for Music Therapy.

Madsen, C. K., & Darrow, A. A. (1989). The relationship between music aptitude and sound conceptualization of the visually impaired. *Journal of Music Therapy, 26,* 71–78.

Madsen, C. K., & Madson, C. H. (1998). *Teaching discipline: A positive approach for educational development* (4th ed.). Raleigh, NC: Contemporary.

Mahler, M. S., Pine, F., & Bergman, A. (1975). *The psychological birth of the human infant.* New York: Basic Books, Inc.

Mark, A. (1988). Metaphoric lyrics as a bridge to the adolescent's world. *Adolescence, 23*(90), 313–323.

Mayer-Johnson, R. (1986). *The picture communication symbols: Book I.* Solana Beach, CA: Mayer Johnson.

McConnell, S. R. (2002). Interventions to facilitate social interactions for young children with autism: Review of available research and recommendations for education intervention and future research. *Journal of Autism and Developmental Disabilities, 32,* 351–372.

McDonald, M. (1973). Transitional tunes and musical development. *The Psychoanalytic Study of the Child, 25,* 503–520.

McFerran-Skewes, K. (2000). From the mouth of babes: The response of six younger, bereaved teenagers to the experience of psychodynamic group music therapy. *Austrailian Journal of Music Therapy, 11,* 3–22.

McGee, G. G., & Menolascino, F. J. (1991). *Beyond gentle teaching: A nonaversive approach to helping those in need.* New York: Plenum.

McGee, G. G. (1992). Gentle teaching's assumptions and paradigm. *Journal of Applied Behavior Analysis, 25,* 869–872.

McGee, G. G., Morrier, M. J., & Daly, T. (1999). An incidental teaching approach to early intervention for toddlers with autism. *Journal of the Association for the Severely Handicapped, 24,* 133–146.

Michel, D. (1968). Music therapy in speech habilitation of cleft-palate children. In E. T. Gaston (Ed.), *Music in therapy* (pp. 162–166). New York: Macmillan.

Michel, D., & Rohrbacher, M. (Eds.). (1982). *Music therapy for handicapped children assessment.* Washington, DC: National Association for Music Therapy.

Michel, D., & Pinson, J. (2005). *Music therapy in principle and practice.* Springfield, IL: Charles C Thomas.

Migliore, M. J. (1991). The Hamilton rating scale for depression and rhythmic competency: A correlational study. *Journal of Music Therapy, 28*(4), 211–221.

Montgomery, C. (2002). Role of dynamic therapy in psychiatry. *Advances in Psychiatric Treatment, 8,* 34–41.

Moog, H. (1976). *The musical experience of the preschool child.* London: Schott.

Moog, H. (1976). The development of musical experience in children of preschool age. *Psychology of Music, 4*(2), 38–45.

Moorhead, G. E., & Pond, D. (1978). *Music of young children.* Santa Barbara, CA: Pillsbury Foundation for Advancement of Music.

Morgenstern, A. M. (1982). Group Therapy: A timely strategy for music therapists. *Music Therapy Perspectives, 1,* 16–20.

Morris, S. (1998). *Songs for speech therapy and beyond.* Boulder, CO: Belle Curve.

Moss, J., & Raposo, J. (1992). *The Sesame Street songbook,* Vol. 2. New York: Macmillan.

Nash, G. (1974). *Creative approaches to child development with music, language and movement.* New York: Alfred.

Nash, G. (1988). *Holidays and special days: A sourcebook of songs, rhymes, and movement for each month of the school year.* New York: Alfred.

Nelson, D., Anderson, V., & Gonzales, A. (1984). Music activities as therapy for children with autism and other pervasive developmental disorders. *Journal of Music Therapy, 21*(3), 100–116.

New Jersey State Department of Education. (2000). *Core curriculum content standards for students with severe disabilities.* Trenton, NJ: NJ State Department of Education.

Nicholls, T. (2002). Could I play a different role? Group music therapy with severely learning disabled adolescents. In A. Davies & E. Richards (Eds.), *Music therapy and group work: Sound company.* London: Jessica Kingsley, Publishers.

Nordoff, P., & Robbins, C. (1962). *The first book of children's play songs.* Bryn Mawr, PA: Theodore Presser.

Nordoff, P., & Robbins, C. (1964). *The three bears: A musi-*

cal adventure for an orchestra and chorus of young children. *Storyteller and piano.* Bryn Mawr, PA: Theodore Presser.

Nordoff, P. & Robbins, C. (1964). *The story of Artaban, the other wise man.* Bryn Mawr, PA: Theodore Presser.

Nordoff, P., & Robbins, C. (1968a). *The second book of children's playsongs.* Bryn Mawr, PA: Theodore Presser.

Nordoff, P., & Robbins, C. (1968b). *Fun for four drums.* Bryn Mawr, PA: Theodore Presser.

Nordoff, P., & Robbins, C. (1968). Improvised music as therapy for autistic children. In E. T. Gaston (Ed.), *Music in therapy* (pp. 191–193). New York: Macmillan.

Nordoff, P., & Robbins, C. (1969). *Pif-paf-poultrie.* Bryn Mawr, PA: Theodore Presser.

Nordoff, P., & Robbins, C. (1970). *The children's Christmas play: For narrator, actors, piano, percussion instruments, and reed horns.* Bryn Mawr, PA: Theodore Presser.

Nordoff, P., & Robbins, C. (1971). *Therapy in music for handicapped children.* New York: St. Martins Press.

Nordoff, P. (1972). *Spirituals for children to sing and play, Vol. I and II.* Bryn Mawr, PA: Theodore Presser.

Nordoff, P., & Robbins, C. (1976). *A message for the king: A story with music for percussion, piano, voices, and narrator.* Bryn Mawr, PA: Theodore Presser.

Nordoff, P., & Robbins, C. (1977). *Creative music therapy: Individualized treatment for the handicapped child.* New York: John Day.

Nordoff, P. (1977). *Folk songs for children to sing and play.* Bryn Mawr, PA: Theodore Presser.

Nordoff, P. (1979). *Fanfares and dances.* Bryn Mawr, PA: Theodore Presser.

Nordoff, P., & Robbins, C. (1980a). *The third book of children's play songs.* Bryn Mawr, PA: Theodore Presser.

Nordoff, P., & Robbins, C. (1980b). *The fourth book of children's play songs.* Bryn Mawr, PA: Theodore Presser.

Nordoff, P., & Robbins, C. (1980c). *The fifth book of children's play songs.* Bryn Mawr, PA: Theodore Presser.

Nordoff, P. (1981). *My Mother Goose: Songs for children to sing and play.* Bryn Mawr, PA: Theodore Presser.

Nordoff, P., & Robbins, C. (1983). *Music therapy in special education.* St. Louis, MO: MMB Music. (Original work published 1973.)

Nordoff, P., & Robbins, C. (2007). *Creative music therapy: A guide to fostering clinical musicianship.* Gilsum, NH: Barcelona.

Noy, P. (1968). The development of musical ability. *Psychoanalytic Study of the Child, 23.*

Oldfield, A. (2006). *Interactive music therapy: A positive approach.* London: Jessica Kingsley, Publishers.

Orff, G. (1980). *The Orff music therapy: Active furthering of the development of the child.* London: Schott.

Orozoco, Jose-Luis (1985). *Canto y Cuento: Latin American childrens' folklore.* Berkeley, CA: Arcoiris.

Orozoco, Jose-Luis (1996). *DeColores.* Berkeley, CA: Arcoiris.

Ostwald, P. (2002). The music lesson. In E. T. Gaston (Ed.), *Music in therapy* (pp. 317–325). New York: Macmillan.

Ostwald, P. F. (1973). Musical behavior in early childhood. *Development of Medical and Child Neurology, 15,* 367–375.

Pachelbel, J. *Canon in D.*

Palmer, H. (1969a). *Learning basic skills through music.* Freeport, NY: Educational Activities.

Palmer, H. (1969b). *Learning basic skills through music, vol. II.* Freeport, NY: Educational Activities.

Palmer, H. (1972). *Getting to know myself.* Freeport, NY: Educational Activities.

Palmer, H. (1981a). *Hap Palmer favorites: Songs for learning through music and movement.* Sherman Oaks, CA: Alfred.

Palmer, H. (1981b). *More baby songs (formerly Tickley-Toddle).* Freeport, NY: Educational Activities.

Palmer, H. (1987). *Hap Palmer songs to enhance the movement vocabulary of young children.* Sherman Oaks, CA: Alfred.

Palmer, H. (1994). *So big: Activity songs for little ones.* Freeport, NY: Educational Activities.

Palmer, H. (2004). *Two little sounds—Fun with phonics and numbers.* Northridge, CA: Hap-Pal Music.

Papousek, M., & Papousek, H. (1981). Musical elements in the infant's vocalization: Their significance for communication, cognition and creativity. In L. P. Lippsett (Ed.), *Advances in infancy research* (L, pp. 164–217). Norwood, NJ: Ablex.

Parette, H. P. (1998). Assistive technology effective practices for students with mental retardation and developmental disabilities. In A. Hilton & R. Ringlaben (Eds.), *Best and promising practices in developmental disabilities* (pp. 205–224). Austin, TX: PRO-ED.

Pasiali, V., De L'Etoile, S., & Tandy, K. (2004). Kindermusik and Music Therapy. In A. A. Darrow (Ed.), *Introduction to approaches in music therapy,* Chapter 4. Silver Spring, MD: American Music Therapy Association.

Pavlicevic, M. (2003). *Groups in music: Strategies from music therapy.* London: Jessica Kingsley Publishers.

Pearce, J. M. S. (2005). Selected Observations on Amusia. *European Neurology, 54,* 145–148.

Pease, T. (1983). *Wobbi-do-wop.* Amberst, WI: Tom Pease.

Pease, T. (1989). *I'm gonna reach.* Amberst, WI: Tom Pease.

Pease T., & Stotts, S. (2003). *Celebrate.* Amherst, WI:

Tom Pease.

Peretz, I., Champod, A. S., & Hyde, K. (2003). Varieties of musical disorders. *The Montreal Battery of Evaluation of Amusia, 7,* 58–75.

Perilli, G. G. (1995). Subjective tempo in adults with and without psychiatric disorders. *Music Therapy Perspectives, 2,* 104–109.

Piaget, J. (1926). *Judgment and reasoning in the child.* New York: Harcourt, Brace & World, Inc.

Piaget, J. (1929). *The child's conception of the world.* New York: Harcourt, Brace & World, Inc.

Piaget, J. (1951). *Play, dreams,and imitation in childhood.* New York: W.W. Norton & Company.

Piaget, J. (1952). *The child's conception of number.* London: Routledge & Kegan.

Piaget, J. (1954). *The construction of reality in the child.* New York: Basic Books Inc.

Piaget, J. (1964). *The early growth of logic in the child.* London: Routledge & Kegan.

Piccirilli, M., Sciarma, T., & Luzzi, S. (2000). Modularity of music [Evidence from a case of pure amusia]. *Journal of Neurology, Neurosurgery, and Psychiatry, 69*(4), 541–545.

Pike, K. L. (1967). Grammar as wave. In E. J. Blansitt, Jr. (Ed.), *Report of the 18th Annual Round Table Meeting on Linguistics and Language Studies, 1–14.* Monograph Series on Lanugages and Linguistics, 20. Washington, DC: Georgetown University Press.

Plach, T. (1980). *The creative use of music in group therapy.* Springfield, IL: Charles C Thomas.

Prebenna, D., Moss, J., & Cooney, J. G. (1992). *Sesame Street songbook: Sixty favorite songs featuring Jim Henson's Sesame Street Muppets.* New York: Scriber.

Presti, G. M. (1984). A levels system approach to music therapy with severely behaviorally handicapped children in the public school system. *Journal of Music Therapy, 2*(3), 117–125.

Pretti-Frontczak, K., & Bricker, D. (2001). Use of the embedding strategy during daily activities by early childhood education and early childhood special education teachers. *Infant and Toddler Intervention: The Transdisciplinary Journal, 11*(2), 29–46.

Priestley, M. 91975). *Music therapy in action.* London: Constable.

Prokofieff, Serge. *Music for Children, opus 65.*

Prokofieff, Serge. *Peter and the Wolf.*

Purvis, J., & Samet, S. (1976). *Music in developmental therapy.* Baltimore: University Park Press.

Radocy, R. E., & Boyle, J. D. (2003). *Psychological foundations of musical behavior* (pp. 411–413). Springfield, IL: Charles C Thomas.

Raffi (1976). *Singable songs for the very young.* Universal City, CA: Troubadour.

Raffi (1977). *More singable songs.* Universal City, CA: Troubadour.

Raffi (1980). *Baby beluga.* Universal City, CA: Troubadour.

Raffi (1982). *Rise and shine.* Universal City, CA: Troubadour.

Raffi (1983). *Baby beluga book.* Toronto, Ontario: McClelland and Stewart.

Raffi (1984). *The Raffi singable songbook.* Ontario, Canada: Chappell.

Raffi (1985). *One light one sun.* Universal City, CA: Troubadour.

Raffi (1986). *The second Raffi songbook.* New York: Crown.

Raffi (1987). *Everything grows (Mary wore her red dress).* Universal City, CA: Troubadour.

Raffi (1989). *Everything grows songbook.* New York: Crown.

Raffi (1994). *Bananaphone.* Universal City, CA: Troubadour.

Ravel, M. *Ma Mere l'oye (Mother Goose).*

Reed, K. (2002). Music therapy treatment groups for mentally disordered offenders (MDO) in a state hospital setting. *Music Therapy Perspectives, 20*(2), 98–104.

Reid, D. K., & Hresko, W. P. (1981). *A cognitive approach to learning disabilities.* New York: McGraw-Hill.

Revesz, G. (1954). *Introduction to the psychology of music.* Norman, OK: University of Oklahoma Press.

Revesz, G. (2001). *Introduction to the psychology of music.* Mineola, NY: Dover.

Rickard-Lauri, R., Groeschel, H., Robbins, C. M., Robbins, C. E., Ritholz, M., & Turry, A. (1997). *Snow White: A guide to child-centered musical theater.* Gilsum, NH: Barcelona.

Rider, M. S. (1981). The assessment of cognitive functioning level through musical perception. *Journal of Music Therapy, 18*(3), 110–119.

Ritholz, M., & Robbins, C. (Eds.). (1999). *Themes for therapy from the Nordoff-Robbins Center for Music Therapy at New York University: New songs and instrumental pieces.* New York: Carl Fischer.

Ritholz, M., & Robbins, C. (Eds.). (2003). *More themes for therapy.* New York: Carl Fischer.

Robb, S. (1996). Techniques in song writing: Restoring emotional and physical well-being in adolescents who have been traumatically injured. *Music Therapy Perspectives, 14*(1), 30–37.

Robb, S. L. (2000). The effect of therapeutic music interventions on the behavior of hospitalized children in isolation: Developing a contextual support model of music therapy. *Journal of Music Therapy, 27,* 118–146.

Robbins, A. (1980). *Expressive therapy: A creative arts approach to depth oriented treatment.* New York: Human

Sciences Press.

Robbins, C. E., & Robbins, C. M. (1980). *Music for the hearing impaired: A resource manual and curriculum guide.* St. Louis: MMB Music.

Robbins, C. (1995). *Greetings and good-byes: A Nordoff-Robbins collection for classroom use.* Bryn Mawr, Pa.:Theodore Presser.

Robbins, C. (Ed.). (1998). *Healing heritage: Paul Nordoff exploring the tonal language of music.* Gilsum, NH: Barcelona.

Robinson, C. R. (1988). Differential modes of choral performance evaluation using traditional procedures and a continuous response digital interface device (Doctoral dissertation, Florida State University). *Dissertation Abstracts International, 49* (10), 2859.

Rogers, F. (1970). *Mister Rogers' songbook.* New York: Random House.

Rogers, L. (1968). Music therapy in a state hospital for crippled children. In Gaston (Ed.), *Music in therapy* (pp. 156–159). New York: Macmillan.

Romanczyk, R. G., Weiner, T., Lockshin, S., & Ekdahl, M. (1999). Research in autism: Myths, controversies and perspectives. In D. B. Zager (Ed.), *Autism: Identitfication, education, and treatment* (2nd ed., pp. 23–61). Mahwah, NJ: Erlbaum.

Rosen, H. (1977). P*iagetian dimensions of clinical relevance.* New York: Columbia University Press.

Rosenthal, L., & Nagelberg, L. (1956). Limitation of activity group therapy. *International Journal of Group Psychotherapy, 6,* 166–170.

Ruttenberg, B., Dratman, M., Fraknoi, J., & Wenar, C. (1966). An instrument for evaluating autistic children. *The Journal of the American Academy of Child Psychiatry.*

Sandness, M. (1991). Developmental sequence in music therapy groups: A review of theoretical models. *Music Therapy Perspectives,* 66–72.

Sausser, S., & Waller, R. J. (2006). A model for music therapy with students with emotional and behavioral disorder. *The Arts in Psychotherapy, v. 33:*1, pp. 1–10.

Scalenghe, R., & Murphy, K. (2000). Music therapy assessment in the managed care environment. *Music Therapy Perspectives, 1,* 123–130.

Schirmer, B. R. (2004). Hearing loss. In R. Turnbull, A. Turnbull, M. Shank, & S. J. Smith (Eds.), *Exceptional lives: Special education in today's schools* (4th ed., pp. 424–454). Upper Saddle River, NJ: Merrill/Prentice Hall.

Schneider, E. H. (1964). Selected articles and research studies relating to music therapy: Music therapy bibliography. *Journal of Music Therapy, 1*(3).

Schneider, E. H. (1968). Music therapy for the cerebral palsied. In Gaston (Ed.), *Music in therapy* (pp.

136–143). New York: Macmillan.

Schumann, R., & Schumann, R. *Forest scenes for piano solo,* opus 82.

Schumann, R. *Kinderscenen* (*Album for the Young, Op. 68* and *Scenes from Childhood, Op. 15*).

Schuppert, M., Munte, T. F., Wieringa, B. M., & Altenmuller, E. (2000). Receptive amusia: Evidence for cross-hemispheric neural networks underlying music processing strategies. *Brain, 123,* 546–559.

Schwartz, I. S., Garfinkle, A. N., & Bauer, J. (1998). The picture exchange communication system: Communicative outcomes for young children with disability. *Topics in Early Childhood Special Education, 18,* 144–159.

Sclesa, G., & Millang, S. (1983). *Greg and Steve Live Together, Vol. 1–5.* Los Angeles, CA: Youngheart.

Sclesa, G., & Millang, S. (1986). W*e all live together.* Milwaukee, WI: Hal Leonard.

Seashore, C. E. (1919). *Manual of instructions and interpretations of measures of musical talent.* Chicago, IL: C. H. Stoelting.

Sharon, Lois, & Bram. (1980). *Elephant jam.* San Francisco: McGraw-Hill.

Schuter, R. (1968). *The psychology of music ability.* London: Methuen & Company.

Shuter-Dyson, R. (1982). Musical ability. In D. Deutsch (Ed.), *The psychology of music.* New York: Academic Press, Inc.

Shuter-Dyson, R., & Gabriel, C. (1981). *The psychology of musical ability* (2nd ed.). New York: Methusen & Co.

Sidman, M. (1994). *Equivalence relations and behavior: A research story.* Boston: Authors Cooperative.

Silver-Burdett (1995). *The Music Connection.* Morristown, NJ.

Simons, G. M. (Ed.). (1978). *Early childhood musical development: A bibliography of research abstracts, 1960–1975.* Reston, VA: Music Educators National Conference.

Skaggs, R. (1997). Music-centered creative arts in a sex offender treatment program for male juveniles. *Music Therapy Perspectives, 15,* 73–78.

Skewes, K., & Thompson, G. (1998). The use of musical interactions to develop social skills in early intervention. *Australian Journal of Music Therapy, 9,* 35–44.

Slavson, S. R. (1943). *An introduction to group therapy.* New York: Commonwealth Fund.

Slavson, S. R., & Schiffer, M. (1975). *Group psychotherapies for children: A textbook.* New York: International Universities Press.

Snell, A. (2002). Music therapy for learners with autism in a public school setting. In B. Wilson (Ed.), *Models of music therapy interventions in school settings.* Silver Spring, MD: American Music Therapy Association.

Sparks, R., Helm, N., & Marin, A. (1974). Aphasia rehabilitation resulting from melodic intonation therapy. *Cortex, 10,* 303–316.

Sparks, R., & Holland, A. (1976). Method: Melodic intonation therapy for aphasia. *Journal of Speech and Hearing Disorders, 41,* 287–297.

Spicknall, H. (1968). Music for deaf and hard of hearing children in public schools. In T. Gaston (Ed.), *Music in therapy* (pp. 314–316). New York: Macmillan.

Spitz, R. A. (1965). *The first year of life.* New York: International Universities Press.

Standley, J. (1996a). A meta-analysis on the effects of music as reinforcement for education/ therapy objectives. *Journal of Research in Music Education, 44,* 105–133.

Standley, J., & Hughes, J. (1996b). Documenting developmentally appropriate objectives and benefits of a music therapy program for early intervention: A behavioral analysis. *Music Therapy Perspectives, 2,* 87–94.

Standley, J., Johnson, C. M., Robb, S. L., Brownell, M. D., & Kim, S. (2004). Behavioral approach to music therapy. In A. A. Darrow (Ed.), *Introduction to approaches in music therapy* (pp. 103–123). Silver Spring, MD: American Music Therapy Association.

Starer, R. *Sketches in color: Seven pieces for piano.* Melville, NY: MCA Music.

Steele, A. L. (1971). Contingent socio-music listening periods in a preschool setting. *Journal of Music Therapy, 8,* 131–139.

Steele, A. L., Vaughan, M., & Dolan, C. (1976). The school support program: Music therapy for adjustment problems in elementary schools. *Journal of Music Therapy, 13,* 87–100.

Steele, L. (1984). Music therapy for the learning disabled. *Music Therapy Perspectives, 1*(3), 2–7.

Stein, J. (1977). Tempo error and mania. *American Journal of Psychiatry, 134*(4).

Steinberg, R., Raith, L., Rossinagl, G., & Eben, E. (1985). Music psychopathology: Musical expression and psychiatric disease. *Psychopathology, 18,* 274–285.

Steiner, R. (1977). *Eurythm as visible music* (2nd ed.). London: Rudolf Steiner Press.

Steiner, R. (1983). *The inner nature of music and the experience of tone.* Spring Valley, NY: Anthroposophic Press.

Stern, D. (1977). *The first relationship–Infant and mother.* Cambridge: Harvard University Press.

Stern, D. N. (1985). *The interpersonal world of the infant.* New York: Basic Books.

Stevens, C. (2003). *The art and heart of drum circles.* New York: Hal Leonard.

Stevens, R., & Rosenshine, B. (1981). Advances in research on teaching. *Exceptional Education Quarterly,* 2, 1–9.

Stewart, G. (1977a). *Beanbag activities and coordination skills.* Long Branch, NJ: Kimbo.

Stewart, G. (1977b). *Playtime parachute fun for childhood.* Long Branch, NJ: Kimbo.

Stewart, G. (1984). *Folkdance fun and simple folk songs and dances.* Long Branch, NJ: Kimbo.

Stewart, G. (1987). *Good morning exercises for kids.* Long Branch, NJ: Kimbo.

Stewart, G. (1991). *Children of the world.* Long Branch, NJ: Kimbo.

Stewart, G. (1992). *Multicultural ryhthm stick fun.* Long Branch, NJ: Kimbo.

Stewart, R. W. (2002). Combined efforts: Increasing social-emotional communication with children with autistic spectrum disorder using psychodynamic music therapy and division TEACCH communication programme. In A. Davies & E. Richards (Eds.), *Music therapy and group work: Sound company.* London: Jessica Kingsley Publishers.

Stone, P. (1997). Educating children who are deaf or hard-of-hearing. *Auditory-oral option* (Report No. 551). (ERIC Document Reproduction Service No. ED 414669).

Strain, P. S., & Schwartz, I. (2001). ABA and the development of meaningful social relations for young children with autism. *Focus on Autism and Other Developmental Disablities, 16,* 120–128.

Sundberg, M., & Partington, J. (1998). *Teaching language to children with autism or other developmental disabilities.* Pleasant Hill, CA: Behavior Analysis.

Sutton, J. (2002). Preparing a potential space for a group of children with special needs. In A. Davies & E. Richards (Eds.), *Music therapy and group work: Sound company.* London: Jessica Kingsley Publishers.

Sutton, K. (1984). The development and implementation of a music therapy physiological measures test. *Music Therapy Perspectives, 1,* 2–7.

Thaut, M. H. (1983). A music therapy treatment model for the autistic child. *Music Therapy Perspectives, 1,* 7–13.

Thaut, M. H. (1985). The use of auditory rhythm and rhythmic speech to aid temporal musical control in children with gross motor dysfunction. *Journal of Music Therapy, 22,* 108–128.

Thaut, M. H. (1999). Music therapy for children with physical disabilities. In Davis, Gfeller, & Thaut (Eds.), *An introduction to music therapy: Theory and practice.*

Thaut, M. H. (1999). Music therapy in neurological rehabilitation. In Davis, Gfeller, & Thaut (Eds.), *An introduction to music therapy: Theory and practice.*

Thomas, A., & Chess, S. (1977). *Temperament and develop-*

ment. New York: Brunner Mazel.

Tomaino, C. (Ed.). (1998). *Clinical applications of music in neurologic rehabilitation.* New York: Beth Abraham Health Services.

Turry, A. (1998). Transference and countertransference in Nordoff-Robbins Music Therapy. In K. Bruscia (Ed.), *The dynamics of music psychotherapy.* Gilsum, NH: Barcelona.

Tyler, H. M. (2002). Working, playing and relating: Issues in group music therapy for children with special needs. In A. Davies & E. Richards (Eds.), *Music therapy and group work: Sound company.* London: Jessica Kingsley, Publishers.

Unkefer, R. (Ed.). (2000). *Music therapy in the treatment of adults with mental disorders,* (2nd ed.). New York: Schirmer.

Venn, M. L., Wolery, M., Werts, M. G., Morris, A., DeCesare, L. D., & Cuffs, M. (1993). Embedding instruction into art activities to teach preschoolers with disabilities to imitate their peers. *Early Childhood Research Quarterly, 8,* 277–294.

Vinter, R. D. (1974). Program activities: Their selection and use in a therapeutic milieu. In P. Glasser, R. Sarri, & R. Vinter (Eds.), *Individual change through small groups* (pp. 244–257). New York: The Free Press.

Voigt, M. (1999). Orff music therapy with multi-handicapped children. In T. Wigram & J. DeBacker (Eds.), *Clinical applications of music therapy: Developmental disability, pediatrics and neurology.* London: Jessica Kingsley, Publishers.

Vort Corporation. (1995). *HELP for preschoolers checklist.* Palo Alto, CA: VORT.

Walker, A. R. (1987). Some differences between pitch perception and basic auditory discrimination in children of different cultural and musical backgrounds. *Council for Research in Music Education, 91,* 166–170.

Wells, K., & Helmus, N. (1968). Music therapy in a children's day-treatment center. In Gaston (Ed.), *Music in therapy* (pp. 159–162). New York: Macmillan.

Wells, N. F., & Stevens, T. (1984). Music as a stimulus for creative fantasy in group psychotherapy with young adolescents. *The Arts in Psychotherapy, 11,* 71–76.

Wells, N. F. (1988). An individual music therapy assessment procedure for emotionally disturbed young adolescents. *The Arts in Psychotherapy, 18*(1), 31–40.

Wheeler, B. (1983). A psychotherapeutic classification of music therapy practices: A continuum of procedures. *Music Therapy Perspectives, 1*(2), 8–16.

Wigram, T. (1995). A model of assessment and differential diagnosis of handicap in children through the medium of music therapy. In T. Wigram, B. Saperston, & R. West (Eds.), *The art and science of*

music therapy: A handbook (pp. 181–193). Switzerland: Harwood Academic.

Wigram, T. (1999). Assessment methods in music therapy: A humanistic or natural science framework. *Nordic Journal of Music Therapy, 8*(1), 7–25.

Wigram, T. (1999). Variability and autonomy in music therapy interaction: Evidence for diagnosis and therapeutic intervention for children with autism and Asperger's syndrome. In R. Pratt & D. Erdonmez–Grocke (Eds.), *Music medicine 3–Music medicine and music therapy: Expanding horizons.*

Wigram, T., & DeBacker, J. (Eds.). (1999). *Clinical applications of music therapy: Developmental disability, pediatrics and neurology.* London: Jessica Kingsley Publishers.

Wigram, T. (2000). A method of music therapy assessment for the diagnosis of autism and communication disorders in children. *Music Therapy Perspectives, 1,* 13–22.

Wigram, T. (2004). *Improvisation: Methods and techniques for music therapy clinicians, educators, and students.* London: Jessica Kingsley Press.

Williams, D. B., & Fox, D. B. (1983). *Toney listens to music* (Computer program). Bellevue, WA: Temporal Acuity Products, Inc.

Wilson, B. L. (Ed.). (2002). Models of music therapy interventions in school settings (2nd ed.). Silver Spring, MD: American Music Therapy Association.

Wilson, B. L., & Smith, D. S. (2000). Music therapy assessment in school settings: A preliminary investigation. *Journal of Music Therapy, 37*(2), 95–117.

Wilson, C. V. (1976). The use of rock music as a reward in behavior therapy with children. *Journal of Music Therapy, 13,* 39–48.

Winnicott, D. W. (1971). *Playing and reality.* London: Tavistock Publications.

Wojcio, M. (1983). *Music in motion: 22 songs in signing exact English for children.* Los Alamitos, CA: Modern Signs Press.

Wolberg, L. R. (1977). *The technique of psychotherapy* (3rd ed.). New York: Grune & Stratton.

Wolery, M., Werts, M., & Holcombe, A. (1994). Current practices with young children who have disabilities: Placement, assessment, and instruction issues. *Focus on Exceptional Children, 26*(6), 1–12.

Wolfe, D., & Hom, C. (1993). Use of melodies as structural prompts for learning and retention of sequential verbal information by preschool students. *Journal of Music Therapy, 30*(2), 100–118.

Wolff, P. H. (1968). The serial organization of sucking in the young infant. *Pediatrics, 42–61.*

Wolff, P. H. (1968). Role of biological rhythms in early psychological development. In S. Chess & A.

Thomas (Eds.), *Annual progress in child psychiatry and child development* (pp. 1–21). New York: Brunner Mazel.

Wood, M. M., Graham, R. M., Swan, W. W., Purvis, J., Gigliotti, C., & Samet, S. (1974). *Developmental music therapy*. Lawrence, KS: National Association for Music Therapy.

Yalom, I. (1985). *The theory and practice of group psy-chotherapy* (3rd ed.). New York: Basic Books.

Yarbrough, C., Charboneau, M., & Wapnick, J. (1977). Music as reinforcement for correct math and attending in ability assigned math classes. *Journal of Music Therapy, 14*(2), 77–88.

Yingling, R. W. (1962). Classification of reaction in listening to music. *Journal of Research in Music Education.*

Name Index

A

Abramson, R., 39, 159, 174, 224, 272
Achey, C., 235–236
Adamek, M., 83, 182, 187, 194, 195, 202
Aigen, K., 116, 191, 194, 235, 240
Alberto, P. A., 192, 201
Allman, T., 7, 72, 86, 106, 179
Anderson, J. C., 46
Anderson, V., 83, 97, 98
Anthony, L. J., 83
Apprey, Z. R., 81
Apprey, M., 81
Arieti, S., 3
Asmus, E. P., 244
Axline, V., 79, 193
Ayres, A. J., 98

B

Baer, D. M., 193
Bailey, J. S., 192
Bauer, J., 192
Bean, K. L., 46
Beer, L., 222, 225
Berger, D. S., 78, 98, 184, 193
Bergman, A., 86
Bion, W. R., 78, 240, 241
Birkenshaw, L., 272
Birkenshaw-Fleming, L., 272
Bitcon, C. H., 236
Bondy, A., 192
Boxill, E., 163
Braswell, C., 44
Brazelton, B., 98
Bricker, D. D., 82, 83
Briggs, C., xi, 86, 87, 88, 89, 93–97, 102, 106, 111, 178, 179, 203
Brooks, B. H., 187, 239
Brooks, D., 44, 191
Brownwell, M. D., 115, 235, 239
Brunk, B., 38, 43, 45, 56, 57, 58, 76, 163, 273
Bruscia, K., xi, 45, 47, 49, 50

C

Carr, E. G., 192
Carr, M., xi
Carter, E., 82
Carter, C. M., 192
Cassity, M., 45, 46, 47, 191
Cassity, J. E., 45, 191
Cattell, R. B., 46
Chadwick, D. M., xi, 3, 162, 202
Charboneau, M., 189
Charoonsathvathana, A., 247
Chase, K., 46, 47, 51, 74
Chess, S., 98
Clair, A., 235, 242
Clark, C., 162, 202
Clarkson, G., 160
Cohen, G., 43
Cohen, N. S., 43
Coleman, K., 38, 43, 45, 56, 57, 58, 76, 136, 163, 179, 187, 213, 273
Colwell, C. M., 187, 235–236
Condon, W. S., 102, 195
Cooke, R., 185
Cooney, J. G., 272
Coons, E., 211
Cooper, J. O., 192
Cripe, F., 184
Crocker, D., 46, 160
Cuffs, M., 83
Cullen, C., 193

D

Daly, T., 192, 193
Darrow, A. A., 83, 182, 187, 194, 195, 199, 200, 202, 235, 239
Daugherty, S., 83
Davis, W., 113
DeBedout, J. K., 182
DeCesare, L. D., 83
Decuir, A., 44

J

Jacobs, K. W., 44
Jamieson, B., 83
Jellison, J., 113, 115, 182, 187, 197, 239, 244, 266
Jenkins, E., 172, 173, 272
Johnson, C. M., 115, 207, 235, 239
Johnson, F., 269
Johnson, F. L., 207
Johnson, R., 197
Jones, E., 76, 78, 80, 81, 116, 209
Joseph, M. R., 76, 81, 98, 209, 210

K

Kangas, K. A., 197
Kaplan, P. R., 44
Kegan, R., 87
Kestenberg, J. S., xi, 3, 102
Kim, J., 187
Kim, S., 235, 239
Kim, Y., 239
Kirsten, I., 197
Klein, M., 241
Koegel, L. K., 192
Koegel, J. L., 192
Kohler, F. W., 83
Kohut, H., 241
Kolodney, R. L., 76, 78, 80, 81, 116, 209
Kranowitz, C., 184
Kwak, E., 239

L

Laing, S., 190
Lathom-Radocy, W., 46, 50, 83, 182
Layman, D., 45, 50, 190
Levin, G., 23, 28, 29, 39, 141, 154, 156, 157, 165, 170, 172, 186, 204, 213, 222, 223, 228, 234, 271
Levin, H., 23, 28, 29, 39, 141, 154, 156, 157, 165, 170, 172, 186, 204, 213, 222, 223, 228, 234, 271
Libertore, A. M., 45, 50
Linder, T., 193
Lloyd, L. I., 197
Lockshin, S., 241
Loewy, J., 45
Losardo, A., 83

M

Madsen, C. K., 190, 239
Madsen, C. H., 190

Mahler, M. S., 86
Mark, A., 191
Marin, A., 195
McComas, N. R., 82
McConnell, S. R., 192
McDonald, M., 102
McFerran-Skewes, K., 191
McGee, G. G., 120, 192, 193
Morrier, M. J., 192, 193
Michel, D., xi, 6, 46, 47, 49, 50, 72, 73, 74, 76
Milgliore, M. J., 46
Millang, S., 172, 272
Miller, C. K., 239
Montello, L., 211
Montgomery, C., 78
Moore, J. R., 46
Morgenstern, A. M., 81
Morris, A., 83
Morris, S., 272
Moss, J., 38, 39, 154, 171, 174, 212, 222, 223, 272
Mudford, O. C., 193
Murphy, K., 43

N

Nagelberg, L., 79
Nash, G., 169, 272
Nelson, D., 81, 97, 98
Nicholls, T., 77
Nordoff, P., 3, 23, 24, 25, 27, 28, 29, 30, 31, 38, 39, 44, 46, 47, 50, 52, 53, 54, 55, 56, 58, 76, 84, 85, 95, 103, 115, 116, 143, 144, 151, 152, 153, 154, 155, 156, 157, 160, 163, 167, 170, 172, 176, 183, 187, 188, 191, 193, 194, 212, 213, 221, 222, 223, 224, 230, 232, 235, 239, 240, 245, 271
Noy, P., 102, 103

O

Oldfield, A., 77, 82, 83, 179, 191, 208
Opper, S., 178, 179
O'Reilly, K., 7, 72, 86, 106, 179
Orozoco, J. L., 272
Ostwald, P., 102, 103

P

Palmer, H., 27, 101, 154, 159, 160, 163, 171, 172, 173, 223, 272
Papousek, M., 102
Papousek, H., 102
Parette, H. P., 202

Subject Index

A

Ancillary materials during music therapy, 162
  Augmentative communication devices as, 162
  Manipulative visuals with songs as, 162
  Materials to supplement movement, 163
  Puppets as, 163
  Songboards, purpose and creation of as, 163
Antiphonal songs, 151
Assessment, 6-7, 42-76
  AMTA Clinical Standards regarding, 42
  Choice of assessment tool, 47
    Issues concerning, 6-7, 47
  Defined, 42
  Developmental Prerequisites for, 49, 50
    Assessment tool examples, 49
  Differences for individual and group, 75
  In group music therapy, 75, 76
  Introduction to topic of, 42
  Methodology for, 51
    Related to philosophy and purpose, 51
  Named assessments, 43
  Needs of music therapists in using, 51
  Of music behaviors, 46
    Normalcy vs. pathology, 46
    Rhythmic response, 46
  Of nonmusic and music behaviors, 46
  Of nonmusic behaviors, 47
    Common areas of concern, 47
    In sample assessment tools, 47
    Rationale for, 43
  Philosophical Orientation, 50, 51
    Behavioral, 50
      Case example, *see* SEMTAP
    Developmental, 50
      Case example, *see* MTAP
    Eclectic, 50
    Humanistic/Client-Centered, 50
      Case example, *see* Nordoff-Robbins
    Psychodynamic, 50
      Case example, *see* MAT-ED
  Possibility of, 6-7
  Published assessment tools, 52-74

  Purposes of, 47
    Changes in, 47, 48
    Descriptive, 47
    Diagnostic, 47
    For eligibility on IEP, 48
    Interpretive, 47
    Prescriptive, 47
  Reasons for, 43
  Scope of, 51
    Global, defined, 51
    Specific purpose, defined, 51
  Time to administer, 51
  Types of, 43
Auditory-Motor Perception Test, 45

B

Beginning therapist, 25, 31
Behavioral goals, 10, 36,
Behavior, measurable, 9
Behavior, Nonmusical and music, 46-47
Behavioral, philosophy, 50, 56-57

C

Case examples, 5-40, 48, 55, 57, 66, 72-73, 94-96,
    99-101, 103-106, 107-113, 123-127, 127-132,
    132-135, 142-147, 149, 158, 160, 164, 165, 166,
    167, 204-205, 208, 214-235, 247-266
  Assessment, 48, 55, 57, 66, 72-73
  Child psychiatric, 132-135, 147-149
  Continuum of musical response, 164, 165, 166, 167
  Developmental appropriateness for group, 94-96
  Developmentally delayed preschoolers, 120-123,
    140-144
  Evaluation, 247-266
  Multiply handicapped, 5-40, 127-132, 144-147,
    214-235
  Musical appropriateness for group, 103-106
  Practical considerations for group, 107-113
  Preschool autistic spectrum disorder, 123-127,
    142-144
  Related to instrumental assignment, 158

ABOUT THE AUTHOR

Karen D. Goodman, M.S., R.M.T., L.C.A.T., Associate Professor of Music Therapy and Coordinator of the Graduate Music Therapy Training Program at the John J. Cali School of Music, Montclair State University, is credentialed as a music therapist, a creative arts therapist, and a special education teacher. She received her Bachelors in English Literature from the University of Wisconsin–Madison, her music therapy certification training from Montclair State University, her full fellowship Masters in Special Education from Hunter College–City University of New York, and her subsequent training in neurology, child psychology, and music from New York University. She is trained as a pianist and vocalist and was drawn to music therapy through her introductory training in the Nordoff-Robbins approach.

Professor Goodman, who has directed the music therapy programs at Montclair for over 15 years, is the recipient of 14 descriptive research awards related to her ongoing clinical work and training of music therapy students. Her research interests, based on her clinical experience with autistic, multiply handicapped, and child psychiatric populations, have included the following: projective music therapy assessment in differential diagnoses of disturbed children, music therapy assessment for the IEP, the use of Developmental Individual Differences Relationship Based (DIR) Greenspan theory in music therapy with autistic children, core considerations in group music therapy with children, sensory integration through music therapy, infant musical development in the context of child development, the process of making music relative to the psychodynamic development of the schizophrenic client, and the reflective model of teaching in training music therapy students.

Professor Goodman has published an original assessment based on her work with emotionally disturbed children, served as editor of *Music Therapy–The Journal of the A.A.M.T.,* and authored the seminal chapter on music therapy in *The American Handbook of Psychiatry.* She is the only music therapist named to the Advisory Board of The Creativity Foundation founded by Dr. Silvano Arieti as well as the Advisory Board of The Center for Parents and Children founded by Dr. Judith Kestenberg. She presents regularly at national and international music therapy conferences, and consults to multiple school districts in New Jersey, as well as Oxford University Press and Educational Testing Service.

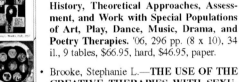

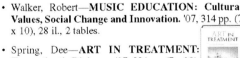